Network Fundamentals
CCNA Exploration Companion Guide

Mark A. Dye
Rick McDonald
Antoon W. Rufi

Cisco Press

800 East 96th Street

Indianapolis, Indiana 46240 USA

Network Fundamentals, CCNA Exploration Companion Guide

Mark A. Dye ▪ Rick McDonald ▪ Antoon W. Rufi

Copyright© 2008 Cisco Systems, Inc.

Cisco Press logo is a trademark of Cisco Systems, Inc.

Published by:
Cisco Press
800 East 96th Street
Indianapolis, IN 46240 USA

Printed in the United States of America

First Printing December 2011

Library of Congress Cataloging-in-Publication Data

Dye, Mark A.

  Network fundamentals : CCNA exploration companion guide/Mark A. Dye, Rick McDonald, Antoon W. Rufi.

     p. cm.

  ISBN-13: 978-1-58713-208-7 (hbk. : CD-ROM)

  ISBN-10: 1-58713-208-7 (hbk. : CD-ROM) 1. Electronic data processing personnel—Certification. 2. Computer networks—Examinations—Study guides. I. McDonald, Rick. II. Rufi, Antoon W. III. Title. IV. Title: CCNA exploration companion guide.

  QA76.3.D94 2007

  004.6—dc22

                    2007038852

ISBN-13: 978-1-58713-348-0
ISBN-10: 1-58713-348-2

Trademark Acknowledgments

Publisher
Paul Boger

Associate Publisher
Dave Dusthimer

Cisco Representative
Anthony Wolfenden

Cisco Press Program Manager
Jeff Brady

Executive Editor
Mary Beth Ray

Managing Editor
Patrick Kanouse

Development Editor
Dayna Isley

Project Editor
Tonya Simpson

Copy Editor
Written Elegance, Inc.

Technical Editors
Martin S. Anderson,
Gerlinde Brady

Editorial Assistant
Vanessa Evans

Book Designer
Louisa Adair

Composition
Mark Shirar

Indexer
Tim Wright

Proofreader
Gill Editorial Services

Warning and Disclaimer

This book is designed to provide information about the Cisco Network Fundamentals CCNA Exploration course. Every effort has been made to make this book as complete and as accurate as possible, but no warranty or fitness is implied.

The information is provided on an "as is" basis. The authors, Cisco Press, and Cisco Systems, Inc., shall have neither liability nor responsibility to any person or entity with respect to any loss or damages arising from the information contained in this book or from the use of the discs or programs that may accompany it.

The opinions expressed in this book belong to the author and are not necessarily those of Cisco Systems, Inc.

Corporate and Government Sales

The publisher offers excellent discounts on this book when ordered in quantity for bulk purchases or special sales, which may include electronic versions and/or custom covers and content particular to your business, training goals, marketing focus, and branding interests. For more information, please contact:

U.S. Corporate and Government Sales   1-800-382-3419   corpsales@pearsontechgroup.com

For sales outside the United States please contact:
International Sales   international@pearsoned.com

Feedback Information

At Cisco Press, our goal is to create in-depth technical books of the highest quality and value. Each book is crafted with care and precision, undergoing rigorous development that involves the unique expertise of members from the professional technical community.

Readers' feedback is a natural continuation of this process. If you have any comments regarding how we could improve the quality of this book, or otherwise alter it to better suit your needs, you can contact us through email at feedback@ciscopress.com. Please make sure to include the book title and ISBN in your message.

We greatly appreciate your assistance.

Americas Headquarters
Cisco Systems, Inc.
170 West Tasman Drive
San Jose, CA 95134-1706
USA
www.cisco.com
Tel: 408 526-4000
800 553-NETS (6387)
Fax: 408 527-0883

Asia Pacific Headquarters
Cisco Systems, Inc.
168 Robinson Road
#28-01 Capital Tower
Singapore 068912
www.cisco.com
Tel: +65 6317 7777
Fax: +65 6317 7799

Europe Headquarters
Cisco Systems International BV
Haarlerbergpark
Haarlerbergweg 13-19
1101 CH Amsterdam
The Netherlands
www-europe.cisco.com
Tel: +31 0 800 020 0791
Fax: +31 0 20 357 1100

Cisco has more than 200 offices worldwide. Addresses, phone numbers, and fax numbers are listed on the Cisco Website at **www.cisco.com/go/offices.**

©2007 Cisco Systems, Inc. All rights reserved. CCVP, the Cisco logo, and the Cisco Square Bridge logo are trademarks of Cisco Systems, Inc.; Changing the Way We Work, Live, Play, and Learn is a service mark of Cisco Systems, Inc.; and Access Registrar, Aironet, BPX, Catalyst, CCDA, CCDP, CCIE, CCIP, CCNA, CCNP, CCSP, Cisco, the Cisco Certified Internetwork Expert logo, Cisco IOS, Cisco Press, Cisco Systems, Cisco Systems Capital, the Cisco Systems logo, Cisco Unity, Enterprise/Solver, EtherChannel, EtherFast, EtherSwitch, Fast Step, Follow Me Browsing, FormShare, GigaDrive, GigaStack, HomeLink, Internet Quotient, IOS, IP/TV, iQ Expertise, the iQ logo, iQ Net Readiness Scorecard, iQuick Study, LightStream, Linksys, MeetingPlace, MGX, Networking Academy, Network Registrar, Packet, PIX, ProConnect, RateMUX, ScriptShare, SlideCast, SMARTnet, StackWise, The Fastest Way to Increase Your Internet Quotient, and TransPath are registered trademarks of Cisco Systems, Inc. and/or its affiliates in the United States and certain other countries.

All other trademarks mentioned in this document or Website are the property of their respective owners. The use of the word partner does not imply a partnership relationship between Cisco and any other company. (0609R)

About the Authors

Mark A. Dye was the technology manager and training manager for the Bevill Center at Gadsden State Community College, where he also managed and taught in the Cisco Academy program. He now works full time as an assessment and curriculum developer with Cisco. Mark also has maintained a private information technology consulting business since 1985. Mark's 30+-year career has included roles as biomedical instrumentation technician, field service engineer, customer service supervisor, network engineer, and instructor.

Rick McDonald teaches computer and networking courses at the University of Alaska Southeast in Ketchikan, Alaska. He is developing methods for delivering hands-on training via distance in Alaska using web-conferencing and NETLAB tools. Rick worked in the airline industry for several years before returning to full-time teaching. He taught CCNA and CCNP courses in the Cisco Networking Academy in North Carolina and was a CCNA instructor trainer.

Antoon "Tony" W. Rufi currently is the associate dean of computer and information science for all the ECPI College of Technology campuses. He also teaches the Cisco Networking Academy CCNA, CCNP, Network Security, Fundamentals of Wireless LAN, and IP Telephony curricula. Before becoming an instructor for ECPI, he spent almost 30 years in the United States Air Force, working on numerous electronic projects and computer programs.

About the Technical Reviewers

Martin S. Anderson is an instructor and program director for computer science technology at BGSU Firelands. BGSU Firelands, located in Huron, Ohio, is a regional branch college of Bowling Green State University. He has more than 30 years of experience in network computers, beginning with his family's small business in the mid-1970s. He has taught the CCNA curriculum at BGSU Firelands since 2002.

Gerlinde Brady has been teaching Cisco CCNA and CCNP courses at Cabrillo College, a Cisco Regional Networking Academy, since 1999. She holds a masters degree in education from the University of Hannover, Germany, and a masters degree in translation (English/German) from the Monterey Institute of International Studies. Her IT industry experience includes LAN design, network administration, technical support, and training.

Dedications

To my wonderful wife of more than 30 years. Frances, your zeal for life and compassion for people put a spark in this nerd's life. To my children, Jacob, Jonathan, Joseph, Jordan, Julianna, and Johannah, who share the many adventures of our lives. Also, to the young ladies that my sons have chosen to be my daughters, Barbie and Morgan. Finally, to my grandson Jacob Aiden; there truly is a reason why they are called grand. —*Mark Dye*

To my mother, Fran McDonald, who is an inspirational life-long learner. —*Rick McDonald*

To my wife, Linda. Without her understanding and support, I would not have been able to spend the amount of time required to produce something like this. —*Tony Rufi*

Acknowledgments

From Mark Dye:

I want to thank Mary Beth Ray and Dayna Isley with Cisco Press, whose unending patience made this book possible. I also want to thank the technical editors, Marty Anderson and Gerlinde Brady, for their insight. Additionally, I want to thank the other authors, Rick McDonald and Tony Rufi, who quietly and professionally made their portions of the book come together.

I want to say a special thanks to Telethia Wills with Cisco, who I have worked with for a number of years. Telethia has guided me through many different projects and allowed me to work with so many wonderful people.

From Rick McDonald:

I wish to thank my two talented coauthors, Mark and Tony, who were generous with their time and knowledge. They were under heavy workloads when the project began and held up throughout. Mary Beth did me a great kindness in bringing me to the table with you.

Gerlinde Brady and Marty Anderson did an excellent job as technical editors for my contributions. I am aware of the time and effort it took to cover so much so thoroughly, and your suggestions and corrections have had a direct impact on the quality of the content.

Mary Beth Ray has been the calming and guiding force behind the publication of this book. I wish to thank her for her vision and for her encouragement when I lost sight of it. Mary Beth's ability to guide the project and adapt to the ever-changing needs of students is to be loudly applauded. Mary Beth, thank you for your confidence and patience. You had to use both quite generously, and I appreciate it.

Dayna Isley once again amazed me with her ability to spot errors and clarify the unnecessarily complex sentences I would submit to her. There were times on the phone I was sure I could hear her eyes rolling, but she kept patiently guiding me through the processes of publishing with humor and kindness.

I wish to also thank Sarah Strickling at the University of Alaska Southeast for her helpful feedback and suggestions. Thanks also to Chris Lott and Christen Bouffard of the Center for Distance Education at the University of Alaska at Fairbanks for helping me understand some of the many ways imagination and technology are changing the way people think, learn, and work. I have tried to pass some of those ideas on within this book.

From Tony Rufi:

I would like to thank my coauthors, Mark Dye and Rick McDonald, for helping make writing this book such a joy. I would also like to thank ECPI College of Technology for all the support through the years, especially in reference to my quest for Cisco knowledge.

Contents at a Glance

Introduction   xx

Chapter 1   Living in a Network-Centric World   1

Chapter 2   Communicating over the Network   33

Chapter 3   Application Layer Functionality and Protocols   63

Chapter 4   OSI Transport Layer   99

Chapter 5   OSI Network Layer   135

Chapter 6   Addressing the Network: IPv4   171

Chapter 7   OSI Data Link Layer   243

Chapter 8   OSI Physical Layer   279

Chapter 9   Ethernet   313

Chapter 10   Planning and Cabling Networks   367

Chapter 11   Configuring and Testing Your Network   409

Appendix   Check Your Understanding and Challenge Questions
Answer Key   471

Glossary   495

Index   515

Contents

Introduction   xx

Chapter 1   Living in a Network-Centric World   1

Objectives   1

Key Terms   1

Communicating in a Network-Centric World   2

Networks Supporting the Way We Live   2

Examples of Today's Popular Communication Tools   4

Networks Supporting the Way We Learn   5

Networks Supporting the Way We Work   7

Networks Supporting the Way We Play   8

Communication: An Essential Part of Our Lives   8

What Is Communication?   8

Quality of Communication   9

The Network as a Platform   10

Communicating over Networks   10

Elements of a Network   10

Converged Networks   15

The Architecture of the Internet   16

The Network Architecture   17

Fault-Tolerant Network Architecture   19

Scalable Network Architecture   20

Providing Quality of Service   21

Providing Network Security   23

Trends in Networking   25

Where Is It All Going?   25

Networking Career Opportunities   27

Summary   28

Activities and Labs   28

Check Your Understanding   29

Challenge Questions and Activities   32

To Learn More   32

Chapter 2   Communicating over the Network   33

Objectives   33

Key Terms   33

The Platform for Communications   34

The Elements of Communication   35

Communicating the Messages   35

Components of the Network   37

End Devices and Their Role on the Network   37

Intermediary Devices and Their Role on the Network   38
Network Media   39

LANs, WANs, and Internetworks   41
Local-Area Networks   41
Wide-Area Networks   41
The Internet: A Network of Networks   42
Network Representations   43

Protocols   44
Rules That Govern Communications   44
Network Protocols   45
Protocol Suites and Industry Standards   46
Interaction of Protocols   46
Technology-Independent Protocols   47

Using Layered Models   47
The Benefits of a Layered Model   48
Protocol and Reference Models   48
TCP/IP Model   49
Communication Process   50
Protocol Data Units and Encapsulation   51
Sending and Receiving Process   52
OSI Model   53
Comparing the OSI Model to the TCP/IP Model   54

Network Addressing   55
Addressing in the Network   55
Getting Data to the End Device   55
Getting Data Through the Internetwork   56
Getting Data to the Right Application   57

Summary   58

Activities and Labs   58

Check Your Understanding   59

Challenge Questions and Activities   61

To Learn More   62

Chapter 3   Application Layer Functionality and Protocols   63
Objectives   63
Key Terms   63
Applications: The Interface Between the Networks   65
OSI and TCP/IP Model   66
Application Layer Software   69
User Applications, Services, and Application Layer Protocols   70
Application Layer Protocol Functions   71

Making Provisions for Applications and Services   71

Client/Server Model   72

Servers   72

Application Layer Services and Protocols   73

Peer-to-Peer (P2P) Networking and Applications   74

Application Layer Protocols and Services Examples   76

DNS Services and Protocol   77

WWW Service and HTTP   81

E-Mail Services and SMTP/POP Protocols   83

E-Mail Server Processes: MTA and MDA   84

FTP   86

DHCP   87

File-Sharing Services and SMB Protocol   89

P2P Services and Gnutella Protocol   90

Telnet Services and Protocol   91

Summary   93

Activities and Labs   93

Check Your Understanding   94

Challenge Questions and Activities   96

To Learn More   97

Chapter 4   OSI Transport Layer   99

Objectives   99

Key Terms   99

Roles of the Transport Layer   101

Purpose of the Transport Layer   101

Supporting Reliable Communication   105

TCP and UDP   107

Port Addressing   108

Segmentation and Reassembly: Divide and Conquer   112

TCP: Communicating with Reliability   114

Making Conversations Reliable   114

TCP Server Processes   115

TCP Connection Establishment and Termination   116

TCP Three-Way Handshake   116

TCP Session Termination   118

TCP Acknowledgment with Windowing   120

TCP Retransmission   121

TCP Congestion Control: Minimizing Segment Loss   122

UDP: Communicating with Low Overhead   124
UDP: Low Overhead Versus Reliability   124
UDP Datagram Reassembly   125
UDP Server Processes and Requests   126
UDP Client Processes   126

Summary   128

Labs   129

Check Your Understanding   130

Challenge Questions and Activities   132

To Learn More   133

Chapter 5   OSI Network Layer   135

Objectives   135

Key Terms   135

IPv4   136
Network Layer: Communication from Host to Host   136
IPv4: Example Network Layer Protocol   140
IPv4 Packet: Packaging the Transport Layer PDU   142
IPv4 Packet Header   143

Networks: Dividing Hosts into Groups   144
Creating Common Groups   145
Why Separate Hosts into Networks?   148
Dividing Networks from Networks   152

Routing: How Data Packets Are Handled   153
Device Parameters: Supporting Communication Outside the Network
153
IP Packets: Carrying Data End to End   154
Gateway: The Way Out of the Network   155
Route: A Path to a Network   156
Destination Network   160
Next Hop: Where the Packet Goes Next   161
Packet Forwarding: Moving the Packet Toward Its Destination   162

Routing Processes: How Routes Are Learned   163
Static Routing   163
Dynamic Routing   164
Routing Protocols   164

Summary   166

Labs   167

Check Your Understanding   167

Challenge Questions and Activities   170

To Learn More   170

Chapter 6   Addressing the Network: IPv4   171

    Objectives   171

    Key Terms   171

    IPv4 Addresses   173

        Anatomy of an IPv4 Address   173

        Binary-to-Decimal Conversion   174

        Decimal-to-Binary Conversions   178

        Addressing Types of Communication: Unicast, Broadcast, Multicast   183

    IPv4 Addresses for Different Purposes   188

        Types of Addresses in an IPv4 Network Range   188

        Subnet Mask: Defining the Network and Host Portions of the Address   190

        Public and Private Addresses   192

        Special Unicast IPv4 Addresses   194

        Legacy IPv4 Addressing   196

    Assigning Addresses   198

        Planning to Address the Network   198

        Static or Dynamic Addressing for End-User Devices   200

        Selecting Device Addresses   202

        Internet Assigned Numbers Authority (IANA)   204

        ISPs   205

    Calculating Addresses   206

        Is the Host on My Network?   207

        Calculating Network, Hosts, and Broadcast Addresses   209

        Basic Subnetting   211

        Subnetting: Dividing Networks into Right Sizes   216

        Subnetting a Subnet   220

    Testing the Network Layer   228

        Ping 127.0.0.1: Testing the Local Stack   228

        Ping Gateway: Testing Connectivity to the Local LAN   229

        Ping Remote Host: Testing Connectivity to Remote LAN   230

        Traceroute (tracert): Testing the Path   231

        ICMPv4: The Protocol Supporting Testing and Messaging   232

    Overview of IPv6   235

    Summary   237

    Labs   237

    Check Your Understanding   238

    Challenge Questions and Activities   240

    To Learn More   241

Chapter 7   OSI Data Link Layer   243

    Objectives   243

    Key Terms   243

    Data Link Layer: Accessing the Media   244

        Supporting and Connecting to Upper-Layer Services   245

        Controlling Transfer Across Local Media   247

        Creating a Frame   248

        Connecting Upper-Layer Services to the Media   249

        Standards   251

    MAC Techniques: Placing Data on the Media   252

        MAC for Shared Media   252

        MAC for Nonshared Media   254

        Logical Topology Versus Physical Topology   255

    MAC: Addressing and Framing Data   258

        Data Link Layer Protocols: The Frame   258

        Framing: Role of the Header   259

        Addressing: Where the Frame Goes   260

        Framing: Role of the Trailer   260

        Sample Data Link Layer Frames   262

    Putting It All Together: Following Data Through an Internetwork   267

    Summary   274

    Labs   274

    Check Your Understanding   274

    Challenge Questions and Activities   276

    To Learn More   277

Chapter 8   OSI Physical Layer   279

    Objectives   279

    Key Terms   279

    Physical Layer: Communication Signals   280

        Purpose of the Physical Layer   280

        Physical Layer Operation   281

        Physical Layer Standards   282

        Physical Layer Fundamental Principles   283

    Physical Signaling and Encoding: Representing Bits   284

        Signaling Bits for the Media   285

        Encoding: Grouping Bits   287

        Data-Carrying Capacity   290

    Physical Media: Connecting Communication   292

        Types of Physical Media   292

        Copper Media   293

        Media Connectors   304

Summary   307

Labs   307

Check Your Understanding   308

Challenge Questions and Activities   310

To Learn More   311

Chapter 9   **Ethernet   313**

Objectives   313

Key Terms   313

Overview of Ethernet   315

Ethernet: Standards and Implementation   315

Ethernet: Layer 1 and Layer 2   316

Logical Link Control: Connecting to the Upper Layers   317

MAC: Getting Data to the Media   317

Physical Implementations of Ethernet   319

Ethernet: Communication Through the LAN   320

Historic Ethernet   320

Legacy Ethernet   321

Current Ethernet   322

Moving to 1 Gbps and Beyond   323

Ethernet Frame   324

Frame: Encapsulating the Packet   324

Ethernet MAC Address   326

Hexadecimal Numbering and Addressing   328

Another Layer of Addressing   331

Ethernet Unicast, Multicast, and Broadcast   331

Ethernet MAC   334

MAC in Ethernet   334

CSMA/CD: The Process   334

Ethernet Timing   338

Interframe Spacing and Backoff   341

Ethernet Physical Layer   342

10- and 100-Mbps Ethernet   343

1000-Mbps Ethernet   345

Ethernet: Future Options   346

Hubs and Switches   347

Legacy Ethernet: Using Hubs   347

Ethernet: Using Switches   349

Switches: Selective Forwarding   351

Address Resolution Protocol (ARP)   355

Resolving IPv4 Addresses to MAC Addresses   355

Maintaining a Cache of Mappings   356

ARP Broadcast Issues   360

Summary   362

Labs   362

Check Your Understanding   363

Challenge Questions and Activities   365

To Learn More   365

Chapter 10   Planning and Cabling Networks   367

Objectives   367

Key Terms   367

LANs: Making the Physical Connection   368

Choosing the Appropriate LAN Device   368

Device Selection Factors   370

Device Interconnections   374

LAN and WAN: Getting Connected   374

Making LAN Connections   380

Making WAN Connections   384

Developing an Addressing Scheme   388

How Many Hosts in the Network?   388

How Many Networks?   389

Designing the Address Standard for Your Internetwork   390

Calculating the Subnets   391

Calculating Addresses: Case 1   391

Calculating Addresses: Case 2   397

Device Interconnections   398

Device Interfaces   398

Making the Device Management Connection   400

Summary   402

Labs   402

Check Your Understanding   403

Challenge Questions and Activities   405

To Learn More   407

Chapter 11   Configuring and Testing Your Network   409

Objectives   409

Key Terms   409

Configuring Cisco Devices: IOS Basics   410

Cisco IOS   410

Access Methods   411

Configuration Files   413

Introducing Cisco IOS Modes   414

Basic IOS Command Structure   418

Using CLI Help   420

IOS Examination Commands   426

IOS Configuration Modes   428

Applying a Basic Configuration Using Cisco IOS   429

Naming Devices   429

Limiting Device Access: Configuring Passwords and Banners   431

Managing Configuration Files   436

Configuring Interfaces   440

Verifying Connectivity   444

Test the Stack   444

Testing the Interface   446

Testing the Local Network   449

Testing Gateway and Remote Connectivity   451

Tracing and Interpreting Trace Results   453

Monitoring and Documenting Networks   458

Basic Network Baselines   458

Capturing and Interpreting Trace Information   459

Learning About the Nodes on the Network   461

Summary   464

Labs   465

Check Your Understanding   467

Challenge Questions and Activities   468

To Learn More   469

Appendix   Check Your Understanding and Challenge Questions Answer Key   471

Chapter 1   471

Chapter 2   472

Chapter 3   473

Chapter 4   478

Chapter 5   479

Chapter 6   481

Chapter 7   483

Chapter 8   487

Chapter 9   488

Chapter 10   489

Chapter 11   493

Glossary   495

Index   515

Icons Used in This Book

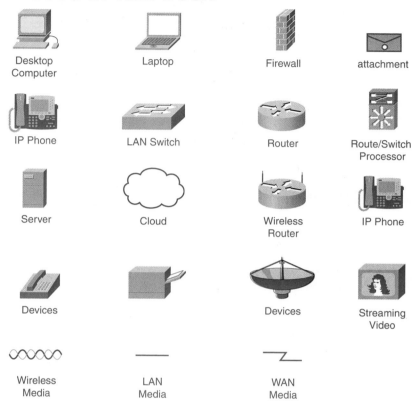

Desktop Computer	Laptop	Firewall	attachment
IP Phone	LAN Switch	Router	Route/Switch Processor
Server	Cloud	Wireless Router	IP Phone
Devices		Devices	Streaming Video
Wireless Media	LAN Media	WAN Media	

Command Syntax Conventions

The conventions used to present command syntax in this book are the same conventions used in the *IOS Command Reference*. The *Command Reference* describes these conventions as follows:

- **Boldface** indicates commands and keywords that are entered literally as shown. In actual configuration examples and output (not general command syntax), boldface indicates commands that are manually input by the user (such as a **show** command).

- *Italics* indicate arguments for which you supply actual values.

- Vertical bars (|) separate alternative, mutually exclusive elements.

- Square brackets [ ] indicate optional elements.

- Braces { } indicate a required choice.

- Braces within brackets [{ }] indicate a required choice within an optional element.

Introduction

Cisco Networking Academy is a comprehensive e-learning program that delivers information technology skills to students around the world. The Cisco CCNA Exploration curriculum consists of four courses that provide a comprehensive overview of networking, from fundamentals to advanced applications and services. The curriculum emphasizes theoretical concepts and practical application, while providing opportunities for you to gain the skills and hands-on experience needed to design, install, operate, and maintain networks in small- to medium-size businesses, as well as enterprise and service provider environments. The Network Fundamentals course is the first course in the curriculum and is based on a top-down approach to networking.

Network Fundamentals, CCNA Exploration Companion Guide is the official supplemental textbook for the first course in v4.x of the CCNA Exploration online curriculum of the Networking Academy. As a textbook, this book provides a ready reference to explain the same networking concepts, technologies, protocols, and devices as the online curriculum.

This book emphasizes key topics, terms, and activities and provides many alternate explanations and examples as compared with the course. You can use the online curriculum as directed by your instructor and then use this Companion Guide's study tools to help solidify your understanding of all the topics.

Goal of This Book

First and foremost, by providing a fresh, complementary perspective of the online content, this book helps you learn all the required materials of the first course in the Networking Academy CCNA Exploration curriculum. As a secondary goal, individuals who do not always have Internet access can use this text as a mobile replacement for the online curriculum. In those cases, you can read the appropriate sections of this book, as directed by your instructor, and learn the topics that appear in the online curriculum. Another secondary goal of this book is to serve as your offline study material to help prepare you for the CCNA exam.

Audience for This Book

This book's main audience is anyone taking the first CCNA Exploration course of the Networking Academy curriculum. Many Networking Academies use this textbook as a required tool in the course, while other Networking Academies recommend the Companion Guides as an additional source of study and practice materials.

Book Features

The educational features of this book focus on supporting topic coverage, readability, and practice of the course material to facilitate your full understanding of the course material.

Topic Coverage

The following features give you a thorough overview of the topics covered in each chapter so that you can make constructive use of your study time:

- **Objectives:** Listed at the beginning of each chapter, the objectives reference the core concepts covered in the chapter. The objectives match the objectives stated in the corresponding chapters of the online curriculum; however, the question format in the Companion Guide encourages you to think about finding the answers as you read the chapter.

- **"How-to" feature:** When this book covers a set of steps that you need to perform for certain tasks, the text lists the steps as a how-to list. When you are studying, the icon helps you easily refer to this feature as you skim through the book.

- **Notes, tips, cautions, and warnings:** These are short sidebars that point out interesting facts, timesaving methods, and important safety issues.

- **Chapter summaries:** At the end of each chapter is a summary of the chapter's key concepts. It provides a synopsis of the chapter and serves as a study aid.

Readability

The authors have compiled, edited, and in some cases rewritten the material so that it has a more conversational tone that follows a consistent and accessible reading level. In addition, the following features have been updated to assist your understanding of the networking vocabulary:

- **Key terms:** Each chapter begins with a list of key terms, along with a page-number reference from inside the chapter. The terms are listed in the order in which they are explained in the chapter. This handy reference allows you to find a term, flip to the page where the term appears, and see the term used in context. The Glossary defines all the key terms.

- **Glossary:** This book contains an all-new Glossary with more than 250 terms.

Practice

Practice makes perfect. This new Companion Guide offers you ample opportunities to put what you learn to practice. You will find the following features valuable and effective in reinforcing the instruction that you receive:

- **Check Your Understanding questions and answer key:** Updated review questions are presented at the end of each chapter as a self-assessment tool. These questions match the style of questions that you see in the online course. Appendix A, "Check Your Understanding and Challenge Questions Answer Key," provides an answer key to all the questions and includes an explanation of each answer.

- **(NEW) Challenge questions and activities:** Additional—and more challenging—review questions and activities are presented at the end of chapters. These questions are purposefully designed to be similar to the more complex styles of questions you might see on the CCNA exam. This section might also include activities to help prepare you for the exams. Appendix A provides the answers.

- **Packet Tracer activities:** Interspersed throughout the chapters you'll find many activities to work with the Cisco Packet Tracer tool. Packet Tracer allows you to create networks, visualize how packets flow in the network, and use basic testing tools to determine whether the network would work. When you see this icon, you can use Packet Tracer with the listed file to perform a task suggested in this book. The activity files are available on this book's CD-ROM; Packet Tracer software, however, is available through the Academy Connection website. Ask your instructor for access to Packet Tracer.

Labs and Study Guide

The supplementary book *Network Fundamentals, CCNA Exploration Labs and Study Guide*, by Cisco Press (ISBN: 1-58713-2036), contains all the labs from the curriculum plus additional challenge labs and study guide material. At the end of each chapter of this Companion Guide, icons indicate what hands-on activities, labs, and Packet Tracer activities are available in the Labs and Study Guide.

- **Lab and Activity references:** This icon notes the hands-on labs and other activities created for this chapter in the online curriculum. Within *Network Fundamentals, CCNA Exploration Labs and Study Guide*, you will also find additional labs and study guide material created by the authors of that book.

- **(NEW) Packet Tracer Companion activities:** Many of the hands-on labs include Packet Tracer Companion activities, where you can use Packet Tracer to complete a simulation of the lab. Look for this icon in *Network Fundamentals, CCNA Exploration Labs and Study Guide* for hands-on labs that have a Packet Tracer Companion.

- **(NEW) Packet Tracer Skills Integration Challenge activities:** These activities require you to pull together several skills learned from the chapter to successfully complete one comprehensive exercise. Look for this icon in *Network Fundamentals, CCNA Exploration Labs and Study Guide* for instructions on how to perform the Packet Tracer Skills Integration Challenge for this chapter.

A Word About Packet Tracer Software and Activities

Packet Tracer is a self-paced, visual, interactive teaching and learning tool developed by Cisco. Lab activities are an important part of networking education. However, lab equipment can be a scarce resource. Packet Tracer provides a visual simulation of equipment and network processes to offset the challenge of limited equipment. Students can spend as much time as they like completing standard lab exercises through Packet Tracer, and have the option to work from home. Although Packet Tracer is not a substitute for real equipment, it allows students to practice using a command-line interface. This "e-doing" capability is a fundamental component of learning how to configure routers and switches from the command line.

Packet Tracer v4.x is available only to Cisco Networking Academies through the Academy Connection website. Ask your instructor for access to Packet Tracer.

The course includes essentially three different types of Packet Tracer activities. This book uses an icon system to indicate which type of Packet Tracer activity is available to you. The icons are intended to give you a sense of the purpose of the activity and the amount of time you need to allot to complete it. The three types of Packet Tracer activities follow:

- **Packet Tracer Activity:** This icon identifies straightforward exercises interspersed throughout the chapters where you can practice or visualize a specific topic. The activity files for these exercises are available on the book's CD-ROM. These activities take less time to complete than the Packet Tracer Companion and Challenge activities.

- **Packet Tracer Companion:** This icon identifies exercises that correspond to the hands-on labs of the course. You can use Packet Tracer to complete a simulation of the hands-on lab or complete a similar "lab." The Companion Guide points these out at the end of each chapter, but look for this icon and the associated exercise file in *Network Fundamentals, CCNA Exploration Labs and Study Guide* for hands-on labs that have a Packet Tracer Companion.

- **Packet Tracer Skills Integration Challenge:** This icon identifies activities that require you to pull together several skills learned from the chapter to successfully complete one comprehensive exercise. The Companion Guide points these out at the end of each chapter, but look for this icon in *Network Fundamentals, CCNA Exploration Labs and Study Guide* for instructions on how to perform the Packet Tracer Skills Integration Challenge for this chapter.

How This Book Is Organized

This book covers the major topics in the same sequence as the online curriculum for the CCNA Exploration Network Fundamentals course. The online curriculum has 11 chapters for Network Fundamentals, so this book has 11 chapters with the same names and numbers as the online course chapters.

To make it easier to use this book as a companion to the course, the major topic headings in each chapter match, with just a few exceptions, the major sections of the online course chapters. However, the Companion Guide presents many topics in slightly different order inside each major heading. Additionally, the book occasionally uses different examples than the course. As a result, students get more detailed explanations, a second set of examples, and different sequences of individual topics, all to aid the learning process. This new design, based on research into the needs of the Networking Academies, helps typical students lock in their understanding of all the course topics.

Chapters and Topics

The book has 11 chapters, as follows:

- **Chapter 1, "Living in a Network-Centric World,"** presents the basics of communication and describes how networks support the way we live. This chapter introduces the concepts of data networks, scalability, quality of service (QoS), security issues, network collaboration tools, and Packet Tracer.

- **Chapter 2, "Communicating over the Network,"** introduces the devices, media, and protocols that enable network communication. This chapter introduces the OSI and TCP/IP models, the importance of addressing and naming schemes, and the process of data encapsulation. You also learn about the tools designed to analyze and simulate network functionality, such as Wireshark.

- **Chapter 3, "Application Layer Functionality and Protocols,"** introduces you to the top network model layer, the application layer. In this context, you will explore the interaction of protocols, services, and applications, with a focus on HTTP, DNS, DHCP, SMTP/POP, Telnet, and FTP.

- **Chapter 4, "OSI Transport Layer,"** focuses on the role of the transport layer as it provides the end-to-end transfer of data between applications. You learn how TCP and UDP apply to common applications.

- **Chapter 5, "OSI Network Layer,"** introduces the concepts of routing packets from a device on one network to a device on a different network. You learn important concepts related to addressing, path determination, data packets, and IP.

- **Chapter 6, "Addressing the Network: IPv4,"** focuses on network addressing in detail and describes how to use the address mask, or prefix length, to determine the number of subnetworks and hosts in a network. This chapter also introduces Internet Control Message Protocol (ICMP) tools, such as ping and trace.

- **Chapter 7, "OSI Data Link Layer,"** discusses how the OSI data link layer prepares network layer packets for transmission and controls access to the physical media. This chapter includes a description of the encapsulation processes that occur as data travels across the LAN and the WAN.

- **Chapter 8, "OSI Physical Layer,"** explores the functions, standards, and protocols associated with the physical layer (Layer 1). You discover how data sends signals and is encoded for travel across the network. You learn about bandwidth and also about the types of media and their associated connectors.

- **Chapter 9, "Ethernet,"** examines the technologies and operation of Ethernet. Topics include the evolution of Ethernet technologies, MAC, and Address Resolution Protocol (ARP).

- **Chapter 10, "Planning and Cabling Networks,"** focuses on designing and cabling a network. You will apply the knowledge and skills developed in the previous chapters to determine which cables to use, how to connect devices, and how to develop an addressing and testing scheme.

- **Chapter 11, "Configuring and Testing Your Network,"** describes how to connect and configure a small network using basic Cisco IOS commands for routers and switches.

This book also includes the following:

- **Appendix, "Check Your Understanding and Challenge Questions Answer Key,"** provides the answers to the Check Your Understanding questions that you find at the end of each chapter. It also includes answers for the challenge questions and activities that conclude most chapters.

- The **Glossary** provides a compiled list of all the key terms that appear throughout this book.

About the CD-ROM

The CD-ROM included with this book provides many useful tools and information to support your education:

- **Packet Tracer Activity files:** These are files to work through the Packet Tracer activities referenced throughout the book, as indicated by the Packet Tracer Activity icon.

- **Other files**: A couple files referenced in this book are on the accompanying CD-ROM:

  VLSM_Subnetting_Chart.pdf

  Exploration_Supplement_Structured_Cabling.pdf

- **Taking Notes:** This section includes a .txt file of the chapter objectives to serve as a general outline of the key topics of which you need to take note. The practice of taking clear, consistent notes is an important skill not only for learning and studying the material but for on-the-job success as well. Also included in this section is "A Guide to Using a Networker's Journal" PDF booklet providing important insight into the value of the practice of using and organizing a professional journal and some best practices on what, and what not, to take note of in your journal.

- **IT Career Information:** This section includes a Student Guide to applying the toolkit approach to your career development. Learn more about entering the world of Information Technology as a career by reading two informational chapters excerpted from *The IT Career Builder's Toolkit:* "Information Technology: A Great Career" and "Breaking into IT."

- **Lifelong Learning in Networking:** As you embark on a technology career, you will notice that it is ever changing and evolving. This career path provides exciting opportunities to learn new technologies and their applications. Cisco Press is one of the key resources to plug into on your quest for knowledge. This section of the CD-ROM provides an orientation to the information available to you and tips on how to tap into these resources for lifelong learning.

CHAPTER 1

Living in a Network-Centric World

Objectives

Upon completion of this chapter, you will be able to answer the following questions:

- How do networks impact our daily lives?

- What is the role of data networking in the human network?

- What are the key components of a data network?

- What are the opportunities and challenges posed by converged networks?

- What are the characteristics of network architectures?

Key Terms

This chapter uses the following key terms. You can find the definitions in the Glossary.

data network   *page 3*

network   *page 3*

Internet   *page 3*

download   *page 4*

instant messaging   *page 4*

real-time   *page 4*

blogs   *page 4*

podcasts   *page 5*

wikis   *page 5*

collaboration tool   *page 6*

Packet Tracer   *page 6*

intranet   *page 7*

extranet   *page 7*

wireless technology   *page 7*

standards   *page 11*

bits   *page 12*

binary   *page 12*

source   *page 12*

router   *page 13*

cloud   *page 13*

IP (Internet Protocol)   *page 14*

TCP (Transmission Control Protocol)   *page 14*

convergence   *page 15*

fault tolerance   *page 17*

redundancy   *page 17*

scalability   *page 17*

internetwork   *page 17*

packet   *page 19*

quality of service (QoS)   *page 21*

bandwidth   *page 21–22*

priority queuing   *page 22*

authentication   *page 24*

firewall   *page 25*

single point of failure   *page 25*

We now stand at a critical turning point in the use of technology to extend and empower the human network. The globalization of the Internet has succeeded faster than anyone could have imagined. The manner in which social, commercial, political, and personal interactions occur is rapidly changing to keep up with the evolution of this global network. In the next stage of our development, innovators will use the Internet as a starting point for their efforts—creating new products and services specifically designed to take advantage of the network capabilities. As developers push the limits of what is possible, the capabilities of the interconnected networks that form the Internet will play an increasing role in the success of these projects.

This chapter introduces the platform of data networks upon which social and business relationships increasingly depend. The material lays the groundwork for exploring the services, technologies, and issues encountered by network professionals as they design, build, and maintain the modern network.

Communicating in a Network-Centric World

Humans are social animals who depend on the interaction with others for daily needs. Throughout human history, people, with few exceptions, have depended on the structure of various community networks for safety, food, and companionship. People have been networking for a very long time.

The ways in which humans interact are constantly changing. As technical developments throughout history have come about, the methods of human communication have developed as well. At one time, sounds and gestures were all humans used to communicate, but now the Internet allows people to instantaneously share all types of communication—documents, pictures, sound, and video—with thousands of people near and far away using computers.

Networks Supporting the Way We Live

Just a few years ago, people communicated mostly on a local level because communicating with people far away was complicated and expensive. People talked in person or used the telephone for most voice communication, the postal service delivered most of the written messages, and the television broadcast one-way video communication. Each of these methods is still working, but all three of them are converging into web-based communication technologies. The extended reach and the reduced cost of communication through the Internet has changed the way businesses interact with their customers, the way people share information and resources, and the way friends and families stay close to each other.

As with every advance in communication technology, the creation and interconnection of robust data networks are having a profound effect. Early *data networks* were limited to exchanging character-based information between connected computer systems. Current *networks* have evolved to carry voice, video streams, text, and graphics between many different types of devices. Previously separate and distinct communication forms have converged onto a common platform. This platform provides access to a wide range of alternative and new communication methods that enable people to interact directly with each other almost instantaneously.

The use of the *Internet* spread quickly as connectivity became available in the 1990s. The early users of the World Wide Web were mostly university researchers exchanging information, but other people and businesses quickly figured out how to take advantage of web-based communications. This sparked the creation of many new businesses and careers.

The immediate nature of communications over the Internet encourages the formation of global communities. These communities foster social interaction that is independent of location or time zone.

Technology is perhaps the most significant change agent in the world today, as it helps to create a world in which national borders, geographic distances, and physical limitations become less relevant and present ever-diminishing obstacles. The creation of online communities for the exchange of ideas and information has the potential to increase productivity opportunities across the globe. As the Internet connects people and promotes unfettered communication, it presents the platform on which to run businesses, to address emergencies, to inform individuals, and to support education, science, and government.

The Internet has quickly become an integral part of our daily routines. The complex interconnection of electronic devices and media that comprises the network is transparent to the millions of users who make it a valued and personal part of their lives.

Data networks that were once the transport of information from business to business are now also used to improve the quality of life for people everywhere. In the course of a day, resources available through the Internet can help you do the following:

- Decide what to wear using online current weather conditions

- Find the least-congested route to your destination, displaying weather and traffic video from webcams

- Check your bank balance and pay bills electronically

- Receive and send e-mail at an Internet cafe over lunch

- Obtain health information and nutritional advice from experts all over the world, and post to a forum to share related health or treatment information
- *Download* new recipes and cooking techniques to create a spectacular dinner
- Post and share your photographs, home videos, and experiences with friends or with the world
- Use Internet phone services
- Shop and sell at online auctions
- Use instant messaging and chat for both business and personal use

Examples of Today's Popular Communication Tools

As in the past with novel technologies like the telephone and television, the general public readily adapted the Internet into daily use. The existence and broad adoption of the Internet has ushered in new forms of communication that empower individuals to create information that can be accessed by a global audience. Popular communication tools include instant messaging, blogs, podcasts, and wikis.

Instant messaging (IM) is not a new technology, but recent enhancements have increased its user base. IM is *real-time* text communication between two or more users. Based on the earlier service known as Internet Relay Chat (IRC), it has expanded to include voice, photo and video sharing, and file transfers. IM is different from e-mail in that e-mail can be delayed when sent, but IM is, as its name implies, instantaneous. IM is an increasingly popular tool used by customer service centers to assist customers and friends in communicating with each other.

The first generation of web use was as a place for people to find static information, educational resources, and business information. But web content is changing from a place for people to get information to a place for people to contribute information as well. The users of the web are, in many ways, becoming the creators of the content. The emergence and use of social software tools such as blogs, podcasts, and wikis enable the interaction and contribution of users.

Blogs, also known as weblogs, are web pages where people can publish their personal opinions and thoughts about any conceivable topic. Blogs, for better or worse, allow unfiltered and unedited publication of ideas from experts and nonexperts alike. This is important because it demonstrates a shift from reliance on traditional media content from experts to a reliance on other users to provide their personal knowledge.

Podcasting is an audio-based medium that originally enabled people to record audio and convert it for use with iPods—small, portable devices for audio playback manufactured by Apple. The ability to record audio and save it to a computer file is not new. However, podcasting allows people to deliver their recordings to a wide audience. The audio file is placed on a website (or blog or wiki), where others can download it and play the recording on their computers, laptops, and iPods.

Wikis are another example of publicly created web content. Individuals create blogs, but wiki web pages are created and edited by groups of people sharing information. The best known example of a wiki is the Wikipedia, an online encyclopedia made up of public contributions edited by public users. Thousands of people contribute their specialized knowledge to the Wikipedia, and anyone can access the information at no cost. Many groups create their own wikis for member instruction, and many organizations create limited wikis as an internal collaboration tool. A *collaboration tool* is web-based software that allows people to work together on a project over the web.

Networks Supporting the Way We Learn

The advances in the Internet and collaboration tools have been the force behind major changes in education. As web reliability and access have increased, more institutions have come to depend on technology to perform core educational functions. For example, distance education was once limited to correspondence, videos, or video and audio conferences. With newer collaboration tools and stronger web technologies, online learning can engage remote students in interactive learning and real-time assessment. The classes can use document sharing, wikis, online video, and online testing software to enhance learning opportunities. Student learning is becoming less dependent on location and schedule, which opens courses to potential students who previously could not attend classes.

The methods of both face-to-face and online instruction are changing with the introduction of web tools such as wikis. Traditionally, a teacher provided course content and the class might have benefited from some discussions. With online tools equally available to all students, many classes focus on sharing the opinions and expertise of students. This is a significant change for many students and instructors, but it is an example of the impact of technical change on society's traditions.

The administration side of instruction has also changed. You might have enrolled in this course on the web and paid with an online bank account. Your final grades might be posted on a school website, and you might never have a face-to-face meeting with your advisor. This is the business side of education, and it is changing as new management tools become available.

The structure of this course is an example of the influence that the changes of the web have had on instruction. The Cisco Networking Academy Program, which offers this course, is an example of a global online learning experience. The instructor provides a syllabus and establishes a preliminary schedule for completing the course content. The Academy program supplements the expertise of the instructor with an interactive curriculum that provides many forms of learning experiences. The program provides text, graphics, animations, and a simulated networking environment tool called *Packet Tracer*. Packet Tracer provides a way to build virtual representations of networks and emulate many of the functions of networking devices.

Students can communicate with the instructor and fellow students using online tools like e-mail, bulletin/discussion boards, chat rooms, and instant messaging. Links provide access to learning resources outside the courseware. Blended e-learning provides the benefits of computer-based training while retaining the advantages of an instructor-led curriculum. Students have the opportunity to work online at their own pace and skill level while still having access to an instructor and other live resources.

In addition to the benefits for the student, networks have improved the management and administration of courses as well. Some of these online functions include enrollment, assessment delivery, and grade books.

In the business world, the use of networks to provide efficient and cost-effective employee training is increasing in acceptance. Online learning opportunities can decrease time-consuming and costly travel yet still ensure that all employees are adequately trained to perform their jobs in a safe and productive manner.

Online courseware and delivery offer many benefits to businesses, including the following:

- **Current and accurate training materials:** Collaboration among vendors, equipment manufacturers, and training providers ensures that the courseware is up to date with the latest processes and procedures. When errors in materials are found and corrected, the new courseware is immediately available to all employees.

- **Availability of training to a wide audience:** Online training is not dependent on travel schedules, instructor availability, or physical class size. Employees can be given deadlines by which training is to be completed, and they can access the courseware when it is convenient.

- **Consistent quality of instruction:** The quality of the instruction does not vary as it would if different instructors were delivering an in-person course. The online curriculum provides a consistent core of instruction to which instructors can add additional expertise.

- **Cost reduction:** In addition to reducing the cost of travel and the lost time associated with travel, there are other cost-reducing factors for business related to online training. It is usually less expensive to revise and update online courseware than it is to update paper-based material. Facilities to support in-person training can also be reduced or eliminated.

Many businesses also provide customer training online. This courseware enables the customers to use the products and services provided by the business in the best manner, reducing calls to the help lines or customer service centers.

Networks Supporting the Way We Work

Advances in computer networks have had a tremendous impact on businesses. Many economists attribute much of the economic growth of the past couple of decades to increased productivity in business stemming from improved business technologies.

Many companies use collaboration software packages that allow distributed work groups—people working together but not in the same physical location—to interactively create documents and contribute to projects in real time. These collaboration tools demonstrate the global nature of online business and are now essential to large and small businesses alike.

Different companies use different types of networks. Employees can meet on the Internet, or they can join a restricted group on a company *intranet*, which allows only internal employee access. Another type of network is an *extranet*, a type of network that allows outside vendors special access to limited information in a company.

To reap the benefits of these technology tools, businesses must provide the continuing training and education of workers. The ability to learn and adopt new ways to implement technology into the workplace is a valuable skill sought after by most employers.

Most of the preceding examples highlight the benefits that larger corporations experience from computer networks. Networks also have enabled small businesses to achieve success. Consider these scenarios based on small businesses stories:

- A small bookstore owner has been struggling to survive in a business location that sees a decline in foot traffic and forecasts going out of business within a year. As he prepares to close the store, he lists his rare book inventory on the web. Over a couple of months, the web traffic grows, and he gets better prices for his books. Soon the web traffic outpaces foot traffic. Within four months, he relocates to a much less expensive location and shifts the business focus to web-based retailing of rare books. By adapting to changing technologies, the bookseller is thriving in a more lucrative sector of the business.

- On a fishing boat off the coast of Alaska, the crew picks the best fish from a catch and puts them, still alive, into a special holding tank on the boat. Looking into the tank is a webcam, connected to the web using *wireless technology* through satellite. Meanwhile, at a top-quality restaurant in Washington, D.C., the owner wants only the finest-quality fish served on her menu. She browses the web to her favorite provider, who links her to the fisherman on his boat in Alaska. She is able to pick the fish she wants. Arrangements are made with a shipping company for overnight delivery. The restaurant owner tracks the shipment on the web, and when she sees that it will arrive in time for dinner, she edits and prints the menu. In this scenario, two businesses thousands of miles apart use networks to work together to provide a top-quality product for the best price.

Not more than a decade or so ago, neither of these scenarios would have been possible. These success stories, along with thousands of others like them, happened because people used networking technologies in imaginative ways to succeed in business.

Networks Supporting the Way We Play

You have learned how networks provide learning and business opportunities, but they offer plenty of recreation options as well. Travel sites can respond to last-minute market conditions for hotel, flight, and cruise availability, which benefits both sellers and consumers. Media and entertainment companies provide websites that offer books, games, TV shows, and movies. The music industry provides songs for download. While the web has helped the music industry reach new audiences and cut costs, record companies have also faced new challenges, such as music-sharing sites and copyright issues. Online auction sites provide an excellent venue for hobbyists and collectors to exchange information and items safely and securely.

Some of the most innovative developments in network technology come about trying to satisfy the voracious appetite of the entertainment sector. Online game companies are constantly pushing for better bandwidth and faster processing to improve their products, and online gamers are willing to spend the money necessary to buy the latest equipment that will improve their gaming experience.

Movie rentals and video-sharing and -distribution systems are newer web technologies that are quickly evolving as faster web connections become more widespread.

Communication: An Essential Part of Our Lives

Communication in our daily lives takes many forms and occurs in many environments. We have different expectations depending on whether we are chatting through the Internet or participating in a job interview. Each situation has its corresponding expected behaviors and styles.

These expectations are the rules of communication, and some of the elements are universal. Taking a closer look at the way humans communicate will introduce many of the necessary elements of network communication as well.

What Is Communication?

People have many ways of communicating with each other. Whether the communication is verbal or nonverbal, face-to-face or over the telephone, or in a handwritten letter or in a chat room, successful communication requires common rules.

The rules of communication are also known as protocols. Some of the protocols required for communication to occur include the presence of

- An identified sender and receiver

- An agreed-upon method of communicating (face-to-face, telephone, letter, photograph, and so on)

- Common language and grammar

- An agreed-upon speed and timing of delivery (for example, "Please slow down so that I can understand you.")

- Confirmation or acknowledgment requirements (for example, "Is that clear?" "Yes, thank you.")

Not all communications have the same agreed-upon protocols. For example, an important legal letter can require a signature and response from the recipient, but personal letters need no such acknowledgment.

People are unaware of many of the rules they follow while communicating because they are ingrained in language and culture. Tone of voice, pausing between thoughts, and polite ways to interrupt are just a few examples of implicit rules that humans follow.

Quality of Communication

Computers and computer networks have no such ingrained communication knowledge, but similar protocols are still required for network devices to communicate. Successful communication between computer network devices, just as is true with communication between people, occurs when the meaning of the message understood by the recipient matches the meaning intended by the sender.

There are many potential barriers to successful communication between computers on a network. The process of sending a message on a computer network can be complex and have many steps and conditions, and any step poorly performed or condition not properly met can potentially ruin the message. The steps and conditions, or factors, can be separated into internal and external groups.

The external factors stem from the complexity of the network and the number of devices handling the message en route to the destination. Examples of external factors include the following:

- The quality of the pathway between the sender and the recipient

- The number of times the message has to change form

- The number of times the message has to be redirected or readdressed

- The number of other messages being transmitted simultaneously on the communication network

- The amount of time allotted for successful communication

Internal factors include the following:

- The size of the message

- The complexity of the message

- The importance of the message

More complex messages can be more difficult for the recipient to understand, and larger messages have a greater potential to be distorted or incomplete at the destination.

The Network as a Platform

The ability to reliably communicate to anyone, anywhere, is becoming increasingly important to our personal and business lives. Adding to the demand of immediacy is the requirement that different types of messages, such as phone, text, and video, be accommodated as normal forms of communication. To support the immediate delivery of the millions of various messages being exchanged among people all over the world, we rely on a web of interconnected networks. The following sections describe communication over networks, different elements that make up a network, and convergence.

Communicating over Networks

Networks directly impact how we live, and the role of networks is increasingly important to people in all parts of the world. The task of reliably delivering millions of messages simultaneously would be too much for any one network to perform. Therefore, a web of smaller, interconnected networks of various sizes and capabilities delivers the many messages and data streams around the world.

Elements of a Network

The webs of data or information networks vary in size and capabilities, but all networks have four basic elements in common:

- **Rules or agreements:** Rules or agreements (protocols) govern how the messages are sent, directed, received, and interpreted.

- **Messages:** The messages or units of information travel from one device to another.

- **Medium:** A medium is a means of interconnecting these devices, that is, a medium can transport the messages from one device to another.

- **Devices:** Devices on the network exchange messages with each other.

Figure 1-1 depicts a small network featuring rules, messages, a medium, and two devices.

Figure 1-1   Elements of a Network

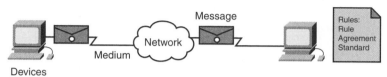

Early networks had varying *standards* and, as a result, could not communicate easily with each other. Now global standardization of these elements enables easy communication between networks regardless of the equipment manufacturer.

People use many technologies and devices that they do not completely understand. Driving a car, for example, is a common function for many people. When a driver starts a car, puts it into gear, and steps on the gas, many systems begin to work together. The car moves because an ignition system started the car, a fuel system regulates power, electrical systems run lights and gauges, and a complex transmission chooses appropriate gears to make the car move as directed by the driver. All of this happens under the hood and out of sight and mind to the driver, who focuses on the task of driving safely to a destination. Most drivers know little or nothing about how a car works but are still able to use it effectively for their own purpose.

Computer networks are similar to cars in the example. Two people communicating on end devices in different networks can do so only if many complex processes are successfully completed. These processes include a message, some form of media, various devices, and protocols working together.

Message

Messages is a generic term that encompasses web pages, e-mail, instant messages, telephone calls, and other forms of communication enabled by the Internet. The message must be one that the network can carry. First, the messages must be supported in software at the end devices. Instant messaging and chat, for example, require some software setup before a session can begin. Different software is required for audio and video conferencing. These software programs that support communication functions are called services, and to initiate a message, a service must be installed. Examples of services include e-mail, IP telephony, and use of the World Wide Web.

It does not matter whether the message is text, voice, or video, because all forms are converted into *bits*, *binary*-coded digital signals, to be carried over a wireless, copper, or fiber-optic connection. The digital signal can change with the media, but the original message content will remain intact.

Medium

The medium that physically carries the message can change several times between the sender and the receiver. Network connections can be wired or wireless.

In wired connections, the medium is either copper, which carries electrical signals, or optical fiber, which carries light signals. The copper medium includes cables, such as twisted-pair telephone wire, coaxial cable, or most commonly, what is known as Category 5 unshielded twisted-pair (UTP) cable. Optical fibers, thin strands of glass or plastic that carry light signals, are another form of networking media.

In wireless connections, the medium is the Earth's atmosphere, or space, and the signals are microwaves. Wireless media can include the home wireless connection between a wireless router and a computer with a wireless network card, the terrestrial wireless connection between two ground stations, or the communication between devices on Earth and satellites. In a typical journey across the Internet, a message can travel across a variety of media.

Devices

Several devices, such as switches and routers, work to see that the message is properly directed from the *source*, or originating device, to the destination device. At the destination network there can be more switches, cable, or perhaps a wireless router that will deliver the instant message to the receiver.

Graphics and icons are common when reading about networks. Icons, or small pictures arranged to represent a network's layout, can greatly clarify information about the design of the network. Figure 1-2 shows various network device symbols. The desktop, laptop, and IP phone represent end-user devices, whereas the rest of the icons depict network equipment or media used to connect the end devices. These icons do not refer to specific models or features on devices, which can vary greatly. Table 1-1 briefly describes the network symbols.

Figure 1-2   Network Device Symbols

Table 1-1   Internal and External Factors Affecting Successful Communication

Symbol	Description
Desktop computer	A common computer used in a home or office
Laptop	A portable computer
Server	A computer dedicated to providing application services to end users on a network
IP phone	A digital telephone that carries voice as data over data networks instead of analog phone lines
LAN media	Local-area network media, usually copper cable
Wireless media	Depicts local-area network wireless access
LAN switch	The most common device for interconnecting local-area networks
Firewall	A device that provides security to networks
Router	A device that helps direct messages between networks
Wireless router	A specific type of router often found in home networks
Cloud	A symbol used to summarize a group of networking devices out of local management control, often the Internet itself
WAN media	One form of wide-area network (WAN) interconnection, represented by the lightning bolt–shaped line

The standardization of the various elements of the network enables equipment and devices created by different companies to work together. Experts in various technologies can contribute their best ideas on how to develop an efficient network, without regard to the brand or manufacturer of the equipment.

Rules

All communication processes happen, as far as humans can tell, in an instant, and tens of thousands of processes can happen in a single second. To work properly, the network processes must be tightly controlled. Rules govern every step of the process, from the way cables are designed to the way the digital signals are sent. These rules are called protocols, and the communications industry has standardized most of them to allow people in different places with different equipment to communicate. The most common protocols are *IP (Internet Protocol)* and *TCP (Transmission Control Protocol)*. These protocols work together and are usually known as the TCP/IP protocol stack. TCP/IP works along other protocols, for example, Extensible Messaging and Presence Protocol (XMPP), which is an instant messaging protocol, to provide communication rules involving different services. Table 1-2 lists some common services and the protocols that support them.

Table 1-2   Services and Their Protocols

Service	Protocol ("Rule")
World Wide Web (WWW)	HTTP (Hypertext Transport Protocol)
E-mail	SMTP (Simple Mail Transport Protocol) and POP (Post Office Protocol)
Instant message (Jabber, AIM)	XMPP (Extensible Messaging and Presence Protocol) and OSCAR (Open System for Communication in Realtime)
IP telephony	SIP (Session Initiation Protocol)

People often only picture networks in the abstract sense: We create and send a text message, and it almost immediately shows up on the destination device. Although we know that between our sending device and the receiving device there is a network over which our message travels, we rarely think about all the parts and pieces that make up that infrastructure. The following list ties together how the elements of networks—devices, media, and services—are connected by rules to deliver a message:

1. An end user types an instant message to a friend using an application on a PC.

2. The instant message gets converted into a format that can be transmitted on the network. All types of message formats—text, video, voice, or data—must be converted to bits before being sent to their destinations. After the instant message is converted to bits, it is ready to be sent onto the network for delivery.

3. The network interface card (NIC) inside the PC generates electrical signals to represent the bits and places the bits on the medium so that they can travel to the first network device.

4. The bits are passed from device to device in the local network.

5. If the bits need to leave the local network, they leave through a router connecting to a different network. There can be dozens, even hundreds, of devices handling the bits as they are routed to their destination.

6. As the bits get close to their destination, they once again get passed through local devices.

7. Finally, the NIC on the destination device accepts the bits and converts them back into a readable text message.

Converged Networks

Communication technologies evolved at different times and in different places in the twentieth century. Many developments in radio broadcast technology were driven by military necessity, yet developments in broadcast television grew to answer a market demand. The telephone evolved as a wired technology and then as a wireless technology. Computer communication developments came much later in the century. For example, the first text e-mail message was sent in the 1960s, but e-mail did not become popular until the 1980s. Now it is quite common to use a computer for instant messaging, telephone calls, and video sharing.

The technology and protocols of each of these communication methods developed largely independent of each other, and most users of TV, telephone, and computer services pay different providers for each service. But recent developments in each area have driven broadcast and telephony to the digital technology already used by computers. This coming together of technologies onto a digital platform is called *convergence*.

Convergence occurs when telephones, broadcasts, and computer communications all use the same rules, devices, and media to transport their messages. On a converged network, or platform, different devices, such as televisions or cell phones, will use a common network infrastructure to communicate.

Figure 1-3 demonstrates the concept of nonconverged systems on the left and a converged network on the right.

Figure 1-3   Convergence

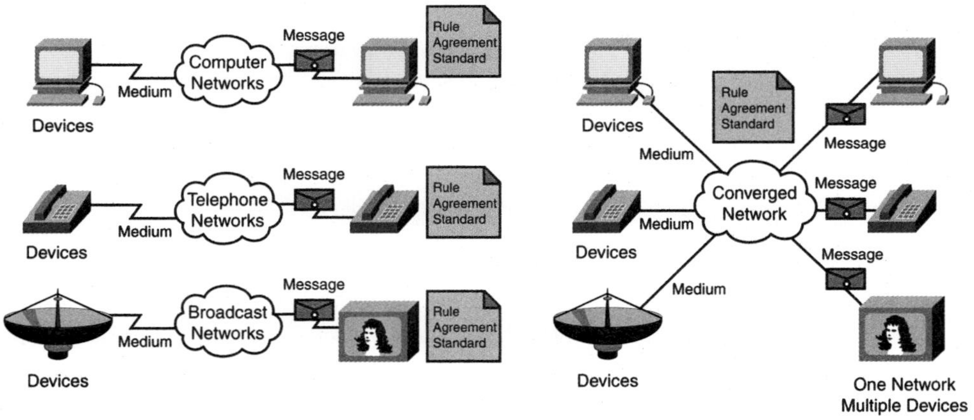

Network technologies are still evolving and converging. As improvements occur, the services offered will expand beyond communications and into shared applications. The convergence of the different types of communications networks onto one platform represents the first phase in building the intelligent information network. We are currently in this phase of network evolution. The next phase will be to consolidate not only the different types of messages onto a single network but also to consolidate the applications that generate, transmit, and secure the messages onto integrated network devices. Not only will voice and video be transmitted over the same network, the devices that perform the telephone switching and video broadcasting will be the same devices that route the messages through the network. The resulting communications platform will provide high-quality application functionality at a reduced cost.

The Internet is the prime example of converging technologies. Websites on which users interact through web phone and video-sharing sites are among the most popular on the web, and few existed just a couple of years ago. Considering how quickly these services became popular on the web, it makes sense to expect new services to change the way people work and play on the web.

The Architecture of the Internet

The term *network architecture* refers to the conceptual plans on which a physical network is built. Just as a building's architect must consider the function of the building and the expected needs of a building's users, so too must network architects design the Internet to accommodate the needs of the web and its users. The Internet has far exceeded the original expectations of size and use, which is a testament to how strong the foundations of the Internet were planned and implemented.

The Network Architecture

The Internet's design meets four fundamental expectations: fault tolerance, scalability, quality of service (QoS), and security. These topics are introduced here, and their implementation is discussed in the following section.

Fault tolerance, simply stated, means that the Internet will continue to function normally even when some of the components of the network fail. ***Redundancy***, or the duplication of equipment and media, is a key factor in fault tolerance. If a server fails, a redundant server performing the same functions should be able to pick up the work until repairs are made. If a data link fails on a fault-tolerant network, messages will be routed to the destination on a duplicate route. Figure 1-4 depicts a fault-tolerant network with a failed network router.

Figure 1-4   Fault Tolerance

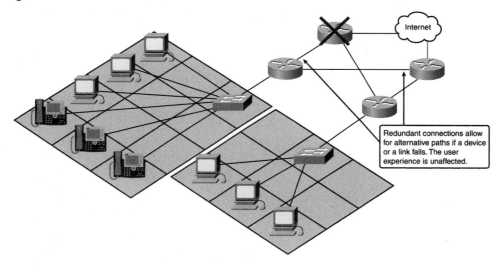

Redundant connections allow for alternative paths if a device or a link fails. The user experience is unaffected.

Scalability describes the network's ability to grow and react to future changes. A scalable network can accept new users and equipment without having to start over on the design. As mentioned earlier, it is certain that changes in the ways networks are used will occur, and having an adaptable, or scalable, network will allow the insertion of new users without having to rebuild the entire network. A scalable network will be able to grow internally and externally, joining other networks to form an ***internetwork*** that can grow to keep pace with user demand.

QoS indicates the performance level of services offered through the network. Services such as live video or voice can require more resources than services such as e-mail. Because many technologies are converged onto one platform, the separation of types of services on that platform can allow higher priority for one service over another. For example, a network administrator can determine that the data from attendees of a web meeting has priority over e-mail service. Configuring devices to prioritize types of data is an example of QoS.

Network security is essential if the public is to have confidence when using the Internet. People using the Internet to do business demand security for their financial transactions, and government and businesses that require personal information (for example, a hospital or doctor's office) must provide the protection of their clients' privacy. Just as citizens of a town expect safety and security, so does the community of web users. Without it, just like citizens of a town, the users will find another place to do business. Encrypted messages and the use of security devices at the gate of a local network are methods of implementing security.

Encryption and firewalls are not necessarily enough to protect a network, however. The security and privacy expectations that result from the use of internetworks to exchange confidential and business-critical information exceed what the current architecture can deliver. As a result, much effort is being devoted to this area of research and development. In the meantime, many tools and procedures are being implemented to combat inherent security flaws in the network architecture.

Figure 1-5 indicates how firewall settings on a router add security to network architecture by controlling network access.

Figure 1-5   Network Security

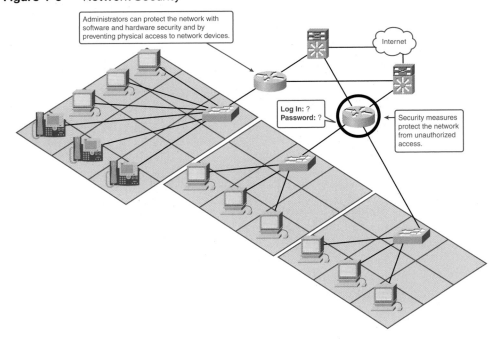

Fault-Tolerant Network Architecture

The architects of the Internet began their designs with fault tolerance as a high priority. The Internet came about when the United States Department of Defense (DoD) planners wanted to design a communication medium that could withstand widespread destruction of telephone and other communication infrastructure.

Circuit-Switched, Connection-Oriented Networks

The existing infrastructure at the time was a circuit-switched, connection-oriented network. Phone operators and primitive dial systems connected telephone calls by setting up a temporary circuit that was a physical connection on which the phone signal would travel from sender to receiver. The technology was connection oriented because any physical disconnect or service problem between the two users would drop the call. This would require initiating a new call and provisioning a new circuit.

The circuit-switched design provided new service to customers, but it had flaws as well. For example, only one phone call occupied each circuit, and no other calls could use the circuit until the previous call ended. This inefficiency limited the capacity of the phone system and made it expensive, especially for long-distance calls. From the DoD perspective, the system was vulnerable to easy disruption from enemy attacks.

Packet-Switched, Connectionless Networks

The answer to the fault tolerance issue was converting to a packet-switched, connectionless network. On a packet-switched network, a single message is broken into small blocks of data, known as *packets*, which address information for the sender and the receiver. The packets then travel through one or more networks along various paths and reassemble at the destination.

The packets travel independently of each other and often take different routes to a destination. Messages are usually broken into thousands of packets, and it is common for some of them to be lost along the way. Protocols allow for this and contain methods for requesting retransmission of packets lost en route.

Packet-switched technology is connectionless because it does not require an active connection for the call to go through. This allows more efficiency than circuit-switched networks because multiple users can use network circuits simultaneously. Packet-switched technology is fault tolerant because it avoids the perils of relying on a single circuit for service reliability. If one network path fails, another network path can deliver the entire message.

Figure 1-6 depicts a packet-switched network with several alternative routes between the source and destination.

Figure 1-6   Packet-Switched Network

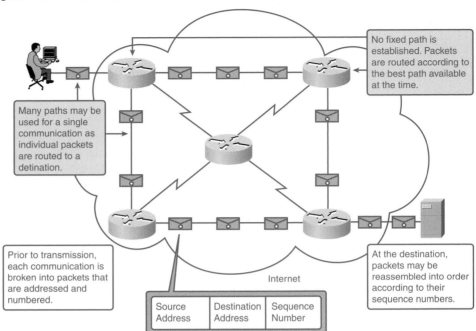

Packet-switched networks are the standard for the Internet, but a niche market remains for circuit-switched networks. Circuit-switched networks today allow circuit failure and session reestablishment, and some customers like the reliability and security that come from modern dedicated circuits. Circuit-switched connections are more expensive than packet-switched networks, but many institutions require the constant circuit availability and security and are willing to pay the extra price.

Scalable Network Architecture

A scalable network is able to grow without undergoing fundamental change at its core. The Internet is an example of scalable design. The Internet has grown exponentially in the past decade or so, and the core design is unchanged. The Internet is a collection of many private and public networks interconnected by routers.

Large tier-1 Internet service providers (ISP) house the largest domain servers that track Internet addresses. That information is replicated and shared in the lower tiers in the system. This hierarchical, multitiered design allows most traffic to be processed away from the upper-tier servers. This distribution of processing work means that changes made at the lower tiers, such as adding a new ISP, do not affect the upper levels.

Figure 1-7 demonstrates the hierarchical design of the web. Traffic between lower tiers can bypass the upper-tier servers in the Internet. This allows upper tiers to work more efficiently as well as to provide alternate paths for peak web traffic.

Figure 1-7   Hierarchical Internet

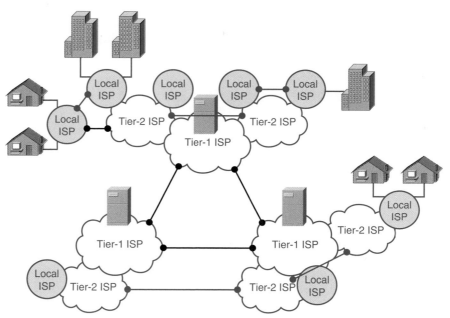

Although the Internet is a collection of independently managed networks, the growth of the web is possible because of individual network managers adhering to standards that allow interconnectivity and scalability. The network managers must also be adaptable to new standards and protocols that enhance the usability of the Internet. Networks that do not adhere to standards can encounter communication problems when connecting to the Internet.

Providing Quality of Service

When the Internet first came into public use, people were amazed at the new tasks they could do and were tolerant of delays and dropped messages. Now, however, users have adapted to higher speeds and a greater *quality of service (QoS)*.

QoS refers to the mechanisms that manage congested network traffic. Congestion is caused when the demand on the network resources exceeds the available capacity. There are some constraints on network resources that cannot be avoided. Constraints include technology limitations, costs, and the local availability of high-bandwidth service. Network *bandwidth* is the measure of the data-carrying capacity of the network. When simultaneous communications are attempted across the network, the demand for network bandwidth can exceed its availability. The obvious fix for this situation is to increase the amount of available bandwidth. But, because of the previously stated constraints, this is not always possible.

Using QoS, a manager can choose which traffic gets priority for processing in the network. For example, most people expect telephone service to be reliable and clear. Many companies want to save money by moving their long-distance phone calls onto the Internet using Voice over Internet Protocol (VoIP) services. If the users cannot distinguish any difference between regular phones and VoIP phones, they will not mind the change. But if network congestion causes the VoIP phones to experience delays and dropped calls, users will return to the old expensive service. The network administrator must ensure that the quality of voice service is as high as possible, and she can do this by giving voice traffic priority over other web traffic.

Different companies and institutions have different needs and priorities. Some companies might prioritize voice traffic, others might want to give priority to video traffic, and still others might want to give priority to traffic carrying financial data. These various needs can be met by classifying network traffic and assigning priorities to each classification.

Classification of traffic means putting web traffic into categories. Because so many types of web traffic exist, assigning each its own priority is not practical. Thus, using one category for time-sensitive traffic such as voice and video and another category for less sensitive traffic like e-mail and document transfers is a way to sort traffic into manageable groups. Not every network will have the same priorities, and different institutions will assign data types into different categories according to their needs. After traffic types are categorized, they can be put into queues.

Examples of priority decisions for an organization might include

- **Time-sensitive communication:** Increase priority for services like telephony or video distribution.

- **Non-time-sensitive communication:** Decrease priority for web page retrieval or e-mail.

- **High importance to organization:** Increase priority for production control or business transaction data.

- **Undesirable communication:** Decrease priority or block unwanted activity, like peer-to-peer file sharing or live entertainment.

Getting into a queue means getting into a line. An example of *priority queuing* can be found at an airport check-in counter. There are two classes of passengers in queues: a queue for coach passengers and a separate queue at the end of the counter for first-class passengers. When airline agents become available, they will choose to help passengers from the first-class queue ahead of someone who has been waiting longer in the coach class queue. The coach class passengers are still important, and the agents will eventually help them, but the airlines give priority to first-class passengers because they value the extra revenue those customers bring to the company.

In networking priority, queuing is much the same as the airline ticket counter process. Network managers assign priorities to traffic categories and allow the more important categories to have better access to the network's bandwidth. Figure 1-8 demonstrates different classes of traffic having different priority access to bandwidth.

Figure 1-8   Priority Queuing

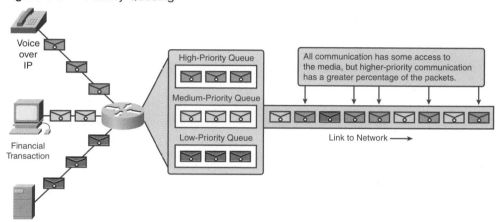

Consider the earlier example of VoIP traffic at a company. If voice traffic has better access to company bandwidth than other traffic, the voice quality will be better and the users will more likely be satisfied. Satisfied users will use the VoIP service and save the company money. Reduced costs and better service are the major incentives for network managers to provide QoS.

Providing Network Security

The Internet has proven to be fertile ground for business, and business-to-business transactions and e-commerce are sustaining significant growth every year. The same environment that attracts legitimate business, however, also attracts scam artists and vandals. Compromising the integrity of company assets could have serious business and financial repercussions. As a result, network security is a major concern of web providers and users, and web safety is a key part of any network management plan.

A network security breach can lead to a variety of serious consequences, including the following:

- Network outage, causing a loss of communication and business transactions

- Loss of personal or business funds

- Theft of intellectual property such as project bids, patents, and strategic plans

- Exposure of confidential customer data

Each of these examples could cause a customer to lose confidence in the company and hasten a move to a more reliable vendor. To provide security, a network manager must address two areas:

- Network infrastructure security

- Content security

Securing the network infrastructure means protecting the devices from outside contact. Locking computer room doors and using quality password protection on network equipment and software are simple steps that can go a long way to securing an infrastructure.

Securing network content means protection of data stored on network devices and the protection of packets carrying data into or out of the network. Content security on a network means ensuring confidentiality, maintaining communication integrity, and ensuring network availability.

Ensuring Confidentiality

Data privacy is maintained by allowing only the intended and authorized recipients—individuals, processes, or devices—to read the data. Different methods ensure data confidentiality. Having a strong system for user *authentication*, enforcing passwords that are difficult to guess, and requiring users to change passwords frequently help restrict access to communications and to data stored on network-attached devices. Where appropriate, encrypting content ensures confidentiality and minimizes unauthorized disclosure or theft of information.

Maintaining Communication Integrity

Data integrity means having the assurance that the information has not been altered in transmission, from origin to destination. Data integrity can be compromised when information has been corrupted—willfully or accidentally—before the intended recipient receives it.

Source integrity is the assurance that the identity of the sender has been validated. Source integrity is compromised when a user or device fakes its identity and supplies incorrect information to a recipient.

Digital signatures, hashing algorithms, and checksum mechanisms provide source and data integrity across a network to prevent unauthorized modification of information.

Ensuring Availability

Making sure that resources are available to authorized users is an important part of a security plan. If a network is unavailable to a company using web-based business practices, the business can be slowed to a halt. Computer virus attacks and denial of service (DoS) attacks can bring a network down. A DoS attack occurs when outside computers flood a network with so many requests for service that valid users cannot access the network resources. Tools to combat virus and DoS attacks include antivirus software on servers and desktops, and *firewalls*, which are routers and servers that are network gatekeepers that analyze traffic entering and exiting a network. Building fully redundant network infrastructures, with few *single points of failure* that can bring the network down, can reduce the impact of these threats.

Fault tolerance, scalability, quality of service, and security are foundations on which to build a reliable and useful network. You will learn more about these in greater depth in this book and online course and in later courses.

Trends in Networking

Making precise predictions about the distant future of technology is a difficult task. Looking at current trends can show near-term developments that are on the horizon and the career opportunities that can be available to you.

Where Is It All Going?

The convergence of the many different communication media onto a single network platform is fueling exponential growth in network capabilities. Three major trends are contributing to the future shape of complex information networks:

- Increasing number of mobile users

- Proliferation of network-capable devices

- Expanding range of services

The following sections describe each trend and its possible impact.

Mobile Users

The trend of mobile use is contributing to changes in the traditional workplace from one where workers travel to a central office to one where the office travels with the worker. More mobile workers can use handheld devices such as cell phones, laptops, and personal digital assistants (PDA), which have evolved from luxury gadgets to necessary tools. Increased wireless service in metropolitan areas has unleashed people from their wired computers and freed them to work away from their desks.

Mobile workers and those who rely on handheld devices require more mobile connectivity to data networks. This demand has created a market for wireless services that have greater flexibility, coverage, and security.

New and More Capable Devices

The computer is only one of many devices on today's information networks. A proliferation of new technologies takes advantage of available network services.

Homes and small offices have access to services such as wireless technology and increased bandwidth that were once available only to corporate offices and educational institutions. Web-enabled phones give users access to Internet applications and e-mail anywhere in cell phone range.

The functions performed by cell phones, PDAs, organizers, and pagers are converging into single handheld devices with continuous connectivity to providers of services and content. These devices, once thought of as "toys" or luxury items, are now an integral part of how people communicate. In addition to mobile devices, we have VoIP devices, gaming systems, and a large assortment of household and business gadgets that can connect and use network services.

Increased Availability of Services

The widespread acceptance of technology and the fast pace of innovation in network-delivered services create a spiraling dependence. To meet user demands, new services are introduced and older services are enhanced. As the users come to trust these expanded services, they want even more capabilities. The network then grows to support the increasing demand. People depend on the services provided over the network, and therefore depend on the availability and reliability of the underlying network infrastructure.

These highly mobile users and their increasingly capable devices require more complex services that are reliable and secure. As these improved tools and services become available to the public, the public demand for network bandwidth will increase as well.

These increases in demand point to growing networks and the new opportunities that will come with them. The challenge of keeping pace with an ever-expanding network of users and services is the responsibility of trained network and IT professionals.

Networking Career Opportunities

The implementation of new technologies is constantly changing the fields of information technology (IT). Network architects, information security managers, and e-commerce specialists are joining software engineers and database administrators in the IT workplace.

As non-IT fields, such as hospital management and education, become more technical in nature, the need for IT professionals with backgrounds in diverse fields such as medicine and education will increase.

Summary

Data networks play an increasing role in the way humans communicate with each other. The Internet and local networks directly impact the way people live, learn, and work.

The process for delivering messages across a computer network involves protocols defining agreements on how to deliver the message between user devices across a medium. The type of media and the devices used to deliver the message are subject to appropriate protocols as well.

Converged data networks can provide different types of services, including text, voice, and video messages between end users. Converged networks provide businesses with an opportunity to reduce costs and offer users a variety of services and content. However, the design and management of converged networks require extensive networking knowledge and skills if all services are to be delivered as expected to users.

A network's architecture must provide scalability, fault tolerance, quality of service, and security.

QoS is an important part of network planning that can affect user productivity. Prioritization of network data can allow an efficient balance of data types flowing through the network.

Security of network infrastructure and content will continue to be an essential element of a successful network, as it directly affects user confidence.

Activities and Labs

The activities and labs available in the companion *Network Fundamentals, CCNA Exploration Labs and Study Guide* (ISBN 1-58713-203-6) provide hands-on practice with the following topics introduced in this chapter:

Activity 1-1: Using Google Earth to View the World (1.1.1.4)

Use satellite imagery available through the Internet to explore your world.

Activity 1-2: Identifying Top Security Vulnerabilities (1.4.5.3)

Upon completion of this activity, you will be able to use the SANS site to quickly identify Internet security threats and explain how threats are organized.

Lab 1-1: Using Collaboration Tools—IRC and IM (1.6.1.1)

In this lab, you will define Internet Relay Chat (IRC) and Instant Messaging (IM). You also will list several misuses and data security issues involving IM.

Lab 1-2: Using Collaboration Tools—Wikis and Web Logs (1.6.2.1)

In this lab, you will define the terms *wiki* and *blog*. You will also explain the purpose of a wiki and blog and how these technologies are used for collaboration.

Many of the hands-on labs include Packet Tracer companion activities where you can use Packet Tracer to complete a simulation of the lab. Look for this icon in the *Network Fundamentals, CCNA Exploration Labs and Study Guide* (ISBN 1-58713-203-6) for hands-on labs that have Packet Tracer companion activities.

Check Your Understanding

Complete all the review questions listed here to test your understanding of the topics and concepts in this chapter. The appendix, "Check Your Understanding and Challenge Questions Answer Key," lists the answers.

1. Which form of communication is a real-time, text-based communication type used between two or more people who use mostly text to communicate?

   A. Weblogs

   B. Wikis

   C. Instant messaging

   D. Podcasting

2. Which type of network provides customers with limited access to corporate data such as inventory, parts lists, and orders?

   A. Intranet

   B. Extranet

   C. Internetwork

   D. Internet

3. _____ are collaborative web pages created and edited by users.

4. What prioritizes traffic and its characteristics to manage data?

   A. Network administration

   B. Network traffic

   C. QoS strategy

   D. Network evaluation

5. Rules that govern the process of network communication are called _____.

6. What network traffic processes must be in place for quality of service strategies to work correctly? (Choose two.)

   A. Traffic is classified based on quality of service requirements.

   B. Priorities are assigned to each classification of application data.

   C. Web traffic is always assigned to a high-priority queue for processing.

   D. Digital movies are always assigned to the high-priority queue for processing.

   E. E-mail traffic is always assigned to the low-priority queue.

7. Copper cables and fiber-optic cables are two types of network _____.

8. What are two components of network architecture? (Choose two.)

   A. People that comprise the human network

   B. Built-in growth potential

   C. Data transfer across the network

   D. Redundant technologies

   E. Corporations that operate and maintain the data network

9. Symbols that graphically represent network devices and media are called _____.

10. For which three reasons were circuit-switched, connection-oriented technologies rejected when the Internet was being developed? (Choose three.)

   A. Circuit-switched technologies required that a single message be broken up into multiple message blocks that contain addressing information.

   B. Early circuit-switched networks did not automatically establish alternative circuits in the event of circuit failure.

   C. Circuit-switched technologies required that an open circuit between network endpoints be established even if data was not being actively transferred between locations.

   D. The quality and consistency of messages transmitted across a connection-oriented, circuit-switched network cannot be guaranteed.

   E. The establishment of simultaneous open circuits for fault tolerance is costly.

11. For which three reasons was a packet-switched, connectionless data communications technology used when developing the Internet? (Choose three.)

   A. It can rapidly adapt to the loss of data transmission facilities.

   B. It efficiently utilizes the network infrastructure to transfer data.

   C. Data packets can travel multiple paths through the network simultaneously.

   D. It allows billing of network use by the amount of time a connection is established.

   E. It requires that a data circuit between the source and destination be established before data can be transferred.

12. A _____ is a device that helps direct messages between networks.

13. What is the role of QoS in a converged network?

   A. Ensures that all traffic above available bandwidth levels is dropped

   B. Establishes delivery priorities for different types of communication in a network

   C. Determines precise priorities for all types of network communication

   D. Allows unused bandwidth to be shared by other organizations within the network

14. Which term describes a common platform for diverse communication types?

   A. Scalability

   B. Convergence

   C. Fault tolerance

   D. Quality of service

15. Connectionless messages are broken into _____.

16. Which of the following pertains to network infrastructure security?

   A. A competitor accesses sensitive information through an unsecured wireless network.

   B. Builders accidentally cut a network cable while digging.

   C. A disgruntled employee alters information in a customer database.

   D. A secretary sends confidential information in a reply to an e-mail that falsely appears to come from her boss.

Challenge Questions and Activities

These questions require a deeper application of the concepts covered in this chapter. You can find the answers in the appendix.

1. A worker is assigned to work on a project with another employee from a different city. During online meetings, there are periods of sketchy video and garbled voice communications. Which combination of the following conditions could cause this?

   A. Poor scalability in network design

   B. Poor security, allowing someone to download music and video files at work

   C. Lack of redundant links to the firewall

   D. Poor QoS

2. Which pair of terms describes a network communication in which a bank has 24-hour exclusive access to an ATM? (Choose one.)

   A. Connectionless and packet-switched

   B. Packet-switched and connection-oriented

   C. Circuit-switched and connection-oriented

   D. Circuit-switched and connectionless

| Packet Tracer |
| ☐ **Challenge** |

Look for this icon in *Network Fundamentals, CCNA Exploration Labs and Study Guide* (ISBN 1-58713-203-6) for instructions on how to perform the Packet Tracer Skills Integration Challenge for this chapter.

To Learn More

To learn more about a milestone in the history of communications, read about Claude Shannon and his famous paper, "A Mathematical Theory of Communication."

CHAPTER 2

Communicating over the Network

Objectives

Upon completion of this chapter, you will able to answer the following questions:

- What is the structure of a network, including devices and media necessary for communications?

- What function do protocols perform in network communications?

- What are the advantages of using a layered model to describe network functionality?

- What is the role of each layer in the OSI network model and the TCP/IP network model?

- What is the importance of addressing and naming schemes in network communications?

Key Terms

This chapter uses the following key terms. You can find the definitions in the Glossary.

channel   page 35

segmentation   page 35

multiplexing   page 36

switch   page 37

end device   page 37

host   page 37

client   page 37

host address   page 38

physical address   page 38

intermediary device   page 38

encoding   page 39

local-area network (LAN)   page 41

Internet service provider (ISP)   page 42

protocols   page 44

protocol suite   page 45

Institute of Electrical and Electronics Engineers (IEEE)   page 46

Internet Engineering Task Force (IETF)   page 46

layered models   page 47

TCP/IP   page 48

encapsulation   page 51

decapsulation   page 51

protocol data unit (PDU)   page 51

segment   page 51

frame   page 51

Open Systems Interconnection (OSI)   page 53

International Organization for Standardization (ISO)   page 53

port   page 57

More and more, networks connect us. People communicate online from everywhere. Efficient, dependable technology enables networks to be available whenever and wherever we need them. As the human network continues to expand, the platform that connects and supports it must also grow.

Rather than developing unique and separate systems for the delivery of each new service, the network industry as a whole has developed the means to both analyze the existing platform and enhance it incrementally. This ensures that existing communications are maintained while new services are introduced that are both cost effective and technologically sound.

This book focuses on these aspects of the information network:

- Devices that make up the network

- Media that connect the devices

- Messages that are carried across the network

- Rules and processes that govern network communications

- Tools and commands for constructing and maintaining networks

Central to the study of networks is the use of generally accepted models that describe network functions. These models provide a framework for understanding current networks and for facilitating the development of new technologies to support future communications needs.

Within this book, you learn about these models and the tools designed to analyze and simulate network functionality. Two of the tools that will enable you to build and interact with simulated networks are Packet Tracer 4.1 software and Wireshark network protocol analyzer.

In this chapter, you explore the fundamentals of communication and learn how they apply to communication in and between data networks. You also learn about two important models that describe the process of network communication and the devices used to achieve communication between network hosts.

The Platform for Communications

Networks are becoming the foundation to human communication over distance. In the past decade or so, personal letters have become e-mails, typed and handwritten documents have become word processing files, photographs have become digital, and phone calls are moving from analog to digital. This transformation to a digital platform is possible because computer networks have grown in size, reliability, and diversity, enabling people to take advantage of the benefits of digital communication. The following sections focus on the platform for this digital communication that is built upon fundamental communication concepts. These concepts are applied to devices and media that enable the sending of data messages between end users.

The Elements of Communication

People exchange ideas using many different communication methods. All of these methods have three elements in common:

- **Message source, or sender:** Message sources are people, or electronic devices, that need to send a message to other individuals or devices.

- **Destination, or receiver of the message:** The destination receives the message and interprets it.

- *Channel*: A channel consists of the media that provides the pathway over which the message can travel from source to destination.

This model of sending a message through a channel to the receiver is also the basis of network communication between computers. The computers encode the message into binary signals and transport them across a cable or through wireless media to the receiver, which knows what rules to follow to understand the original message.

The basic model of communication between people and between computers is illustrated in Figure 2-1.

Figure 2-1   Elements of Network Communication

In this book, the term *network* refers to data networks carrying messages containing text, voice, video, and other types of data.

Communicating the Messages

Computer networks carry messages large and small. Devices often exchange updates that are small and require very little bandwidth, yet are very important. Other messages, for example, high-quality photos, can be very large and consume a lot of network resources. Sending a large photograph in one continuous stream of data might mean that a device misses an important update or other communication that will need to be re-sent, using even more bandwidth.

The answer to this problem is a process called *segmentation*, in which all messages are broken into smaller pieces that can be easily transported together across a medium. Segmenting messages has two primary benefits:

- Multiplexing

- Increased efficiency of network communications

Multiplexing occurs when the segments of two or more messages can shuffle into each other and share the medium. Figure 2-2 depicts how messages can be broken into smaller pieces and multiplexed onto a single medium.

Figure 2-2   Multiplexing Messages on a Network

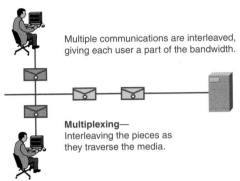

Multiple communications are interleaved, giving each user a part of the bandwidth.

Multiplexing—
Interleaving the pieces as they traverse the media.

A second benefit of segmentation is that networks can more efficiently send the message through different routes if necessary. This can happen because the Internet is always adjusting routes for efficiency. For example, consider what happens if someone in Las Vegas e-mails a picture of her new kitten to a friend in Boston. First, the picture of the kitten is segmented into small pieces and each piece is given, among other things, a destination address and a code telling where the piece belongs in the big picture. When the message is under way, the pieces might not travel along the same route. Traffic conditions on the Internet are constantly changing, and a large file with many segments can take a couple different routes. Depending on traffic conditions, the data containing the kitten's ears might go through Chicago on the way to Boston, the paws might go through Denver, and the whiskers and tail might travel through Atlanta. It doesn't matter which way the pieces travel as long as they all get to Boston and the destination computer can reassemble them into one photograph.

The downside to using segmentation and multiplexing to transmit messages across a network is the level of complexity that is added to the process. Imagine if you had to send a 100-page letter, but each envelope would hold only one page. The process of addressing, labeling, sending, receiving, and opening the entire hundred envelopes would be time consuming for both the sender and the recipient.

In network communications, each segment of the message must go through a similar process to ensure that it gets to the correct destination and can be reassembled into the content of the original message.

Various types of devices throughout the network participate in ensuring that the pieces of the message arrive reliably at their destination.

Components of the Network

The path that a message takes from source to destination can be as simple as a single cable connecting one computer to another or as complex as a network that literally spans the globe. This network infrastructure is the platform that supports our human network. It provides the stable and reliable channel over which our communications can occur.

Devices and media are the physical elements or hardware of the network. Hardware is often the visible components of the network platform such as a laptop, a PC, a *switch*, or the cabling used to connect the devices. Occasionally, some components might not be so visible. In the case of wireless media, messages are transmitted through the air using invisible radio frequency or infrared waves.

Services and processes are the communication programs, called software, that run on the networked devices. A network service provides information in response to a request. Services include many of the common network applications people use every day, like e-mail hosting services and web hosting services. Processes provide the functionality that directs and moves the messages through the network. Processes are less obvious to us but are critical to the operation of networks.

End Devices and Their Role on the Network

An *end device* refers to a piece of equipment that is either the source or the destination of a message on a network. Network users usually only see and touch an end device, which is most often a computer. Another generic term for an end device that sends or receives messages is a *host*. A host can be one of several pieces of equipment performing a wide variety of functions. Examples of hosts and end devices are as follows:

- Computers, including workstations, laptops, and servers connected to a network
- Network printers
- Voice over Internet Protocol (VoIP) phones
- Cameras on a network, including webcams and security cameras
- Handheld devices such as PDAs and handheld scanners
- Remote monitoring stations for weather observation

An end user is a person or group using an end device. Not all end devices are operated by people all of the time, though. For example, file servers are end devices that are set up by people but perform their tasks on their own. Servers are hosts that are set up to store and share information with other hosts called *clients*. Clients request information and services, like e-mail and web pages, from servers, and servers reply with the requested information if they recognize the client.

When hosts communicate with each other, they use addresses to find each other. The *host address* is a unique *physical address* used by hosts inside a local-area network (LAN), and when a host sends a message to another host, it uses the physical address of the destination device.

Intermediary Devices and Their Role on the Network

End devices are the hosts that initiate communications and are the ones that people are most familiar with. But getting a message from the source to the destination can be a complex task involving several *intermediary devices* along the way. Intermediary devices connect the individual hosts to the network and can connect multiple individual networks to form an internetwork.

Intermediary devices are not all the same. Some work inside the LAN performing switching functions, and others help route messages between networks. Table 2-1 lists some intermediary devices and their functions.

Table 2-1   Intermediary Devices

Device Type	Description
Network access devices	Connect end users to their network. Examples are hubs, switches, and wireless access points.
Internetwork devices	Connect one network to one or more other networks. Routers are the main example.
Communication servers	Route services such as IPTV and wireless broadband.
Modems	Connect users to servers and networks through telephone or cable.
Security devices	Secure the network with devices such as firewalls that analyze traffic exiting and entering networks.

The management of data as it flows through the network is also a role of the intermediary devices. These devices use the destination host address, in conjunction with information about the network interconnections, to determine the path that messages should take through the network. Processes running on the intermediary network devices perform these functions:

- Regenerate and retransmit data signals

- Maintain information about what pathways exist through the network and internetwork

- Notify other devices of errors and communication failures

- Direct data along alternate pathways when there is a link failure

- Classify and direct messages according to quality of service (QoS) priorities

- Permit or deny the flow of data, based on security settings

Figure 2-3 depicts two LANs with end devices connected by intermediary switches in the LANs and routers between the LANs.

Figure 2-3   LANs Connected by Routers

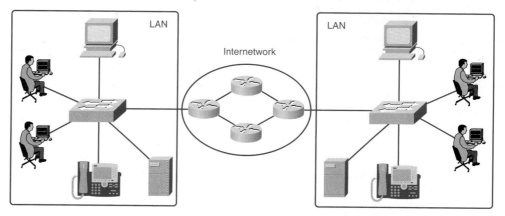

Network Media

Communication across a network is carried on a medium. The medium provides the channel over which the message travels from source to destination. The three main types of media in use in a network are

- Copper

- Fiber-optic cable

- Wireless

Each of these media has vastly different physical properties and uses different methods to encode messages. *Encoding* messages refers to the way data is converted to patterns of electrical, light, or electromagnetic energy and carried on the medium. Each medium is briefly described in Table 2-2.

Table 2-2   Networking Media

Media	Example	Encoding
Copper	Twisted-pair cable usually used as LAN media	Electrical pulses
Fiber-optic	Glass or plastic fibers in a vinyl coating usually used for long runs in a LAN and as a trunk	Light pulses
Wireless	Connects local users through the air	Electromagnetic waves

The differences in the media make each one ideal for different roles in networking situations. When choosing network media, administrators must consider the following:

- The distance the media can carry the signal

- The environment in which the media works

- The bandwidth requirements for users

- The cost of installation

- The cost of connectors and compatible equipment

Fiber, copper, and wireless media are shown in Figure 2-4.

Figure 2-4   Network Media

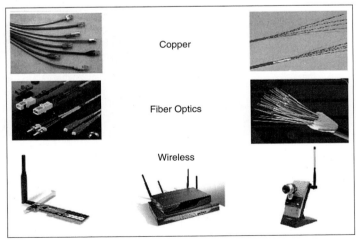

LANs, WANs, and Internetworks

Networks come in many sizes and serve a wide variety of functions. Following are some of the basic differences:

- The size of the area covered
- The number of users connected
- The number and types of services available

Three distinct groups of networks accommodate different groups and extend geographic boundaries: local-area networks (LANs), wide-area networks (WANs), and internetworks.

Local-Area Networks

A *local-area network (LAN)* is a group of end devices and users under the control of a common administration. The term *local* first meant that the computers were grouped geographically close together and had the same purpose in an organization. This is still true in many situations, but as technologies evolve, the definition of local has evolved as well. A LAN can consist of one group of users on one floor, but the term can also be used to describe all users on a multibuilding campus.

Wide-Area Networks

A wide-area network (WAN) is a network that is used to connect LANs that are located geographically far apart. If a company has offices in different cities, it will contract with a telecommunications service provider (TSP) to provide data lines between LANs in each city. The leased lines will vary in service and bandwidth, depending on the terms of the contract. The TSP is responsible for the intermediary devices on the WAN that transports messages, while LANs at both ends are controlled by the company. The sole purpose of WANs is to connect LANs, and there are usually no end users on WANs. Figure 2-5 depicts two LANs connected by a WAN.

Figure 2-5   Network with a WAN Connection

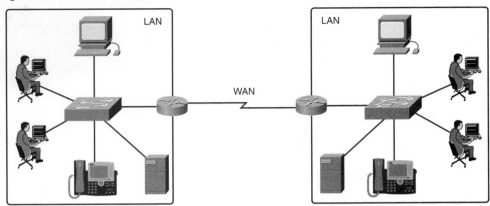

The Internet: A Network of Networks

In years past, LANs changed the way people worked, but they were limited to the resources within each network. Now workers who are not restricted to their own LAN can access other LANs on an internetwork. An *internetwork* is a collection of two or more LANs connected by WANs. Internetworks are referred to interchangeably as *data networks* or simply *networks*. The most popular internetwork is the Internet, which is open to public use.

With LANs able to communicate with other LANs using WANs, many organizations developed intranets. A term often confused with the Internet, an *intranet* is a private web of networks closed to the public but open for employees to browse. For example, many companies use intranets to share company information and training across the globe to far-away employees. Documents are shared and projects are managed securely over great distances on an intranet.

Internet service providers (ISP), which are often also TSPs, connect their customers to the Internet. The customer can be a home user, a company, or a government institution. All Internet users access the web through ISPs. The ISPs cooperate with TSPs and other ISPs to make sure that all users have access to the web. This involves implementing rules and standards that enable any user to communicate with any other user regardless of location and equipment type. Figure 2-6 demonstrates how many WANs connect to form the Internet. Note the difference in symbols representing LAN connections to routers and the WAN connections between routers.

Figure 2-6   Internetworks Made Up of LANs and WANs

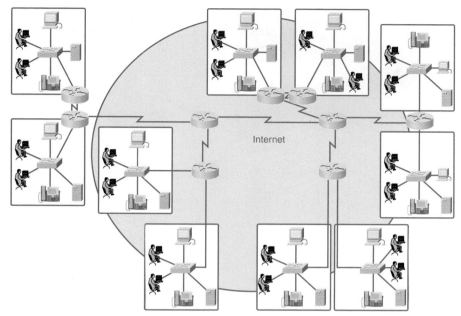

Network Representations

Chapter 1, "Living in a Network-Centric World," introduced many common data network symbols pictured in Figure 2-7. When discussing how devices and media connect to each other, remember these important terms:

- **Network interface card (NIC):** A *NIC*, or *LAN adapter*, provides the physical connection to the network at the PC or other host device. The media connecting the PC to the networking device plugs directly into the NIC. Each NIC has a unique physical address that identifies it on the LAN.

- **Physical port:** A *physical port* is a connector or outlet on a networking device where the media is connected to a host or other networking device. You can assume that all network host devices used in this book have a physical port that allows a connection to the network.

- **Interface:** The term *interface* refers to how the device can allow two different networks to communicate. Routers connect to different networks, and the specialized NICs on routers are simply called interfaces. The interface on a router device has a unique physical address and appears as a host on the local network.

Figure 2-7   Network Device and Media Symbols

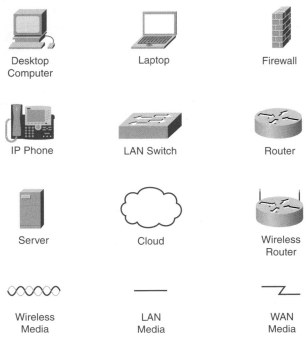

Desktop Computer   Laptop   Firewall

IP Phone   LAN Switch   Router

Server   Cloud   Wireless Router

Wireless Media   LAN Media   WAN Media

Packet Tracer
☐ Activity

Network Representations (2.2.4.2)

In this activity, you will gain experience with data network symbols by creating a simple logical topology. Use file e1-2242.pka on the CD-ROM that accompanies this book to perform this activity using Packet Tracer.

Protocols

All communication, whether face-to-face or over a network, is governed by predetermined rules called *protocols*. These protocols are specific to the characteristics of the conversation. Network communication follows protocols similar to those used in human communication.

Rules That Govern Communications

Protocols are rules used by anyone who communicates with another. During a conversation, people usually don't think about protocols until someone breaks one, but many levels of behavior are important for successful communication. For example, the clothing and informal language that is appropriate when you're with your close friends is not appropriate in a formal setting with a court official. Being improperly dressed for the communication situation could derail the message before any words are spoken. Also, people who interrupt conversations, speak too loudly, or walk away from conversations without the proper closing words like "thank you" or "good-bye" are considered rude, and the rude behavior can distract from the importance of the message. In addition, if a person tries to communicate in a language that the receiver does not understand, attempts at verbal communication will likely fail.

The protocols in human communication are separate rules about appearance, speaking, listening, and understanding. All these rules, also called protocols of conversation, represent different layers of communication. They work together to help people successfully communicate.

You can use these examples to understand three different layers of a simple conversation. Consider two people communicating face to face. The bottom layer, the physical layer, has two people, each with a voice that can utter words aloud. The second layer, the rules layer, has an agreement to speak in a common language. The top layer, the content layer, has the words actually spoken, that is, the content of the communication.

Were you to witness this conversation, you would not see the layers. It is important to understand that the use of layers is a model and, as such, layers provide a way to conveniently break a complex task into parts and describe how they work.

The need for protocols also applies to network devices. Computers have no way of learning protocols, so network engineers have written rules for communication that must be strictly followed for successful host-to-host communication. These rules apply to different layers of sophistication such as which physical connections to use, how hosts listen, how to interrupt, how to say good-bye, what language to use, and many others. These rules, or protocols, that work together to ensure successful communication are grouped into what is known as a *protocol suite*.

Network Protocols

For devices to communicate on a network, they must follow different protocols that perform the many tasks to be completed. The protocols define the following:

- The format of the message, such as how much data to put into each segment
- The way intermediary devices share information about the path to the destination
- The method to handle update messages between intermediary devices
- The process to initiate and terminate communications between hosts

The authors of the protocols might be writing them for a specific company that will own the protocol. The protocol is treated like a copyright and can be licensed to other companies to use. Protocols controlled by a company and not for public use are considered proprietary. Other protocols are written for public use at no charge and are considered open source protocols.

Protocol Suites and Industry Standards

In the early days of networking, each manufacturer had proprietary network equipment and protocols to support it. This worked well as long as the company that purchased the equipment did not need to share data outside its own network. As companies started to do business with other companies who were using different network systems, the need for a cross-platform standard for network communication became apparent.

People from the telecommunications industry gathered to standardize the way network communication works by writing common protocols. These standards are practices that are endorsed by representatives from industry groups and are followed to ensure interoperability between vendors. For example, Microsoft, Apple, and Linux operating systems each have a way to implement the TCP/IP protocol stack. This allows the users of different operating systems to have common access to network communication. The organizations that standardize networking protocols are the *Institute of Electrical and Electronics Engineers (IEEE)* and the *Internet Engineering Task Force (IETF)*.

Interaction of Protocols

An example of the use of a protocol suite in network communications is the interaction between a web server and a web browser. This interaction uses a number of protocols and standards in the process of exchanging information between them. The different protocols work together to ensure that the messages are received and understood by both parties. Examples of these protocols are as follows:

- **Hypertext Transfer Protocol (HTTP):** HTTP is a common protocol that governs the way that a web server and a web client interact. HTTP defines the content and formatting of the requests and responses exchanged between the client and server. Both the client and the web server software implement HTTP as part of the application. The HTTP protocol relies on other protocols to govern how the messages are transported between client and server.

- **Transport protocol:** Transmission Control Protocol (TCP) is the transport protocol that manages the individual conversations between web servers and web clients. TCP divides the HTTP messages into smaller pieces, called segments, to be sent to the destination client. It is also responsible for controlling the size and rate at which messages are exchanged between the server and the client.

- **Internetwork protocol:** The most common internetwork protocol is Internet Protocol (IP). IP is responsible for taking the formatted segments from TCP, encapsulating them into packets, assigning the appropriate addresses, and selecting the best path to the destination host.

- **Network access protocols:** Network access protocols describe two primary functions: data-link management and the physical transmission of data on the media. Data-link management protocols take the packets from IP and format them to be transmitted over the media. The standards and protocols for the physical media govern how the signals are sent over the media and how they are interpreted by the receiving clients. Transceivers on the network interface cards implement the appropriate standards for the media that is being used.

Technology-Independent Protocols

Protocols that guide the network communication process are not dependent on any specific technology to carry out the task. Protocols describe what must be done to communicate, not how the task is to be completed. For example, in a classroom, the protocol for asking a question might be to raise a hand for attention. The protocol instructs students to raise their hands, but it does not specify how high to raise them or specify whether the right hand or left hand is better or whether waving the hand is helpful. Each student can raise his or her hand in a slightly different way, but if the hand is raised, the teacher will likely give attention to the student.

So network communication protocols state what tasks must be completed, not how to complete them. This is what enables different types of devices, such as telephones and computers, to use the same network infrastructure to communicate. Each device has its own technology, but it is able to interact with different devices at the network level. In the previous example of Apple, Microsoft, and Linux, the operating systems must find a way to present data to others using TCP/IP, but each operating system will have its own way to do it.

Using Layered Models

The IT industry uses *layered models* to describe the complex process of network communication. Protocols for specific functions in the process are grouped by purpose into well-defined layers.

The Benefits of a Layered Model

By breaking the network communication process into manageable layers, the industry can benefit in the following ways:

- Defines common terms that describe the network functions to those working in the industry and allows greater understanding and cooperation.

- Segments the process to allow technologies performing one function to evolve independently of technologies performing other functions. For example, advancing technologies of wireless media is not dependent on advances in routers.

- Fosters competition because products from different vendors can work together.

- Provides a common language to describe networking functions and capabilities.

- Assists in protocol design, because protocols that operate at a specific layer have defined information that they act upon and a defined interface to the layers above and below.

As an IT student, you will benefit from the layered approach as you build your understanding of the network communication process.

Protocol and Reference Models

Networking professionals use two networking models to communicate within the industry: protocol models and reference models. Both were created in the 1970s when network communication was in its infancy.

A protocol model provides a model that closely matches the structure of a particular protocol suite. The hierarchical set of related protocols in a suite typically represents all the functionality required to interface the human network with the data network. The *TCP/IP* model is a protocol model because it describes the functions that occur at each layer of protocols within the TCP/IP suite.

A reference model provides a common reference for maintaining consistency within all types of network protocols and services. A reference model is not intended to be an implementation specification or to provide a sufficient level of detail to define precisely the services of the network architecture. The primary purpose of a reference model is to aid in clearer understanding of the functions and process involved. The Open Systems Interconnection (OSI) model is the most widely known internetwork reference model.

The OSI model describes the entire communication process in detail, and the TCP/IP model describes the communication process in terms of the TCP/IP protocol suite and the way it functions. It is important to know details of the OSI model to understand the entire network communication process and to know the TCP/IP model to understand how the process is implemented in current networks.

The OSI model is used to reference the process of communication, not to regulate it. Many protocols in use today apply to more than one layer of the OSI model. This is why some of the layers of the OSI model are combined in the TCP/IP model. Some manufacturers use variations on these models to demonstrate the functions of their products within the industry. Figure 2-8 shows both OSI and TCP/IP models.

Figure 2-8   OSI and TCP/IP Models

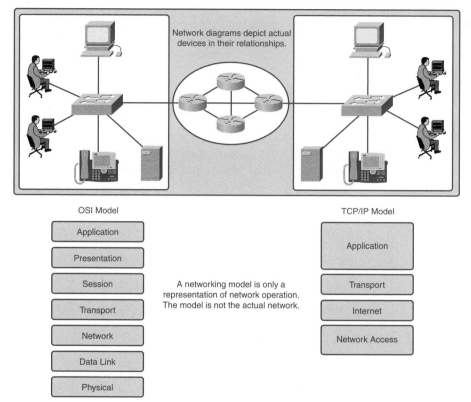

TCP/IP Model

The TCP/IP model defines the four communication functions that protocols perform. TCP/IP is an open standard, which means that one company does not control it. The rules and implementations of the TCP/IP model were cooperatively developed by members of the industry using Request for Comments (RFC) documents. RFC documents are publicly accessible documents that define specifications and policies of the protocols and of the Internet in general. Solicitation and maintenance of RFCs are the responsibility of the IETF. Table 2-3 briefly describes the functions of each layer of the TCP/IP model.

Table 2-3   Layers of the TCP/IP Model

Layer	Description
Application	Represents application data to the user. For example, the HTTP presents data to the user in a web browser application like Internet Explorer.
Transport	Supports communication between devices and performs error correction.
Internet	Finds the best path through the network.
Network access	Controls hardware devices and media.

Communication Process

The TCP/IP model describes the functionality of the protocols that make up the TCP/IP protocol suite. These protocols, which are implemented on both the sending and receiving hosts, interact to provide end-to-end delivery of applications over a network.

A complete communication process includes these steps:

1. Creation of data at the application layer of the originating source end device.

2. Segmentation and encapsulation of data as it passes down the protocol stack in the source end device.

3. Generation of the data onto the media at the network access layer of the stack.

4. Transportation of the data through the internetwork, which consists of media and any intermediary devices.

5. Reception of the data at the network access layer of the destination end device.

6. Decapsulation and reassembly of the data as it passes up the stack in the destination device. You learn more about the encapsulation and decapsulation processes in the next section.

7. Passing this data to the destination application at the application layer of the destination end device.

Protocol Data Units and Encapsulation

For application data to travel uncorrupted from one host to another, header (or control data), which contains control and addressing information, is added to the data as it moves down the layers. The process of adding control information as it passes through the layered model is called *encapsulation*. *Decapsulation* is the process of removing the extra information and sending only the original application data up to the destination application layer.

Each layer adds control information at each step. The generic term for data at each level is *protocol data unit (PDU)*, but a PDU is different at each layer. For example, a PDU at the internetwork layer is different from the PDU at the transport layer, because internetwork layer data has been added to the transport layer data. The different names for PDUs at each layer are listed in Table 2-4.

Table 2-4   Protocol Data Unit Naming Conventions

PDU Name	Layer
Data	Application layer PDU
Segment	Transport layer PDU
Packet	Internetwork layer PDU
Frame	Network access layer PDU
Bits	PDU used for the physical transmission of binary data over media

Figure 2-9 depicts the encapsulation process and shows how PDUs are modified.

Figure 2-9   Encapsulation

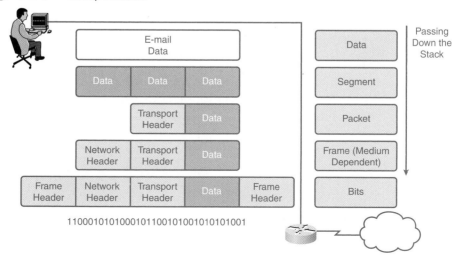

Sending and Receiving Process

The common task of sending an e-mail has many steps in the process. Using the proper terms for PDUs and the TCP/IP model, the process of sending the e-mail is as follows:

1. An end user, using an e-mail application, creates data. The application layer codes the data as e-mail and sends the data to the transport layer.

2. The message is segmented, or broken into pieces, for transport. The transport layer adds control information in a header so that it can be assigned to the correct process and all segments put into proper order at the destination. The segment is sent down to the internetwork layer.

3. The internetwork layer adds IP addressing information in an IP header. The segment is now an addressed packet that can be handled by routers en route to the destination. The internetwork layer sends the packet down to the network access layer.

4. The network access layer creates an Ethernet frame with local network physical address information in the header. This enables the packet to get to the local router and out to the web. The frame also contains a trailer with error-checking information. After the frame is created, it is encoded into bits and sent onto the media to the destination.

5. At the destination host, the process is reversed. The frame is decapsulated to a packet, then to a segment, and then the transport layer puts all segments into the proper order.

6. When all data has arrived and is ready, it is sent to the application layer, and then the original application data goes to the receiver's e-mail application. The message is successful.

Figure 2-10 depicts these steps as an encapsulated message travels down the TCP/IP model on the source and is en route to the destination for decapsulation.

Figure 2-10   Steps in the Communication Process

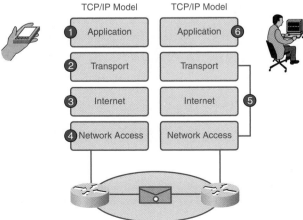

OSI Model

The *Open Systems Interconnection (OSI)* model, known as the OSI model, provides an abstract description of the network communication process. Developed by the *International Organization for Standardization (ISO)* to provide a road map for nonproprietary protocol development, the OSI model did not evolve as readily as the TCP/IP model. Many of the OSI protocols are no longer in use, but knowledge of the model as a reference is a basic expectation for networking professionals. Many professionals refer to the layers by number rather than name, so it is important to know both.

The OSI model is just a reference model, so manufacturers have been free to create protocols and products that combine functions of one or more layers. New protocols might not exactly match the functions described at each layer but might fit into parts of two different layers.

As designed, the communication process begins at the application layer of the source, and data is passed down to each lower layer to be encapsulated with supporting data until it reaches the physical layer and is put out on the media. When the data arrives at the destination, it is passed back up through layers and decapsulated by each layer. Each layer provides data services to the layer directly above by preparing information coming down the model or going up.

Table 2-5 briefly describes each layer of the OSI model. Each layer will be explored in its own chapter later in this book.

Table 2-5   OSI Model

No.	Layer Name	Description
7	Application	Performs services for the applications used by the end users.
6	Presentation	Provides data format information to the application. For example, the presentation layer tells the application layer whether there is encryption or whether it is a .jpg picture.
5	Session	Manages sessions between users. For example, the session layer will synchronize multiple web sessions and voice and video data in web conferences.
4	Transport	Defines data segments and numbers them at the source, transfers the data, and reassembles the data at the destination.
3	Network	Creates and addresses packets for end-to-end delivery through intermediary devices in other networks.
2	Data Link	Creates and addresses frames for host-to-host delivery on the local LANs and between WAN devices.
1	Physical	Transmits binary data over media between devices. Physical layer protocols define media specifications.

Comparing the OSI Model to the TCP/IP Model

The TCP/IP model evolved faster than the OSI model and is now more practical in describing network communication functions. The OSI model describes in detail functions that occur at the upper layers on the hosts, while networking is largely a function of the lower layers. Figure 2-11 shows the two models side by side for comparison.

Figure 2-11   Comparing the OSI and TCP/IP Models

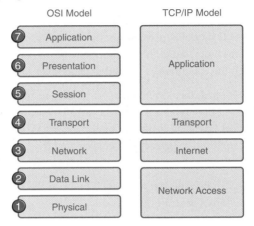

When juxtaposed, you can see that the functions of the application, presentation, and session layers of the OSI model are combined into one application layer in the TCP/IP model.

The bulk of networking functions reside at the transport and the network layers, so they remain individual layers. TCP operates at the transport layer, and IP operates at the Internet layer.

The data link and physical layers of the OSI model combine to make the network access layer of the TCP/IP model.

Use of the TCP/IP Protocols and the OSI Model in Packet Tracer (2.4.8.2)

In this activity, you will see how Packet Tracer uses the OSI model as a reference to display the encapsulation details of a variety of the TCP/IP protocols. Use file e1-2482.pka on the CD-ROM that accompanies this book to perform this activity using Packet Tracer.

Network Addressing

Successful communication requires that a sender and a receiver know how to get messages to each other. Postal systems use geography to deliver mail to physical addresses, but getting messages between computers is a more complicated matter. With the Internet, computers can communicate regardless of physical location.

Instead of using a geographical addressing scheme for computers, engineers devised a logical addressing scheme using numeric network addresses. The following sections introduce the addressing process. Chapter 6, "Addressing the Network: IPv4," explores network addressing in greater detail.

Addressing in the Network

There are millions of computers in use on the web and billions of messages traversing networks at any given time, so proper addressing is essential to make sure that the sent message arrives intact at the proper destination. Addressing of data happens in three different layers of the OSI model. The PDU at each layer adds address information for use by the peer layer at the destination. Figure 2-12 depicts the different addressing information added by each layer.

Figure 2-12   Addressing Added at Each Layer

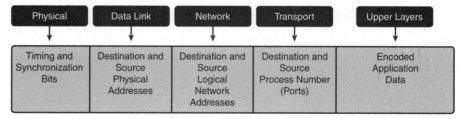

Getting Data to the End Device

During the process of encapsulation, address identifiers are added to the data as it travels down the protocol stack on the source host. There are two layers of addressing added to ensure that data is delivered to the destination.

The first identifier, the host physical address, is contained in the header of the Layer 2 PDU, called a frame. Layer 2 is concerned with the delivery of messages on a single local network. The Layer 2 address is unique on the local network and represents the address of the end device on the physical media. The physical address comes from codes placed on the NIC by the manufacturer. In a LAN using Ethernet, this address is called the MAC address. The terms *physical address* and *MAC address* are often used interchangeably. When two end devices communicate on the local Ethernet network, the frames that are exchanged between them contain the destination and source MAC addresses. After a frame is success-fully received by the destination host, the Layer 2 address information is removed as the data is decapsulated and moved up the protocol stack to Layer 3.

Getting Data Through the Internetwork

Layer 3 protocols are primarily designed to move data from one local network to another local network within an internetwork. Whereas Layer 2 addresses are only used to commu-nicate between devices on a single local network, Layer 3 addresses must include identifiers that enable intermediary network devices to locate hosts on different networks. In the TCP/IP protocol suite, every IP host address contains information about the network where the host is located.

At the boundary of each local network, an intermediary network device, usually a router, decapsulates the frame to read the destination host address contained in the header of the packet, the Layer 3 PDU. Routers use the network identifier portion of this address to deter-mine which path to use to reach the destination host. When the path is determined, the router encapsulates the packet in a new frame and sends it on its way toward the destination end device. When the frame reaches its final destination, the frame and packet headers are removed and the data moved up to Layer 4. The journey from source to destination is depicted in Figure 2-13.

Figure 2-13   IP Addressing

The Protocol Data Unit header also contains the network address.

Getting Data to the Right Application

At Layer 4, information contained in the PDU header does not identify a destination host or a destination network. What it does identify is the specific process or service running on the destination host device that will act on the data being delivered. Hosts, whether they are clients or servers on the Internet, can run multiple network applications simultaneously. People using PCs often have an e-mail client running at the same time as a web browser, an instant messaging program, some streaming media, and perhaps even a game. All these separately running programs are examples of individual processes.

Viewing a web page invokes at least one network process. Clicking a hyperlink causes a web browser to communicate with a web server. At the same time, in the background, an e-mail client can be sending and receiving e-mail, and a colleague or friend can be sending an instant message.

Think about a computer that has only one network interface on it. All the data streams created by the applications that are running on the PC enter and leave through that one interface, yet instant messages do not pop up in the middle of a word processor document or e-mail showing up in a game.

This is because the transport layer adds *port* numbers to its segment header information to ensure that the destination host knows which application process is to receive the packet. The end host assigns a port number to each type of traffic going in and out. A user can send and receive many types of traffic over a single network interface, and using port numbers for each segment keeps traffic for web pages separate from e-mail traffic and so on. The segment contains both source and destination ports in case the receiver needs to contact the sender. Figure 2-14 shows different data types for two different services on an end device.

Figure 2-14   Port Addressing

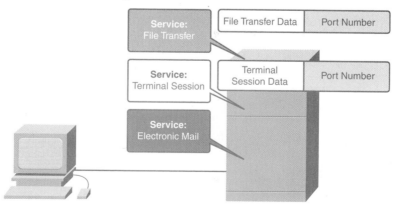

Summary

Communication in data networks requires a source device and a destination device with a medium connecting the two. For messages to travel to other networks, intermediary devices such as routers are necessary.

The devices that handle messages and the media that carry them comply with communication rules called protocols. Many protocols can work together in a stack to complete the process of network communication.

Layered models describe the various steps that must occur for successful communication. The OSI and TCP/IP models are the most common models used in networking and can serve as a guide to the different protocols and devices used at each layer. Models are useful for students and companies in analyzing and troubleshooting networks as well as for future development of protocols.

Application data is sent down the protocol stacks and is encapsulated at each layer with addressing and control information. The data is segmented into pieces, addressed, and then encoded on the media. The process is reversed at the destination.

Activities and Labs

The activities and labs available in the companion *Network Fundamentals, CCNA Exploration Labs and Study Guide* (ISBN 1-58713-203-6) provide hands-on practice with the following topics introduced in this chapter:

Activity 2-1: Using NeoTrace to View Internetworks (2.2.5.1)

In this activity, you will observe the flow of information across the Internet. This activity should be performed on a computer that has Internet access and access to a command line. You will use the Windows embedded **tracert** utility and then the more enhanced NeoTrace program. This lab also assumes you have the installation of NeoTrace.

Lab 2-1: Topology Orientation and Building a Small Network (2.6.1.1)

This lab begins by having you construct two small networks. It then shows how they are connected to the larger hands-on lab network used throughout the course. This network is a simplified model of a section of the Internet and will be used to develop your practical networking skills.

Lab 2-2: Using Wireshark to View Protocol Data Units (2.6.2.1)

In this lab, you will begin learning about the Wireshark tool by capturing ("sniffing") traffic off the model network.

Packet Tracer
☐ Companion

Many of the hands-on labs include Packet Tracer companion activities where you can use Packet Tracer to complete a simulation of the lab. Look for this icon in the *Network Fundamentals, CCNA Exploration Labs and Study Guide* (ISBN 1-58713-203-6) for hands-on labs that have Packet Tracer companion activities.

Check Your Understanding

Complete all the review questions listed here to test your understanding of the topics and concepts in this chapter. The appendix, "Check Your Understanding and Challenge Questions Answer Key," lists the answers.

1. Which OSI layer is associated with IP addressing?

    A. 1

    B. 2

    C. 3

    D. 4

2. The elements of communication include a message source, a message destination, and a _____, or medium, to transport the message.

3. Which type of addressing is found at the OSI Layer 2? (Choose two.)

    A. Logical

    B. Physical

    C. MAC

    D. IP

    E. Port

4. When a server responds to a web request, what occurs next in the encapsulation process after the web page data is formatted and separated into TCP segments?

    A. The client decapsulates the segment and opens the web page.

    B. The client adds the appropriate physical address to the segments so that the server can forward the data.

    C. The server converts the data to bits for transport across the medium.

    D. The server adds the source and destination IP address to each segment header to deliver the packets to the destination.

    E. The server adds the source and destination physical addresses to the packet header.

5. Which term describes a specific set of rules that determine the formatting of messages and the process of encapsulation used to forward data?

    A. Segmentation

    B. Protocol

    C. Multiplexing

    D. QoS

    E. Reassembly

6. A limited-use protocol owned by a company is considered to be

    _____.

7. Which one of the following is associated with Layer 4 of the OSI model?

    A. IP

    B. TCP

    C. FTP

    D. TFTP

8. The device that connects a device to the media is called a/an

    _____.

9. Which of the following terms defines dividing data streams into smaller pieces suitable for transmission?

    A. Protocol

    B. Multiplexing

    C. Segmentation

    D. Encapsulation

10. A device that moves data between networks is a _____.

11. Which of the following is the process for interweaving multiple data streams onto one shared communication channel or network medium?

    A. Multicasting

    B. Multiplexing

    C. Encapsulation

    D. Multidirecting

12. Which of the following is associated with the network layer?

    A. IP address

    B. Frames

    C. MAC address

    D. Physical addressing

13. Which of the following is the correct "top down" order of the OSI model?

    A. Application, presentation, session, network, transport, data link, physical

    B. Application, presentation, session, transport, network, data link, physical

    C. Application, session, presentation, transport, network, data link, physical

    D. Application, presentation, session, network, data link, transport, physical

14. Which layer of the OSI model is concerned with end-to-end message delivery over the network?

    A. Network

    B. Transport

    C. Data link

    D. Application

Challenge Questions and Activities

These questions require a deeper application of the concepts covered in this chapter. You can find the answers in the appendix.

  1. Which layers of the OSI model are combined into other layers of the TCP/IP model? (Choose all that apply.)

    A. Network

    B. Presentation

    C. Internet

    D. Data link

    E. Application

    F. Physical

    G. Session

    H. Network access

    I. Transport

2. Which of the following are true about LANs and WANs? (Choose two.)

   A. LANs connect groups of networks using ISPs.

   B. LANs consist of hosts communicating with logical addresses.

   C. WANs connect groups of networks using TSPs.

   D. WANs connect LANs.

   E. Hosts on a LAN use physical addressing to communicate.

Look for this icon in *Network Fundamentals, CCNA Exploration Labs and Study Guide* (ISBN 1-58713-203-6) for instructions on how to perform the Packet Tracer Skills Integration Challenge for this chapter.

To Learn More

The following questions encourage you to reflect on the topics discussed in this chapter. Your instructor might ask you to research the questions and discuss your findings in class.

1. How are the classifications LAN, WAN, and Internet still useful, and how might they be problematic in classifying networks?

2. What are strengths and weaknesses of the OSI and TCP/IP models? Why are both models still used?

3. Metaphors and analogies can be powerful aids to learning but must be used with care. Consider issues of devices, protocols, and addressing in the following systems:

   Standard postal service
   Express parcel delivery service
   Traditional (analog) telephone system
   Internet telephony
   Containerized shipping services
   Terrestrial and satellite radio systems
   Broadcast and cable television

4. Discuss what you see as common factors among these systems. Apply any similarities to other networks.

5. How could you apply these common concepts to developing new communications systems and networks?

CHAPTER 3

Application Layer Functionality and Protocols

Objectives

Upon completion of this chapter, you will be able to answer the following questions:

- How do the functions of the three upper OSI model layers provide network services to end-user applications?

- How do the TCP/IP application layer protocols provide the services specified by the upper layers of the OSI model?

- How do people use the application layer to communicate across the information network?

- What are the functions of well-known TCP/IP applications, such as the World Wide Web and e-mail, and their related services (HTTP, DNS, DHCP, STMP/POP, and Telnet)?

- What are the file-sharing processes that use peer-to-peer applications and the Gnutella protocol?

- How do protocols ensure that services running on one kind of device can send to and receive from many different network devices?

- How can you use network analysis tools to examine and explain how common user applications work?

Key Terms

This chapter uses the following key terms. You can find the definitions in the Glossary.

data   page 67

source device   page 67

Domain Name System (DNS)   page 68

Request for Comments (RFC)   page 68

syntax   page 70

session   page 71

client   page 72

server   page 72

daemon   page 73

peer   page 75

scheme   page 76

IP address   page 77

domain name   page 77

network address   page 78

resource record   page 78

DNS resolver   page 78

nslookup   page 78

query   page 78

cache   page 79

authoritative   page 81

plug-in   page 82

HTTP   page 82

distributed   page 82

collaborative   page 82

encryption   page 82

Post Office Protocol (POP)   page 83

Simple Mail Transfer Protocol (SMTP)   page 83

Mail User Agent (MUA)   page 83

spam   page 85

gateway   page 85

*Dynamic Host Configuration Protocol (DHCP)
 page 87*

subnet mask   page 87

broadcast   page 88

Server Message Block (SMB)   page 89

UNIX   page 89

Interpret as Command (IAC)   page 91

The world experiences the Internet through the use of the World Wide Web, e-mail, and file-sharing programs. These applications, as well as others, provide the human interface to the underlying network, allowing you to send and receive information with relative ease. Most of the applications are intuitive; they can be accessed and used without the need to know how they work. As you continue to study the world of networking, it becomes more important to know how an application is able to format, transmit, and interpret messages that are sent and received across the network.

Visualizing the mechanisms that enable communication across the network is made easier if you use the layered framework of the Open System Interconnection (OSI) model. Figure 3-1 depicts that framework. The OSI model is a seven-layer model, designed to help explain the flow of information from layer to layer.

Figure 3-1   Interfacing Human and Data Networks

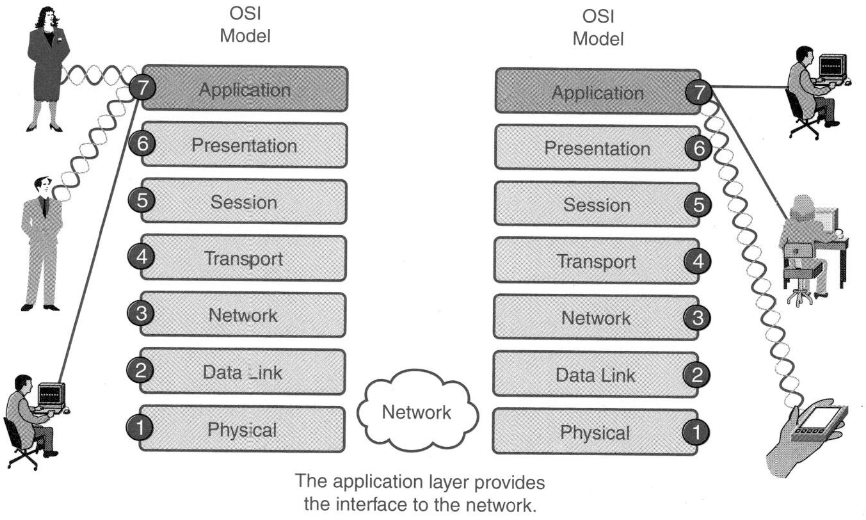

The application layer provides
the interface to the network.

This chapter focuses on the role of Layer 7, the application layer, and its components: applications, services, and protocols. You explore how these three elements make the robust communication across the information network possible.

Applications: The Interface Between the Networks

This section introduces two important concepts:

- **Application layer:** The application layer of the OSI model provides the first step of getting data onto the network.

- **Application software:** Applications are the software programs used by people to communicate over the network. Examples of application software, including HTTP, FTP, e-mail, and others, are used to explain the differences between these two concepts.

OSI and TCP/IP Model

The OSI reference model is a layered, abstract representation created as a guideline for network protocol design and instruction. The OSI model divides the networking process into seven logical layers, each of which has unique functionality and to which are assigned specific services and protocols.

In the OSI model, information is passed from one layer to the next, starting at the application layer on the transmitting host and proceeding down the hierarchy to the physical layer, then passing over the communications channel to the destination host, where the information proceeds back up the hierarchy, ending at the application layer. Figure 3-2 depicts the steps in this process. The following explains the six steps:

1. People create the communication.

2. The application layer prepares human communication for transmission over the data network.

3. Software and hardware convert communication to a digital format.

4. Application layer services initiate the data transfer.

5. Each layer plays its role. The OSI layers encapsulate data down the stack. Encapsulated data travels across the media to the destination. OSI layers at the destination unencapsulate the data up the stack.

6. The application layer receives data from the network and prepares it for human use.

Figure 3-2   OSI Encapsulation Process

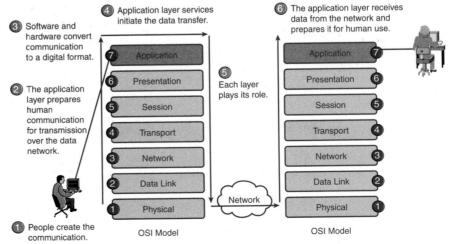

The application layer, Layer 7, is the top layer of both the OSI and TCP/IP models. (Refer to the section "Protocol and Reference Models" in Chapter 2, "Communicating over the Network," for more information about the TCP/IP model.) Layer 7 provides the interface between the applications you use to communicate and the underlying network over which your messages are transmitted. Application layer protocols are used to exchange *data* between programs running on the source and destination hosts. There are many application layer protocols, and new protocols are always being developed. (Refer to the section "User Applications, Services, and Application Layer Protocols," later in this chapter, for examples.)

Although the TCP/IP protocol suite was developed prior to the definition of the OSI model, the functionality of the TCP/IP application layer protocols fits roughly into the framework of the top three layers of the OSI model: application, presentation, and session.

Most applications, such as web browsers or e-mail clients, incorporate functionality of the OSI Layers 5, 6, and 7. A comparison of the OSI and TCP/IP model is shown in Figure 3-3.

Figure 3-3   OSI and TCP/IP Model

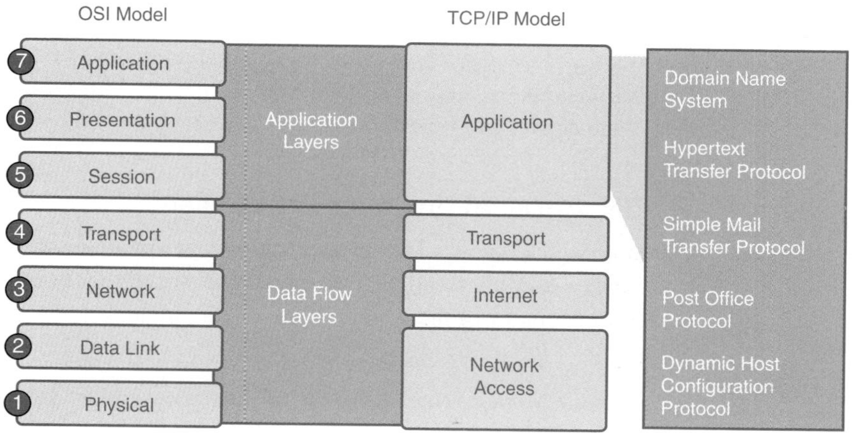

Most TCP/IP application layer protocols were developed before the emergence of personal computers, GUIs, and multimedia objects. As a result, these protocols implement little of the functionality that is specified in the OSI model presentation and session layers. The next sections describe the OSI presentation and session layers in more detail.

Presentation Layer

The presentation layer has three primary functions:

- Coding and conversion of application layer data to ensure that data from the *source device* can be interpreted by the appropriate application on the destination device

- Compression of the data in a manner that can be decompressed by the destination device

- Encryption of the data for transmission and decryption of data upon receipt by the destination

Presentation layer implementations are not typically associated with a particular protocol stack. The standards for video and graphics are examples. Some well-known standards for video include QuickTime and Motion Picture Experts Group (MPEG). QuickTime is an Apple Computer specification for video and audio, and MPEG is a standard for video compression and coding.

Among the well-known graphic image formats are Graphics Interchange Format (GIF), Joint Photographic Experts Group (JPEG), and Tagged Image File Format (TIFF). GIF and JPEG are compression and coding standards for graphic images, and TIFF is a standard coding format for graphic images.

Session Layer

Functions at the session layer create and maintain dialogs between source and destination applications. The session layer handles the exchange of information to initiate dialogs and keep them active, and to restart sessions that are disrupted or idle for a long period of time.

TCP/IP Application Layer Protocols

The most widely known TCP/IP application layer protocols are those that provide the exchange of user information. These protocols specify the format and control information necessary for many of the common Internet communication functions. Among these TCP/IP protocols are the following:

- *Domain Name System (DNS)* is used to resolve Internet names to IP addresses.

- Hypertext Transfer Protocol (HTTP) is used to transfer files that make up the web pages of the World Wide Web.

- Simple Mail Transfer Protocol (SMTP) is used for the transfer of mail messages and attachments.

- Telnet, a terminal emulation protocol, is used to provide remote access to servers and networking devices.

- File Transfer Protocol (FTP) is used for interactive file transfer between systems.

The protocols in the TCP/IP suite are generally defined by *Requests for Comments (RFC)*. The Internet Engineering Task Force (IETF) maintains the RFCs as the standards for the TCP/IP suite.

Application Layer Software

The functions associated with the application layer protocols in both the OSI and the TCP/IP models enable the human network to interface with the underlying data network. When you open a web browser or an instant message window, an application is started, and the program is put into the device memory, where it is executed. Each executing program loaded on a device is referred to as a *process*.

Within the application layer, there are two forms of software programs or processes that provide access to the network: applications and services. This concept is shown in Figure 3-4.

Figure 3-4   Software Processes

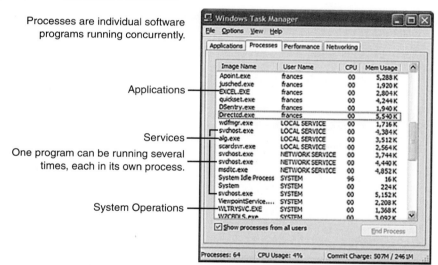

Network-Aware Applications

Some end-user applications are network aware, meaning that they implement the application layer protocols and are able to communicate directly with the lower layers of the protocol stack. E-mail clients and web browsers are examples of these types of applications.

Application Layer Services

Other programs, such as file transfer or network print spooling, might need the assistance of application layer services to use network resources. Although transparent to the user, these services interface with the network and prepare the data for transfer. Different types of data—whether it is text, graphics, or video—require different network services to ensure that it is properly prepared for processing by the functions occurring at the lower layers of OSI model.

Each application or network service uses protocols that define the standards and data formats to be used. A service provides the function for doing something, and a protocol provides the rules the service uses. To understand the *function* of various network services, you need to become familiar with the underlying protocols that govern their operation.

User Applications, Services, and Application Layer Protocols

The application layer uses protocols that are implemented within applications and services. Applications provide people with a way to create messages, application layer services establish an interface to the network, and protocols provide the rules and formats that govern how data is treated, as shown in Figure 3-5. A single executable program can use all three components. For example, when discussing "Telnet," you could be referring to the Telnet application, the Telnet service, or the Telnet protocol.

Figure 3-5   Interfacing Human and Data Networks

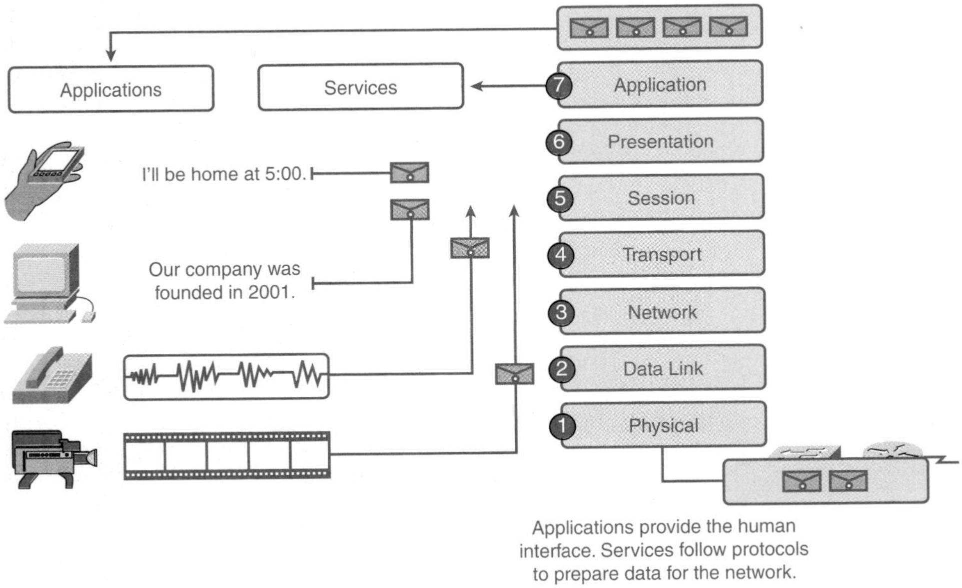

Applications provide the human interface. Services follow protocols to prepare data for the network.

In the OSI model, applications that interact directly with people are considered to be at the top of the stack, as are the people themselves. Like all layers within the OSI model, the application layer relies on the functions of the lower layers to complete the communication process. Within the application layer, protocols specify what messages are exchanged between the source and destination hosts, the *syntax* of the control commands, the type and format of the data being transmitted, and the appropriate methods for error notification and recovery.

Application Layer Protocol Functions

Both the source and destination devices use application layer protocols during a communication *session*. For the communications to be successful, the application layer protocols implemented on the source and destination host must match.

Protocols perform the following tasks:

- Establish consistent rules for exchanging data between applications and services loaded on the participating devices.

- Specify how data inside the messages is structured and the types of messages that are sent between source and destination. These messages can be requests for services, acknowledgments, data messages, status messages, or error messages.

- Define message dialogues, ensuring that a message being sent is met by the expected response and that the correct services are invoked when data transfer occurs.

Many different types of applications communicate across data networks. Therefore, application layer services must implement multiple protocols to provide the desired range of communication experiences. Each protocol has a specific purpose and contains the characteristics required to meet that purpose. The right protocol details in each layer must be followed so that the functions at one layer interface properly with the services in the lower layer.

Applications and services can also use multiple protocols in the course of a single conversation. One protocol might specify how to establish the network connection, and another might describe the process for the data transfer when the message is passed to the next lower layer.

Making Provisions for Applications and Services

When people attempt to access information on their device, whether it is a PC, laptop, PDA, cell phone, or some other device connected to a network, the data might not be physically stored on their device. If that is the case, a request to access that information must be made to the device where the data resides. The following sections cover three topics that will help you understand how the request for data can occur and how the request is filled:

- Client/server model

- Application layer services and protocols

- Peer-to-peer networking and applications

Client/Server Model

In the client/server model, the device requesting the information is called a *client* and the device responding to the request is called a server. Client and *server* processes are considered to be in the application layer. The client begins the exchange by requesting data from the server, which responds by sending one or more streams of data to the client. Application layer protocols describe the design of the requests and responses between clients and servers. In addition to the actual data transfer, this exchange can require control information, such as user authentication and the identification of a data file to be transferred.

One example of a client/server network is a corporate environment where employees use a company e-mail server to send, receive, and store e-mail. The e-mail client on an employee computer issues a request to the e-mail server for any unread mail. The server responds by sending the requested e-mail to the client.

Although data is typically described as flowing from the server to the client, some data always flows from the client to the server. Data flow can be equal in both directions or can even be greater in the direction going from the client to the server. For example, a client might transfer a file to the server for storage purposes. Data transfer from a client to a server is referred to as an *upload*, and data from a server to a client is a *download*. Figure 3-6 shows the client/server model concept.

Figure 3-6 Client/Server Model

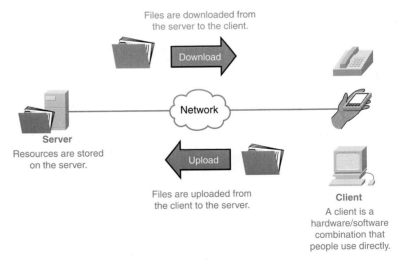

Servers

In a general networking context, any device that responds to requests from client applications is functioning as a server. A server is usually a computer that contains information to be shared with many client systems. For example, web pages, documents, databases, pictures, video, and audio files can all be stored on a server and delivered to requesting clients. In other cases, such as a network printer, the print server delivers the client print requests to the specified printer.

Different types of server applications can have different requirements for client access. Some servers can require authentication of user account information to verify whether the user has permission to access the requested data or to use a particular operation. Such servers rely on a central list of user accounts and the authorizations, or permissions (both for data access and operations), granted to each user. When using an FTP client, for example, if you request to upload data to the FTP server, you might have permission to write to your individual folder but not to read other files on the site.

In a client/server network, the server runs a service, or process, sometimes called a server *daemon*. Like most services, daemons typically run in the background and are not under an end user's direct control. Daemons are described as "listening" for a request from a client, because they are programmed to respond whenever the server receives a request for the service provided by the daemon. When a daemon "hears" a request from a client, it exchanges appropriate messages with the client, as required by its protocol, and proceeds to send the requested data to the client in the proper format.

Figure 3-7 shows the clients requesting services from the server; specifically, one client is requesting an audio file (.wav) and the other client is requesting a video file (.avi). The server responds by sending the requested files to the clients.

Figure 3-7   Servers

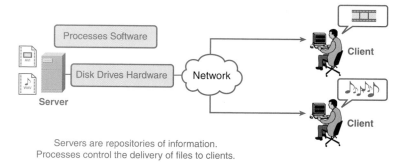

Servers are repositories of information.
Processes control the delivery of files to clients.

Application Layer Services and Protocols

A single application can employ many different supporting application layer services. Thus, what appears to the user as one request for a web page might, in fact, amount to dozens of individual requests. For each request, multiple processes can be executed. For example, the FTP requires a client to initiate a control process and a data stream process to a server.

Additionally, servers typically have multiple clients requesting information at the same time, as shown in Figure 3-8. For example, a Telnet server can have many clients requesting connections to it. These individual client requests must be handled simultaneously and separately for the network to succeed. The application layer processes and services rely on support from lower-layer functions to successfully manage the multiple conversations.

Figure 3-8   Multiple Clients' Service Requests

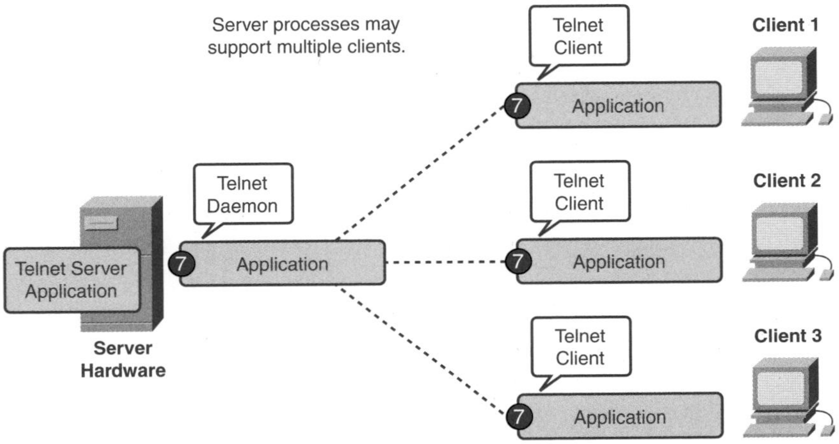

Client Server Interaction (3.2.3.2)

In this activity, you will study a simple example of client/server interaction, which can serve as a model for more complex interactions later in the course. Use file e1-3232.pka on the CD-ROM that accompanies this book to perform this activity using Packet Tracer.

Peer-to-Peer (P2P) Networking and Applications

In addition to the client/server model for networking, there is a peer-to-peer (P2P) model. P2P networking involves two distinct forms: peer-to-peer network design and peer-to-peer applications. Both forms have similar features but in practice work very differently.

P2P Networks

In a peer-to-peer network, two or more computers are connected through a network and can share resources such as printers and files without having a dedicated server. Every connected end device, known as a peer, can function as either a server or a client. One computer might assume the role of server for one transaction while simultaneously serve as a client for another. The roles of client and server are set on a per-request basis, as shown in Figure

3-9. The figure shows one peer asking the other peer to provide print services, while at the same time acting as a file server that shares one of its files.

Figure 3-9   Peer-to-Peer Networking

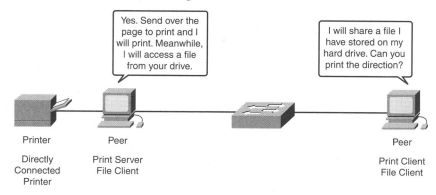

In a peer-to-peer exchange, both devices are considered equal in the communication process.

A simple home network with two connected computers sharing a printer is an example of a peer-to-peer network. Each person can set his or her computer to share files, enable networked games, or share an Internet connection. Another example of peer-to-peer network functionality is two computers connected to a large network that use software applications to share resources between one another through the network.

Unlike the client/server model, which uses dedicated servers, peer-to-peer networks decentralize the resources on a network. Instead of locating information to be shared on dedicated servers, information can be located anywhere on any connected device. Most of the current operating systems support file and print sharing without requiring additional server software. Because peer-to-peer networks usually do not use centralized user accounts, permissions, or monitors, it is difficult to enforce security and access policies in networks containing more than just a few computers. User accounts and access rights must be set individually on each *peer* device.

P2P Applications

A P2P application, unlike a peer-to-peer network, allows a device to act as both a client and a server within the same communication session. In this model, every client is a server and every server a client, as shown in Figure 3-10. Figure 3-10 shows two phones belonging to the same network sending an instant message. The blue lines at the top of the figure depict the digital traffic between the two phones. Both can initiate a communication and are considered equal in the communication process. However, peer-to-peer applications require that each end device provide a user interface and run a background service. When you launch a specific peer-to-peer application, it invokes the required user interface and background services. After that, the devices can communicate directly.

Figure 3-10   Peer-to-Peer Applications

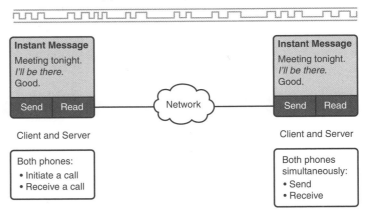

A type of peer-to-peer application is the P2P hybrid system, which utilizes a centralized directory called an index server even though the files being shared are on the individual host machines. Each peer accesses the index server to get the location of a resource stored on another peer. The index server can also help connect two peers, but after they are connected, the communication takes place between the two peers without additional communication to the index server.

Peer-to-peer applications can be used on peer-to-peer networks, in client/server networks, and across the Internet.

Application Layer Protocols and Services Examples

Now that you have a better understanding of how applications provide an interface for the user and provide access to the network, you will take a look at some specific commonly used protocols.

As you will see later in this book, the transport layer uses an addressing *scheme* called a port number. Port numbers identify applications and application layer services that are the source and destination of data. Server programs generally use predefined port numbers that are commonly known by clients. As you examine the different TCP/IP application layer protocols and services, you will be referring to the TCP and UDP port numbers normally associated with these services. Some of these services are

- **Domain Name System (DNS):** TCP/UDP port 53

- **HTTP:** TCP port 80

- **Simple Mail Transfer Protocol (SMTP):** TCP port 25
- **Post Office Protocol (POP):** UDP port 110
- **Telnet:** TCP port 23
- **DHCP:** UDP port 67
- **FTP:** TCP ports 20 and 21

The next sections take a closer look at DNS, world wide web services, and HTTP.

DNS Services and Protocol

In data networks, devices are assigned *IP addresses* so that they can participate in sending and receiving messages over the network. However, most people have a hard time remembering this numeric address. Hence, domain names were created to convert the numeric address into a simple, recognizable name.

On the Internet, these domain names, such as http://www.cisco.com, are much easier for people to remember than 198.132.219.25, which, at the time of this writing, is the numeric address for this server. Also, if Cisco decides to change the numeric address, it is transparent to the user, because the *domain name* will remain http://www.cisco.com. The new address will simply be linked to the existing domain name and connectivity is maintained, as shown in Figure 3-11. When networks were small, it was a simple task to maintain the mapping between domain names and the addresses they represented. However, as networks began to grow and the number of devices increased, this manual system became unworkable.

Figure 3-11   Resolving DNS Addresses

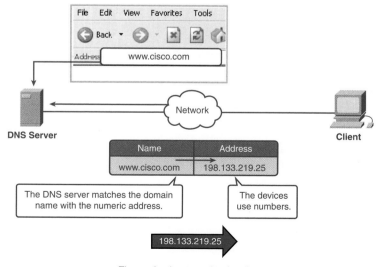

The number is returned to the client
for use in making requests of the server.

DNS was created for domain name–to–address resolution for these networks. DNS uses a distributed set of servers to resolve the names associated with these numbered addresses.

How DNS Works

The DNS protocol defines an automated service that matches resource names with the required numeric *network address*. It includes the format for queries, responses, and data formats. DNS protocol communications use a single format called a message. This message format is used for all types of client queries and server responses, error messages, and the transfer of *resource record* information between servers.

DNS is a client/server service; however, it differs from the other client/server services that you are examining. Whereas other services use a client that is an application (web browser, e-mail client, and so on), the DNS client runs as a service itself. The DNS client, sometimes called the *DNS resolver*, supports name resolution for the other network applications and other services that need it.

When configuring a network device, you generally provide one or more DNS server addresses that the DNS client can use for name resolution. Usually the Internet service provider (ISP) gives you the addresses to use for the DNS servers. When a user's application requests to connect to a remote device by name, the requesting DNS client queries one of these DNS servers to resolve the name to a numeric address.

Computer operating systems also have a utility called *nslookup* that allows the user to manually *query* the name servers to resolve a given host name. You also can use this utility to troubleshoot name resolution issues and to verify the current status of the name servers.

In Example 3-1, when the **nslookup** command is issued, the default DNS server configured for your host is displayed. In this example, the DNS server is dns-sjk.cisco.com, which has an address of 171.68.226.120.

Example 3-1 nslookup Command

```
Microsoft Windows XP [Version 5.1.2600]
 Copyright 1985-2001 Microsoft Corp.


C:\> nslookup

Default Server: dns-sjk.cisco.com
Address: 171.68.226.120
>www.cisco.com
Server: dns-sj.cisco.com
Address: 171.70.168.183


Name:   www.cisco.com
Address: 198.133.219.25
```

You can then type the name of a host or domain for which you want to get the address. In the first query in Example 3-1, a query is made for www.cisco.com. The responding name server provides the address of 198.133.219.25.

Although the queries shown in Example 3-1 are only simple tests, the **nslookup** command has many options available to do extensive testing and verification of the DNS process.

Name Resolution and Caching

A DNS server provides the name resolution using the name daemon, which is often called *named* (pronounced name-dee). The DNS server acts as the phone book for the Internet: It translates human-readable computer host names, for example, http://www.cisco.com, into the IP addresses that networking equipment needs for delivering information.

The DNS server stores different types of resource records used to resolve names. These records contain the name, address, and type of record.

Some of these record types are

- **A:** An end device address

- **NS:** An authoritative name server

- **CNAME:** The canonical name (or fully qualified domain name [FQDN]) for an alias; used when multiple services have the single network address but each service has its own entry in DNS

- **MX:** Mail exchange record; maps a domain name to a list of mail exchange servers for that domain

When a client makes a query, the "named" process first looks at its own records to see whether it can resolve the name. If it is unable to resolve the name using its stored records, it contacts other servers to resolve the name.

The request can be passed along to a number of servers, which can take extra time and consume bandwidth. When a match is found and returned to the original requesting server, the server temporarily stores the numbered address that matches the name in the *cache*.

If that same name is requested again, the first server can return the address by using the value stored in its name cache. Caching reduces both the DNS query data network traffic and the workloads of servers higher up the hierarchy. The DNS client service on Windows PCs optimizes the performance of DNS name resolution by storing previously resolved names in memory, as well. The **ipconfig/displaydns** command displays all the cached DNS entries on a Windows XP or 2000 computer system.

DNS Hierarchy

DNS uses a hierarchical system to create a name database to provide name resolution. The hierarchy looks like an inverted tree with the root at the top and branches below.

At the top of the hierarchy, the root servers maintain records about how to reach the top-level domain servers, which in turn have records that point to the secondary-level domain servers and so on.

The different top-level domains represent either the type of organization or the country of origin. The following are examples of top-level domains are:

- **.au:** Australia
- **.co:** Colombia
- **.com:** A business or industry
- **.jp:** Japan
- **.org:** A nonprofit organization

After top-level domains are second-level domain names, and below them are other lower-level domains. A great example of that is the domain name http://www.cisco.netacad.net. The .net is the top-level domain, .netacad is the second-level domain, and .cisco is at the lower level.

Each domain name is a path down this inverted tree starting from the root. For example, as shown in Figure 3-12, the root DNS servers might not know exactly where the e-mail server mail.cisco.com is located, but they maintain a record for the .com domain within the top-level domain. Likewise, the servers within the .com domain might not have a record for mail.cisco.com, but they do have a record for the cisco.com secondary-level domain. The servers within the cisco.com domain have a record (an MX record to be precise) for mail.cisco.com.

Figure 3-12   DNS Server Hierarchy

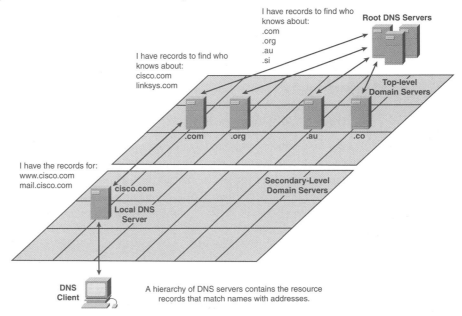

DNS relies on this hierarchy of decentralized servers to store and maintain these resource records. The resource records list domain names that the server can resolve and alternative servers that can process requests. If a given server has resource records that correspond to its level in the domain hierarchy, it is said to be *authoritative* for those records.

For example, a name server in the cisco.netacad.net domain would not be authoritative for the mail.cisco.com record because that record is held at a higher-domain-level server, specifically the name server in the cisco.com domain.

Note

Two links to the DNS protocol RFCs are

- http://www.ietf.org/rfc/rfc1034.txt
- http://www.ietf.org/rfc/rfc1035.txt

Request for Comments (RFC) are standards documents encompassing new research, innovations, and methodologies applicable to Internet technologies. These RFCs are very technical in nature, but they can provide you with some insight to how detailed these standards really are.

WWW Service and HTTP

When a web address (or URL) is typed into a web browser, the web browser establishes a connection to the web service running on the server using HTTP. URLs and URIs (uniform resource identifiers) are the names most people associate with web addresses.

The URL http://www.cisco.com/index.html refers to a specific resource—a web page named index.html on a server identified as cisco.com.

Web browsers are the client applications computers use to connect to the World Wide Web and access resources stored on a web server. As with most server processes, the web server runs as a background service and makes different types of files available.

To access the content, web clients make connections to the server and request the desired resources. The server replies with the resources and, upon receipt, the browser interprets the data and presents it to the user.

Browsers can interpret and present many data types, such as plain text or HTML, the language in which web pages are constructed). Other types of data, however, might require another service or program, typically referred to as a *plug-in* or add-on. To help the browser determine what type of file it is receiving, the server specifies what kind of data the file contains.

To better understand how the web browser and web client interact, you can examine how a web page is opened in a browser. For this example, consider the URL http://www.cisco.com/web-server.htm.

First, the browser interprets the three parts of the URL:

- http: The protocol or scheme
- www.cisco.com: The server name
- web-server.htm: The specific filename requested

The browser then checks with a name server to convert http://www.cisco.com into a numeric address, which it uses to connect to the server. Using the HTTP requirements, the browser sends a GET request to the server and asks for the file web-server.htm. The server in turn sends the HTML code for this web page to the browser. Finally, the browser deciphers the HTML code and formats the page for the browser window.

HTTP, one of the protocols in the TCP/IP suite, was originally developed to publish and retrieve HTML pages and is now used for *distributed, collaborative* information systems. HTTP is used across the world wide web for data transfer and is one of the most used application protocols.

HTTP specifies a request/response protocol. When a client, typically a web browser, sends a request message to a server, the HTTP protocol defines the message types the client uses to request the web page and the message types the server uses to respond. The three common message types are:

- GET
- POST
- PUT

GET is a client request for data. A web browser sends the GET message to request pages from a web server. As shown in Figure 3-13, when the server receives the GET request, it responds with a status line, such as HTTP/1.1 200 OK, and a message of its own, the body of which can be the requested file, an error message, or some other information.

POST and PUT are used to send messages that upload data to the web server. For example, when the user enters data into a form embedded in a web page, POST includes the data in the message sent to the server. PUT uploads resources or content to the web server.

Although it is remarkably flexible, HTTP is not a secure protocol. The POST messages upload information to the server in plain text that can be intercepted and read. Similarly, the server responses, typically HTML pages, are unencrypted.

For secure communication across the Internet, the Secure HTTP (HTTPS) protocol is used for accessing and posting web server information. HTTPS can use authentication and *encryption* to secure data as it travels between the client and server. HTTPS specifies additional rules for passing data between the application layer and the transport layer.

Figure 3-13 HTTP Protocol Using GET

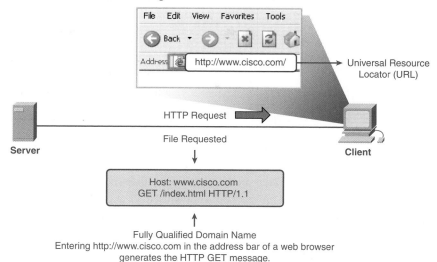

Network Representations (3.3.2.3)

In this activity, you will configure DNS and HTTP services, and then study the packets that result when a web page is requested by typing a URL. Use file e1-3323.pka on the CD-ROM that accompanies this book to perform this activity using Packet Tracer.

Packet Tracer
☐ Activity

E-Mail Services and SMTP/POP Protocols

E-mail, the most popular network service, has revolutionized how people communicate through its simplicity and speed. Yet to run on a computer or other end device, e-mail requires several applications and services. Two examples of application layer protocols are *Post Office Protocol (POP)* and *Simple Mail Transfer Protocol (SMTP)*. As with HTTP, these protocols define client/server processes.

POP and POP3 (Post Office Protocol, version 3) are inbound mail delivery protocols and are typical client/server protocols. They deliver e-mail from the e-mail server to the client (MUA).

SMTP, on the other hand, governs the transfer of outbound e-mail from the sending client to the e-mail server (MDA), as well as the transport of e-mail between e-mail servers (MTA). (These acronyms are defined in the next section.) SMTP enables e-mail to be transported across data networks between different types of server and client software and makes e-mail exchange over the Internet possible.

When people compose e-mail messages, they typically use an application called a *Mail User Agent (MUA)*, or e-mail client. The MUA allows messages to be sent and places received messages into the client mailbox, both of which are distinct processes, as shown in Figure 3-14.

Figure 3-14   E-Mail Client (MUA)

To receive e-mail messages from an e-mail server, the e-mail client can use POP. Sending e-mail from either a client or a server uses message formats and command strings defined by the SMTP protocol. Usually an e-mail client provides the functionality of both protocols within one application.

E-Mail Server Processes: MTA and MDA

The e-mail server operates two separate processes:

- Mail Transfer Agent (MTA)

- Mail Delivery Agent (MDA)

The Mail Transfer Agent (MTA) process is used to forward e-mail. As shown in Figure 3-15, the MTA receives messages from the MUA or from another MTA on another e-mail server. Based on the message header, it determines how a message has to be forwarded to reach its destination. If the mail is addressed to a user whose mailbox is on the local server, the mail is passed to the MDA. If the mail is for a user not on the local server, the MTA routes the e-mail to the MTA on the appropriate server.

Figure 3-15   E-Mail Server: MTA

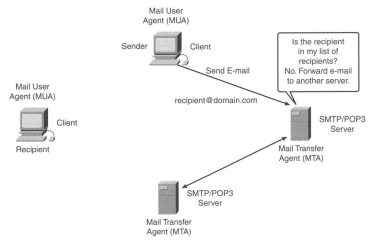

In Figure 3-16, you see that the Mail Delivery Agent (MDA) accepts a piece of e-mail from a Mail Transfer Agent (MTA) and performs the delivery. The MDA receives all the inbound mail from the MTA and places it into the appropriate users' mailboxes. The MDA can also resolve final delivery issues, such as virus scanning, *spam* filtering, and return-receipt handling.

Figure 3-16   E-Mail Server: MDA

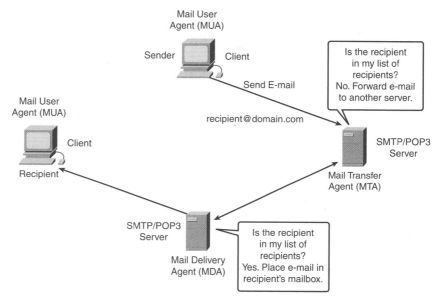

Most e-mail communications use the MUA, MTA, and MDA applications. However, there are other alternatives for e-mail delivery. A client can be connected to a corporate e-mail system, such as IBM Lotus Notes, Novell Groupwise, or Microsoft Exchange. These systems often have their own internal e-mail format, and their clients typically communicate with the e-mail server using a proprietary protocol.

The server sends or receives e-mail through the Internet through the product's Internet mail *gateway*, which performs any necessary reformatting. If, for example, two people who work for the same company exchange e-mail with each other using a proprietary protocol, their messages can stay completely within the corporate e-mail system of the company.

As another alternative, computers that do not have an MUA can still connect to a mail service on a web browser to retrieve and send messages in this manner. Some computers can run their own MTA and manage interdomain e-mail themselves.

The SMTP protocol message format uses a rigid set of commands and replies. These commands support the procedures used in SMTP, such as session initiation, mail transaction, forwarding mail, verifying mailbox names, expanding mailing lists, and the opening and closing exchanges.

Some of the commands specified in the SMTP protocol are:

- **HELO:** Identifies the SMTP client process to the SMTP server process
- **EHLO:** Is a newer version of HELO, which includes services extensions
- **MAIL FROM:** Identifies the sender
- **RCPT TO:** Identifies the recipient
- **DATA:** Identifies the body of the message

FTP

FTP is another commonly used application layer protocol. FTP was developed to allow file transfers between a client and a server. An FTP client is an application that runs on a computer that is used to push and pull files from a server running the FTP daemon (FTPd).

To successfully transfer files, FTP requires two connections between the client and the server: one for commands and replies, and the other for the actual file transfer.

The client establishes the first connection to the server on TCP port 21. This connection is used for control traffic, consisting of client commands and server replies.

The client establishes the second connection to the server over TCP port 20. This connection is for the actual file transfer and is created every time a file is transferred.

The file transfer can happen in either direction, as shown in Figure 3-17. The client can download (pull) a file from the server or upload (push) a file to the server.

Figure 3-17   FTP Process

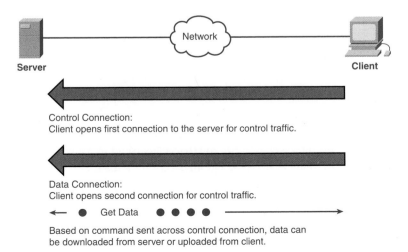

DHCP

The *DHCP* enables clients on a network to obtain IP addresses and other information from a DHCP server. The protocol automates the assignment of IP addresses, subnet masks, gateway, and other IP networking parameters.

DHCP allows a host to obtain an IP address dynamically when it connects to the network. The DHCP server is contacted by sending a request, and an IP address is requested. The DHCP server chooses an address from a configured range of addresses called a *pool* and assigns it to the host client for a set period.

On larger networks, local networks, or where the user population changes frequently, DHCP is preferred. New users might arrive with laptops and need a connection. Others have new workstations that need to be connected. Rather than have the network administrator assign IP addresses for each workstation, it is more efficient to have IP addresses assigned automatically using DHCP.

When a DHCP-configured device boots up or connects to the network, the client broadcasts a DHCP DISCOVER packet to identify any available DHCP servers on the network. A DHCP server replies with a DHCP OFFER, which is a lease offer message with an assigned IP address, *subnet mask*, DNS server, and default gateway information as well as the duration of the lease.

DHCP-distributed addresses are not permanently assigned to hosts but are only leased for a period of time. If the host is powered down or taken off the network, the address is returned to the pool for reuse. This is especially helpful with mobile users who come and go on a network. Users can freely move from location to location and re-establish network connections. The host can obtain an IP address after the hardware connection is made, either through a wired or wireless LAN.

DHCP makes it possible for you to access the Internet using wireless hotspots at airports or coffee shops. As you enter the area, your laptop DHCP client contacts the local DHCP server through a wireless connection. The DHCP server assigns an IP address to your laptop.

Various types of devices can be DHCP servers when running DHCP service software. The DHCP server in most medium to large networks is usually a local dedicated PC-based server.

With home networks, the DHCP server is usually located at the ISP, and a host on the home network receives its IP configuration directly from the ISP.

Many home networks and small businesses use an Integrated Services Router (ISR) device to connect to the ISP. In this case, the ISR is both a DHCP client and a server. The ISR acts as a client to receive its IP configuration from the ISP and then acts a DHCP server for internal hosts on the local network.

Figure 3-18 shows the different ways of having DHCP servers arranged.

Figure 3-18   DHCP Servers

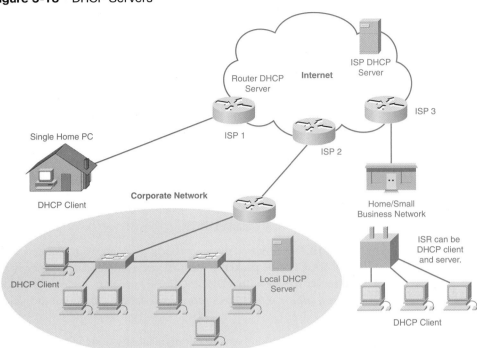

DHCP can pose a security risk because any device connected to the network can receive an address. This risk makes physical security an important factor when determining whether to use dynamic or static (manual) addressing.

Dynamic and static addressing have their places in network designs. Many networks use both DHCP and static addressing. DHCP is used for general-purpose hosts such as end-user devices, and static, or fixed, addresses are used for network devices such as gateways, switches, servers, and printers.

The client can receive multiple DHCP OFFER packets if the local network has more than one DHCP server. The client must choose between them and *broadcast* a DHCP REQUEST packet that identifies the explicit server and lease offer that it is accepting. A client can choose to request an address that it had previously been allocated by the server.

Assuming that the IP address requested by the client, or offered by the server, is still valid, the chosen server would return a DHCP ACK (acknowledgment) message. The ACK message lets the client know that the lease is finalized. If the offer is no longer valid for some reason, perhaps because of a timeout or another client allocating the lease, the chosen server must respond to the client with a DHCP NAK (negative acknowledgment) message. When the client has the lease, it must be renewed prior to the lease expiration through another

DHCP REQUEST message. The DHCP server ensures that all IP addresses are unique. (An IP address cannot be assigned to two different network devices simultaneously.)

File-Sharing Services and SMB Protocol

Server Message Block (SMB) is a client/server file-sharing protocol. IBM developed SMB in the late 1980s to describe the structure of shared network resources, such as directories, files, printers, and serial ports. It is a request/response protocol. Unlike the file sharing supported by FTP, clients establish a long-term connection to servers. After the connection is established, the user of the client can access the resources on the server as if the resource is local to the client host.

SMB file-sharing and print services have become the mainstay of Microsoft networking. With the introduction of the Windows 2000 series of software, Microsoft changed the underlying structure for using SMB. In previous versions of Microsoft products, the SMB services used a non-TCP/IP protocol to implement name resolution. Beginning with Windows 2000, all subsequent Microsoft products use DNS naming. This allows TCP/IP protocols to directly support SMB resource sharing, as shown in Figure 3-19.

Figure 3-19   File Sharing Using the SMB Protocol

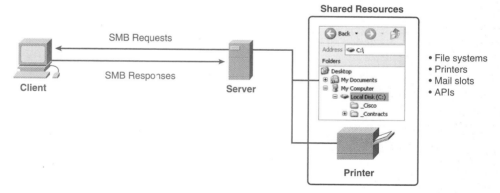

The Linux and *UNIX* operating systems also provide a method of sharing resources with Microsoft networks using a version of SMB called SAMBA. The Apple Macintosh operating systems also support resource sharing using the SMB protocol.

The SMB protocol describes file system access and indicates how clients can make requests for files. It also describes the SMB protocol interprocess communication. All SMB messages share a common format. This format uses a fixed-sized header followed by a variable-sized parameter and data component.

SMB messages can perform the following tasks:

- Start, authenticate, and terminate sessions

- Control file and printer access

- Allow an application to send or receive messages to or from another device

P2P Services and Gnutella Protocol

You learned about FTP and SMB as ways of obtaining files. This section describes another application protocol, Gnutella. Sharing files over the Internet has become extremely popular. With P2P applications based on the Gnutella protocol, people can make files on their hard disks available to others for downloading. Gnutella-compatible client software allows users to connect to Gnutella services over the Internet and to locate and access resources shared by other Gnutella peers.

Many client applications are available for accessing the Gnutella network, including BearShare, Gnucleus, LimeWire, Morpheus, WinMX, and XoloX. Although the Gnutella Developer Forum maintains the basic protocol, application vendors often develop extensions to make the protocol work better on their applications.

Many P2P applications do not use a central database to record all the files available on the peers. Instead, the devices on the network each tell the other what files are available when queried and use the Gnutella protocol and services to support locating resources, as shown in Figure 3-20. When a user is connected to a Gnutella service, the client applications will search for other Gnutella nodes to connect to. These nodes handle queries for resource locations and replies to those requests. They also govern control messages, which help the service discover other nodes. The actual file transfers usually rely on HTTP services.

Figure 3-20 Gnutella Protocol

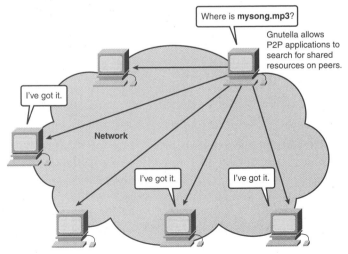

The Gnutella protocol defines five different packet types:

- **ping:** For device discovery
- **pong:** As a reply to a ping
- **query:** For file location
- **query hit:** As a reply to a query
- **push:** As a download request

Telnet Services and Protocol

Long before desktop computers with sophisticated graphical interfaces existed, people used text-based systems that were often just display terminals physically attached to a central computer. After networks were available, people needed a way to remotely access the computer systems in the same manner that they did with the directly attached terminals.

Telnet was developed to meet that need. It dates back to the early 1970s and is among the oldest of the application layer protocols and services in the TCP/IP suite. Telnet is a client/server protocol that provides a standard method of emulating text-based terminal devices over the data network. Both the protocol itself and the client software that implements the protocol are commonly referred to as Telnet. The Telnet service is depicted in Figure 3-21.

Figure 3-21   Telnet Service

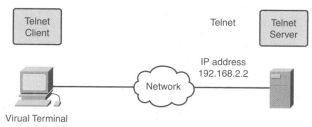

Appropriately enough, a connection using Telnet is called a *VTY* (Virtual Terminal) *session*, or *connection*. Telnet specifies how a VTY session is established and terminated. It also provides the syntax and order of the commands used to initiate the Telnet session, and it provides control commands that can be issued during a session. Each Telnet command consists of at least 2 bytes. The first byte is a special character called the *Interpret as Command (IAC)* character. As its name implies, the IAC character defines the next byte as a command rather than text. Rather than using a physical device to connect to the server, Telnet uses software to create a virtual device that provides the same features of a terminal session with access to the server command-line interface (CLI).

To support Telnet client connections, the server runs a service called the Telnet daemon. A virtual terminal connection is established from an end device using a Telnet client application. Most operating systems include an application layer Telnet client. On a Microsoft Windows PC, Telnet can be run from the command prompt. Other common terminal applications that run as Telnet clients are HyperTerminal, Minicom, and TeraTerm.

When a Telnet connection is established, users can perform any authorized function on the server, just as if they were using a command-line session on the server itself. If authorized, they can start and stop processes, configure the device, and even shut down the system.

The following are some sample Telnet protocol commands:

- **Are You There (AYT):** Enables the user to request that a response, usually a prompt icon, appear on the terminal screen to indicate that the VTY session is active.

- **Erase Line (EL):** Deletes all text from the current line.

- **Interrupt Process (IP):** Suspends, interrupts, aborts, or terminates the process to which the virtual terminal is connected. For example, if a user started a program on the Telnet server through the VTY, he or she could send an IP command to stop the program.

Although the Telnet protocol supports user authentication, it does not support the transport of encrypted data. All data exchanged during a Telnet session is transported as plain text across the network. This means that the data can be intercepted and easily understood.

The Secure Shell (SSH) protocol offers an alternate and secure method for server access. SSH provides the structure for secure remote login and other secure network services. It also provides stronger authentication than Telnet and supports the transport of session data using encryption. As a best practice, network professionals should use SSH in place of Telnet, whenever possible.

Summary

The application layer is responsible for directly accessing the underlying processes that manage and deliver communication to the human network. This layer serves as the source and destination of communications across data networks. The application layer applications, protocols, and services enable users to interact with the data network in a way that is meaningful and effective.

Applications are computer programs with which the user interacts and that initiate the data transfer process at the user's request.

Services are background programs that provide the connection between the application layer and the lower layers of the networking model.

Protocols provide a structure of agreed-upon rules, much like grammar and punctuation provide "rules" in a language. These protocol rules ensure that services running on one particular device can send and receive data from a range of different network devices.

Delivery of data over the network can be requested from a server by a client. In a peer-to-peer arrangement, either device can function as a client or server, and data is delivered depending on the client/server relationship established. Messages are exchanged between the application layer services at each end device in accordance with the protocol specifications to establish and use these relationships.

Protocols like HTTP, for example, support the delivery of web pages to end devices. SMTP/POP protocols support sending and receiving e-mail. SMB enables users to share files. DNS resolves the human-legible names used to refer to network resources into numeric addresses usable by the network. Telnet provides remote, text-based access to devices. DHCP provides dynamic allocation of IP addresses and other network-enabling parameters. P2P allows two or more computers to share resources over the network.

Activities and Labs

The activities and labs available in the companion *Network Fundamentals, CCNA Exploration Labs and Study Guide* (ISBN 1-58713-203-6) provide hands-on practice with the following topics introduced in this chapter:

Activity 3-1: Data Stream Capture (3.4.1.1)

In this activity, you will use a computer that has a microphone and Microsoft Sound Recorder or Internet access so that an audio file can be downloaded.

Lab 3-1: Managing a Web Server (3.4.2.1)

In this lab, you will download, install, and configure the popular Apache web server. You will use a web browser to connect to the server and Wireshark to capture the communication. Analyzing the capture will help you understand how HTTP operates.

Lab 3-2: E-mail Services and Protocols (3.4.3.1)

In this lab, you will configure and use an e-mail client application to connect to eagle-server network services. You will then monitor the communication with Wireshark and analyze the captured packets.

Many of the hands-on labs include Packet Tracer companion activities where you can use Packet Tracer to complete a simulation of the lab. Look for this icon in the *Network Fundamentals, CCNA Exploration Labs and Study Guide* (ISBN 1-58713-203-6) for hands-on labs that have Packet Tracer companion activities.

Check Your Understanding

Complete all the review questions listed here to test your understanding of the topics and concepts in this chapter. The appendix, "Check Your Understanding and Challenge Questions Answer Key," lists the answers.

1. The application layer is _____ of the OSI model.

    A. Layer 1

    B. Layer 3

    C. Layer 4

    D. Layer 7

2. The TCP/IP application layer consists roughly of which three OSI layers?

    A. Application, session, transport

    B. Application, presentation, session

    C. Application, transport, network

    D. Application, network, data link

3. HTTP is used to do which of the following?

    A. Resolve Internet names to IP addresses

    B. Provide remote access to servers and networking devices

    C. Transfer files that make up the web pages of the World Wide Web

    D. Transfer the mail messages and attachments

4. Post Office Protocol (POP) uses which port?

   A. TCP/UDP port 53

   B. TCP port 80

   C. TCP port 25

   D. UDP port 110

5. What is GET?

   A. A client request for data

   B. A protocol that uploads resources or content to the web server

   C. A protocol that uploads information to the server in plain text that can be intercepted and read

   D. A response from a server

6. Which is the most popular network service?

   A. HTTP

   B. FTP

   C. Telnet

   D. E-mail

7. FTP requires _____ connection(s) between client and server to successfully transfer files.

   A. 1

   B. 2

   C. 3

   D. 4

8. DHCP enables clients on a network to do which of the following?

   A. Have unlimited telephone conversations

   B. Play back video streams

   C. Obtain IP addresses

   D. Track intermittent denial of service attacks

9. The Linux and UNIX operating systems use SAMBA, which is a version of which protocol?

   A. SMB

   B. HTTP

   C. FTP

   D. SMTP

10. Which of the following is a connection using Telnet?

   A. File Transfer Protocol (FTP) session

   B. Trivial File Transfer Protocol (TFTP) session

   C. Virtual Terminal (VTY) session

   D. Auxiliary (AUX) session

11. Is eBay a peer-to-peer or client/server application?

12. In the client/server model, the device requesting the service is referred to as the
    _____.

13. HTTP is referred to as a request/response protocol. What are three typical message formats?

14. DHCP allows the automation of what?

15. What does FTP stand for, and what is it used for?

Challenge Questions and Activities

These questions require a deeper application of the concepts covered in this chapter. You can find the answers in the appendix.

1. List the six-step process for converting human communications to data.

2. Describe the two forms of application software and the purpose of each.

3. Elaborate on the meaning of the terms server and client in the context of data networks.

4. Compare and contrast client/server with peer-to-peer data transfer over networks.

5. List five general functions that application layer protocols specify.

6. Give the specific purposes of the DNS, HTTP, SMB, and SMTP/POP application layer protocols.

7. Compare and contrast the messages that application layer protocols such as DNS, HTTP, SMB, and SMTP/POP exchange between devices to enable data transfers to occur.

To Learn More

The following questions encourage you to reflect on the topics discussed in this chapter. Your instructor might ask you to research the questions and discuss your findings in class.

1. Why is it important to distinguish between a particular application layer application, the associated service, and the protocol? Discuss this in the context of network reference models.

2. What if it was possible to include all application layer services with a single all-encompassing protocol? Discuss the advantages and disadvantages of having one such protocol.

3. How would you develop a new protocol for a new application layer service? What would have to be included? Who would have to be involved in the process, and how would the information be disseminated?

CHAPTER 4

OSI Transport Layer

Objectives

Upon completion of this chapter, you will be able to answer the following questions:

- Why is there a need for the transport layer?

- What is the role of the transport layer as it provides the end-to-end transfer of data between applications?

- What is the role of two TCP/IP transport layer protocols: TCP and UDP?

- How do the key functions of the transport layer protocol, including reliability, port addressing, and segmentation, work?

- How do TCP and UDP handle the key functions?

- When is it appropriate to use TCP or UDP, and what are some examples of applications that use each protocol?

Key Terms

This chapter uses the following key terms. You can find the definitions in the Glossary.

flow control   page 104

control data   page 106

Internet Assigned Numbers Authority (IANA)
  page 110

well-known ports   page 110

registered ports   page 111

dynamic or private ports   page 111

URG   page 117

ACK   page 117

PSH   page 117

RST   page 117

SYN   page 117

FIN   page 117

acknowledgment   page 118

window size   page 121

Data networks and the Internet support the human network by supplying seamless, reliable communication among people—both locally and around the globe. On a single device, people can use multiple services, such as e-mail, the web, and instant messaging, to send messages or retrieve information. Applications such as e-mail clients, web browsers, and instant messaging clients allow people to use computers and networks to send messages and find information.

Data from each of these applications is packaged, transported, and delivered to the appropriate server daemon or application on the destination device. The processes described in the OSI transport layer accept data from the application layer and prepare it for addressing at the network layer. The transport layer is responsible for the overall end-to-end transfer of application data, as shown in Figure 4-1.

Figure 4-1   OSI Transport Layer

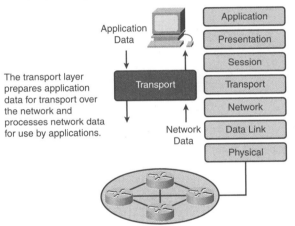

This chapter examines the role of the transport layer in encapsulating application data for use by the network layer. The transport layer also encompasses these functions:

- Enables multiple applications to communicate over the network at the same time on a single device

- Ensures that, if required, all the data is received reliably and in order by the correct application

- Employs error-handling mechanisms

Roles of the Transport Layer

The transport layer provides transparent transfer of data between end users, providing reliable data transfer services to the upper layers. The transport layer controls the reliability of a given link through flow control, segmentation/desegmentation, and error control. Some protocols are state and connection oriented. This means that the transport layer can keep track of the segments and retransmit those that fail.

Purpose of the Transport Layer

The following are the primary responsibilities of the transport layer:

- Tracking the individual communications between applications on the source and destination hosts

- Segmenting data and managing each piece

- Reassembling the segments into streams of application data

- Identifying the different applications

- Performing flow control between end users

- Enabling error recovery

- Initiating a session

The transport layer enables applications on devices to communicate, as shown in Figure 4-2.

Figure 4-2   Enabling Applications on Devices to Communicate

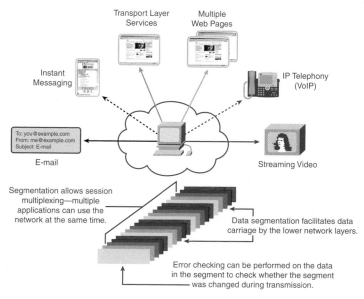

The next sections describe the different roles of the transport layer and data requirements for transport layer protocols.

Tracking Individual Conversations

Any host can have multiple applications that are communicating across the network. Each of these applications will be communicating with one or more applications on remote hosts. It is the responsibility of the transport layer to maintain the multiple communication streams between these applications.

Consider a computer connected to a network that is simultaneously receiving and sending e-mail and instant messages, viewing websites, and conducting a Voice over IP (VoIP) phone call, as shown in Figure 4-3. Each of these applications is sending and receiving data over the network at the same time. However, data from the phone call is not directed to the web browser, and text from an instant message does not appear in an e-mail.

Figure 4-3   Tracking the Conversations

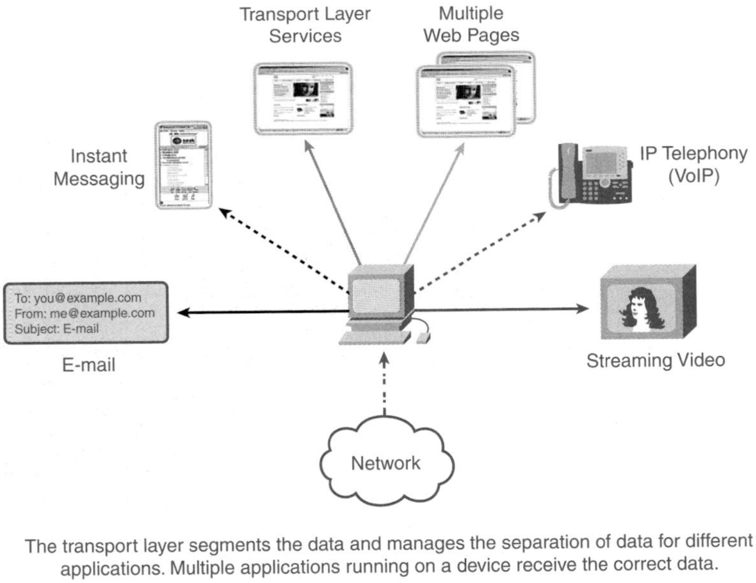

The transport layer segments the data and manages the separation of data for different applications. Multiple applications running on a device receive the correct data.

Segmenting Data

The application layer passes large amounts of data to the transport layer. The transport layer has to break the data into smaller pieces, better suited for transmission. These pieces are called segments.

This process includes the encapsulation required on each piece of data. Each piece of application data requires headers to be added at the transport layer to indicate to which communication it is associated.

Segmentation of the data, as shown in Figure 4-4, in accordance with transport layer protocols, provides the means to both send and receive data when running multiple applications concurrently on a computer. Without segmentation, only one application, the streaming video, for example, would be able to receive data. You could not receive e-mails, chat on instant messenger, or view web pages while also viewing the video.

Figure 4-4   Segmentation

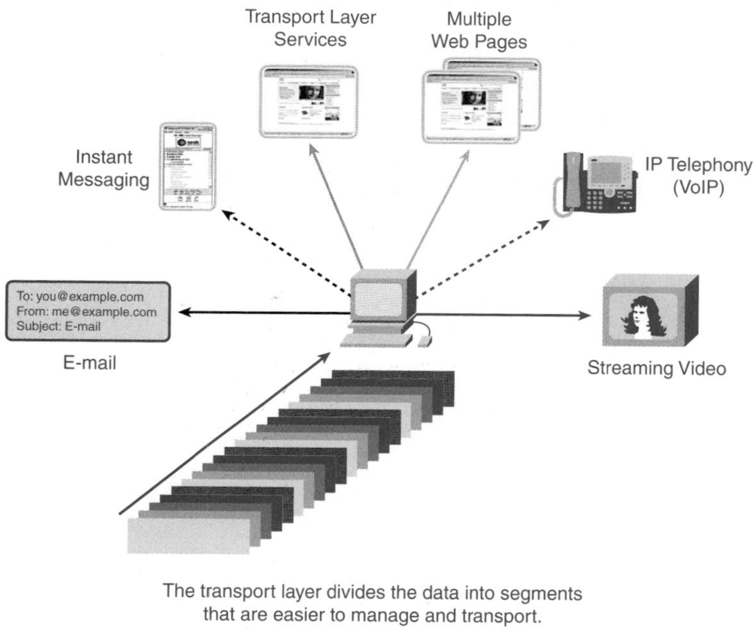

The transport layer divides the data into segments
that are easier to manage and transport.

Reassembling Segments

Because networks can provide multiple routes that can have different transmission times, data can arrive in the wrong order. By numbering and sequencing the segments, the transport layer can ensure that these segments are reassembled into the proper order.

At the receiving host, each segment of data must be reassembled in the correct order and then directed to the appropriate application.

The protocols at the transport layer describe how the transport layer header information is used to reassemble the data pieces into in-order data streams to be passed to the application layer.

Identifying the Applications

To pass data streams to the proper applications, the transport layer must identify the target application. To accomplish this, the transport layer assigns an identifier to an application.

The TCP/IP protocols call this identifier a *port number*. Each software process that needs to access the network is assigned a port number unique in that host. This port number is used in the transport layer header to indicate to which application that piece of data is associated.

At the transport layer, each particular set of pieces flowing between a source application and a destination application is known as a *conversation*. Dividing data into small parts, and sending these parts from the source to the destination, enables many different communications to be interleaved (multiplexed) on the same network.

The transport layer is the link between the application layer and the lower layers that are responsible for network transmission. This layer accepts data from different conversations and passes it down to the lower layers as manageable pieces that can be eventually multiplexed over the media.

Applications do not need to know the operational details of the network in use. The applications generate data that is sent from one application to another, without regard to the destination host type, the type of media over which the data must travel, the path taken by the data, the congestion on a link, or the size of the network.

Additionally, the lower layers are not aware that multiple applications are sending data on the network. Their responsibility is to deliver data to the appropriate device. The transport layer then sorts these pieces before delivering them to the appropriate application.

Flow Control

Network hosts have limited resources, such as memory or bandwidth. When the transport layer is aware that these resources are overtaxed, some protocols can request that the sending application reduce the rate of data flow. This is done at the transport layer by regulating the amount of data the source transmits as a group. *Flow control* can prevent the loss of segments on the network and avoid the need for retransmission.

As the protocols are discussed in this chapter, this service will be explained in more detail.

Error Recovery

For many reasons, it is possible for a piece of data to become corrupted, or lost, as it is transmitted over the network. The transport layer can ensure that all pieces reach their destination by having the source device retransmit any data that is lost.

Initiating a Session

The transport layer can provide connection orientation by creating a session between the applications. These connections prepare the applications to communicate with each other before any data is transmitted. Within these sessions, the data for a communication between the two applications can be closely managed.

Data Requirements Vary

Multiple transport layer protocols exist to meet the requirements of different applications. For example, users require that an e-mail or web page be completely received and presented for the information to be considered useful. Slight delays are considered acceptable to ensure that the complete information is received and presented.

In contrast, occasionally missing small parts of a telephone conversation might be considered acceptable. You can either infer the missing audio from the context of the conversation or ask the other person to repeat what he said. This is considered preferable to the delays that would result from asking the network to manage and resend missing segments. In this example, the user, not the network, manages the resending or replacement of missing information.

In today's converged networks, where the flow of voice, video, and data travels over the same network, applications with very different transport needs can be communicating on the same network. The different transport layer protocols have different rules allowing devices to handle these diverse data requirements.

Some protocols, such as UDP (User Datagram Protocol), provide just the basic functions for efficiently delivering the data pieces between the appropriate applications. These types of protocols are useful for applications whose data is sensitive to delays.

Other transport layer protocols, such as TCP (Transmission Control Protocol), describe processes that provide additional features, such as ensuring reliable delivery between the applications. While these additional functions provide more robust communication at the transport layer between applications, they have additional overhead and make larger demands on the network.

To identify each segment of data, the transport layer adds to the piece a header containing binary data. This header contains fields of bits. The values in these fields enable different transport layer protocols to perform different functions.

Supporting Reliable Communication

Recall that the primary function of the transport layer is to manage the application data for the conversations between hosts. However, different applications have different requirements for their data, and therefore different transport protocols have been developed to meet these requirements.

TCP is a transport layer protocol that can be implemented to ensure reliable delivery of the data. In networking terms, reliability means ensuring that each piece of data that the source sends arrives at the destination. At the transport layer, the three basic operations of reliability are

- Tracking transmitted data
- Acknowledging received data
- Retransmitting any unacknowledged data

The transport layer of the sending host tracks all the data pieces for each conversation and retransmits any data that the receiving host did not acknowledge. These reliability processes place additional overhead on the network resources because of the acknowledgment, tracking, and retransmission. To support these reliability operations, more *control data* is exchanged between the sending and receiving hosts. This control information is contained in the Layer 4 header.

This creates a trade-off between the value of reliability and the burden it places on the network. Application developers must choose which transport protocol type is appropriate based on the requirements of their applications, as shown in Figure 4-5. At the transport layer, protocols specify methods for either reliable, guaranteed delivery or best-effort delivery. In the context of networking, best-effort delivery is referred to as unreliable, because the destination does not acknowledge whether it received the data.

Figure 4-5   Transport Layer Protocols

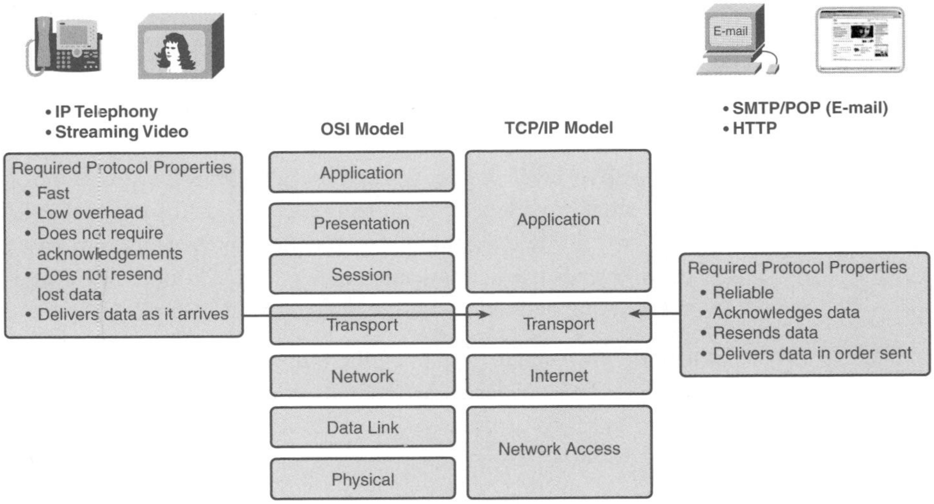

Applications, such as databases, web pages, and e-mail, require that all the sent data arrive at the destination in its original condition for the data to be useful. Any missing data could cause a corrupt communication that is either incomplete or unreadable. Therefore, these applications are designed to use a transport layer protocol that implements reliability. The additional network overhead is considered to be required for these applications.

Other applications are more tolerant of the loss of small amounts of data. For example, if one or two segments of a video stream fail to arrive, it would only create a momentary disruption in the stream. This can appear as distortion in the image but might not even be noticeable to the user. Imposing overhead to ensure reliability for this application could reduce the usefulness of the application. The image in a streaming video would be greatly degraded if the destination device had to account for lost data and delay the stream while waiting for its arrival. It is better to render the best image possible at the time with the segments that arrive and forego reliability. If reliability is required for some reason, these applications can provide error checking and retransmission requests.

TCP and UDP

The two most common transport layer protocols of the TCP/IP protocol suite are Transmission Control Protocol (TCP) and User Datagram Protocol (UDP). Both protocols manage the communication of multiple applications. The differences between the two are the specific functions that each protocol implements.

User Datagram Protocol (UDP)

UDP is a simple, connectionless protocol, described in RFC 768. It has the advantage of providing low-overhead data delivery. The segments of communication in UDP are called *datagrams*. UDP sends datagrams as "best effort."

Applications that use UDP include

- Domain Name System (DNS)

- Video streaming

- Voice over IP (VoIP)

Figure 4-6 illustrates a UDP datagram.

Figure 4-6   UDP Datagram

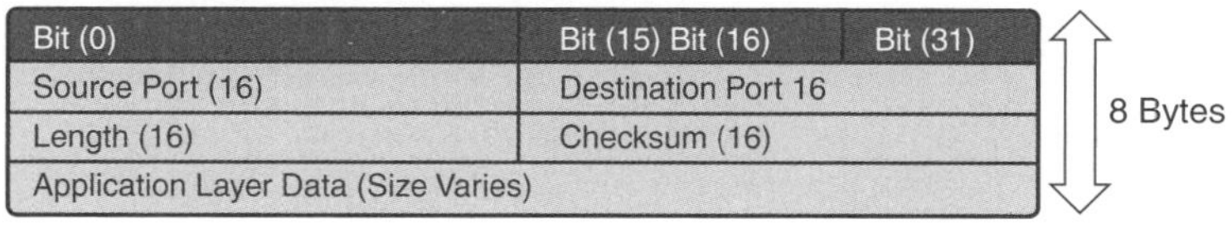

Bit (0)		Bit (15) Bit (16)	Bit (31)	
Source Port (16)		Destination Port 16		8 Bytes
Length (16)		Checksum (16)		
Application Layer Data (Size Varies)				

Transmission Control Protocol (TCP)

TCP is a connection-oriented protocol, described in RFC 793. TCP incurs additional overhead to gain functions. Additional functions specified by TCP are same-order delivery, reliable delivery, and flow control. Each TCP segment has 20 bytes of overhead in the header encapsulating the application layer data, whereas each UDP segment has only 8 bytes of overhead. Figure 4-7 shows the TCP datagram.

Figure 4-7   TCP Datagram

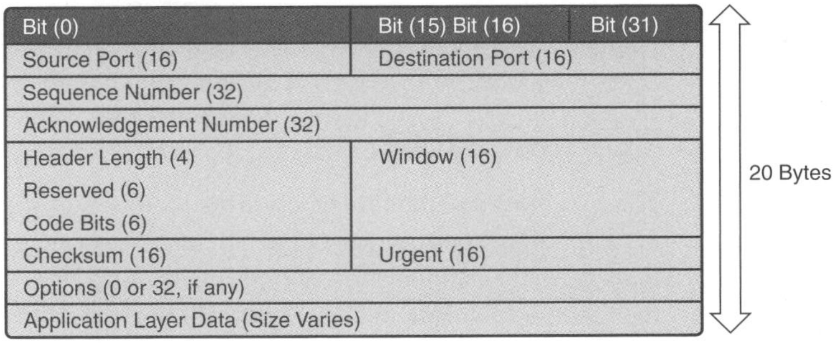

Bit (0)		Bit (15) Bit (16)	Bit (31)	
Source Port (16)		Destination Port (16)		
Sequence Number (32)				
Acknowledgement Number (32)				
Header Length (4) Reserved (6) Code Bits (6)		Window (16)		20 Bytes
Checksum (16)		Urgent (16)		
Options (0 or 32, if any)				
Application Layer Data (Size Varies)				

The following applications use TCP:

- Web browsers

- E-mail

- File transfers

Port Addressing

Consider the earlier example of a computer simultaneously receiving and sending e-mail, instant messages, web pages, and a VoIP phone call.

The TCP- and UDP-based services keep track of the various applications that are communicating. To differentiate the segments and datagrams for each application, both TCP and UDP have header fields that can uniquely identify these applications.

Identifying the Conversations

The header of each segment or datagram contains a source and destination port. The source port number is the number for this communication associated with the originating application on the local host. The destination port number is the number for this communication associated with the destination application on the remote host.

Port numbers are assigned in various ways, depending on whether the message is a request or a response. While server processes have static port numbers assigned to them, clients dynamically choose a port number for each conversation.

When a client application sends a request to a server application, the destination port contained in the header is the port number that is assigned to the service daemon running on the remote host. The client software must know what port number is associated with the server process on the remote host. This destination port number is configured, either by default or manually. For example, when a web browser application makes a request to a web server, the browser uses TCP and port number 80 unless otherwise specified. TCP port 80 is the default port assigned to web-serving applications. Many common applications have default port assignments.

The source port in a segment or datagram header of a client request is randomly generated. As long as it does not conflict with other ports in use on the system, the client can choose any port number. This port number acts like a return address for the requesting application. The transport layer keeps track of this port and the application that initiated the request so that when a response is returned, it can be forwarded to the correct application. The requesting application port number is used as the destination port number in the response coming back from the server.

The combination of the transport layer port number and the network layer IP address assigned to the host uniquely identifies a particular process running on a specific host device. This combination is called a *socket*. Occasionally, you can find the terms *port number* and *socket* used interchangeably. In the context of this book, the term *socket* refers only to the unique combination of IP address and port number. A socket pair, consisting of the source and destination IP addresses and port numbers, is also unique and identifies the conversation between the two hosts.

For example, an HTTP web page request being sent to a web server (port 80) running on a host with a Layer 3 IPv4 address of 192.168.1.20 would be destined to socket 192.168.1.20:80.

If the web browser requesting the web page is running on host 192.168.100.48 and the dynamic port number assigned to the web browser is 49152, the socket for the web page would be 192.168.100.48:49152.

These unique identifiers are the port numbers, and the process of identifying the different conversations through the use of port numbers is shown in Figure 4-8.

Figure 4-8   Identifying Conversations

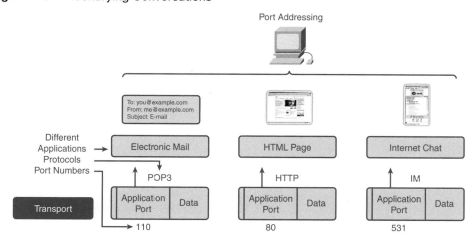

Port Addressing Types and Tools

The *Internet Assigned Numbers Authority (IANA)* assigns port numbers. IANA is a standards body that is responsible for assigning various addressing standards.

The different types of port numbers are

- Well-known ports (numbers 0 to 1023)

- Registered ports (numbers 1024 to 49151)

- Dynamic or private ports (numbers 49152 to 65535)

The following sections describe the three types of port numbers and examples of when both TCP and UDP might use the same port number. You also learn about the netstat network utility.

Well-Known Ports

Well-known ports (numbers 0 to 1023) are reserved for services and applications. They are commonly used for applications such as HTTP (web server), POP3/SMTP (e-mail server), and Telnet. By defining these well-known ports for server applications, client applications can be programmed to request a connection to that specific port and its associated service. Table 4-1 lists some well-known ports for TCP and UDP.

Table 4-1   Well-Known Ports

Well-Known Port	Application	Protocol
20	File Transfer Protocol (FTP) Data	TCP
21	File Transfer Protocol (FTP) Control	TCP
23	Telnet	TCP
25	Simple Mail Transfer Protocol (SMTP)	TCP
69	Trivial File Transfer Protocol (TFTP)	UDP
80	Hypertext Transfer Protocol (HTTP)	TCP
110	Post Office Protocol 3 (POP3)	TCP
194	Internet Relay Chat (IRC)	TCP
443	Secure HTTP (HTTPS)	TCP
520	Routing Information Protocol (RIP)	UDP

Registered Ports

Registered ports (numbers 1024 to 49151) are assigned to user processes or applications. These processes are primarily individual applications that a user has chosen to install rather than common applications that would receive a well-known port. When not used for a server resource, a client can dynamically select a registered port as its source port. Table 4-2 lists registered ports for TCP and UDP.

Table 4-2   Registered Ports

Registered Port	Application	Protocol
1812	RADIUS Authentication Protocol	UDP
1863	MSN Messenger	TCP
2000	Cisco Skinny Client Control Protocol (SCCP, used in VoIP applications)	UDP
5004	Real-Time Transport Protocol (RTP, a voice and video transport protocol)	UDP
5060	Session Initiation Protocol (SIP, used in VoIP applications)	UDP
8008	Alternate HTTP	TCP
8080	Alternate HTTP	TCP

Dynamic or Private Ports

Dynamic or private ports (numbers 49152 to 65535), also known as ephemeral ports, are usually assigned dynamically to client applications when initiating a connection. It is not common for a client to connect to a service using dynamic or private ports (although some peer-to-peer file-sharing programs do).

Using Both TCP and UDP

Some applications can use both TCP and UDP. For example, the low overhead of UDP enables DNS to serve many client requests very quickly. Sometimes, however, sending the requested information can require the reliability of TCP. In this case, both protocols use the well-known port number of 53 with this service. Table 4-3 lists examples of registered and well-known TCP and UDP common ports.

Table 4-3   TCP/UDP Common Ports

Common Port	Application	Port Type
53	DNS	Well-known TCP/UDP common port
161	SNMP	Well-known TCP/UDP common port
531	AOL Instant Messenger, IRC	Well-known TCP/UDP common port
1433	MS SQL	Registered TCP/UDP common port
2948	WAP (MMS)	Registered TCP/UDP common port

netstat Command

Sometimes it is necessary to know which active TCP connections are open and running on a networked host. The **netstat** command is an important network utility that you can use to verify those connections. **netstat** lists the protocol in use, the local address and port number, the destination address and port number, and the state of the connection.

Unexplained TCP connections can indicate that something or someone is connected to the local host, which is a major security threat. Additionally, unnecessary TCP connections can consume valuable system resources, thus slowing the host's performance. Use **netstat** to examine the open connections on a host when performance appears to be compromised.

Many useful options are available for the **netstat** command. Example 4-1 shows **netstat** output.

```
Example 4-1 netstat Command
C:\> netstat


Active Connections
Proto     Local Address      Foreign Address          State
TCP       kenpc:3126         192.168.0.2:netbios-ssn  ESTABLISHED
TCP       kenpc:3158         207.138.126.152:http     ESTABLISHED
TCP       kenpc:3159         207.138.126.169:http     ESTABLISHED
TCP       kenpc:3160         207.138.126.169:http     ESTABLISHED
TCP       kenpc:3161         sc.msn.com:http          ESTABLISHED
TCP       kenpc:3166         www.cisco.com:http       ESTABLISHED
C:\>
```

Segmentation and Reassembly: Divide and Conquer

Chapter 2, "Communicating over the Network," explained how an application passes data down through the various protocols to create a protocol data unit (PDU) that is then transmitted on the medium. At the application layer, the data is passed down and is segmented into pieces. A UDP segment (piece) is called a *datagram*. A TCP segment (piece) is called a *segment*. A UDP header provides source and destination (ports). A TCP header provides source and destination (ports), sequencing, acknowledgments, and flow control. At the destination host, this process is reversed until the data can be passed up to the application. Figure 4-9 provides an example.

Figure 4-9   Transport Layer Functions

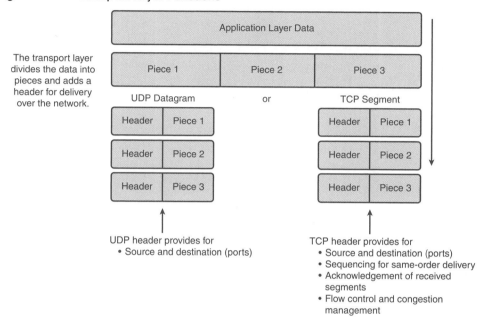

Some applications transmit large amounts of data—in some cases, many gigabytes. Sending all this data in one large piece would be impractical. A large piece of data could take minutes or even hours to send, and no other network traffic could be transmitted at the same time. In addition, if errors occurred during the transmission, the entire data file would be lost or would have to be re-sent. Network devices would not have memory buffers large enough to store this much data while it is being transmitted or received. The size of the segment varies depending on the networking technology and specific physical medium in use.

Dividing application data into segments both ensures that data is transmitted within the limits of the media and that data from different applications can be multiplexed onto the media. TCP and UDP handle segmentation differently.

In TCP, each segment header contains a sequence number. This sequence number allows the transport layer functions on the destination host to reassemble segments in the order in which they were transmitted. This ensures that the destination application has the data in the exact form the sender intended.

Although services using UDP also track the conversations between applications, they are not concerned with the order in which the information was transmitted or in maintaining a connection. The UDP header does not include a sequence number. UDP is a simpler design and generates less overhead than TCP, resulting in a faster transfer of data.

Information can arrive in a different order than it was transmitted because different packets can take different paths through the network. An application that uses UDP must tolerate the fact that data might not arrive in the order in which it was sent.

UDP and TCP Port Numbers (4.1.6.2)

In this activity, you will "look inside" packets to see how DNS and HTTP use port numbers. Use file e1-4162.pka on the CD-ROM that accompanies this book to perform this activity using Packet Tracer.

TCP: Communicating with Reliability

TCP is often referred to as a connection-oriented protocol, a protocol that guarantees reliable and in-order delivery of data from sender to receiver.

In the following sections, you explore how this is managed. Connection establishment and termination are discussed, along with the use of three-way handshake. Flow control, the use of windowing as congestion control, and retransmission of data are presented.

Making Conversations Reliable

The key distinction between TCP and UDP is reliability. The reliability of TCP communication is performed using connection-oriented sessions. Before a host using TCP sends data to another host, the transport layer initiates a process to create a connection with the destination. This connection enables the tracking of a session, or communication stream, between the hosts. This process ensures that each host is aware of and prepared for the communication. A complete TCP conversation requires the establishment of a session between the hosts in both directions.

After a session has been established, the destination sends acknowledgments to the source for the segments that it receives. These acknowledgments form the basis of reliability within the TCP session. As the source receives an acknowledgment, it knows that the data has been successfully delivered and can quit tracking that data. If the source does not receive an acknowledgment within a predetermined amount of time, it retransmits that data to the destination.

Part of the additional overhead of using TCP is the network traffic generated by acknowledgments and retransmissions. The establishment of the sessions creates overhead in the form of additional segments being exchanged. Additional overhead is the result of keeping track of acknowledgments and the retransmission process the host must undertake if no acknowledgment is received.

Reliability is achieved by having fields in the TCP segment, each with a specific function. These fields will be discussed in later sections.

TCP Server Processes

As discussed in Chapter 3, "Application Layer Functionality and Protocols," application processes run on servers. These processes wait until a client initiates communication with a request for information or other services.

Each application process running on the server is configured to use a port number, either by default or manually by a system administrator. An individual server cannot have two services assigned to the same port number within the same transport layer services. A host running a web server application and a file transfer application cannot have both configured to use the same port (for example, TCP port 8080).

When an active server application is assigned to a specific port, that port is considered to be "open" on the server. This means that the transport layer accepts and processes segments addressed to that port. Any incoming client request addressed to the correct socket is accepted, and the data is passed to the server application. There can be many simultaneous ports open on a server, one for each active server application. It is common for a server to provide more than one service, such as a web server and an FTP server, at the same time.

One way to improve security on a server is to restrict server access to only those ports associated with the services and applications that should be accessible to authorized requestors.

Figure 4-10 shows the typical allocation of source and destination ports in TCP client/server operations.

Figure 4-10   Clients Sending TCP Requests

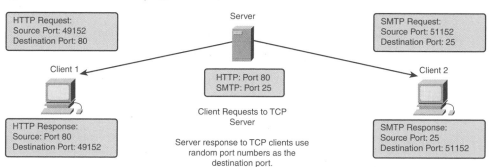

TCP Connection Establishment and Termination

When two hosts communicate using TCP, a connection is established before data can be exchanged. After the communication is completed, the sessions are closed and the connection is terminated. The connection and session mechanisms enable TCP's reliability function.

TCP Three-Way Handshake

The host tracks each data segment within a session and exchanges information about what data is received by each host using the information in the TCP header.

Each connection represents two one-way communication streams, or sessions. To establish the connection, the hosts perform a three-way handshake. Control bits in the TCP header indicate the progress and status of the connection. The three-way handshake performs the following functions:

- Establishes that the destination device is present on the network

- Verifies that the destination device has an active service and is accepting requests on the destination port number that the initiating client intends to use for the session

- Informs the destination device that the source client intends to establish a communication session on that port number

In TCP connections, the host serving as a client initiates the session to the server. The three steps in TCP connection establishment are as follows:

1. The initiating client sends a segment containing an initial sequence value, which serves as a request to the server to begin a communications session.

2. The server responds with a segment containing an acknowledgment value equal to the received sequence value plus 1, plus its own synchronizing sequence value. The acknowledgment value is 1 greater than the sequence number because there is no data contained to be acknowledged. This acknowledgment value enables the client to tie the response back to the original segment that it sent to the server.

3. The initiating client responds with an acknowledgment value equal to the sequence value it received plus 1. This completes the process of establishing the connection.

Figure 4-11 shows the steps to establish a TCP connection.

Figure 4-11   TCP Connection Establishment: SYN ACK

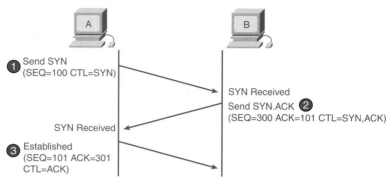

To understand the three-way handshake process, it is important to look at the various values that the two hosts exchange. Within the TCP segment header, the following six 1-bit fields contain control information used to manage the TCP processes:

- *URG*: Urgent pointer field significant

- *ACK*: Acknowledgment field significant

- *PSH*: Push function

- *RST*: Reset the connection

- *SYN*: Synchronize sequence numbers

- *FIN*: No more data from sender

These fields are referred to as *flags*, because the value of one of these fields is only 1 bit and, therefore, has only two values: 1 or 0. When a bit value is set to 1, it indicates what control information is contained in the segment.

The next sections describe each step of the three-way handshake in more detail.

Step 1: SYN

A TCP client begins the three-way handshake by sending a segment with the SYN control flag set, indicating an initial value in the sequence number field in the header. This initial value for the sequence number, known as the initial sequence number (ISN), is randomly chosen and is used to begin tracking the flow of data from the client to the server for this session. The ISN in the header of each segment is increased by 1 for each byte of data sent from the client to the server as the data conversation continues. The SYN control flag is set and the relative sequence number is at 0.

Step 2: SYN and ACK

The TCP server needs to acknowledge the receipt of the SYN segment from the client to establish the session from the client to the server. To do so, the server sends a segment back to the client with the ACK flag set, indicating that the acknowledgment number is significant. With this flag set in the segment, the client recognizes this as an acknowledgment that the server received the SYN from the TCP client.

The value of the *acknowledgment* number field is equal to the client ISN plus 1. This establishes a session from the client to the server. The ACK flag will remain set for the balance of the session. The conversation between the client and the server is two one-way sessions: one from the client to the server and the other from the server to the client. In this second step of the three-way handshake, the server must initiate the response from the server to the client. To start this session, the server uses the SYN flag in the same way that the client did. It sets the SYN control flag in the header to establish a session from the server to the client. The SYN flag indicates that the initial value of the sequence number field is in the header. This value will be used to track the flow of data in this session from the server back to the client.

Step 3: ACK

Finally, the TCP client responds with a segment containing an ACK that is the response to the TCP SYN sent by the server. This segment does not include user data. The value in the acknowledgment number field contains one more than the ISN received from the server. After both sessions are established between client and server, all additional segments exchanged in this communication will have the ACK flag set.

You can add security to the data network by doing the following:

- Denying the establishment of TCP sessions
- Allowing sessions to be established for specific services only
- Allowing traffic only as a part of already established sessions

You can implement this security for all TCP sessions or only for selected sessions.

TCP Session Termination

To close a connection, the FIN control flag in the segment header must be set. To end each one-way TCP session, a two-way handshake is used, consisting of a FIN segment and an ACK segment. Therefore, to terminate a single conversation supported by TCP, four exchanges are needed to end both sessions:

1. When the client has no more data to send in the stream, it sends a segment with the FIN flag set.

2. The server sends an ACK to acknowledge the receipt of the FIN to terminate the session from client to server.

3. The server sends a FIN to the client, to terminate the server-to-client session.

4. The client responds with an ACK to acknowledge the FIN from the server.

Figure 4-12 shows the steps used to terminate a TCP connection.

Figure 4-12   TCP Connection Termination: FIN ACK

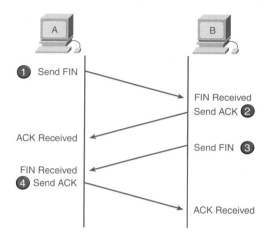

> **Note**
>
> In this explanation, the terms *client* and *server* are used in this description as a reference for simplicity, but the termination process can be initiated by any two hosts that complete the session.

When the client end of the session has no more data to transfer, it sets the FIN flag in the header of a segment. Next, the server end of the connection will send a normal segment containing data with the ACK flag set using the acknowledgment number, confirming that all the bytes of data have been received. When all segments have been acknowledged, the session is closed.

The session in the other direction is closed using the same process. The receiver indicates that there is no more data to send by setting the FIN flag in the header of a segment sent to the source. A return acknowledgment confirms that all bytes of data have been received and that the session is, in turn, closed.

It is also possible to terminate the connection by a three-way handshake. When the client has no more data to send, it sends a FIN to the server. If the server also has no more data to send, it can reply with both the FIN and ACK flags set, combining two steps into one. The client replies with an ACK.

TCP Session Establishment and Termination (4.2.5.2)

In this activity, you will study the TCP three-way handshake for session establishment and the TCP process for session termination. Many application protocols use TCP, and visualizing the session establishment and termination processes with Packet Tracer will deepen your understanding. Use file e1-4252.pka on the CD-ROM that accompanies this book to perform this activity using Packet Tracer.

TCP Acknowledgment with Windowing

One of TCP's functions is to make sure that each segment reaches its destination. The TCP services on the destination host acknowledge the data that they have received to the source application.

The segment header sequence number and acknowledgment number are used together to confirm receipt of the bytes of data contained in the segments. The sequence number indicates the relative number of bytes that have been transmitted in this session, including the bytes in the current segment. TCP uses the acknowledgment number in segments sent back to the source to indicate the next byte in this session that the receiver expects to receive. This is called *expectational acknowledgment*.

The source is informed that the destination has received all bytes in this data stream up to, but not including, the byte indicated by the acknowledgment number. The sending host is expected to send a segment that uses a sequence number that is equal to the acknowledgment number.

Remember, each connection is actually two one-way sessions. Sequence numbers and acknowledgment numbers are being exchanged in both directions.

In Figure 4-13, the host on the left is sending data to the host on the right. It sends a segment containing 10 bytes of data for this session and a sequence number equal to 1 in the header.

Host B receives the segment at Layer 4 and determines that the sequence number is 1 and that it has 10 bytes of data. Host B then sends a segment back to host A to acknowledge the receipt of this data. In this segment, the host sets the acknowledgment number to 11 to indicate that the next byte of data it expects to receive in this session is byte number 11.

When host A receives this acknowledgment, it can now send the next segment containing data for this session starting with byte number 11.

Figure 4-13   Acknowledgment of TCP Segments

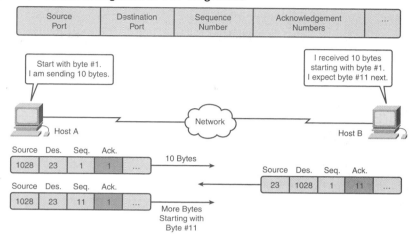

Looking at this example, if host A had to wait for acknowledgment of the receipt of each 10 bytes, the network would have a lot of overhead. To reduce the overhead of these acknowledgments, multiple segments of data can be sent and acknowledged with a single TCP message in the opposite direction. This acknowledgment contains an acknowledgment number based on the total number of segments received in the session.

For example, starting with a sequence number of 2000, if 10 segments of 1000 bytes each were received, an acknowledgment number of 12001 would be returned to the source.

The amount of data that a source can transmit before an acknowledgment must be received is called the *window size*. Window size is a field in the TCP header that enables the management of lost data and flow control.

TCP Retransmission

No matter how well designed a network is, data loss will occasionally occur. Therefore, TCP provides methods of managing these segment losses, including a mechanism to retransmit segments with unacknowledged data.

A destination host service using TCP usually only acknowledges data for contiguous sequence bytes. If one or more segments are missing, only the data in the segments that complete the stream is acknowledged. For example, if segments with sequence numbers 1500 to 3000 and 3400 to 3500 were received, the acknowledgment number would be 3001, because segments with the sequence numbers 3001 to 3399 have not been received.

When TCP at the source host has not received an acknowledgment after a predetermined amount of time, it will go back to the last acknowledgment number that it received and retransmit data from that point forward. The retransmission process is not specified by RFC 793 but is left up to the particular implementation of TCP.

For a typical TCP implementation, a host can transmit a segment, put a copy of the segment in a retransmission queue, and start a timer. When the data acknowledgment is received, the segment is deleted from the queue. If the acknowledgment is not received before the timer expires, the segment is retransmitted.

Hosts today can also employ an optional feature called *selective acknowledgments*. If both hosts support selective acknowledgments, it is possible for the destination to acknowledge bytes in noncontiguous segments, and the host would only need to retransmit the missing data.

TCP Congestion Control: Minimizing Segment Loss

TCP provides congestion control through the use of flow control and dynamic window sizes. The following sections discuss how these techniques minimize segment loss that minimizes network overhead caused by retransmission of lost segments.

Flow Control

Flow control assists the reliability of TCP transmission by adjusting the effective rate of data flow between the two services in the session. When the source is informed that the specified amount of data in the segments is received, it can continue sending more data for this session.

The window size field in the TCP header specifies the amount of data that can be transmitted before an acknowledgment must be received. The initial window size is determined during the session startup through the three-way handshake.

The TCP feedback mechanism adjusts the effective rate of data transmission to the maximum flow that the network and destination device can support without loss. TCP attempts to manage the rate of transmission so that all data will be received and retransmissions will be minimized.

Figure 4-14 shows a simplified representation of window size and acknowledgments. In this example, the initial window size for a TCP session represented is set to 3000 bytes. When the sender has transmitted 3000 bytes, it waits for an acknowledgment of these bytes before transmitting more segments in this session. After the sender has received this acknowledgment from the receiver, the sender can transmit an additional 3000 bytes.

Figure 4-14   TCP Segment Acknowledgment and Window Size

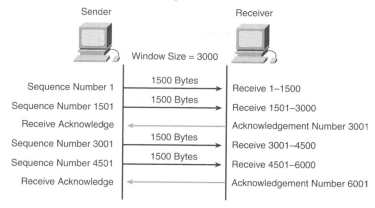

During the delay in receiving the acknowledgment, the sender will not send additional segments for this session. In periods when the network is congested or the resources of the receiving host are strained, the delay can increase. As this delay grows longer, the effective transmission rate of the data for this session decreases. The slowdown in data rate helps reduce the resource contention.

Dynamic Window Sizes

Another way to control the data flow is to use dynamic window sizes. When network resources are constrained, TCP can reduce the window size to require that received segments be acknowledged more frequently. This effectively slows the rate of transmission because the source must wait for data to be acknowledged.

The TCP receiving host sends the window size value to the sending TCP to indicate the number of bytes that it is prepared to receive as a part of this session. If the destination needs to slow the rate of communication because of limited buffer memory, it can send a smaller window size value to the source as part of an acknowledgment.

As shown in Figure 4-15, if a receiving host has congestion, it can respond to the sending host with a segment with a reduced window size. Figure 4-15 shows a loss of one of the segments. The receiver changed the window size field in the TCP header of the returning segments in this conversation from 3000 to 1500. This caused the sender to reduce the window size to 1500.

Figure 4-15   TCP Congestion and Flow Control

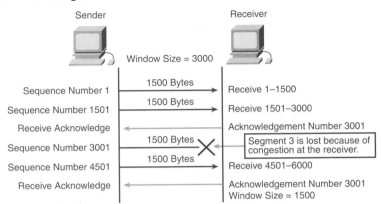

After periods of transmission with no data losses or constrained resources, the receiver will begin to increase the window size field. This reduces the overhead on the network because fewer acknowledgments need to be sent. Window size will continue to increase until data loss occurs, which will cause the window size to be decreased.

This dynamic increasing and decreasing of window size is a continuous process in TCP, which determines the optimum window size for each TCP session. In highly efficient networks, window sizes can become very large because data is not being lost. In networks where the underlying infrastructure is being stressed, the window size will likely remain small.

UDP: Communicating with Low Overhead

UDP is a simple protocol that provides the basic transport layer functions. It has much lower overhead than TCP, because it is not connection oriented and does not provide the sophisticated retransmission, sequencing, and flow control mechanisms. The following sections compare how UDP handles low overhead and reliability, data reassembly, server processes and requests, and client processes.

UDP: Low Overhead Versus Reliability

Because UDP has low overhead and does not provide the functionality that TCP provides for reliability, care must be taken when you choose to use UDP. Applications that use UDP are not always unreliable. Using UDP simply means that reliability is not provided by the transport layer protocol and must be implemented elsewhere if required.

Some applications, such as online games or VoIP, can tolerate loss of some data. If these applications used TCP, they might experience large delays while TCP detects data loss and retransmits data. These delays would be more detrimental to the application than small data losses. Some applications, such as DNS, will simply retry the request if they do not receive a response, and therefore they do not need TCP to guarantee the message delivery. The low overhead of UDP makes it desirable for such applications.

UDP Datagram Reassembly

Because UDP is connectionless, sessions are not established before communication takes place as they are with TCP. UDP is transaction based. In other words, when an application has data to send, it simply sends the data.

Many applications that use UDP send small amounts of data that can fit in one segment. However, some applications will send larger amounts of data that must be split into multiple segments The UDP PDU is referred to as a datagram, although the terms *segment* and *datagram* are sometimes used interchangeably to describe a transport layer PDU.

When multiple datagrams are sent to a destination, they can take different paths and arrive in the wrong order, as shown in Figure 4-16. UDP does not keep track of sequence numbers the way TCP does. UDP has no way to reorder the datagrams into their transmission order. Therefore, UDP simply reassembles the data in the order that it was received and forwards it to the application. If the sequence of the data is important to the application, the application will have to identify the proper sequence of the data and determine how it should be processed.

Figure 4-16   UDP Data Reassembly

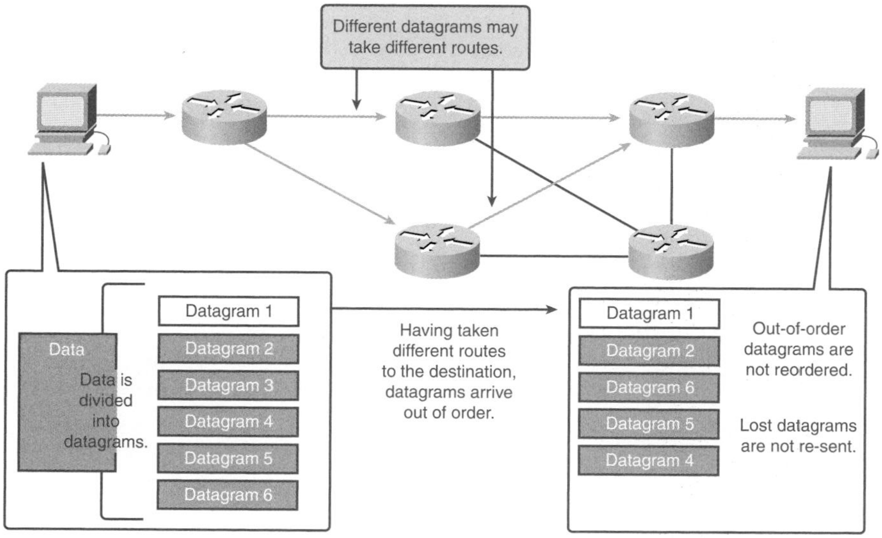

UDP Server Processes and Requests

Like TCP-based applications, UDP-based server applications are assigned well-known or registered port numbers. When these applications or processes are running, they will accept the data matched with the assigned port number. When UDP receives a datagram destined for one of these ports, it forwards the application data to the appropriate application based on its port number.

UDP Client Processes

As with TCP, client/server communication is initiated by a client application that is requesting data from a server process. The UDP client process randomly selects a port number from the dynamic range of port numbers and uses this as the source port for the conversation. The destination port will usually be the well-known or registered port number assigned to the server process.

Randomized source port numbers also help with security. If there is a predictable pattern for destination port selection, an intruder can more easily simulate access to a client by attempting to connect to the port number most likely to be open.

Because UDP does not create a session, as soon as the data is ready to be sent and the ports are identified, UDP can form the datagram and pass it to the network layer to be addressed and sent on the network.

Remember, after a client has chosen the source and destination ports, the same pair of ports is used in the header of all datagrams used in the transaction. For the data returning to the client from the server, the source and destination port numbers in the datagram header are reversed. Figure 4-17 shows the clients sending UDP requests.

Figure 4-17   Clients Sending UDP Requests

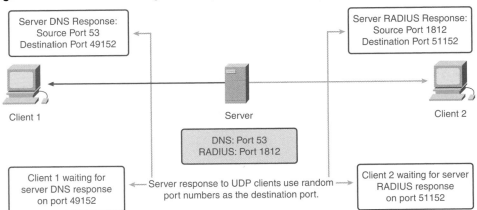

Packet Tracer
☐ **Activity**

UDP Operation (4.4.4.2)

In this activity, you examine how DNS uses UDP. Use file e1-4442.pka on the CD-ROM that accompanies this book to perform this activity using Packet Tracer.

Summary

The transport layer provides data network needs by

- Tracking the individual communications between applications on the source and destination hosts

- Segmenting data and managing each piece

- Reassembling the segments into streams of application data

- Identifying the different applications

- Performing flow control between end users

- Enabling error recovery

- Initiating a session

UDP and TCP are common transport layer protocols. UDP datagrams and TCP segments have headers prefixed to the data that include a source port number and destination port number. These port numbers enable data to be directed to the correct application running on the destination computer.

TCP does not pass data to the network until it knows that the destination is ready to receive it. TCP then manages the flow of the data and resends any data segments that are not acknowledged as being received at the destination. TCP uses mechanisms of the three-way handshake, timers, acknowledgments, and dynamic windowing to achieve these reliable features. This reliability does, however, impose overhead on the network in terms of much larger segment headers and more network traffic between the source and destination managing the data transport.

If the application data needs to be delivered across the network quickly, or if network bandwidth cannot support the overhead of control messages being exchanged between the source and the destination systems, UDP is the developer's preferred transport layer protocol. UDP does not track or acknowledge the receipt of datagrams at the destination; it just passes received datagrams to the application layer as they arrive. UDP does not resend lost datagrams; however, this does not necessarily mean that the communication itself is unreliable. The application layer protocols and services can process lost or delayed datagrams if the application has these requirements.

The choice of transport layer protocol is made by the developer of the application to best meet the user requirements. The developer bears in mind, though, that all the other layers play a part in data network communications and will influence its performance.

Labs

The labs available in the companion *Network Fundamentals, CCNA Exploration Labs and Study Guide* (ISBN 1-58713-203-6) provide hands-on practice with the following topics introduced in this chapter:

Lab 4-1: Observing TCP and UDP Using netstat (4.5.1.1)

In this lab, you will examine the **netstat** (network statistics utility) command on a host computer and adjust **netstat** output options to analyze and understand TCP/IP transport layer protocol status.

Lab 4-2: TCP/IP Transport Layer Protocols, TCP and UDP (4.5.2.1)

In this lab, you will use Wireshark to capture and identify TCP header fields and operation during an FTP session and UDP header fields and operation during a TFTP session.

Lab 4-3: Application and Transport Layer Protocols (4.5.3.1)

In this lab, you will use Wireshark to monitor and analyze client application (FTP and HTTP) communications between a server and clients.

Packet Tracer
☐ Companion

Many of the hands-on labs include Packet Tracer companion activities, where you can use Packet Tracer to complete a simulation of the lab. Look for this icon in *Network Fundamentals, CCNA Exploration Labs and Study Guide* (ISBN 1-58713-203-6) for hands-on labs that have Packet Tracer companion activities.

Check Your Understanding

Complete all the review questions listed here to test your understanding of the topics and concepts in this chapter. Appendix A, "Check Your Understanding and Challenge Questions Answer Key," lists the answers.

1. Which port number is used by HTTP?

   A. 23

   B. 80

   C. 53

   D. 110

2. Which port number is used with SMTP?

   A. 20

   B. 23

   C. 25

   D. 143

3. Which characteristics are part of TCP? (Choose two.)

   A. Reliable

   B. Connectionless

   C. No flow control

   D. Resends anything not received

4. At the transport layer, which of the following controls is used to keep a transmitting host from overflowing the buffers of a receiving host?

   A. Best effort

   B. Encryption

   C. Flow control

   D. Congestion avoidance

5. End systems use port numbers to select the proper application. What is the lowest port number that can be dynamically assigned by the host system?

   A. 1

   B. 128

   C. 256

   D. 1024

6. During data transfer, what is the receiving host responsible for? (Choose the best two answers.)

    A. Encapsulation

    B. Bandwidth

    C. Segmentation

    D. Acknowledgment

    E. Reassembly

7. What are the transport layer's responsibilities?

8. Why does TCP use a sequence number in the header?

    A. To reassemble the segments into data

    B. To identify the application layer protocol

    C. To indicate the number of the next expected byte

    D. To show the maximum number of bytes allowed during a session

9. Which of the following determines how much data a sending host running TCP/IP can transmit before it must receive an acknowledgment?

    A. Segment size

    B. Transmission rate

    C. Bandwidth

    D. Window size

10. What is the purpose of TCP/UDP port numbers?

    A. To indicate the beginning of a three-way handshake

    B. To reassemble the segments into the correct order

    C. To identify the number of data packets that can be sent without acknowledgment

    D. To track the different conversations crossing the network at the same time

11. What does segmentation provide to communications?

12. In networking terms, what is reliability?

13. List three network applications that use TCP.

14. List three network applications that use UDP.

15. What is contained in the header of each segment or datagram?

16. What is the purpose of sequence numbers?

Challenge Questions and Activities

These questions require a deeper application of the concepts covered in this chapter. You can find the answers in Appendix A.

1. Which acknowledgment number should be sent by the receiver shown in Figure 4-18?

Figure 4-18   Challenge Question 1

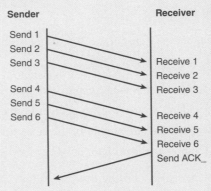

2. What is the protocol number for UDP?

   A. 1

   B. 3

   C. 6

   D. 17

3. What is the default DNS port number?

   A. 1025

   B. 53

   C. 110

   D. 143

4. What is the netstat utility used for on a host?

5. Explain an expectational acknowledgment.

Look for this icon in *Network Fundamentals, CCNA Exploration Labs and Study Guide* (ISBN 1-58713-203-6) for instructions on how to perform the Packet Tracer Skills Integration Challenge for this chapter.

Analyzing the Application and Transport Layers

In this activity, a process that occurs every time you request a web page on the Internet—the interaction of DNS, HTTP, UDP, and TCP—is examined in depth.

To Learn More

Discuss the requirements of an application layer application that would determine whether the developer selected UDP or TCP as the transport layer protocol to be used.

If a network application required its data to be delivered reliably, discuss how UDP could be used as the transport layer protocol and under what circumstances this would be used.

For an introduction to internetworking, read Internetworking Basics at Cisco.com: http://www.cisco.com/univercd/cc/td/doc/cisintwk/ito_doc/introint.htm.

CHAPTER 5

OSI Network Layer

Objectives

Upon completion of this chapter, you will be able to answer the following questions:

- What is the method described by the network layer for routing packets from a device on one network to a device on a different network?

- How does the Internet Protocol (IP) work at the network layer to provide connectionless, best-effort service to the upper layers of the OSI model?

- How are devices grouped into physical and logical networks?

- How do the hierarchical addresses of devices allow communication between networks?

- How do routers use next-hop addresses to select a path for packets to reach their destination?

- How do routers forward packets?

Key Terms

This chapter uses the following key terms. You can find the definitions in the Glossary.

route   page 136

source IP address   page 137

destination IP address   page 137

IP header   page 137

routing   page 138

hop   page 138

directly connected network   page 138

connection oriented   page 140

connectionless   page 140

overhead   page 140

best-effort   page 141

media independent   page 141

maximum transmission unit (MTU)   page 141

fragmentation   page 142

Time to Live (TTL)   page 143

subnetwork   page 145

subnet   page 145

broadcast domain   page 149

hierarchical addressing   page 151

octets   page 152

default gateway   page 153

routing table   page 156

default route   page 158

static route   page 163

dynamic routing   page 164

routing protocols   page 164

Previous chapters explained how application data from an end device traveling to another network is first encapsulated in added bits that indicate presentation, session, and transport layer information and instructions. When the transport layer sends the protocol data unit (PDU) down to the network layer, the PDU needs the essentials of any successful journey: a destination address and directions on how to arrive efficiently and safely.

This chapter describes the process the network layer uses to convert transport layer segments into packets and get them started on their journey down the right path across different networks to the destination network. You learn how the network layer divides networks into groups of hosts to manage the flow of data packets. You also consider how communication between networks is facilitated. This facilitation of communication between networks is called *routing*.

IPv4

The network layer, or Open Systems Interconnection (OSI) Layer 3, provides services to exchange the individual pieces of data over the network between identified end devices. To accomplish this end-to-end transport, Layer 3 uses the processes outlined in the following sections to address the packet to the proper destination, encapsulate the packet with necessary data for delivery, route the packet through the web of connected networks that will deliver the packet to the destination network for delivery, and finally, have the destination host decapsulate the data for processing. The details of these processes are explored further in the next sections.

Network Layer: Communication from Host to Host

The network layer, or OSI Layer 3, receives segments of data, or PDUs, from the transport layer. These bits of data have been processed into a transportable size and numbered for reliability. It is now up to the network layer to use protocols to add addressing and other information to the PDU and send it to the next router along the best path, or *route*, to the destination network.

Network layer protocols, such as the widely used IP, are rules and instructions that devices use to enable sharing of upper-layer information between hosts. When the hosts are in different networks, additional routing protocols are used to choose routes between networks. Network layer protocols specify the addressing and packaging of a transport layer PDU and describe how the PDU is to be carried with minimum overhead.

The network layer describes four tasks to be performed:

1. Addressing packets with an IP address

2. Encapsulation

3. Routing

4. Decapsulation

The next sections describe each task in more detail and describe popular network layer protocols.

Addressing

IP requires each sending and receiving device to have a unique IP address. Devices in IP networks that have IP addresses are called *hosts*. The IP address of the sending host is known as the *source IP address*, and the IP address of the receiving host is referred to as the *destination IP address*. The conventions of IP addressing will be explored in greater detail in Chapter 6, "Addressing the Network: IPv4."

Encapsulation

Each PDU sent between networks needs to be identified with source and destination IP addresses in an *IP header*. The IP header contains the address information and some other bits that identify the PDU as a network layer PDU. This process of adding information is called *encapsulation*. When an OSI Layer 4 PDU has been encapsulated at the network layer, it is referred to as a *packet*.

Figure 5-1 displays how segments are encapsulated at the network layer and become IP packets. The process is reversed at the destination.

Figure 5-1   Network Layer Encapsulation

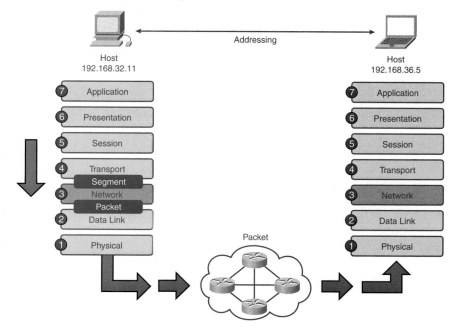

Routing

When a packet is encapsulated at the network layer, it contains all the information necessary to travel to networks near and far. The journey between networks can be very short and relatively simple, or it can be complex and involve many steps between routers connected to different networks.

Routers are devices that connect networks. They specialize in understanding OSI Layer 3 packets and protocols as well as calculating the best path for the packets. *Routing* is the process routers perform when receiving packets, analyzing the destination address information, using the address information to select a path for the packet, and then forwarding the packet on to the next router on the selected network. Each route that a packet takes to reach the next device is called a *hop*. A packet can hop between several different routers en route to the destination. Each router examines the address information in the packet, but neither the IP address information nor the encapsulated transport layer data in the packet is changed or removed until the packet reaches the destination network.

Figure 5-2 shows how there can be several different paths in the internetwork cloud between a source host and a destination host.

Figure 5-2   Multiple Network Paths Between Hosts

At the network layer, the router opens the packet and looks in the packet header for IP address information. The router, depending on how it is configured and what it knows about the destination network, will choose the best network to deliver the packet. The router then forwards the packet out of the interface connected to the chosen network. The last router along the path will realize that the packet belongs to a *directly connected network* and will forward it out the correct network interface for final delivery on the local network.

For a network layer packet to travel between hosts, it must be handed down to the data link layer (OSI Layer 2) for another layer of encapsulation called *framing*, and then encoded and put onto the physical layer (OSI layer 1) to be sent to the next router. Details of how these two layers handle the data are the subject of Chapter 7, "OSI Data Link Layer," and Chapter 8, "OSI Physical Layer."

Decapsulation

An IP packet arrives at a router's network interface encapsulated in a Layer 2 frame on the physical OSI layer. The router's network interface card (NIC) accepts the packet, removes the Layer 2 encapsulation data, and sends the packet up to the network layer. The process of removing encapsulation data at different layers is referred to as *decapsulation*.

Encapsulation and decapsulation occur at all layers of the OSI model. As a packet travels from network to network to its destination, there can be several instances in which Layers 1 and 2 are encapsulated and decapsulated by routers. The network layer only decapsulates the IP packet at the final destination after examining the destination addresses and determining that the journey is over. The IP packet is no longer useful, so it is discarded by the destination host.

When the IP packet is decapsulated, the information in the packet is handed up to the upper layers for delivery and processing.

Network Layer Protocols

IP is the most common network layer protocol, but it is important to understand that other protocols are available that offer different features than IP. At one time, network protocols were largely proprietary, and communication was limited to a manufacturer's specific equipment. Internet Protocol version 4 (IPv4), however, is open source and allows devices from various manufacturers to communicate with each other. Table 5-1 lists some of the common network layer protocols.

Table 5-1   Common Network Protocols

Protocol	Description
Internet Protocol version 4 (IPv4)	Most widely used network protocol. Basic protocol of the Internet.
Internet Protocol version 6 (IPv6)	Currently in use in some areas. Will work with IPv4 and likely replace it.
Novell IPX	Part of Novell NetWare, a widely popular internetworking protocol in the 1980s and 1990s.
AppleTalk	Apple Computer's proprietary networking protocol.
Connectionless Network Service (CLNS)	A protocol used in telecommunication networks that does not require established circuits.

The IPv4 protocol describes services and packet structure that are used to encapsulate User Datagram Protocol (UDP) datagrams or TCP segments handed down from the transport layer of the OSI model. Because the Internet Protocol (IPv4 and IPv6) is the most widely used Layer 3 data-carrying protocol, it is the focus of this book. Discussion of the other protocols is minimal.

IPv4: Example Network Layer Protocol

Version 4 of IP (IPv4) is currently the most widely used version of IP. It is the only Layer 3 protocol that is used to carry user data over the Internet and is the focus of the CCNA. Therefore, it will be the example you use for network layer protocols in this course.

IP version 6 (IPv6) is developed and being implemented in some areas. IPv6 will operate alongside IPv4 and might replace it in the future. The services provided by IP, as well as the packet header structure and contents, are specified by either IPv4 or IPv6.

The characteristics of IPv4 and IPv6 are different. Understanding these characteristics will allow you to understand the operation of the services described by this protocol.

IP was designed as a protocol with low overhead. It provides only the functions that are necessary to deliver a packet from a source to a destination over an interconnected system of networks. The protocol was not designed to track and manage the flow of packets. These functions are performed by other protocols in other layers.

IPv4 basic characteristics include the following:

- **Connectionless:** IPv4 does not establish a connection before sending data packets.

- **Best effort (unreliable):** IPv4 does not use processes that guarantee packet delivery, which reduces processing time on routers and saves the bandwidth that acknowledgment messages would otherwise require.

- **Media independent:** IPv4 operates independently of the medium carrying the data.

The next sections describe these three traits in greater detail.

Connectionless

As you learned in Chapter 4, "OSI Transport Layer," TCP's reliability comes from being *connection oriented*. TCP uses a connection between the sender and the receiver to exchange control data and ensure reliability of packet delivery.

IP is *connectionless*, meaning that there is no established connection between the sender and the receiver. IP simply sends packets without informing the receiver. Lacking a connection is not a problem for IP and is part of the "best effort" design. This is why IP and TCP work together so well in a TCP/IP stack: If a packet is lost or late, TCP will correct the problem at Layer 4, and IP can work more efficiently at Layer 3.

Because IP does not have to be accountable for reliability or keep a connection, it does not need as much information in the header as a TCP segment does. Because IP requires less data to perform the required tasks, it uses much less processing power and bandwidth, called *overhead*, than TCP.

Best Effort

In Chapter 4, you also learned that TCP is reliable. It is reliable because communication is established with the receiver and receipt of the data is confirmed by the receiver. If packets are lost, the receiver communicates with the sender to request a retransmission. The TCP segment contains information that allows reliability to be ensured.

IP is an unreliable, *best-effort* protocol in that it is unaware of the quality of job it is performing. IP packets are sent without certainty that they will be received. The IP protocol makes a "best effort" to deliver packets, but it has no way of determining whether the packets are delivered successfully or whether they are lost en route. IP has no way to inform the sender of reliability problems. TCP can be relied on to inform the sender of delivery problems.

Media Independent

IP is *media independent*, which means it is not concerned with the physical medium that carries the packet. Internetwork communication is likely to be a multimedia journey using a combination of wireless, Ethernet cable, fiber-optic cable, and other OSI Layer 1 media. The arrangement of bits in the IP packet and header will not be changed as the packet transfers from wireless to fiber or any other media.

Figure 5-3 shows how there can be several different physical layer media between the source host and destination host.

Figure 5-3   IP Packets Are Media Independent

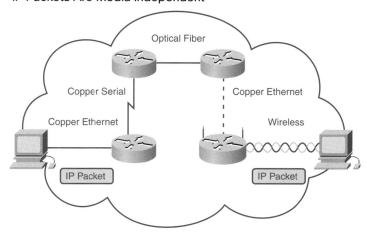

One important consideration, however, is the size of the PDU. Some networks have media restrictions and must enforce a *maximum transmission unit (MTU)*. The MTU is determined by the OSI data link layer, and that requirement is passed to the network layer.

The network layer then builds the packets according to specification. Should the packet come across a network that requires smaller packets, the router connected to the network will fragment the packets before forwarding them on the network's medium. This process is called *fragmentation*.

The process of sending a packet across the web with the IP protocol is analogous to someone sending a surprise gift to a friend using a package delivery service. The gift, in this example three boxes strapped together, is taken to the delivery office already wrapped. The delivery service does not know (nor does it care) what is in the package. The package is an acceptable size, so the delivery workers add a label with the destination and return address and some of their own routing codes to the package. They place the gift in a standard container used for easy shipping. To keep costs low, the sender chooses simple service, which means nothing is guaranteed and the sender cannot track the package on the web. The container with the package travels by car to the dock terminal and then by boat to its destination terminal. From there it travels by truck to a city delivery office. The final local delivery is by bicycle. The package is too large for the bicycle carrier, so it is broken into three pieces for separate delivery. All pieces arrive at the destination, and the job of the delivery service is complete. Later the sender receives a thank-you note from her friend, and she is assured that the gift was delivered.

In this analogy, the gift was a surprise, so it was sent without notification (connectionless). It was encapsulated in the shipping office by adding source, destination, and control information (header). To reduce cost (overhead), the gift was sent "best effort" without guarantee. The service was media independent (traveled by car, boat, truck, and bicycle), but at one point, the package had to be fragmented into the original three boxes (but the gift itself was not altered). The delivery service did not assure the sender that the package was successfully delivered, but the sender relied on the higher-level protocol of good manners to receive notification that the package was delivered.

IPv4 Packet: Packaging the Transport Layer PDU

IPv4 encapsulates, or packages, the transport layer segment or datagram so that the network can deliver it to the destination host. The IPv4 encapsulation remains in place from the time the packet leaves the network layer of the originating host until it arrives at the network layer of the destination host.

The process of encapsulating data by layer enables the services at the different layers to develop and scale without affecting other layers. This means that transport layer segments can be readily packaged by existing network layer protocols, such as IPv4 and IPv6, or by any new protocol that might be developed in the future.

network to and from the same or different hosts. The routing performed by these intermediary devices only considers the contents of the packet header that encapsulates the segment.

In all cases, the data portion of the packet—that is, the encapsulated transport layer PDU—remains unchanged during the network layer processes.

IPv4 Packet Header

The IP header holds the delivery and handling instructions for an IP packet. For example, when a packet arrives on a router's interface, the router needs to know whether the packet is IPv4 or IPv6. The router looks to a specific field in the header to see which type is arriving. The header also contains addressing information and other data about how to handle the packet along the way.

Figure 5-4 shows an outline of an IP packet header. There are several fields in the packet, and not every network uses every field. There are highlighted fields that are important to understanding how the IP header helps routers route IP packets successfully.

Figure 5-4   Components of an IP Header

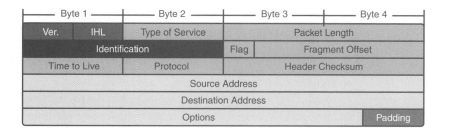

The key fields are as follows:

- **IP Source Address:** Contains a 32-bit binary value that represents the IPv4 address of the host sending the packet.*

- **IP Destination Address:** Contains a 32-bit binary value that represents the host that will receive the packet. Routers will use this data to forward the packet to the correct network.

- *Time to Live (TTL):* The 8-bit TTL field describes the maximum hops the packet can take before it is considered "lost" or undeliverable. Each router that handles the packet decrements the TTL field by at least 1. The packet will be dropped if the TTL value reaches 0. This keeps the Internet from being cluttered with lost packets.

---

*This field enables the destination host to respond to the source if necessary.

- **Type of Service (ToS):** Each of the 8 bits in this field describes a level of throughput priority a router should use in processing the packet. For example, a packet containing IP voice data gets precedence over a packet containing streaming music. The way a router handles a packet from this data is known as *QoS*, or *quality of service*.

- **Protocol:** This 8-bit field indicates the upper-layer protocol—for example, TCP, UDP, or ICMP—that will receive the packet when it is decapsulated and given to the transport layer.

- **Flag and Fragment Offset:** A router might have to fragment a packet when forwarding it from one medium to another medium that has a smaller MTU. When fragmentation occurs, the IPv4 packet uses the Fragment Offset field and the MF flag in the IP header to reconstruct the packet when it arrives at the destination host. The Fragment Offset field identifies the order in which to place the packet fragment in the reconstruction.

Other fields are as follows:

- **Version:** Indicates IP version 4 or 6.

- **Internet Header Length (IHL):** Tells the router how long the header is. The length is not always the same because of variable data in the Options field.

- **Packet Length:** This is the total length of the datagram, including the header. The minimum length of a packet is 20 bytes (header with no data), and the maximum length with data is 65,535 bytes.

- **Identification:** Sent by the source to help reassemble any fragments.

- **Header Checksum:** This data is used to indicate the length of the header and is checked by each router along the way. An algorithm is run by each router, and if the checksum is invalid, the packet is assumed to be corrupted and is dropped. Because the TTL value is changed by each router that handles the packet, the header checksum is recalculated at each hop.

- **Options:** A rarely used field that can provide special routing services.

- **Padding:** Padding is used to fill in bits when header data does not end on a 32-bit boundary.

Networks: Dividing Hosts into Groups

Networks are communities of computers and other hosts, but in many ways, they are like human communities. When people live in a small town, it is usually easy for community members to find and communicate with each other. A small town does not need large roads and expensive traffic signals, and in general does not require as many services as a large community. In a small town, many members also know and trust each other, and many consider smaller communities to be safer than big cities. As a town grows, however, it needs to scale its services to the needs of the increasing number of citizens. As the number of streets grows and the number of dwellings increases, a system for citizens to find each other easily must be designed and implemented. Finding other members gets more complex as a town becomes a city, and at some point, the city divides into more manageable neighborhoods, often connected by major roads, to better govern, serve, and secure the community members.

Computer communities are similar to human communities in that as they grow, they become more complex, and at some point, dividing the large networks into smaller, more manageable groups can make sense. As networks grow and divide, hosts still need to find each other to communicate. One of the major roles of the network layer is to provide a mechanism for addressing hosts in a way that allows all member hosts to find each other. As the number of hosts on the network grows, more planning is required to address the network so that it can be managed efficiently.

Creating Common Groups

Just as cities can be divided into geographic neighborhoods, large computer networks can be separated into internetworks. Departments and groups that share computers and servers are good candidates for dividing into groups from the large network into a common ***subnetwork***, or ***subnet***. Membership in a subnet requires following the rules of communication provided by the TCP/IP protocols.

Historically, large computer networks were divided geographically, like city neighborhoods, because workers with common tasks tended to be clustered into workgroups. The early technology for computer network communication was designed for workgroups that were close together. As networking technology evolved, the nature of the workgroups began to change. Now network members can be grouped not just by physical attributes, but by abstract attributes such as purpose and ownership.

Grouping Hosts Geographically

Grouping network hosts geographically is an economical way to improve communications by reducing overhead for the users, especially if most of their communication stays in the neighborhood. When communication leaves the subnet, it can be subject to external bandwidth issues. Figure 5-5 shows an example of grouping by office locations.

Figure 5-5   Grouping by Physical Location

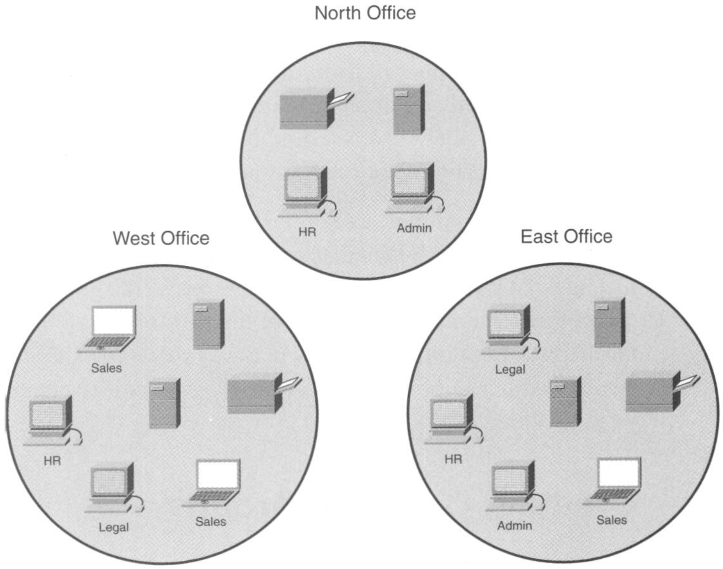

The simple fact of wiring together the physical network can make
geographic location a logical place to start when segmenting a network.

Grouping Hosts for a Specific Purpose

People on a large network will likely use computers for many different reasons. The tools
people use for work are increasingly software based and are requiring ever-increasing
amounts of computing power to perform work tasks. The purpose of these tasks can be cler-
ical, design, education, government administration, or e-commerce. Each purpose can have
specialized software that can consume substantial resources. Whatever the purpose, a network must provide sufficient resources to allow people to work. It can make sense for a network manager to divide a network by purpose instead of geography so that people sharing a
common purpose are also sharing common resources.

In Figure 5-6, the business employs salespersons who can only log in once a day to record
their sales transactions, which generates minimal network traffic. The art department has
very different functions and requires different computing resources. In this scenario, the
best use of network resources would be to create a network for artists to access and another
one for the salespeople to use.

Figure 5-6   Grouping by Purpose

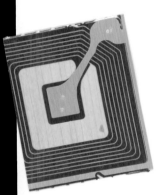

Grouping Hosts for Ownership

Ownership of (and access to) information is another way to group users. Grouping by purpose and geography is concerned with efficient resources and reduced network overhead. In an ownership group, the main concern is security. In a large network, it is much more difficult to define and limit the responsibility and access for the network personnel. Dividing hosts into separate networks provides a boundary for security enforcement and management of each network.

In the previous example, networks were grouped by their differing functions. In Figure 5-7, corporate records and the public website are kept separate, because it was determined that their need for security is more important than their physical location or group function.

Figure 5-7   Grouping by Ownership

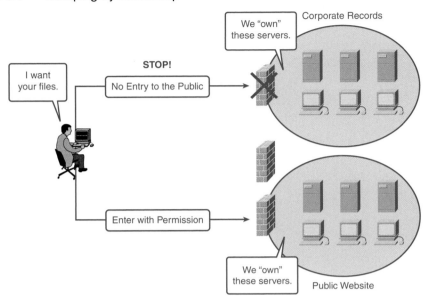

Why Separate Hosts into Networks?

As communities and networks grow larger, they present problems that can be alleviated by dividing the network into smaller, interconnected networks. In growing computer networks, some common issues arise, such as the following:

- Performance degradation

- Security issues

- Address management

Performance

Hosts on a network can be chatty devices. They are designed to broadcast news about themselves to all other users on the network. A *broadcast* is a message sent from one host to all other hosts on the network, and the purpose is usually to share its own information and to request information about other hosts. Broadcasts are a necessary and useful tool used by protocols as part of the communication process. When a group of computers is networked, they generate broadcasts to each other, and the more users on a network, the more broadcasting consumes bandwidth. As users are added, performance quality decreases because the broadcast traffic takes up valuable bandwidth that can otherwise be carrying productive data. Because broadcasts do not travel beyond the network boundary, the network is known as a ***broadcast domain***. Isolating groups of users into smaller networks reduces the size of broadcast domains and restores performance.

Routers Segment Broadcast Domains (5.2.2.2)

In this activity, the replacement of a switch with a router breaks one large broadcast domain into two more manageable ones. Use file e1-5222.pka on the CD-ROM that accompanies this book to perform this activity using Packet Tracer.

Security

As more of the world's businesses and consumers shift their trade onto the Internet, so too are thieves and cyber-pirates finding new ways to exploit the web for criminal gain. Policing a large community like the Internet can be a daunting task, but tending to a small neighborhood's security needs is much more manageable.

The original IP-based network that has now become the Internet once consisted of a small number of trusted users in government agencies and research organizations. In such a small community of known users, security was a fairly simple issue.

Since then, the Internet has grown beyond recognition, and now individuals, businesses, and organizations have developed their own IP networks that can link to the Internet. The hosts, network equipment, and data are the property of those network owners. By isolating themselves from the larger networks and shielding their devices from public access, companies and organizations can better protect themselves from spies and thieves. A local network manager can more easily control outside access to the smaller network.

Internetwork access within a company or organization can be similarly secured. For example, a college network can be divided into administrative, research, and student subnetworks. Dividing a network based on user access is an effective way to protect the organization's interests and employee privacy. Such access restrictions can protect an organization from both unauthorized internal access and malicious external attacks.

Security between networks is controlled in an intermediary device (a router or firewall appliance) at the perimeter of the network. The firewall function can be configured to allow only known, trusted data and users to access the network. Figure 5-8 displays a network with firewalls protecting information while allowing access to the Internet.

Figure 5-8   Firewalls

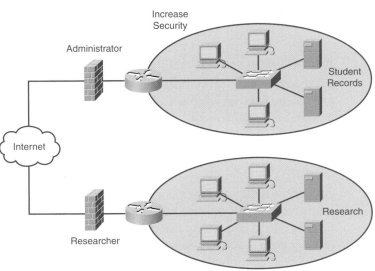

Address Management and Hierarchical Addressing

A group of hosts in a network can be compared to a small neighborhood in a town with a helpful local post office. The postal worker knows all the residents and their streets and street addresses, but he does not share that information with anyone outside the neighborhood.

Just as the neighborhood post office has a postal code that identifies the physical location of the neighborhood, a network has a network address that identifies the logical location of the network on a router. (Because computer networks are not restricted to physical locations, IPv4 provides a logical system of keeping track of networks.) An IPv4 address contains both network bits that identify a logical network address and host bits that contain a local "inside the neighborhood" address of the end device.

In the neighborhood analogy, residents (hosts) can communicate with others in their neighborhood quite easily. They know each other's street addresses and trust each other, and they are constantly chatting and checking up on each other. If they need to send messages somewhere outside the neighborhood, however, they give the message to the postal worker, who figures out how to forward the message to another post office in the neighborhood of the destination. This frees the residents on the inside of the neighborhood from having to know how to communicate with all the possible addresses outside their known neighborhood. The post office serves as a community gateway to communication with the world outside the neighborhood.

When messages arrive from the outside, they are addressed with information containing the address of both the neighborhood post office (the postal code) and the street address (the local address). The helpful postal worker takes all the messages addressed to the neighborhood, sorts them by address, and delivers the message inside the neighborhood to the proper recipient.

This example also describes the basic function of network addressing. Routers act as postal workers at post offices for small networks by taking care of messages going out and serving as a general destination and sorting station for messages coming in. The router a network uses to send and receive messages beyond the network is called a *gateway router*.
Figure 5-9 depicts a gateway router providing local hosts with access to an outside host whose address is unknown inside the network.

Figure 5-9   Gateway Routers Provide Outside Network Access

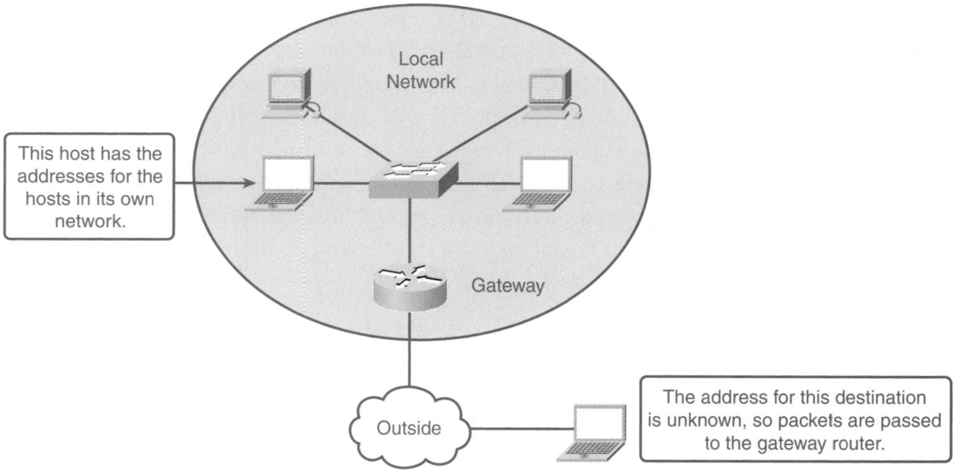

The address is divided into two parts: the network address and the host address. The network portion of the address tells routers where to find the general network, and the host portion is used by the last router for delivery inside the network. The structure of the IP address will be explored in greater detail in Chapter 6.

The type of addressing in the analogy is considered hierarchical. *Hierarchical addressing* is read from the most general information to the most specific. When a letter or package is sent through the postal service, there is an addressing protocol. Figure 5-10 shows an example of a properly addressed letter for the Canadian postal system.

Figure 5-10   Hierarchical Postal Address

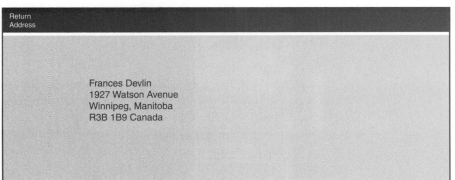

The address in Figure 5-10 will be read by postal workers from the most general information (the country and postal code) to the most specific (the name of the addressee). When the letter is in the hands of the Canadian postal service, the postal code will be used to route the letter to the neighborhood of its destination. (In reality, the first few characters of the postal code include province and city information, so the city and province information in the letter address is redundant.) When the letter is in the neighborhood, the postal worker uses the street address to get to the house, and then the name identifies the person in the house who gets the letter. Postal codes in most countries use the same hierarchical organization.

Dividing Networks from Networks

The IPv4 address is composed of 32 bits divided into two parts: the network address and the host address. The network portion of the address acts like a postal code and tells routers where to find the general neighborhood of a network. Routers forward packets between networks by referring only to the network portion. When the packet arrives at the last router, like a letter arriving at the last postal station, the local portion of the address identifies the destination host.

The IPv4 addressing system is flexible. If a large network needs to be divided into smaller subnets, additional network codes can be created using some of the bits designated for the host in a process called *subnetting*. Network managers use this flexibility to customize their private networks. IPv4's ability to scale to the ever-growing demands of the Internet has contributed to its wide use.

Figure 5-11 shows the basic structure of an IPv4 address. In this address, the three *octets* to the left are the general network address, and the last octet is used by the destination router to identify the local host.

Figure 5-11 Hierarchical IPv4 Address

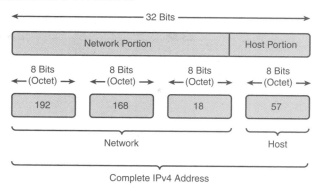

The portion of the address that is network and the portion that is host can vary. The structure of the IP addressing will be explored in greater detail in Chapter 6.

Routing: How Data Packets Are Handled

Communication within a network, or subnet, happens without a network layer device. When a host communicates outside the local network, a router acts as a gateway and performs the network layer function of choosing a path for the packet.

Device Parameters: Supporting Communication Outside the Network

As a part of its configuration, a host has a *default gateway* address defined. As shown in Figure 5-12, this gateway address is the address of a router interface that is connected to the same network as the host. The router interface is actually a host on the local network, so the host IP address and the default gateway address must be on the same network. Figure 5-12 shows that default gateways are members of their own local networks.

Figure 5-12   Gateways Enable Communications Between Networks

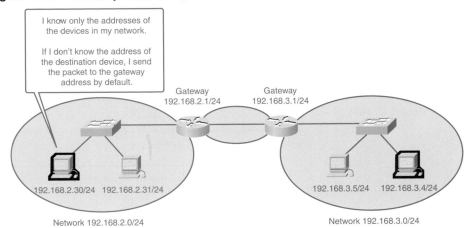

The default gateway is configured on a host. On a Windows computer, the Internet Protocol (TCP/IP) Properties tools are used to enter the default gateway IPv4 address. Both the host IPv4 address and the gateway address must have the same network (and subnet, if used) portion of their respective addresses.

IP Packets: Carrying Data End to End

The role of the network layer is to transfer data from the host that originates the data to the host that uses it. During encapsulation at the source host, an IP packet is constructed at Layer 3 to transport the Layer 4 PDU. If the destination host is in the same network as the source host, the packet is delivered between the two hosts on the local media without the need for a router.

However, if the destination host and source host are not in the same network, the packet can be carrying a transport layer PDU across many networks and through many routers. As it does, the information contained within is not altered by any routers when forwarding decisions are made.

At each hop, the forwarding decisions are based on the information in the IP packet header. The packet with its network layer encapsulation also is basically intact throughout the complete process, from the source host to the destination host.

If communication is between hosts in different networks, the local network delivers the packet from the source to its gateway router. The router examines the network portion of the packet destination address and forwards the packet to the appropriate interface. If the destination network is directly connected to this router, the packet is forwarded directly to that host. If the destination network is not directly connected, the packet is forwarded to a second router that is the next-hop router.

The packet forwarding then becomes the responsibility of this second router. Many routers or hops along the way can process the packet before reaching the destination.

Gateway: The Way Out of the Network

The gateway, also known as the default gateway, is needed to send a packet out of the local network. If the network portion of the destination address of the packet is different from the network of the originating host, the packet has to be routed outside the original network. To do this, the packet is sent to the gateway. This gateway is a router interface connected to the local network. The gateway interface has a network layer address that matches the network address of the hosts. The hosts are configured to recognize that address as the gateway.

Default Gateway

The default gateway is configured on a host. On a Windows computer, the Internet Protocol (TCP/IP) Properties tools are used to enter the default gateway IPv4 address. Both the host IPv4 address and the gateway address must have the same network (and subnet, if used) portion of their respective addresses. Figure 5-13 depicts the Windows TCP/IP Properties configuration.

Figure 5-13   IP Address and Gateway Configuration in Windows

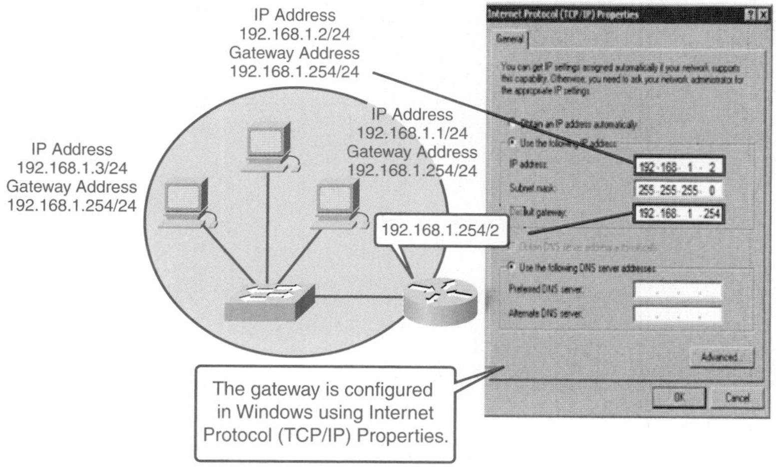

No packet can be forwarded without a route. Whether the packet is originating in a host or being forwarded by an intermediary device, the device must have a route to identify where to forward the packet.

A host must either forward a packet to the host on the local network or to the gateway, as appropriate. To forward the packets, the host must have routes that represent these destinations.

A router makes a forwarding decision for each packet that arrives at the gateway interface. This forwarding process is referred to as *routing*. To forward a packet to a destination network, the router requires a route to that network. If a route to a destination network does not exist, the packet cannot be forwarded.

The destination network can be a number of routers or hops away from the gateway. The route to that network would only indicate the next-hop router to which the packet is to be forwarded, not the final router. The routing process uses a route to map the destination network address to the next hop and then forwards the packet to this next-hop address.

Confirming the Gateway and Route

An easy way to check the host IP address and default gateway is by issuing the **ipconfig** command at the command-line prompt of a Windows XP computer:

Step 1.   Open the command-prompt window by clicking the Windows Start button in the lower-left corner of the desktop.

Step 2.   Choose the Run icon.

Step 3.   In the text box, type **cmd** and press **Enter**.

Step 4.   The c:\Windows\system32\cmd.exe program is running. At the prompt, type **ipconfig** and press Enter. The Windows IP configuration will display with the IP address, subnet mask, and default gateway addresses.

Example 5-1 shows a sample of the **ipconfig** output with the host's IP address information.

Example 5-1 Confirming the IP Address and Gateway Route

```
C:\> ipconfig

Windows IP Configuration
Ethernet adapter Local Area Connection:
        Connection-specific DNS Suffix  .  :
        IP Address........................: 192.168.1.2
        Subnet Mask.......................: 255.255.255.0
        Default Gateway...................: 192.168.1.254
```

Route: A Path to a Network

A route for packets for remote destinations is added using the default gateway address as the next hop. Although it is not usually done, a host can also have routes manually added through configurations.

Like end devices, routers also add routes for the connected networks to their *routing table*. When a router interface is configured with an IP address and subnet mask, the interface becomes part of that network. The routing table now includes that network as a directly connected network. All other routes, however, must be configured or acquired through a routing protocol. To forward a packet, the router must know where to send it. This information is available as routes in a routing table.

The routing table stores information about connected and remote networks. Connected networks are directly attached to one of the router interfaces. These interfaces are the gateways for the hosts on different local networks. Remote networks are networks that are not directly connected to the router. Routes to these networks can be manually configured on the router by the network administrator or learned automatically using dynamic routing protocols.

Routes in a routing table have three main features:

- Destination network

- Next-hop

- Metric

The router matches the destination address in the packet header with the destination network of a route in the routing table and forwards the packet to the next-hop router specified by that route. If there are two or more possible routes to the same destination, the metric is used to decide which route appears on the routing table.

Figure 5-14 shows a sample network with a local router and a remote router. Example 5-2 displays the routing table in the local router, which you can examine with the **show ip route** command from a router's console. From left to right, the output contains the destination network, the metric of [120/1], and the next hop through 192.168.2.2.

Figure 5-14   Confirming the Gateway and Route

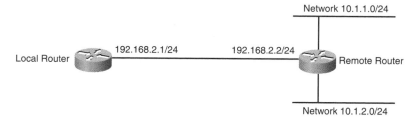

Example 5-2 Router's Routing Table

```
Local_Router# show ip route

10.0.0.0/24 is subnetted, 2 subnets
R     10.1.1.0  [120/1] via 192.168.2.2, 00:00:08, FastEthernet0/0
R     10.1.1.0  [120/1] via 192.168.2.2, 00:00:08, FastEthernet0/0
C 192.168.1.0/24 is directly connected, FastEthernet0/0
```

Note

The routing process and the role of metrics are the subject of a later course and companion book.

As you know, packets cannot be forwarded by the router without a route. If a route representing the destination network is not on the routing table, the packet will be dropped (that is, not forwarded). The matching route could be either a connected route or a route to a remote network. The router can also use a default route to forward the packet. The *default route* is used when the destination network is not represented by any other route in the routing table.

Host Routing Table

Hosts require a local routing table to ensure that network layer packets are directed to the correct destination network. Unlike the routing table in a router, which contains both local and remote routes, the local table of the host typically contains its direct connection or connections (hosts can belong to more than one local network) and its own default route to the gateway. Configuring the default gateway address on the host creates the local default route. Without a default gateway or route, packets destined outside the network will be dropped.

Figure 5-15 shows a simple network for the host routing table example that follows. The routing table of a computer host can be examined at the Windows command line by issuing the **netstat –r** or the **route print** command. Note that the host (192.168.1.2) serves as its own gateway to its own network (192.168.1.0) and has a default gateway for destinations outside the network pointing to the router interface (192.168.1.254).

Figure 5-15 Simple Network for Example 5-3

Follow these steps to display a local routing table on a host:

Step 1. Open the command-prompt window by clicking the Windows Start button in the lower-left corner of the desktop.

Step 2. Choose the Run icon.

Step 3. In the text box, type **cmd** and click the OK button or press **Enter**.

Step 4. The c:\Windows\system32\cmd.exe program is running. At the prompt, type **route print** or **netstat -r** and press Enter. The route table listing all known routes on the host will display.

Example 5-3 shows the host routing table.

```
Example 5-3 Host IP Routing Table Commands
C:\> netstat -r

Route Table
_ _ _ _ _ _ _ _ _ _ _ _ _ _ _ _ _ _ _ _ _ _ _ _ _ _ _ _ _ _ _ _ _ _ _ _ _ _
Interface List
0x2….00 0f fe 26 f7 7b …Gigabit Ethernet – Packet Scheduler Miniport
_ _ _ _ _ _ _ _ _ _ _ _ _ _ _ _ _ _ _ _ _ _ _ _ _ _ _ _ _ _ _ _ _ _ _ _ _ _
Active Routes:
Network Destination    Netmask           Gateway          Interface       Metric
0.0.0.0                0.0.0.0           192.168.1.254    192.168.1.2     20
192.168.1.0            255.255.255.0     192.168.1.2      192.168.1.2     20
Default Gateway:       192.168.1.254
// output omitted //
_ _ _ _ _ _ _ _ _ _ _ _ _ _ _ _ _ _ _ _ _ _ _ _ _ _ _ _ _ _ _ _ _ _ _ _ _ _
```

When a host creates packets, it uses the routes it knows to forward them to the locally connected destination. These local network packets are delivered on the local route within the network without using a router. No packet is forwarded without a route. Whether the packet is originating in a host or being forwarded by an intermediary router, the device must have a route to identify which interface will be used to forward the packet. A host must either forward a packet to the host on the local network or to the gateway, as appropriate.

Routing

Routing is the process a router performs when making forwarding decisions for each packet arriving at the gateway interface. To forward a packet to a destination network, the router requires a route to that network. If a route to a destination network does not exist on the router, the packet will be forwarded to a default gateway. If no default gateway is configured, the packet cannot be forwarded. The destination network can be a number of routers or hops away from the gateway. If the router has an entry for the network in its routing table, it would only indicate the next-hop router to which the packet is to be forwarded, not the exact route to the final router. The routing process uses a routing table to map the destination network address to the next hop and then forwards the packet to this next-hop address. Figure 5-16 depicts a portion of a local router's routing table.

Figure 5-16   Local Router's Routing Table

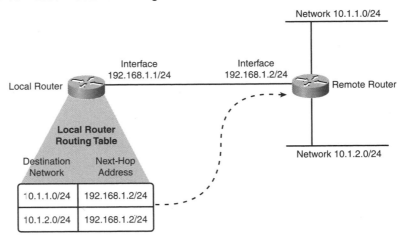

Destination Network

For a router to route a packet to a destination network efficiently, it needs information about the route in its routing table. With millions of routes on the Internet, however, it is not reasonable to expect every route to be known to the router. The following sections describe how routers use information in routing tables and how packets can be forwarded when no information about routes can be found.

Routing Table Entries

The route, or destination network, in a routing table entry represents a range of host addresses and sometimes a range of network and host addresses.

The hierarchical nature of Layer 3 addressing means that one route entry can refer to a large general network and another entry can refer to a subnet of that same network. When forwarding a packet, the router will select the most specific route that it knows. If a specific subnet is not in the routing table but the larger network that holds the subnet is known, the router will send it to the larger network, trusting that another router will find the subnet.

Consider Example 5-4. If a packet arrives at the router with the destination address of 10.1.1.55, the router forwards the packet to a next-hop router associated with a route to network 10.1.1.0. If a route to 10.1.1.0 is not listed in the routing table but a route to 10.1.0.0 is available, the packet is forwarded to the next-hop router for that network.

```
Example 5-4 Routes in a Routing Table
10.0.0.0/24 is subnetted, 2 subnets
R     10.1.1.0  [120/1] via 192.168.2.2, 00:00:08, FastEthernet0/0
R     10.1.1.0  [120/1] via 192.168.2.2, 00:00:08, FastEthernet0/0
C 192.168.1.0/24 is directly connected, FastEthernet0/0
```

The precedence the router uses for route selection for the packet going to 10.1.1.55 is as follows:

1. 10.1.1.0

2. 10.1.0.0

3. 10.0.0.0

4. 0.0.0.0 (default route if configured)

5. Dropped

In this case, the 10.1.1.0 network is known through 192.168.2.2, which is out the FastEthernet 0/0 interface.

Default Route

Remember that a default route is the route used if no specific route is available to be selected for delivery. In IPv4 networks, the address 0.0.0.0 is used for this purpose. Packets with a destination network address that does not match a more specific route in the routing table are forwarded to the next-hop router associated with the default route. The default route is also known as the *gateway of last resort*. When a default route is configured in a router, you can see it in the output, as noted in the first line of Example 5-5.

```
Example 5-5 Gateway of Last Resort
Gateway of Last Resort is 192.168.2.2 to Network 0.0.0.0
10.0.0.0/24 is subnetted, 2 subnets
R     10.1.1.0  [120/1] via 192.168.2.2, 00:00:08, FastEthernet0/0
R     10.1.1.0  [120/1] via 192.168.2.2, 00:00:08, FastEthernet0/0
C 192.168.1.0/24 is directly connected, FastEthernet0/0
S* 0.0.0.0/0 [1/0] via 192.168.2.2
```

Next Hop: Where the Packet Goes Next

The *next hop* is the address of the device that will process the packet next. For a host on a network, the address of the default gateway (router interface) is the next hop for all packets destined for another network.

As each packet arrives at a router, the destination network address is examined and compared to the routes in the routing table. The routing table lists an IP address for the next-hop router for the routes it knows. If a matching route is determined, the router then forwards the packet out the interface to which the next-hop router is connected. Example 5-6 outlines the association of routes with next hops and router interfaces.

```
Example 5-6 Routing Table Output with Next Hops
10.0.0.0/24 is subnetted, 2 subnets
R    10.1.1.0  [120/1] via 192.168.2.2, 00:00:08, FastEthernet0/0
R    10.1.1.0  [120/1] via 192.168.2.2, 00:00:08, FastEthernet0/0
C 192.168.1.0/24 is directly connected, FastEthernet0/0
```

As you can see in Example 5-6, some routes can have multiple next hops. This indicates that there are multiple paths to the same destination network. These are parallel routes that the router can use to select paths and forward packets.

Packet Forwarding: Moving the Packet Toward Its Destination

Routing is performed packet by packet and hop by hop. Each packet is treated independently by each router along the path. At each hop, the router examines the destination IP address for each packet and then checks the routing table for forwarding information. The router will then do one of the following with the packet:

- Forward it to the next-hop router

- Forward it to the destination host

- Drop it

A router takes the following steps to determine the appropriate action:

1. As an intermediary device, a router processes the packet at the network layer. However, packets that arrive at a router's interfaces are encapsulated as a data link layer (Layer 2) PDU. The router first discards the Layer 2 encapsulation so that the IP packet can be examined.

2. The router examines the IP address.

3. The router checks the routing table for a match.

4. The router selects the next hop. In the router, the destination address in a packet header is examined. If a matching route in the routing table shows that the destination network is directly connected to the router, the packet is forwarded to the interface to which that network is connected.

5. The router then does one of the following:

   - **Scenario A: The router forwards the packet.** If the route matching the destination network of the packet is a remote network, the packet is forwarded to the indicated interface, encapsulated by the Layer 2 protocol, and sent to the next-hop address. If the destination network is on a directly connected network, the packet has to be first reencapsulated by the Layer 2 protocol and then forwarded out the proper interface to the local network.

- **Scenario B: The router uses the default route.** If the routing table does not contain a more specific route entry for an arriving packet, the packet is forwarded to the interface indicated by a default route, if one exists. At this interface, the packet is encapsulated by the Layer 2 protocol and sent to the next-hop router. The default route is also known as the *gateway of last resort.*

- **Scenario C: The router drops the packet.** If a packet is dropped, IP, by design, has no provision to return a packet to the sender or previous router. Such a function would detract from the protocol's efficiency and low overhead. Other protocols are used to report such errors.

Router Packet Forwarding (5.3.7.4)

In this activity, the rules (algorithms) that routers use to make decisions on how to process packets, depending on the state of their routing tables when the packet arrives, are examined. Use file e1-5374.pka on the CD-ROM that accompanies this book to perform this activity using Packet Tracer.

Routing Processes: How Routes Are Learned

Routers need information about other networks to build a reliable routing table. Networks and routes are constantly changing, with new networks coming on and routes going down. If a router has bad information about routes, it is likely it will forward packets incorrectly, causing packets to be delayed or dropped. It is vital that routers have current information about neighboring routers to reliably forward packets. The two ways in which a router can learn information about routes is through static routing and dynamic routing. The following sections also introduce common routing protocols used by routers to dynamically share information.

Static Routing

The route information can be manually configured on the router, creating what is known as a *static route*. An example of a static route is a default route. Static routing requires a network administrator for initial setup and for any changes to routes. Static routes are considered very reliable, and the router does not use much overhead to process packets. On the other hand, static routes do not update automatically and have higher continuing administrative costs.

If the router is connected to a number of other routers, knowledge of the internetworking structure is required. To ensure that the packets are routed to use the best possible next hops, each known destination network needs to either have a route or a default route configured. Because packets are forwarded at every hop, every router must be configured with static routes to next hops that reflect its location in the internetwork.

Furthermore, if the internetwork structure changes or if new networks become available, these changes have to be manually updated on every router. If updating is not done in a timely fashion, the routing information can be incomplete or inaccurate, resulting in packet delays and possible packet loss.

Dynamic Routing

Routers can also learn about routes automatically from other routers in the same internetwork, which is known as *dynamic routing*. Dynamic routing updates arrive from other routers and are used by the receiving router without administrative configuration. Dynamic routing has higher router processing overhead but little administrative cost after initial setup.

If dynamic routing is not enabled and configured on a router, static routes to the next hops must be in place for the router to know where to forward packets.

Routing Protocols

It is imperative that all routers in an internetwork have up-to-date and extensive route knowledge. Maintaining the routing table by manual static configuration is not always feasible. Configuring one of several available dynamic routing protocols on network routers is a much more efficient way to keep the routers updated.

Routing protocols are the set of rules by which routers dynamically share their routing information. As routers become aware of changes to the networks for which they act as the gateway, or changes to links between other routers, the information is passed on to other routers. When a router receives information about new or changed routes, it updates its own routing table and, in turn, passes the information to other routers. In this way, all routers have accurate routing tables that are updated dynamically and can learn about routes to remote networks that are many hops away. An example of routers sharing routes is shown in Figure 5-17.

The most common routing protocols used in this book are

- Routing Information Protocol (RIP)

- Enhanced Interior Gateway Protocol (EIGRP)

- Open Shortest Path First (OSPF)

Figure 5-17   Dynamic Route Sharing

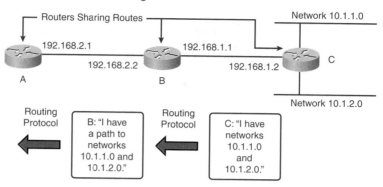

Router B learns about Router C's networks dynamically.
Router B's next hop to 10.1.1.0 and 10.1.2.0 is 192.168.1.2 (Router C).
Router A learns about Router C's networks dynamically from Router B.
Router A's next hop to 10.1.1.0 and 10.1.2.0 is 192.168.2.2 (Router B).

The advantage of routing protocols providing routers with up-to-date routing tables is tempered by added overhead costs. The exchange of route information adds overhead by consuming network bandwidth. This overhead can be an issue with low-bandwidth links between routers. Another cost is the router's processing overhead. Not only does each packet need to be processed and routed, but updates from routing protocols also require complicated algorithmic calculations before the route information can be used in a routing table. This means that routers employing these protocols must have sufficient processing capacity to both implement the protocol's algorithms and to perform timely packet routing and forwarding, which can add to initial network setup costs.

Static routing does not produce network overhead and places entries directly into the routing table with no route processing required by the router. The cost for static routing, as mentioned earlier, is administrative time taken to manually configure and maintain routing tables in a manner that ensures efficient routing.

In most internetworks, a combination of static (including default) and dynamic routes is used to provide efficient routing. The configuration of routing protocols on routers is an integral component of the CCNA and will be covered extensively by *Routing Protocols and Concepts, CCNA Exploration Companion Guide*.

Observing Dynamic Routing Protocol Updates (5.4.3.2)

Packet Tracer
☐ Activity

In this activity, you will examine a simple visualization of a dynamic routing protocol in "action." Use file e1-5432.pka on the CD-ROM that accompanies this book to perform this activity using Packet Tracer.

Summary

The most significant network layer (OSI Layer 3) protocol is the IP. IP version 4 (IPv4) is the network layer protocol that will be used as an example throughout this book, although IPv6 is available and operational in many areas.

Layer 3 IP routing does not guarantee reliable delivery or establish a connection before data is transmitted. This connectionless and unreliable communication is fast and efficient, but upper layers must provide mechanisms to guarantee delivery of data if it is needed.

The role of the network layer is to encapsulate upper-level data into a packet and route it from one host to another, regardless of the type of data. The data is encapsulated in a packet. The packet header has fields that include the source and destination addresses of the packet.

Hierarchical network layer addressing, called an IP address, with network and host portions, allows the division of networks into subnets. The network portion of the IP address is used for forwarding packets between routers toward the destination. Only the last router connected to the destination network uses the host portion of the IP address.

If a host creates a packet with a destination address outside the local network, the packet is sent to the default gateway for forwarding to the destination network. The default gateway is an interface of a router that is on the local network. The gateway router examines the destination address and, if the gateway router has knowledge of a route to the destination network in its routing table, forwards the packet either to a connected network or to the next-hop router. If no routing entry exists, the router can forward the packet on to a default route or, lacking a default route, drop the packet.

Routing table entries are configured either statically on each router to provide static routing and default routes, or dynamically to collect and share route information with other routers automatically by using one or more routing protocols.

The network layer encapsulates data from the transport layer and sends it down to the data link layer (OSI Layer 2). Chapter 6 explores the communication process at the data link layer of the OSI model.

Labs

The labs available in the companion *Network Fundamentals, CCNA Exploration Labs and Study Guide* (ISBN 1-58713-203-6) provide hands-on practice with the following topics introduced in this chapter:

Lab 5-1: Examining a Device's Gateway (5.5.1)

In this lab, you will examine the purpose of a gateway address, configure network parameters on a Windows computer, and then troubleshoot a hidden gateway address problem.

Lab 5-2: Examining a Route (5.5.2)

In this lab, you will use the **route** command to modify a Windows computer route table, use a Windows Telnet client to connect to a Cisco router, and then examine the router's routing table using basic Cisco IOS commands.

Packet Tracer
☐ Companion

Many of the hands-on labs include Packet Tracer companion activities, where you can use Packet Tracer to complete a simulation of the lab. Look for this icon in *Network Fundamentals, CCNA Exploration Labs and Study Guide* (ISBN 1-58713-203-6) for hands-on labs that have Packet Tracer companion activities.

Check Your Understanding

Complete all the review questions listed here to test your understanding of the topics and concepts in this chapter. The appendix, "Check Your Understanding and Challenge Questions Answer Key," lists the answers.

1. Which protocol provides connectionless network layer services?

   A. IP

   B. TCP

   C. UDB

   D. OSI

2. What two commands can be used to view a host's routing table?

3. Select three pieces of information about a route that a routing table contains.

   A. Next-hop

   B. Source address

   C. Metric

   D. Destination network address

   E. Last hop

   F. Default gateway

4. What kinds of problems are caused by excessive broadcast traffic on a network segment? (Choose three.)

   A. Consumes network bandwidth

   B. Increases overhead on network

   C. Requires complex address schemes

   D. Interrupts other host functions

   E. Divides networks based on ownership

   F. Advanced hardware required

5. What are three key factors to consider when grouping hosts into a common network?

6. Which of the following are not functions of the network layer? (Choose two.)

   A. Routing

   B. Addressing packets with an IP address

   C. Delivery reliability

   D. Application data analysis

   E. Encapsulation

   F. Decapsulation

7. Which of the following are true about IP? (Choose two.)

   A. IP stands for International Protocol.

   B. It is the most common network layer protocol.

   C. It analyzes presentation layer data.

   D. It operates at OSI Layer 2.

   E. It encapsulates transport layer segments.

8. What is the name of the process of removing the OSI Layer 2 information from an IP packet?

9. Which of the following is true about IP?

   A. It is connection oriented.

   B. It uses application data to determine the best path.

   C. It is used by both routers and hosts.

   D. It is reliable.

10. Which of the following are true about network layer encapsulation? (Choose two.)

    A. It adds a header to a segment.

    B. It can happen many times on the path to the destination host.

    C. It is performed by the last router on the path.

    D. Both source and destination IP addresses are added.

    E. It converts transport layer information into a frame.

11. Which of the following are true about TCP and IP? (Choose two.)

    A. TCP is connectionless and IP is connection oriented.

    B. TCP is reliable and IP is unreliable.

    C. IP is connectionless and TCP is connection oriented.

    D. TCP is unreliable and IP is reliable.

    E. IP operates at the transport layer.

12. Why is IP "media independent"?

    A. It encapsulates Layer 1 instructions.

    B. It works the same on all Layer 1 media.

    C. It carries both video and voice data.

    D. It works without Layer 1 media.

13. TCP is a _____ layer protocol.

14. How many bits are in an IPv4 address?

15. Which of the following are true about static and dynamic routing? (Choose two.)

    A. Static routing requires a routing protocol such as RIP.

    B. A default route is a dynamic route.

    C. Dynamic routing adds packet-processing overhead.

    D. Administrative overhead is reduced with static routing.

    E. Routers can use static and dynamic routing simultaneously.

Challenge Questions and Activities

These questions require a deeper application of the concepts covered in this chapter. You can find the answers in the appendix.

1. What can happen when the TTL is 1? (Choose two.)

    A. The packet can be successfully delivered if it is destined for a directly connected network.

    B. TCP controls in the packet will add hops to the TTL.

    C. The packet will be dropped by the next router unless that router has an interface on the destination network.

    D. The packet will be returned to the source host.

    E. The packet will be returned to the previous router.

2. IP is connectionless and will occasionally drop a packet en route to a destination IP address. If packets are dropped, how will messages be completed?

    A. Only the IP portion of the packet is dropped, but the TCP portion continues to the last router.

    B. The routing protocols will carry the TCP information to the previous-hop router, which sends a reverse notification to the source.

    C. The routing protocols, such as RIP, are connection oriented and will contact the source host.

    D. The destination host is expecting the packet and will send a request if it does not arrive.

    E. The IP header contains the source address so that the packet can be returned by the router that receives the packet when the TTL is 0.

Look for this icon in *Network Fundamentals, CCNA Exploration Labs and Study Guide* (ISBN 1-58713-203-6) for instructions on how to perform the Packet Tracer Skills Integration Challenge for this chapter.

To Learn More

The following questions encourage you to reflect on the topics discussed in this chapter. Your instructor might ask you to research the questions and discuss your findings in class.

1. How can lost data be re-sent when the network layer uses unreliable and connectionless means of packet forwarding?

2. In what network circumstances would it be more advantageous to use static routing instead of dynamic routing protocols?

CHAPTER 6

Addressing the Network: IPv4

Objectives

Upon completion of this chapter, you will able to answer the following questions:

- What type of addressing structure does IPv4 use?

- What is the 8-bit binary equivalent of a given decimal number?

- What is the decimal equivalent of a given 8-bit binary number?

- What type of address is a given IPv4 address, and how is it used in a network?

- How do administrators assign addresses within networks?

- How are addresses assigned by ISPs?

- What is the network portion of the host address?

- What is the role of the subnet mask in dividing networks?

- What are the appropriate addressing components for IPv4, given addressing design criteria?

- How do you use testing utilities to verify and test network connectivity and operational status of the IP stack on a host?

Key Terms

This chapter uses the following key terms. You can find the definitions in the Glossary.

digital logic   page 173

dotted decimal   page 173

high-order bits   page 174

positional notation   page 174

radix   page 175

low-order bits   page 176

most significant bit   page 178

broadcast address   page 184

directed broadcast   page 184

limited broadcast   page 184

multicast clients   page 187

multicast group   page 187

scope   page 187

reserved link-local addresses   page 187

globally scoped addresses   page 187

administratively scoped addresses   page 187

limited-scope addresses   page 187

Network Time Protocol (NTP)   page 188

prefix length   page 190

slash format   page 190

public addresses   page 192

private addresses   page 192

Network Address Translation (NAT)   page 193

loopback   page 194

link-local addresses   page 194

test-net addresses   page 195

classful addressing   page 197

classless addressing   page 198

address pool   page 201

Regional Internet Registries (RIR)   page 204

Internet backbone   page 205

AND   page 207

round-trip time (RTT)   page 231

*Internet Control Message Protocol (ICMP)
  page 232–233*

Addressing is a key function of network layer protocols. Addressing enables data communication between hosts on the same network or on different networks. Internet Protocol version 4 (IPv4) provides hierarchical addressing for packets that carry your data.

Designing, implementing, and managing an effective IPv4 addressing plan ensures that networks can operate effectively and efficiently. This chapter examines in detail the structure of IPv4 addresses and their application to the construction and testing of IP networks and subnetworks.

IPv4 Addresses

For communication to take place between hosts, the appropriate addresses must be applied to these devices. Managing the addressing of the devices and understanding the IPv4 address structure and its representation are essential.

Anatomy of an IPv4 Address

Each device on a network must be uniquely defined by a network layer address. At this layer, the packets of the communication are also identified with the source and destination addresses of the two end systems. With IPv4, each packet uses a 32-bit source address and a 32-bit destination address in the Layer 3 header.

These addresses are represented in the data network as binary patterns. Inside the devices, *digital logic* is applied for the interpretation of these addresses. For the human network, a string of 32 bits is difficult to interpret and even more difficult to remember. For this reason, IPv4 addresses are represented using *dotted decimal* format.

Dotted Decimal

IPv4 addresses are easier to remember, write, and verbally communicate than strings of 32 bits. Representing IPv4 addresses as dotted decimals begins by separating the 32 bits of the address into bytes. Each byte of the binary pattern, called an *octet*, is separated with a dot. The bytes are called an octet, because each of the decimal numbers represents 1 byte, or 8 bits.

For example, the following address:

10101100000100000000010000010100

is expressed in dotted decimal as

172.16.4.20

Keep in mind that devices use binary logic. The dotted decimal format makes it easier for people to use and remember addresses.

Network and Host Portions

IPv4 addresses have two parts: the network portion and the host portion. For each IPv4 address, some portion of the most significant bits, or *high-order bits*, represents the network address. At Layer 3, a *network* is defined as a group of hosts that have identical bit patterns in the network address portion of their addresses. That is, all the bits in the network portion of their addresses are identical.

In the following example, the two addresses have identical network portions. Therefore, hosts assigned these two addresses would be on the same logical network:

172.16.4.20	172.16.4.32
network host	network host
portion portion	portion portion

Although all 32 bits define the IPv4 host address, a variable number of bits represent the host portion of the address. The number of bits used in this host portion determines the number of hosts within the network. In the previous example, the last octet, the lowest 8 bits, are the host portion. This means that the bits for the upper three octets represent the network portion.

You determine how many bits are required for the host portion based on the number of hosts that a network requires. If a particular network requires at least 200 hosts, you would need to use enough bits in the host portion to be able to represent at least 200 different bit patterns. To assign a unique address to 200 hosts, you would use the entire last octet. With 8 bits, a total of 256 different bit patterns can be achieved. As with the previous example, this means that the bits for the upper three octets represent the network portion. Calculating the number of hosts and determining which portion of the 32 bits of an IPv4 address refers to the network portion will be covered in the section "Calculating Network, Hosts, and Broadcast Addresses," later in this chapter.

Binary-to-Decimal Conversion

To understand the operation of a device in a network, you need to look at addresses and other data the way a network device does: in binary notation. This means that you need to have some skill in binary-to-decimal conversion.

Data represented in binary can represent many different forms of data to the human network. In this discussion, binary is discussed as it relates to IPv4 addressing. This means that each byte (octet) is interpreted as a decimal number in the range of 0 to 255.

Positional Notation

Learning to convert binary to decimal requires an understanding of the mathematical basis of a numbering system called *positional notation*. Positional notation means that a digit represents different values depending on the position it occupies. More specifically, the value that a digit represents is the value of the digit multiplied by the power of the base, or *radix*, represented by the position the digit occupies. Some examples will help to clarify how this system works.

For the decimal number 245, the 2 is in the 100s, or 10^2, position. Therefore, this 2 represents $2*10^2$ (2 times 10 to the power of 2). Positional notation refers to this position as the base^2 position because the base, or radix, is 10 and the power is 2.

Using positional notation in the base 10 number system, 245 represents the following:

$$245 = (2 * 10^2) + (4 * 10^1) + (5 * 10^0)$$

or

$$245 = (2 * 100) + (4 * 10) + (5 * 1)$$

Binary Numbering System

In the binary numbering system, the radix is 2. Therefore, each position represents increasing powers of 2. In 8-bit binary numbers, the positions represent the quantities shown in Table 6-1.

Table 6-1   Binary Positional Values

Powers of 2	2^7	2^6	2^5	2^4	2^3	2^2	2^1	2^0
Decimal Value	128	64	32	16	8	4	2	1

The base 2 numbering system has only two digits: 0 and 1. When a byte is interpreted as a decimal number, the quantity that position represents is added to the total if the digit is a 1, and 0 is added if the digit is a 0.

A 1 in each position means that the value for that position is added to the total. Table 6-2 shows the values of each position with a 1 in the position.

Table 6-2   Binary Positional Notation with Digit of 1

Decimal Value	128	64	32	16	8	4	2	1
Binary Digit	1	1	1	1	1	1	1	1
Position Value	128	64	32	16	8	4	2	1

The value of each position is added to determine the total value of the number. As in Table 6-1, when there is a 1 in each position of an octet, the total is 255, as follows:

$$128 + 64 + 32 + 16 + 8 + 4 + 2 + 1 = 255$$

A 0 in each position indicates that the value for that position is not added to the total. A 0 in every position yields a total of 0, as follows in Table 6-3.

Table 6-3 Binary Positional Notation with Digit of 0

Decimal Value	128	64	32	16	8	4	2	1
Binary Digit	0	0	0	0	0	0	0	0
Position Value	0	0	0	0	0	0	0	0

For the conversion of a 32-bit IPv4 address, you identify the 4 bytes or octets that make up this address. You then convert each of these four octets to decimal. As an example, convert the IPv4 address 10101100000100000000010000010100 to the bytes of a dotted decimal address. The conversion starts with the *low-order bits*, in this case byte 00010100, and continues up to the high-order byte.

Step 1. Divide the 32 bits into 4 octets, as follows:

10101100.00010000.00000100.00010100

Step 2. Convert the low-order byte 00010100 first, as seen in Table 6-4.

Step 3. Convert the next-highest byte, which is 00000100, as seen in Table 6-5.

Step 4. Continue converting with the next byte, 00010000, as seen in Table 6-6.

Step 5. Convert the highest byte, 10101100, as seen in Table 6-7.

Step 6. Write down the four numbers with dots separating the octets, such as 172.16.4.20.

Table 6-4 Conversion of Binary Number 00010100

Decimal Value	128	64	32	16	8	4	2	1
Binary Digit	0	0	0	1	0	1	0	0
Position Value	0	0	0	16	0	4	0	0
Total Value	0 + 0 + 0 + 16 + 0 + 4 + 0 + 0 = 20							

Table 6-5 Conversion of Binary Number 00000100

Decimal Value	128	64	32	16	8	4	2	1
Binary Digit	0	0	0	0	0	1	0	0
Position Value	0	0	0	0	0	4	0	0
Total Value	0 + 0 + 0 + 0 + 0 + 4 + 0 + 0 = 4							

Table 6-6   Conversion of Binary Number 00010000

Decimal Value	128	64	32	16	8	4	2	1
Binary Digit	0	0	0	1	0	0	0	0
Position Value	0	0	0	16	0	0	0	0
Total Value	0 + 0 + 0 + 16 + 0 + 0 + 0 + 0 = 16							

Table 6-7   Conversion of Binary Number 10101100

Decimal Value	128	64	32	16	8	4	2	1
Binary Digit	1	0	1	0	1	1	0	0
Position Value	128	0	32	0	8	4	0	0
Total Value	128 + 0 + 32 + 0 + 8 + 4 + 0 + 0 = 172							

In this example, the binary number 10101100000100000000010000010100 is converted to 172.16.4.20. The address representation 172.16.4.20 is much easier for humans to interpret.

Binary Counting

With the decimal numbering system, counting uses the numbers in the base, 0 through 9. With this system, the digits continue to increase until they reach 9. Then an additional 1 would be included with the addition of a new high-order bit. For example, similar to the way decimal 99 increments to 100 decimal, the next binary number after 11 is 100. Notice, that as the "1" position and "2" position go to 0s, an additional 1 is included in the "4" position.

The binary number system uses only two digits, 0 and 1. Because there are only two digits in the binary numbering system, the counting process is simpler than in other numbering systems. So, counting is only 0 and 1 before a new column is added. Like other numbering systems, leading 0s do not affect the value of the number. However, because we are representing the status of a byte of address or data, we include these as placeholders. Table 6-8 show an example of binary counting.

Table 6-8   Binary Counting

Decimal	Binary	Decimal	Binary	Decimal	Binary
0	00000000	16	00010000	32	00100000
1	00000001	17	00010001	33	00100001
2	00000010	18	00010010	34	00100010
3	00000011	19	00010011	35	00100011

Table 6-8   Binary Counting   *continued*

Decimal	Binary	Decimal	Binary	Decimal	Binary
4	00000100	20	00010100	36	00100100
5	00000101	21	00010101	37	00100101
6	00000110	22	00010110	38	00100110
7	00000111	23	00010111	39	00100111
8	00001000	24	00011000	40	00101000
9	00001001	25	00011001	41	00101001
10	00001010	26	00011010	42	00101010
11	00001011	27	00011011	43	00101011
12	00001100	28	00011100	44	00101100
13	00001101	29	00011101	45	00101101
14	00001110	30	00011110	46	00101110
15	00001111	31	00011111	47	00101111

Decimal-to-Binary Conversions

Not only do you need to be able to convert binary to decimal, but you also need to be able to convert decimal to binary. You often need to examine an individual octet of an address given in dotted decimal notation. Such is the case when the network bits and host bits divide an octet.

As an example, if a host with the address 172.16.4.20 were using 28 bits for the network address, the first 4 bits of the last octet would be network address bits and the last 4 bits would be host bits. To discover that this host is on the network 172.16.4.16, you would need to examine the last octet in binary. This process of extracting the network address from a host address will be explained in the section "IPv4 Addresses for Different Purposes," later in this chapter.

To begin the conversion process, you start by determining whether the decimal number of an octet is equal to or greater than the largest decimal value represented by the ***most significant bit***. Because the representation of addresses is limited to decimal values for a single octet, you examine only the process of converting 8-bit binary to the decimal values of 0 to 255 in this section. In the highest position, you determine whether the value is equal to or greater than 128. If the value is smaller than 128, you place a 0 in the 128-bit position and move to the 64-bit position.

If the value in the 128-bit position is larger than or equal to 128, place a 1 in the 128 position and subtract 128 from the number being converted. You then compare the remainder of this operation to the next smaller value, 64. You continue this process for all the remaining bit positions: 32, 16, 8, 4, 2, and 1. Figure 6-1 demonstrates the steps using the conversion of 172 to 10101100.

Figure 6-1   Decimal-to-Binary Conversion Steps

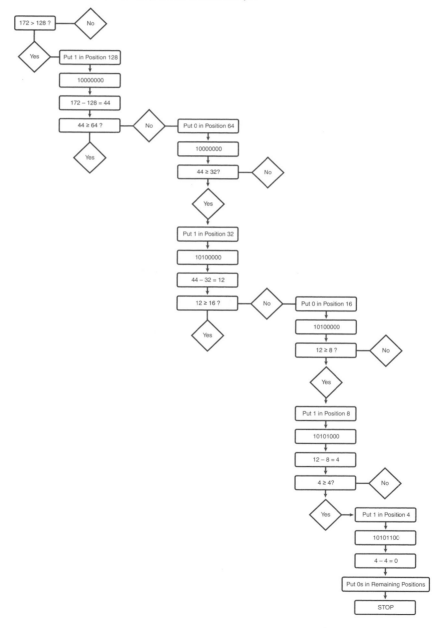

The following is the entire conversion of 172.16.4.20 from dotted decimal notation to binary notation, showing the math in all steps. Although you will learn to short-cut some of these steps, you should study this process carefully to ensure that you can perform these conversions.

To make the conversion, you need to convert each octet individually. This process begins with the conversion of the most significant octet. The following describes the steps of the conversion of decimal 172, as shown in Figure 6-2.

How To 🔍

Step 1.   Because 172 is NOT less than 128, place a 1 in the 128 position and subtract 128 (1 * 128).

Step 2.   Because 44 is less than 64, place a 0 in the 64 position and subtract 0 (0 * 64).

Step 3.   Because 44 is NOT less than 32, place a 1 in the 32 position and subtract 32 (1 * 32).

Step 4.   Because 12 is less than 16, place a 0 in the 16 position and subtract 0 (0 * 16).

Step 5.   Because 12 is NOT less than 8, place a 1 in the 8 position and subtract 8 (1 * 8).

Step 6.   Because 4 is NOT less than 4, place a 1 in the 4 position and subtract 4 (1 * 4).

Step 7.   Because 0 is less than 2, place a 0 in the 2 position and subtract 0 (0 * 2).

Step 8.   Because 0 is less than 1, place a 0 in the 1 position and subtract 0 (0 * 1).

Figure 6-2   Conversion of Decimal 172 to Binary

Step 1 172 NOT < 128	172 − 128	1 128						
Step 2 44 < 64	44 − 0		0 64					
Step 3 44 NOT < 32	44 − 32			1 32				
Step 4 12 < 16	12 − 0				0 16			
Step 5 12 NOT < 8	12 − 8					1 8		
Step 6 4 NOT < 4	4 − 4						1 4	
Step 7 0 < 2	0 − 0							0 2
Step 8 0 < 1	0 − 0								0 1
	0							
	1	0	1	0	1	1	0	0

Answer: 172 = 10101100

The following describes the steps of converting decimal 16, as shown in Figure 6-3:

Step 1. Because 16 is less than 128, place a 0 in the 128 position and subtract 0 (0 * 128).

Step 2. Because 16 is less than 64, place a 0 in the 64 position and subtract 0 (0 * 64).

Step 3. Because 16 is less than 32, place a 0 in the 32 position and subtract 0 (0 * 32).

Step 4. Because 16 is NOT less than 16, place a 1 in the 16 position and subtract 16 (1 * 16).

Step 5. Because 0 is less than 8, place a 0 in the 8 position and subtract 0 (0 * 8).

Step 6. Because 0 is less than 4, place a 0 in the 4 position and subtract 0 (0 * 4).

Step 7. Because 0 is less than 2, place a 0 in the 2 position and subtract 0 (0 * 2).

Step 8. Because 0 is less than 1, place a 0 in the 1 position and subtract 0 (0 * 1).

Figure 6-3   Conversion of Decimal 16 to Binary

		128	64	32	16	8	4	2	1
Step 1 16 < 128	16 − 0	0							
Step 2 16 < 64	16 − 0		0						
Step 3 16 < 32	44 − 0			0					
Step 4 16 NOT < 16	16 − 16				1				
Step 5 0 < 8	0 − 0					0			
Step 6 0 < 4	0 − 0						0		
Step 7 0 < 2	0 − 0							0	
Step 8 0 < 1	0 − 0								0
	0	0	0	0	1	0	0	0	0

Answer: 16 = 00010000

The following describes the steps of converting decimal 4, as shown in Figure 6-4:

Step 1. Because 4 is less than 128, place a 0 in the 128 position and subtract 0 (0 * 128).

Step 2. Because 4 is less than 64, place a 0 in the 64 position and subtract 0 (0 * 64).

Step 3. Because 4 is less than 32, place a 0 in the 32 position and subtract 0 (0 * 32).

Step 4.   Because 4 is less than 16, place a 0 in the 16 position and subtract 0 (0 * 16).

Step 5.   Because 4 is less than 8, place a 0 in the 8 position and subtract 0 (0 * 8).

Step 6.   Because 4 is NOT less than 4, place a 1 in the 4 position and subtract 1 (1 * 4).

Step 7.   Because 0 is less than 2, place a 0 in the 2 position and subtract 0 (0 * 2).

Step 8.   Because 0 is less than 1, place a 0 in the 1 position and subtract 0 (0 * 1).

Figure 6-4   Conversion of Decimal 4 to Binary

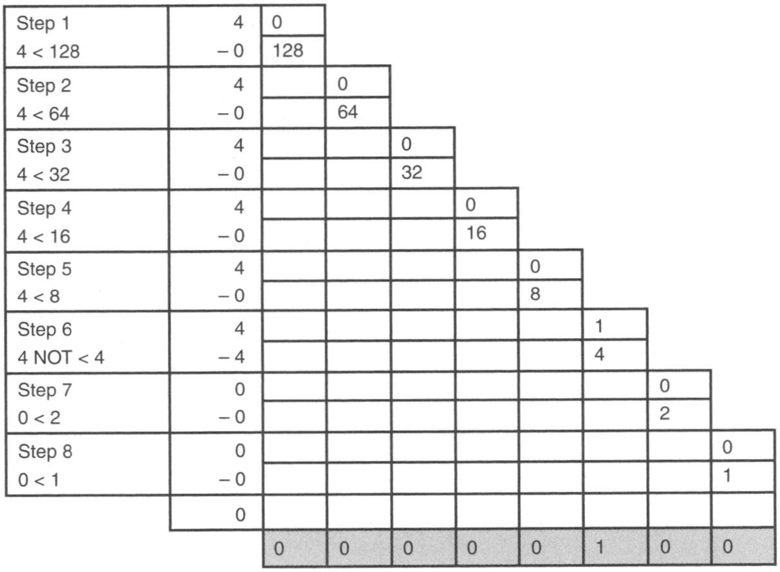

		128	64	32	16	8	4	2	1
Step 1 4 < 128	4 − 0	0 128							
Step 2 4 < 64	4 − 0		0 64						
Step 3 4 < 32	4 − 0			0 32					
Step 4 4 < 16	4 − 0				0 16				
Step 5 4 < 8	4 − 0					0 8			
Step 6 4 NOT < 4	4 − 4						1 4		
Step 7 0 < 2	0 − 0							0 2	
Step 8 0 < 1	0 − 0								0 1
	0	0	0	0	0	0	1	0	0

Answer: 4 = 00000100

The following describes the steps of converting decimal 20, as shown in Figure 6-5:

Step 1.   Because 20 is less than 128, place a 0 in the 128 position and subtract 0 (0 * 128).

Step 2.   Because 20 is less than 64, place a 0 in the 64 position and subtract 0 (0 * 64).

Step 3.   Because 20 is less than 32, place a 0 in the 32 position and subtract 0 (0 * 32).

Step 4.   Because 20 is NOT less than 16, place a 1 in the 16 position and subtract 16 (1 * 16).

Step 5.   Because 4 is less than 8, place a 0 in the 8 position and subtract 0 (0 * 8).

Step 6.   Because 4 is NOT less than 4, place a 1 in the 4 position and subtract 1 (1 * 4).

Step 7.   Because 0 is less than 2, place a 0 in the 2 position and subtract 0 (0 * 2).

Step 8.   Because 0 is less than 1, place a 0 in the 1 position and subtract 0 (0 * 1).

Figure 6-5 Conversion of Decimal 20 to Binary

Step			128	64	32	16	8	4	2	1
Step 1 20 < 128	20 − 0	0 128								
Step 2 20 < 64	20 − 0		0 64							
Step 3 20 < 32	20 − 0			0 32						
Step 4 20 NOT < 16	20 − 16				1 16					
Step 5 4 < 8	4 − 0					0 8				
Step 6 4 NOT < 4	4 − 4						1 4			
Step 7 0 < 2	0 − 0							0 2		
Step 8 0 < 1	0 − 0								0 1	
	0									
		0	0	0	1	0	1	0	0

Answer: 20 = 00010100

Addressing Types of Communication: Unicast, Broadcast, Multicast

In an IPv4 network, the hosts can communicate in one of three different ways:

- **Unicast:** The process of sending a packet from one host to an individual host

- **Broadcast:** The process of sending a packet from one host to all hosts in the network

- **Multicast:** The process of sending a packet from one host to a selected group of hosts

Each of these three types supports different types of communication in the data networks and uses different IPv4 destination addresses. In all three cases, the IPv4 address of the originating host is placed in the packet header as the source address.

Unicast Communication and Addresses

The most common type of communication is unicast. This is the normal host-to-host communication in both a client/server and a peer-to-peer network. For unicast communication, the host addresses assigned to the two end devices are used as the source and destination IPv4 addresses. During the encapsulation process, the source host places its IPv4 address in the unicast packet header as the source host address and the IPv4 address of the destination host in the packet header as the destination address. The communication using a unicast packet can be forwarded through an internetwork using the same addresses.

Figure 6-6 shows an example of IPv4 unicast communication from computer A with the address 172.16.4.1 to the printer with the address 172.16.4.253. In the communication represented, computer A creates a single packet addressed to the Layer 3 address of the printer. This packet is then forwarded by the services at the lower layers to the printer. If a copy of this packet should arrive at an end device whose address does not match this address, that host will discard the packet.

Figure 6-6   Unicast Communication

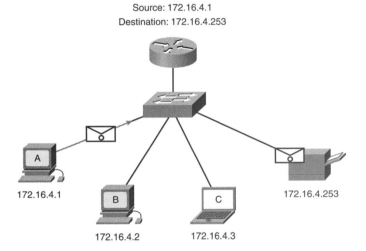

Note

In this book, all communication between devices is unicast communication unless otherwise noted.

Broadcast Communication and Addresses

Layer 4 broadcast communication is the process of sending a packet from one host to all hosts in the network. Unlike unicast communication, which uses the destination host address, broadcast and multicast communication use special addresses as the destination address. This special address, called the ***broadcast address***, allows all the receiving hosts to accept the packet. When a host receives a packet with the broadcast address as the destination, it processes the packet as it would a packet to its unicast address. Using these special addresses, broadcasts are generally restricted to the local network.

Broadcast transmission is used for the location of special services/devices for which the address is not known or when a host needs to provide information to all the hosts on the network. Some examples for using broadcast transmission are as follows:

- Mapping upper-layer addresses to lower-layer addresses

- Requesting an address

- Exchanging routing information by routing protocols

When a host needs information, the host sends a request, called a *query*, to the broadcast address. All hosts in the network receive and process this query. One or more of the hosts with the requested information will respond, typically using unicast. Similarly, when a host needs to send information to the hosts on a network, it creates and sends a broadcast packet with the information.

Unlike unicast, where the packets can be routed throughout the internetwork, broadcast packets are usually restricted to the local network and not forwarded by a router. This restriction is dependent on the configuration of the router that borders the network and the type of broadcast.

There are two types of broadcasts: ***directed broadcast*** and ***limited broadcast***. Each of these two types of broadcasts uses a different method of IPv4 addressing.

Directed Broadcast

A directed broadcast is sent to all hosts on a specific network. This type of broadcast is useful for sending a broadcast to all hosts on a nonlocal network. Directed broadcast uses an IPv4 destination address that is the highest address in a network. This is the network address with all 1s in the host bits. For example, for a host outside the network to communicate with the hosts within the 172.16.4.0 /24 network, the destination address of the packet would be 172.16.4.255. Although routers do not forward directed broadcasts by default, they can be configured to do so.

Limited Broadcast

The limited broadcast is used for communication that is limited to the hosts on the local network. These packets use a destination IPv4 address of all 1s (255.255.255.255). Routers do not forward this broadcast. Packets addressed to the limited broadcast address will only appear on the local network. For this reason, an IPv4 network is also referred to as a broadcast domain. Routers form the boundary for a broadcast domain. As an example, a host within the 172.16.4.0 /24 network would broadcast to all the hosts in its network using a packet with a destination address of 255.255.255.255.

Figure 6-7 represents a limited broadcast from host A with the address 172.16.4.1. In this example, the source host creates a single packet addressed to the Layer 3 broadcast address. The lower-layer services will use a corresponding data link layer address to forward this packet to all the hosts. When a copy of this packet arrives at each end device, the devices recognize that it is addressed to all the devices and processes the packet.

Figure 6-7   Broadcast Communication

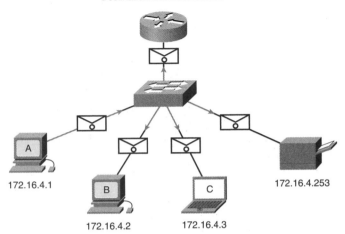

As presented earlier, when a packet is broadcast, it uses resources on the network and forces every host on the network that receives the packet to process it. Therefore, broadcast traffic should be limited so that it does not adversely affect the performance of the network or devices. Because routers separate broadcast domains, subdividing networks with excessive broadcast traffic can improve network performance.

Multicast Communication and Addresses

Multicast transmission is designed to conserve the bandwidth of the IPv4 network. It reduces traffic by allowing a host to send a single packet to a selected set of hosts. To reach multiple destination hosts using unicast communication, a source host would need to send an individual packet addressed to each host. With multicast, the source host can send a single packet that can reach thousands of destination hosts.

The following are some examples of multicast transmission:

- Video and audio broadcasts
- Routing information exchange by some routing protocols
- Distribution of software
- News feeds

Hosts that want to receive particular multicast data are called *multicast clients*. The multi-cast clients use services initiated by a client program to subscribe to the *multicast group*. Each multicast group is represented by a single IPv4 multicast destination address. When an IPv4 host subscribes to a multicast group, the host processes packets addressed to this mul-ticast address as well as packets addressed to its uniquely allocated unicast address. As you will see, IPv4 has set aside a special block of addresses from 224.0.0.0 to 239.255.255.255 as addresses for multicast groups. Unicast packets use the IPv4 host address of the destina-tion host as the destination address and can be routed through an internetwork. The *scope* of multicast traffic is often limited to the local network or routed through an internetwork.

In the multicast communication shown in Figure 6-8, the source host A, with the address 172.16.4.1, creates a single packet addressed to the multicast address 224.10.10.5. In this example, host C and host D have an application or service running that subscribes to this multicast group. When a copy of this packet arrives, these devices will process the packet.

Figure 6-8   Multicast Communication

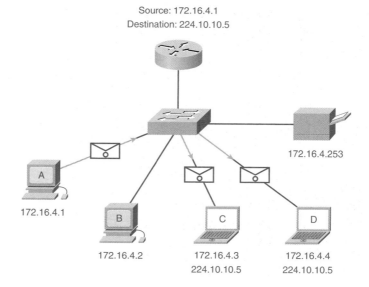

The IPv4 addresses from 224.0.0.0 to 239.255.255.255 are reserved for multicast communi-cation. This multicast address range is subdivided into different types of addresses: *reserved link-local addresses* and *globally scoped addresses*. One additional type of multicast address is the *administratively scoped addresses*, also called *limited-scope addresses*.

The IPv4 multicast addresses 224.0.0.0 to 224.0.0.255 are reserved link-local addresses. These addresses are used for multicast groups on a local network. Packets to these destina-tions are always transmitted with a Time to Live (TTL) value of 1. Therefore, a router that connects the local network should never forward them outside the local network. A typical use of reserved link-local addresses is in routing protocols using multicast transmission to exchange routing information.

The globally scoped addresses are 224.0.1.0 to 238.255.255.255. They can be used to multi-cast data across the Internet. For example, 224.0.1.1 has been reserved for *Network Time Protocol (NTP)* to synchronize the time-of-day clocks of network devices.

Show Unicast, Broadcast, and Multicast Traffic (6.2.3.4)

In this activity, you will be able to visualize unicasts, broadcasts, and multicasts by using Packet Tracer in simulation mode. Use file e1-6234.pka on the CD-ROM that accompanies this book to perform this activity using Packet Tracer.

Note

You can find more information about broadcasts by reading RFC 919, "Broadcasting Internet Datagrams," at http://www.ietf.org/rfc/rfc0919.txt?number=919.

Cisco provides many articles about multicast, including the following:

- http://www.cisco.com/en/US/tech/tk828/technologies_white_paper09186a0080092942.shtml
- http://www.cisco.com/univercd/cc/td/doc/cisintwk/ito_doc/ipmulti.htm#wp1020604

IPv4 Addresses for Different Purposes

Besides the addresses in the IPv4 address range that are reserved for multicast, many of the IPv4 unicast addresses have been reserved for special purposes. Some of these addresses limit the scope or functionality of the hosts to which they are assigned. Other reserved addresses cannot be assigned to hosts. In the next sections, some of these reserved addresses will be presented.

Types of Addresses in an IPv4 Network Range

Within each IPv4 network, there are three types of addresses:

- **Network address:** A special address that refers to the network
- **Broadcast address:** A special address used to send data to all hosts in the network
- **Host addresses:** The unicast addresses assigned to the end devices in the network

Within each network, there are two addresses that cannot be assigned to devices: network address and broadcast address. The other addresses allocated to a network are the host addresses to be assigned to the individual devices.

Network Address

The network address is a standard way to refer to a network. For example, you could refer to the network inside the circle in Figure 6-9 as "the 10.0.0.0 network." This is a much more convenient and descriptive way to refer to the network than using a term like "the first network." All hosts in the 10.0.0.0 network will have the same network bits.

Figure 6-9   Network, Broadcast, and Host Addresses

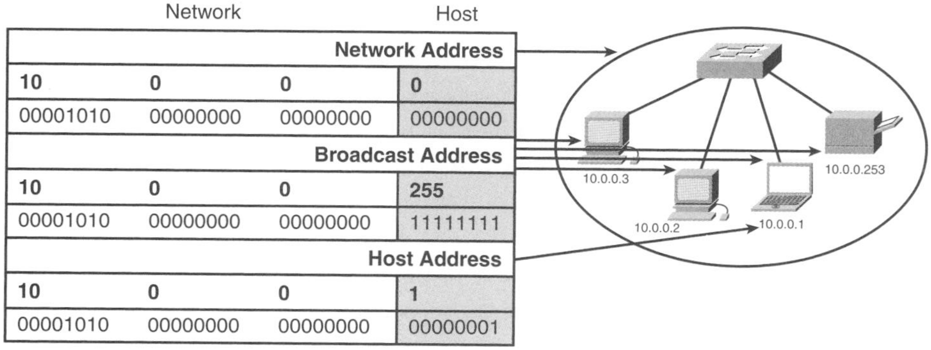

This address cannot be assigned to a device and is, therefore, not used as an address for communication in the network. It is only used as a reference to the network. Within the IPv4 address range of a network, the lowest address is reserved for the network address. This address has a 0 for each host bit in the host portion of the address.

Broadcast Address

The IPv4 broadcast address within a network is the directed broadcast address. Unlike the network address, this address is used in communication to all the hosts in a network. This special address for each network allows a single packet to communicate to all the hosts in that network. To send data to all hosts in a network, a host can send a single packet that is addressed to the broadcast address of the network. For example in Figure 6-9 in the preceding section, to communicate with all the hosts in this network, use a destination address 10.0.0.255, which is the broadcast address for the network.

The broadcast address uses the highest address in the network range. This is the address in which the bits in the host portion are all 1s. For the network 10.0.0.0 with 24 network bits in Figure 6-9, the broadcast address would be 10.0.0.255.

Host Addresses

As described previously, every end device requires a unique unicast address to deliver a packet to that host. In IPv4 addresses, you can assign the values between the network address and the broadcast address to the devices in that network. These are called the host addresses.

In Figure 6-9, the addresses between the network address of 10.0.0.0 and the broadcast address of 10.0.0.255 are the host addresses. This means that the addresses 10.0.0.1 to 10.0.0.254 can be assigned to the hosts in this logical network.

Network Prefixes

When you examine a network address, you might ask, "How do you know how many bits of this address represent the network portion and how many bits represent the host portion?" The answer is the prefix mask. When an IPv4 network address is expressed, you add a *prefix length* to the network address. This prefix length is the number of bits in the address that gives the network portion. This prefix length is written in *slash format*. That is a forward slash (/) followed by the number of network bits. For example, in 172.16.4.0 /24, the /24 is the prefix length. This tells you that the first 24 bits are the network address. The remaining 8 bits, the last octet, are the host portion.

Networks are not always assigned a /24 prefix. Depending on the number of hosts on the network, the prefix assigned can be different. Having a different prefix number changes the host range and broadcast address for each network. Notice that the network addresses in Table 6-9 remain the same, but the host range and the broadcast address are different for the different prefix lengths. You can also see that the number of hosts that can be addressed on the network changes as well.

Table 6-9   Using Different Prefixes for the 172.16.4.0 Network

Network	Network Address	Host Range	Broadcast Address
172.16.4.0 /24	172.16.4.0	172.16.4.1–172.16.4.254	172.16.4.255
172.16.4.0 /25	172.16.4.0	172.16.4.1–172.16.4.126	172.16.4.127
172.16.4.0 /26	172.16.4.0	172.16.4.1–172.16.4.62	172.16.4.63
172.16.4.0 /27	172.16.4.0	172.16.4.1–172.16.4.30	172.16.4.31

Subnet Mask: Defining the Network and Host Portions of the Address

Another question you might ask is, "How do the network devices know how many bits are the network portion and how many bits are the host portion?" The answer to this question is the subnet mask.

The prefix and the subnet mask are different ways of representing the same information: the network portion of an address. The prefix length tells you the number of bits in the address that are the network portion in a way that is easier to communicate to humans. The subnet mask is used in data networks to define this network portion for the devices.

The subnet mask is a 32-bit value used with the IPv4 address that specifies the network portion of the address to the network devices. The subnet mask uses 1s and 0s to indicate which bits of the IPv4 address are network bits and which bits are hosts bits. The subnet mask is expressed in the same dotted decimal format as the IPv4 address.

There is a one-to-one correlation between the bits in the IPv4 address and the subnet mask. The subnet mask is created by placing a binary 1 in each appropriate bit position that represents a network bit of the address and placing a binary 0 in the remaining bit positions that represent the host portion of the address.

A /24 prefix represents a subnet mask of 255.255.255.0 (11111111.11111111.11111111.00000000). The first three octets, the higher-order 24 bits, are all 1s. The remaining low-order bits of the subnet mask are 0s, indicating the host address within the network.

For example, examine the host 172.16.4.35/27 shown in Table 6-10.

Table 6-10   Determining the Network Address for the Host 172.16.4.35 /27

	Dotted Decimal				Binary Octets			
Host	172	16	4	35	10101100	00010000	00000100	00100011
Mask	255	255	255	224	11111111	11111111	11111111	11100000
Network	172	16	4	32	10101100	00010000	00000100	00100000

Because the high-order bits of the subnet masks are contiguous 1s, there are only a limited number of subnet values within an octet. You only need to expand an octet if the network and host division falls within that octet. Therefore, there is a limited number of 8-bit patterns used in address masks. These bit patterns for the subnet masks, the number of network bits and the number of data bits within the octet, are shown in Table 6-11.

Table 6-11   Subnet Mask Values Within an Octet

Mask (Decimal)	Mask (Binary)	Network Bits	Host Bits
0	00000000	0	8
128	10000000	1	7
192	11000000	2	6
224	11100000	3	5
240	11110000	4	4
248	11111000	5	3
252	11111100	6	2
254	11111110	7	1
255	11111111	8	0

If the subnet mask for an octet is represented by 255, all the equivalent bits in that octet of the address are network bits. Similarly, if the subnet mask for an octet is represented by 0, all the equivalent bits in that octet of the address are host bits. In each of these cases, it is not necessary to expand this octet to binary to determine the network and host portions. Similarly, you can use the other patterns to determine the number of network and data bits inside the octet.

IPv4 Experimental Address Range

Expressed in dotted decimal format, the IPv4 address range is 0.0.0.0 to 255.255.255.255. As you have already seen, not all these addresses can be used as unicast host addresses for unicast communication. Recall that the block of addresses from 224.0.0.0 to 239.255.255.255 is reserved for the addressing of multicast groups.

All the IPv4 addresses higher than the multicast range are also reserved for special purposes. Except for the limited broadcast address of 255.255.255.255, the address range of 240.0.0.0 to 255.255.255.254 is the IPv4 experimental addresses. Currently, these addresses are listed as *reserved for future use* (RFC 3330). This suggests that they could be converted to usable addresses. Currently, they cannot be used in IPv4 networks. However, these addresses are used for research or experimentation.

After accounting for the ranges reserved for experimental addresses and multicast addresses, this leaves an address range of 0.0.0.0 to 223.255.255.255 that could be used for IPv4 hosts. However, this range includes many addresses that are already reserved for special purposes. Although some of these addresses have been previously presented, the major reserved addresses are discussed in the next sections.

Public and Private Addresses

Although most IPv4 host addresses are *public addresses* designated for use in networks that are accessible on the Internet, there are blocks of addresses used in networks that require limited or no Internet access. These addresses are called *private addresses*.

The private address blocks are

- 10.0.0.0 /8 (10.0.0.0 to 10.255.255.255)
- 172.16.0.0 /12 (172.16.0.0 to 172.31.255.255)
- 192.168.0.0 /16 (192.168.0.0 to 192.168.255.255)

Private space address blocks are set aside for use in private networks. The use of these addresses need not be unique among outside networks. Hosts that do not require access to the Internet at large can make unrestricted use of private addresses. However, the internal networks still must design network address schemes to ensure that the hosts in the private networks use IP addresses that are unique within their networking environment.

Many hosts in different networks can use the same private space addresses. Packets using these addresses as the source or destination should not appear on the public Internet. The router or firewall device at the perimeter of these private networks must block or translate these addresses. Even if these packets were to make their way to the Internet, the routers would not have routes to forward them to the appropriate private network.

Because packets with private space destination addresses are not routable across the Internet, services to translate packets from hosts using private addresses are required. As represented in Figure 6-10, these services, called *Network Address Translation (NAT)*, can be implemented on a device at the edge of the private network. At the perimeter router, NAT changes the private space addresses in the IPv4 packet header to a public space address.

Figure 6-10   NAT on the Perimeter Device

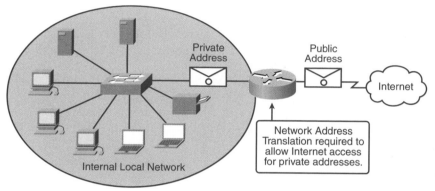

By "borrowing" a public address, these hosts in the private network can communicate to out-side networks. While there are some limitations and performance issues with NAT, clients for most applications can access services over the Internet without noticeable problems.

Note

NAT will be covered in detail in the Accessing the WAN course and companion book.

The addresses in the IPv4 unicast host range are designed for hosts that are publicly acces-sible from the Internet. Even within these address blocks, many addresses are designated for other special purposes, as described in the next section.

Special Unicast IPv4 Addresses

In addition to the addresses that cannot be assigned to hosts, special addresses can also be assigned to hosts but with restrictions on how those hosts can interact within the network. These special addresses include the following:

- Default route
- Loopback address
- Link-local address
- Test-net addresses

The following sections summarize these special IPv4 addresses.

Default Route

The IPv4 default route is 0.0.0.0. This default route is a "catch all" route to route packets when a more specific route is not available. The use of this address also reserves all addresses in the 0.0.0.0 /8 address block (0.0.0.0–0.255.255.255).

Loopback

Another reserved address block is 127.0.0.0 /8 (127.0.0.0 to 127.255.255.255). This is reserved in the IPv4 hosts for the 127.0.0.1 *loopback*. The loopback is a special address that hosts use to direct traffic to themselves. The loopback address creates a shortcut method for TCP/IP applications and services that run on the same device to communicate with one another. By using the loopback address instead of the assigned IPv4 host address, two services on the same host can bypass the lower layers of the TCP/IP stack. You can also ping the loopback address to test the configuration of TCP/IP on the local host.

Although only the single 127.0.0.1 address is used, address block 127.0.0.0 /8 (127.0.0.0 to 127.255.255.255) is reserved. Any address within this block will loop back within the local host. No address within this block should ever appear on any network.

Link-Local Addresses

IPv4 addresses in the 169.254.0.0 /16 address blocks (169.254.0.0 to 169.254.255.255) are designated as *link-local addresses*. These addresses can be automatically assigned to the local host by the operating system in environments where no IP configuration is available. These might be used in a small peer-to-peer network or for a host that could not automatically obtain an address from a Dynamic Host Configuration Protocol (DHCP) server.

Communication using IPv4 link-local addresses is only suitable for communication with other devices connected to the same network. A host *must not* send a packet with an IPv4 link-local destination address to any router for forwarding and should set the IPv4 TTL for these packets to 1.

Link-local addresses do not provide services outside the local network. However, many client/server and peer-to-peer applications will work properly with IPv4 link-local addresses on the local network.

Test-Net Addresses

The *test-net addresses* are set aside for teaching and learning purposes. This is the address block 192.0.2.0 /24 (192.0.2.0 to 192.0.2.255). These addresses can be used in documentation and network examples. Unlike the experimental addresses, network devices *will* accept the test-net addresses in their configurations. You can often find these addresses used with the domain names example.com or example.net in RFCs and vendor and protocol documentation. Addresses within this block should not appear on the Internet.

Table 6-12 is a summary of the reserved and special-purpose IPv4 addresses presented in this section. These do not represent all the special address blocks used in IPv4 networks. Additionally, the status of these blocks can be changed. You should consult the RFCs for any changes.

Table 6-12   Major Reserved and Special-Purpose IPv4 Addresses

Type	Block	Range	Reference
Multicast	224.0.0.0 /4	224.0.0.0–239.255.255.255	RFC 1700
Network address	—	—	One per network
Broadcast address	—	—	One per network plus 255.255.255.255
Experimental addresses	240.0.0.0 /4	240.0.0.0–255.255.255.254	RFC 3330
Private space addresses	10.0.0.0 /8 172.16.0.0 /12 192.168.0.0 /16	10.0.0.0–10.255.255.255 172.16.0.0–172.31.255.255 192.168.0.0–192.168.255.255	RFC 1918
Default route	0.0.0.0 /8	0.0.0.0–0.255.255.255	RFC 1700
Loopback	127.0.0.0 /8	127.0.0.0–127.255.255.255	RFC 1700
Link-local addresses	169.254.0.0 /16	169.254.0.0–169.254.255.255	RFC 3927
Test-net addresses	192.0.2.0 /24	192.0.2.0–192.0.2.255	—

> **Note**
>
> You can find more information about link-local addresses by reading RFC 3927, "Dynamic Configuration of IPv4 Link-Local Addresses," at http://www.ietf.org/rfc/rfc3927.txt.
>
> RFC 3330, "Special-Use IPv4 Addresses," is available at http://www.ietf.org/rfc/rfc3330.txt.

Legacy IPv4 Addressing

In the early 1980s, the IPv4 addressing range was divided into three different classes: class A, class B, and class C. Each class of addresses represented networks of a specific fixed size. At that time in the development of IP, there were no subnet masks to specify the network and host portion of the addresses. To distinguish between the network sizes, each of these classes of addresses was assigned address ranges. Devices could examine the high-order address to determine how many network bits were used to define the network. For example, for the address 192.168.2.2, because this address is in the class C addressing range, a network device recognized this as a class C network and identified the standard class C prefix of /24.

In the late 1980s and early 1990s, the subnet mask was added to the IPv4 addressing scheme to allow these fixed-size networks to be subdivided or subnetted. However, many of the restrictions of these classes remained.

By the mid-1990s, most of the restrictions of this class-based addressing system had been removed from the standards and the equipment operation. However, the associated practices developed over the decade perpetuated this classful system. Even today, some remnants of this addressing system still affect network practices and operation. For this reason, you should be familiar with these network classes. Table 6-13 summarizes the address classes.

Table 6-13   IPv4 Network Classes

Address Class	First Octet Range	Prefix and Mask	Number of Possible Networks	Number of Hosts per Network
A	1 to 127	/8 255.0.0.0	126 (2^7)	16,777,214 (2^{24}–2)
B	128 to 191	/16 255.255.0.0	16,384 (2^{14})	65,534 (2^{16}–2)
C	192 to 223	/24 255.255.255.0	2,097,159 (2^{21})	254 (2^8–2)

Historic Network Classes

RFC 1700 defined the unicast ranges class A, class B, and class C addresses into specific sizes. It also defined class D (multicast) and class E (experimental) addresses, as previously presented in the "Addressing Types of Communication: Unicast, Broadcast, Multicast" and "IPv4 Experimental Address Range" sections.

A company or organization was assigned an entire class A, class B, or class C address block. This use of address space is referred to as *classful addressing*.

Class A Blocks

The class A address block was designed to support extremely large networks with more than 16 million host addresses. Class A IPv4 addresses used a fixed /8 prefix with the first octet to indicate the network address. The remaining three octets were used for host addresses.

To reserve address space for the remaining address classes, all class A addresses required that the most significant bit of the high-order octet be a 0. This meant that there were only 128 possible class A networks, 0.0.0.0 /8 to 127.0.0.0 /8, before taking out the reserved address blocks. Even though the class A addresses reserved one-half of the address space, because of their limit of 128 networks, they could only be allocated to approximately 120 companies or organizations.

Class B Blocks

Class B address space was designed to support the needs of moderate- to large-size networks with more than 65,000 hosts. A class B IP address used the two high-order octets to indicate the network address. The other two octets specified host addresses. As with class A, address space for the remaining address classes needed to be reserved.

For class B addresses, the most significant 2 bits of the high-order octet were 10. This restricted the address block for class B to 128.0.0.0 /16 to 191.255.0.0 /16. Class B had slightly more efficient allocation of addresses than class A because it equally divided 25 percent of the total IPv4 address space among approximately 16,000 networks.

Class C Blocks

The class C address space was the most commonly available of the historic address classes. This address space was intended to provide addresses for small networks with a maximum of 254 hosts.

Class C address blocks used a /24 prefix. This meant that a class C network used only the last octet as host addresses, with the three high-order octets used to indicate the network address.

Class C address blocks set aside address space for class D (multicast) and class E (experimental) by using a fixed value of 110 for the three most significant bits of the high-order octet. This restricted the address block for class C to 192.0.0.0 /16 to 223.255.255.0 /16. Although it occupied only 12.5 percent of the total IPv4 address space, it could provide addresses to 2 million networks.

Limits to the Classful Addressing System

Not all organizations' addressing requirements fit well into one of these three classes. Classful allocation of address space often wasted many addresses, which exhausted the availability of IPv4 addresses. For example, a company that had a network with 260 hosts would need to be given a class B address with more than 65,000 addresses.

Even though this classful system was all but abandoned in the late 1990s, the remnants of it are in effect in networks today. For example, when you assign an IPv4 address to a computer, the operating system examines the address being assigned to determine whether it is a class A, class B, or class C address. The operating system then assumes the prefix used by that class and makes the appropriate subnet mask assignment.

Another example is the assumption of the mask by some routing protocols. When some routing protocols receive an advertised route, it can assume the prefix length based on the class of the address.

Classless Addressing

The system that is currently in use is referred to as *classless addressing*. With the classless system, address blocks appropriate to the number of hosts are assigned to companies or organizations without regard to the unicast class. Associated with this classless addressing system are other practices, such as using networks of fixed sized, that have made IPv4 addressing more viable.

Assigning Addresses

Network personnel must design the addresses scheme for the network. The following sections present the practices and processes of providing addresses for networks.

Planning to Address the Network

The allocation of network layer address space within the corporate network needs to be well designed. Network administrators should not randomly select the addresses used in the networks.

Network administrators should plan and document the allocation of these addresses inside the networks for the following purposes:

- Preventing duplication of addresses
- Providing and controlling access
- Monitoring security and performance

The following sections describe these three reasons for planning and documentation and explain considerations for assigning private addresses within a network. There are many aspects of address planning and many different ways to allocate the addresses. For example, you can group your network addresses for hosts with different types of users. These sections serve as a beginning point to introduce you to the planning process.

Preventing Duplication of Addresses

As you already know, each host in an internetwork must have a unique address. Without the proper planning and documentation of these network allocations, you could easily assign an address to more than one host. Duplicate addresses will impede the operation of the hosts. Duplicate IP addresses will prevent the hosts trying to use the same address from communicating across the network. A duplicate IP address for a vital device on the network, such as an intermediary device or a server, can affect the operation of many other hosts.

Providing and Controlling Access

Some hosts, such as servers, provide resources to the internal network as well as to the external network. Access to these resources can be controlled by the Layer 3 address. If the addresses for these resources are not planned and documented, the security and accessibility of the devices are not easily controlled. For example, if a server has a random address assigned, blocking access to its address is difficult and clients might not be able to locate this resource.

Monitoring Security and Performance

Similarly, you will need to monitor the security and performance of the network hosts and the network as a whole. As part of the monitoring process, you examine network traffic, looking for addresses that are generating or receiving excessive packets. With the properly planned and documented network addressing, you can identify the device on the network that has a problematic address.

Assigning Addresses Within a Network

As you have already learned, hosts are associated with an IPv4 network by a common network portion of the address. Within a network, there are different types of hosts, such as the following:

- End devices for users
- Servers and peripherals
- Hosts that are accessible from the Internet
- Intermediary devices

Each of these different device types should be allocated to a logical block of addresses *within* the address range of the network. An important part of planning an IPv4 addressing scheme is deciding when private addresses are to be used and where they are to be applied. Considerations include the following:

- Will there be more devices connected to the network than public addresses allocated by the network ISP?

- Will the devices need to be accessed from outside the local network?

- If devices that can be assigned private addresses require access to the Internet, is the network capable of providing a Network Address Translation (NAT) service?

If there are more devices than available public addresses, only those devices that will directly access the Internet, such as web servers, require a public address. A NAT service would allow those devices with private addresses to effectively share the remaining public addresses.

Static or Dynamic Addressing for End-User Devices

Addresses in the network can be assigned to hosts statically or dynamically. The decision whether to use static or dynamic assignment for a particular device depends on several factors described in the following sections.

Addresses for User Devices

In most data networks, the largest population of hosts includes the end devices such as PCs, IP phones, printers, and PDAs. Because this population represents the largest number of devices within a network, the largest number of addresses should be allocated to these hosts. IP addresses can be assigned either statically or dynamically.

Static Assignment of Addresses

With a static assignment, the network administrator must manually configure the network information for a host. At a minimum, this includes entering the host IP address, subnet mask, and default gateway. Static addresses for the interface of a Windows-based computer can be set in the IP Properties screen for the network interface, as shown in Figure 6-11.

Static addresses have some advantages over dynamic addresses. For example, they are useful for printers, servers, and other networking devices that need to be accessible to clients on the network. If hosts normally access a server at a particular IP address, it would cause problems if that address changed. Additionally, static assignment of addressing information can provide increased control of network resources. However, it can be time consuming to enter the information on each host.

Figure 6-11   Statically Assigning Host Addresses

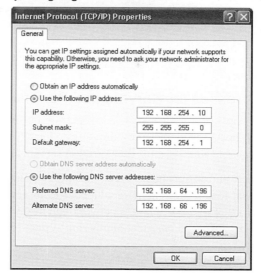

Because a duplicated address affects the host operation, care must be taken not to reuse an address. When using static IP addressing, it is necessary to maintain an accurate list of the IP address assigned to each device.

Dynamic Assignment of Addresses

Because of the challenges associated with static address management, end-user devices often have addresses dynamically assigned, using DHCP.

DHCP enables the automatic assignment of addressing information such as IP address, subnet mask, default gateway, and other configuration information. The configuration of the DHCP server requires that a block of addresses, called an *address pool*, be defined to be assigned to the DHCP clients on a network. Addresses assigned to this pool should be planned so that they exclude any addresses used for the other types of devices.

DHCP is generally the preferred method of assigning IP addresses to hosts on large networks because it reduces the burden on network support staff and virtually eliminates entry errors. Another benefit of DHCP is that an address is not permanently assigned to a host but is only "leased" for a period of time. If the host is powered down or taken off the network, the address is returned to the pool for reuse. This feature is especially helpful for mobile users who come and go on a network.

Selecting Device Addresses

When determining the addresses to be assigned *within* the network, similar devices should be grouped into address ranges. These address ranges should be distinguishable. By examining an address, you should be able to determine what kind of device originates the packet.

Addresses for Servers and Peripherals

Any network resource, such as a server or a printer, should have a static IPv4 address. The client hosts access these resources using the IPv4 addresses of these devices. Therefore, predictable addresses for each of these servers and peripherals are necessary.

Servers and peripherals are a concentration point for network traffic. There are many packets sent to and from the IPv4 addresses of these devices. When monitoring network traffic with a tool like Wireshark, a network administrator should be able to rapidly identify these devices. Using a consistent numbering system for these devices makes the identification easier.

Addresses for Hosts That Are Accessible from the Internet

In most internetworks, only a few devices are accessible by hosts outside the corporation. For the most part, these devices are usually servers of some type. As with all devices in a network that provides network resources, the IPv4 addresses for these devices should be static.

In the case of servers accessible by the Internet, each of these must have a public space address associated with it. Additionally, variations in the address of one of these devices will make this device inaccessible from the Internet. In many cases, these devices are on a network that is numbered using private addresses. This means that the router or firewall at the perimeter of the network must be configured to translate the internal address of the server into a public address. Because of this additional configuration in the perimeter intermediary device, it is even more important that these devices have a predictable address.

Addresses for Intermediary Devices

Intermediary devices are also a concentration point for network traffic. Almost all traffic within or between networks passes through some form of intermediary device. Therefore, these network devices provide an opportune location for network management, monitoring, and security.

Most intermediary devices are assigned Layer 3 addresses, either for the device management or for device operation. Devices such as hubs, switches, and wireless access points do not require IPv4 addresses to operate as intermediary devices. However, to access these devices as hosts to configure, monitor, or troubleshoot network operation, they need to have addresses assigned.

Because you need to know how to communicate with intermediary devices, they should have predictable addresses. Therefore, their addresses are typically assigned manually. Additionally, the addresses of these devices should be in a different range within the network block than user device addresses.

Addresses for Routers and Firewalls

Unlike the other intermediary devices mentioned, routers and firewall devices have an IPv4 address assigned to each interface. Each interface is in a different network and serves as the gateway for the hosts in that network. Typically, the router interface uses either the lowest or the highest address in the network. This assignment should be uniform across all networks in the corporation so that network personnel will always know the gateway of the network no matter which network they are working on.

Router and firewall interfaces are the concentration point for traffic entering and leaving the network. Because the hosts in each network use a router or firewall device interface as the gateway out of the network, many packets flow through these interfaces. Therefore, these devices can play a major role in network security by filtering packets based on source and/or destination IPv4 addresses. Grouping the different types of devices into logical addressing groups makes the assignment and operation of this packet filtering more efficient.

When addresses for devices are grouped by similar functions, you can create rules to address the group of devices instead of having to create individual rules for each device. A single rule can be created using a summary address rather than an individual rule for the address of each device. This allows the devices to have fewer security rules, which greatly streamlines the security function.

Table 6-14 shows an example of designing addressing groups for a network. In this table, we have grouped the devices into four groups: user hosts, servers, peripherals, and networking devices. Each of these device types is assigned to a group of addresses inside its network. Each summary address for each group is shown in the last column. This summary is created for use in security rules. You will learn more about the summary addresses in later courses.

Table 6-14   Device Address Groups Within the 172.16.x.0 /24 Network

Use	Low Address	High Address	Summary Address
User hosts (DHCP pool)	172.16.x.1	172.16.x.127	172.16.x.0 /25
Servers	172.16.x.128	172.16.x.191	172.16.x.128 /26
Peripherals	172.16.x.192	172.16.x.223	172.16.x.192 /27
Networking devices	172.16.x.224	172.16.x.253	172.16.x.224 /27
Router (gateway)	172.16.x.254	—	172.16.x.224 /27

You will also notice in Table 6-14 that the middle octet of the addresses is represented by an *x*. This designates that this same addressing scheme can be used across similar networks in the internetwork. This allows address allocation and security rules to be universally applied in the organization.

Internet Assigned Numbers Authority (IANA)

A company or organization that wants to have network hosts accessible from the Internet must have a block of public addresses assigned. The use of these public addresses is regulated, and the company or organization must have a block of addresses allocated to it. This is true for IPv4, IPv6, and multicast addresses.

IANA (http://www.iana.net) is the master holder of the IP addresses. The IP multicast addresses and the IPv6 addresses are obtained directly from IANA. Until the mid-1990s, all IPv4 address space was managed directly by the IANA. At that time, the IANA allocated remaining IPv4 address space to various other registries to manage for particular purposes or for regional areas. These registration companies are called *Regional Internet Registries (RIR)*. The following are the major registries:

- **AfriNIC (African Network Information Centre):** Africa Region, http://www.afrinic.net

- **APNIC (Asia Pacific Network Information Centre):** Asia/Pacific Region, http://www.apnic.net

- **ARIN (American Registry for Internet Numbers):** North America Region, http://www.arin.net

- **LACNIC (Regional Latin-American and Caribbean IP Address Registry):** Latin America and some Caribbean Islands, http://www.lacnic.net

- **RIPE NCC (Reseaux IP Europeans):** Europe, the Middle East, and Central Asia, http://www.ripe.net

Note

Several resources offer more information about RIRs and the registration process.

To learn more about IPv4 address registries allocations, refer to RFC 1466, "Guidelines for Management of IP Address Space," (http://www.ietf.org/rfc/rfc1466.txt) and RFC 2050, "Internet Registry IP Allocation Guidelines" (http://www.ietf.org/rfc/rfc2050.txt).

The IANA provides information about IPv4 address allocation (http://www.iana.org/ipaddress/ip-addresses.htm).

Look up IP addressing information at ARIN (http://www.arin.net/whois).

ISPs

Most companies or organizations obtain their IPv4 address blocks from an Internet service provider (ISP). An ISP will generally supply a small number of usable IPv4 addresses (6 or 14) to its customers as a part of its services. Larger blocks of addresses can be obtained based on justification of needs and at additional service costs.

In a sense, the ISP loans or rents these addresses to the organization. If you choose to move your Internet connectivity to another ISP, the new ISP will provide you with addresses from the address blocks that have been provided to it. Your previous ISP then returns the blocks loaned to your network to its allocation for loan to another customer.

ISP Services

To get access to the services of the Internet, you have to connect your data network to the Internet using an ISP. ISPs have their own set of internal data networks to manage Internet connectivity and to provide related services. Among the other services that an ISP generally provides to its customers are Domain Name System (DNS) services, e-mail services, and a website. Depending on the level of service required and available, customers use different tiers of an ISP.

ISP Tiers

ISPs are designated by a hierarchy based on their level of connectivity to the *Internet backbone*. Each lower tier obtains connectivity to the backbone through a connection to a higher-tier ISP. Figure 6-12 shows the three tiers of ISPs.

Figure 6-12   Three Tiers of ISPs

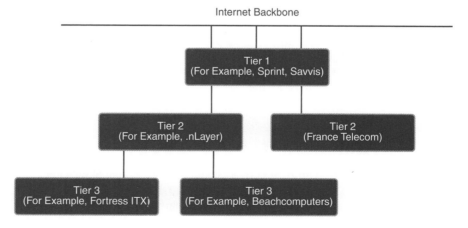

Tier 1

At the top of the ISP hierarchy are tier 1 ISPs. These ISPs are large national or international ISPs directly connected to the Internet backbone. The customers of tier 1 ISPs are either lower-tiered ISPs or large companies and organizations. Because they are at the top of Internet connectivity, they engineer highly reliable connections and services. Among the technologies used to support this reliability are multiple connections to the Internet backbone.

The primary advantages for customers of tier 1 ISPs are reliability and speed. Because these customers are only one connection away from the Internet, there are fewer opportunities for failures or traffic bottlenecks. The drawback for tier 1 ISP customers is the high cost.

Tier 2

Tier 2 ISPs acquire their Internet service from tier 1 ISPs. Tier 2 ISPs generally focus on business customers and usually offer more services than the other two tiers of ISPs. Tier 2 ISPs tend to have the IT resources to operate their own services such as DNS, e-mail servers, and web servers. Other services that tier 2 ISPs can offer include website development and maintenance, e-commerce/e-business, and VoIP.

The primary disadvantage of tier 2 ISPs, as compared to tier 1 ISPs, is slower Internet access. Because tier 2 ISPs are at least one more connection away from the Internet backbone, they also tend to have poorer reliability than tier 1 ISPs.

Tier 3

Tier 3 ISPs purchase their Internet service from tier 2 ISPs. The focus of these ISPs is the retail and home markets in a specific locale. Tier 3 customers typically do not need many of the services required by tier 2 customers. Their primary need is connectivity and support.

These customers often have little or no computer or network expertise. Tier 3 ISPs often bundle Internet connectivity as a part of network and computer service contracts for their customers. Although they might have reduced bandwidth and less reliability than tier 1 and tier 2 providers do, they are often good choices for small- to medium-size companies.

Calculating Addresses

To work with IPv4 networks, you need to be able to develop and determine proper addressing. These skills include the ability to determine whether a particular host is on a network, determine the addresses in a particular network, and determine how to divide an addressing scheme for an internetwork.

In the following sections, you will be presented with techniques to make these determinations. There will also be several examples demonstrating how these are accomplished.

Is the Host on My Network?

As a network associate, one of the determinations you often have to make about a host is "Is it on my network?" or "To what network does this host belong?" To make these determinations, you will need to determine what hosts are in a given network.

ANDing: What Is in Your Network?

Inside data network devices, digital logic is applied for their interpretation of the addresses. When creating or forwarding an IPv4 packet, the destination network address must be extracted from the destination address. This is done by a logic called *AND*.

The IPv4 host address is logically ANDed with its subnet mask to determine the network address to which the host is associated. When this ANDing between the address and the subnet mask is performed, the result yields the network address.

AND Operation

ANDing is one of three basic binary operations used in digital logic. The other two are OR and NOT. While all three are used in data networks, AND is used in determining the network address. Therefore, the discussion in this section is limited to logical AND. Logical AND is the comparison of two bits that yields the following results:

> 1 AND 1 = 1
>
> 1 AND 0 = 0
>
> 0 AND 1 = 0
>
> 0 AND 0 = 0

The result from anything ANDed with a 1 yields a result that is the original bit. That is, 0 AND 1 is 0, and 1 AND 1 is 1. Consequently, anything ANDed with a 0 yields a 0. These properties of ANDing are used with the subnet mask to "mask" the host bits of an IPv4 address. Each bit of the address is ANDed with the corresponding bit of the subnet mask.

Because all the bits of the subnet mask that represent host bits are 0s, the host portion of the resulting network address becomes all 0s. Recall that an IPv4 address with all 0s in the host portion represents the network address. Likewise, all the bits of the subnet mask that indicate the network portion are 1s. When each of these 1s is ANDed with the corresponding bit of the address, the resulting bits are identical to the original address bits.

Reasons to Use AND

An ANDing between the host address and subnet mask is performed by devices in a data network for various reasons. Routers use ANDing to determine an acceptable route for an incoming packet. The router checks the destination address and attempts to associate this address with a next hop. As a packet arrives at a router, the router performs ANDing on the IP destination address in the incoming packet and with the subnet mask of potential routes. This yields a network address that is compared to the route from the routing table whose subnet mask was used.

An originating host must determine whether a packet should be sent directly to a host in the local network or be directed to the gateway. To make this determination, a host must first know its own network address.

A host extracts its network address by ANDing its address with its subnet mask. A logical AND is also performed by an originating host between the destination address of the packet and the subnet mask of the host. This yields the network address of the destination. If this network address matches the network address of the local host, the packet is sent directly to the destination host. If the two network addresses do not match, the packet is sent to the gateway.

Importance of AND

If the routers and end devices calculate these processes without your intervention, why do you need to learn how to AND? The answer is, you need to understand the operation of the network devices. The more you are able to predict the operation of a network, the better equipped you are to design and administer one.

In network verification and troubleshooting, you often need to determine what IPv4 network a host is on or whether two hosts are on the same IP network. You need to make this determination from the perspective of the network devices. Because of improper configuration, a host might see itself on a network that was not the intended one. This can create an operation that seems erratic unless diagnosed by examining the ANDing processes used by the host.

In addition, a router might have many different routes that can satisfy the forwarding of packets to a given destination. The selection of the route used for any given packet is a complex operation. For example, the prefix forming these routes is not directly associated with the networks assigned to the host. This means that a route in the routing table can represent many networks. If there were issues with routing packets, you would need to determine how the router would make the routing decision. Although there are subnet calculators available, it is helpful for a network administrator to know how to manually calculate subnets.

Note

When planning a network implementation, a subnet calculator like the VLSM (CIDR) subnet calculator at http://vlsm-calc.net can be useful. However, no calculators are permitted during certification exams.

ANDing Process

Figure 6-13 shows the ANDing of 192.0.0.1 with a subnet mask of 255.255.255.0. For the first two octets, the subnet mask bits are all 1s (255). For the AND of each of these bits to the host address, the result is the host address bit. For the last two octets, the subnet mask bits are 0s (0). For these AND processes, all the resultants are 0.

Figure 6-13   Applying the Subnet Mask

	Dotted Decimal				Binary Octets			
Host	192	0	0	1	11000000	00000000	00000000	00000001
Mask	255	255	0	0	11111111	11111111	00000000	00000000
AND								
Network	192	0	0	0	11000000	00000000	00000000	00000000

Calculating Network, Hosts, and Broadcast Addresses

Now you might be asking, "How do you determine the network, hosts, and broadcast addresses for a network?" This calculation process requires you to examine these addresses in binary. Calculating the address assignments requires the following steps:

Step 1.   Calculate the network address.

Step 2.   Calculate the lowest host address.

Step 3.   Calculate the broadcast address.

Step 4.   Calculate the highest host address.

Step 5.   Determine the host address range.

In the following sections, you examine address assignments for the 172.16.20.0 /25 network.

Calculating the Network Address

First, determine the network address. The network address is the lowest address in the address block. To represent a network address, all the host bits are 0. With a 25-bit prefix, the last 7 bits are host bits and are 0s.

Figure 6-14 shows the network address for the 172.16.20.0 /25 network.

Figure 6-14 Network Address for the 172.16.20.0 /25 Network

172	16	20	0	
1 0 1 0 1 1 0 0	0 0 0 1 0 0 0 0	0 0 0 1 0 1 0 0	0	0 0 0 0 0 0 0
Network				Host

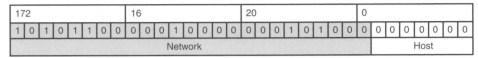

Host bits are all 0s: 0+0+0+0+0+0+0+0=0. So, the network address is 172.16.20.0. This makes the last octet of the address 0. Therefore, the network address is 172.16.20.0.

Calculating the Lowest Host Address

Next, you should calculate the lowest host address. This is always 1 greater than the network address. Therefore, using binary counting, you increment the 1s bit, making the last host bit a 1. Figure 6-15 shows the lowest host address for the network 172.16.20.0 /25.

Figure 6-15 Lowest Host Address for the 172.16.20.0 /25 Network

172	16	20	1	
1 0 1 0 1 1 0 0	0 0 0 1 0 0 0 0	0 0 0 1 0 1 0 0	0	0 0 0 0 0 0 1
Network				Host

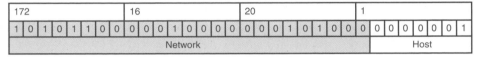

All host bits except the least significant address are all 0s: 0+0+0+0+0+0+0+1=1. With the lowest bit of the host address set to a 1, the address is 172.16.20.1. So, the lowest host address is 172.16.20.1.

Calculating the Broadcast Address

Although it can seem a little out of sequence, it is often easier to calculate the broadcast address before calculating the highest host address. The broadcast address of a network is the highest address in the address block. It requires all the host bits to be set. Therefore, all seven host bits used in this example network are 1s, as shown in Figure 6-16.

Figure 6-16 Broadcast Address for the 172.16.20.0 /25 Network

172	16	20	127	
1 0 1 0 1 1 0 0	0 0 0 1 0 0 0 0	0 0 0 1 0 1 0 0	0	1 1 1 1 1 1 1
Network				Host

All host bits are 1s: 64+32+16+8+4+2+1=127. From the calculation, the value of the last octet is 127. This gives you a broadcast address of 172.16.20.127 for the network 172.16.20.0 /25.

Calculating the Highest Host Address

After determining the broadcast address, you can easily determine the highest host address. It is 1 less than the broadcast address. In Figure 6-17, with a broadcast address of 172.16.20.127, the highest host address would be 172.16.20.126. To determine the highest host address, make the lowest host bit a 0 and all other host bits a 1.

Figure 6-17   Highest Host Address for the 172.16.20.0 /25 Network

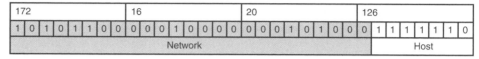

All host bits, except the lowest address, are all 1s: 64+32+16+8+4+2+0=126. This makes the highest host address in this example 172.16.20.126.

Note

Although, for this example, all the octets are expanded, you only need to examine the content of a divided octet, that is, an octet that contains network bits and host bits.

Determining the Host Address Range

Finally, you need to determine the host range for the network. The host range of the network includes all the addresses from the lowest host address to the highest host address inclusive. Therefore in this network, the address range is

172.16.20.1 to 172.16.20.126

These IPv4 unicast addresses can be assigned to the hosts in the logical network 172.16.20.0 /25. A host that is assigned any other address will be in a different logical network.

Tip

Notice that the least significant bit of the network address and the least significant bit of the highest host address are always 0. That makes these values even.

Similarly, the least significant bit of the lowest address and the least significant bit of the broadcast address are always 1. This makes these values odd.

This is a quick check to help you determine whether you have the correct values.

Basic Subnetting

Another IPv4 addressing skill helpful for a network associate is the ability to plan the subnetting of a network. The address range used in an internetwork needs to be divided into networks. Each of these networks must be assigned a portion of these addresses called a subnet. Many factors and techniques are used to create a subnetting plan. These sections will present some of these factors and techniques.

Subnetting allows creating multiple logical networks from a single address block. Because a router connects these networks, each interface on a router must have a unique network ID. Every node on that link is on the same network.

You create the subnets by reassigning one or more of the host bits as network bits. This is done by extending the prefix to "borrow" some of the bits from the host portion of the address to create additional network bits. The more host bits borrowed, the more subnets that can be defined. For each bit borrowed, you double the number of subnetworks available. For example, if you borrow 1 bit, you can define two subnets. If you borrow 2 bits, you can have four subnets.

However, with each bit you borrow, you have fewer host bits to define the host addresses in each subnet. Therefore, there are fewer host addresses available per subnet. Additionally, because you have two addresses for each network—network address and broadcast address—that cannot be assigned to hosts, the total number of hosts in the entire network decreases.

Creating Two Subnets

Router A in Figure 6-18 has two interfaces to interconnect two networks. Given an address block of 192.168.1.0 /24, you will create two subnets. You borrow 1 bit from the host portion by using a subnet mask of 255.255.255.128, instead of the original 255.255.255.0 mask. This makes the most significant bit in the last octet a network bit instead of a host bit. This bit is used to distinguish between the two subnets. For one of the subnets, this bit is a 0, and for the other subnet, this bit is a 1. The information for these two subnets is shown in Table 6-15.

Figure 6-18   Borrowing a Bit to Create Two Subnets

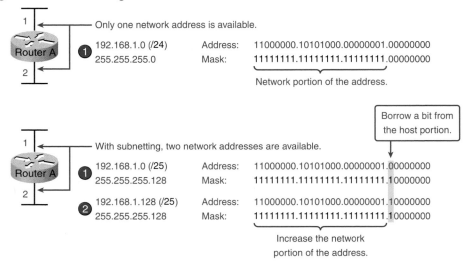

Table 6-15   Subnets for the 192.168.1.0 /24 Network with 1 Borrowed Bit

Subnet	Network Address	Host Range	Broadcast Address
1	192.168.1.0/25	192.168.1.1–192.168.1.126	192.168.1.127
2	192.168.1.128/25	192.168.1.129–192.168.1.254	192.168.1.255

Use this formula to calculate the number of subnets:

2^n, where n = the number of bits borrowed

In the example of Figure 6-18 and Table 6-15, the calculation is

$2^1 = 2$ subnets

For each subnet, examine the last octet of the subnet address in binary. The values in these octets for the two networks are

Subnet 1: **0**0000000 = 0

Subnet 2: **1**0000000 = 128

To calculate the number of hosts per network, you use the formula of $2^n - 2$, where n = the number of bits left for hosts.

Applying this formula to the two-subnet example in Figure 6-18 and Table 6-15, $2^7 - 2 = 126$ shows that each of these subnets can have 126 hosts.

Creating Three Subnets

Beginning with the previous example, consider an internetwork that requires three subnets. The network in Figure 6-19 starts with the same 192.168.1.0 /24 address block. Borrowing a single bit would only provide two subnets. To provide more networks, you change the subnet mask to 255.255.255.192 and borrow 2 bits. These 2 bits will provide four subnets. These networks are shown in Table 6-16. The calculations follow.

Figure 6-19   Borrowing 2 Bits to Create Subnets

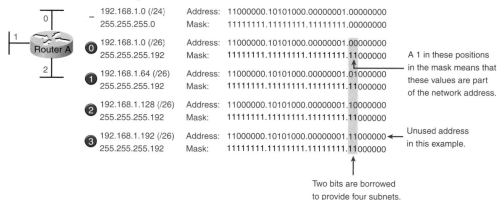

Table 6-16   Subnets for the 192.168.1.0 /24 Network with 2 Borrowed Bits

Subnet	Network Address	Host Range	Broadcast Address
0	192.168.1.0/26	192.168.1.1–192.168.1.62	192.168.1.63
1	192.168.1.64/26	192.168.1.65–192.168.1.126	192.168.1.127
2	192.168.1.128/26	192.168.1.129–192.168.1.190	192.168.1.191
3	192.168.1.192/26	192.168.1.193–192.168.1.254	192.168.1.255

Calculate the number of subnets with this formula:

$2^2 = 4$ subnets

To calculate the number of hosts, begin by examining the last octet. Notice these subnets:

Subnet 1:   0 = **00**000000

Subnet 2:   64 = **01**000000

Subnet 3:   128 = **10**000000

Subnet 4:   192 = **11**000000

Apply the host calculation formula:

$2^6 - 2 = 62$ hosts per subnet

Creating Six Subnets

Consider the example in Figure 6-20 with five LANs and a WAN, for a total of six networks. The network information for this example is shown in Table 6-17, and the calculations follow.

Table 6-17   Subnets for the 192.168.1.0 /24 Network with 3 Borrowed Bits

Subnet	Network Address	Host Range	Broadcast Address
0	192.168.1.0/27	192.168.1.1–192.168.1.30	192.168.1.31
1	192.168.1.32/27	192.168.1.33–192.168.1.62	192.168.1.63
2	192.168.1.64/27	192.168.1.65–192.168.1.94	192.168.1.95
3	192.168.1.96/27	192.168.1.97–192.168.1.126	192.168.1.127
4	192.168.1.128/27	192.168.1.129–192.168.1.158	192.168.1.159
5	192.168.1.160/27	192.168.1.161–192.168.1.190	192.168.1.191
6	192.168.1.192/27	192.168.1.193–192.168.1.222	192.168.1.223
7	192.168.1.224/27	192.168.1.225–192.168.1.254	192.168.1.255

Figure 6-20   Borrowing 3 Bits to Create Subnets

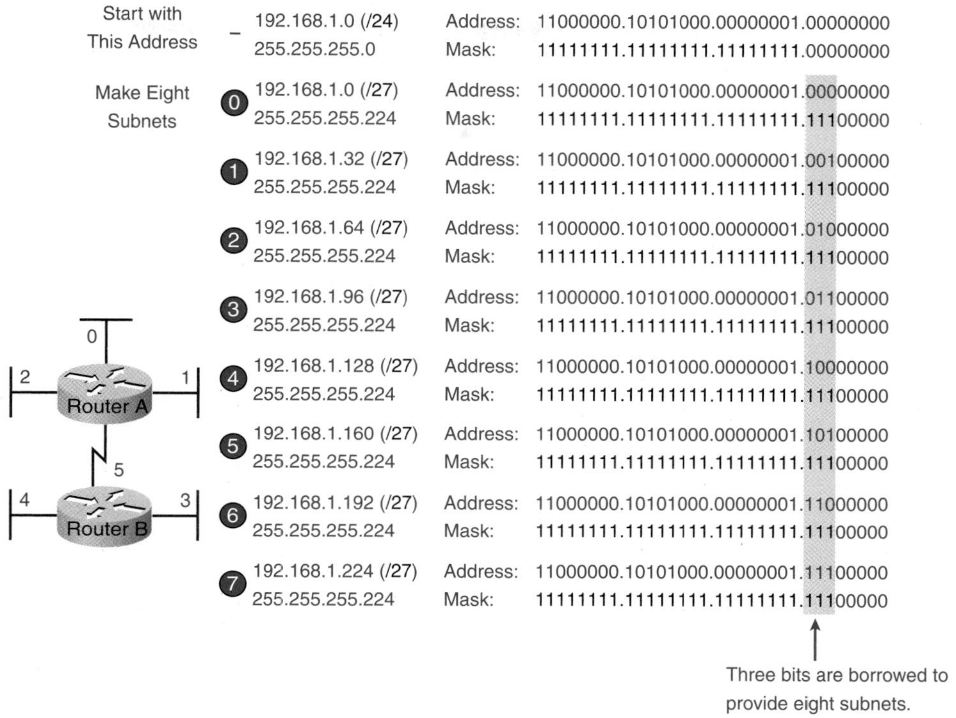

Start with This Address	192.168.1.0 (/24) 255.255.255.0	Address: Mask:	11000000.10101000.00000001.00000000 11111111.11111111.11111111.00000000
Make Eight Subnets	⓪ 192.168.1.0 (/27) 255.255.255.224	Address: Mask:	11000000.10101000.00000001.00000000 11111111.11111111.11111111.11100000
	① 192.168.1.32 (/27) 255.255.255.224	Address: Mask:	11000000.10101000.00000001.00100000 11111111.11111111.11111111.11100000
	② 192.168.1.64 (/27) 255.255.255.224	Address: Mask:	11000000.10101000.00000001.01000000 11111111.11111111.11111111.11100000
	③ 192.168.1.96 (/27) 255.255.255.224	Address: Mask:	11000000.10101000.00000001.01100000 11111111.11111111.11111111.11100000
	④ 192.168.1.128 (/27) 255.255.255.224	Address: Mask:	11000000.10101000.00000001.10000000 11111111.11111111.11111111.11100000
	⑤ 192.168.1.160 (/27) 255.255.255.224	Address: Mask:	11000000.10101000.00000001.10100000 11111111.11111111.11111111.11100000
	⑥ 192.168.1.192 (/27) 255.255.255.224	Address: Mask:	11000000.10101000.00000001.11000000 11111111.11111111.11111111.11100000
	⑦ 192.168.1.224 (/27) 255.255.255.224	Address: Mask:	11000000.10101000.00000001.11100000 11111111.11111111.11111111.11100000

Three bits are borrowed to provide eight subnets.

To accommodate six networks, subnet 192.168.1.0 /24 into address blocks using this formula:

$$2^3 = 8$$

To get at least six subnets, borrow 3 host bits. A subnet mask of 255.255.255.224 provides the 3 additional network bits.

To calculate the number of hosts, begin by examining the last octet. Notice these subnets:

$$0 = 00000000$$

$$32 = 00100000$$

$$64 = 01000000$$

$$96 = 01100000$$

$$128 = 10000000$$

$$160 = 10100000$$

$$192 = \mathbf{11}000000$$

$$224 = \mathbf{111}00000$$

Apply the host calculation formula:

$$2^5 - 2 = 30 \text{ hosts per subnet}$$

Subnetting: Dividing Networks into Right Sizes

Every network within the internetwork of a corporation or organization is designed to accommodate a finite number of hosts. Some networks, such as point-to-point WAN links, only require a maximum of two hosts. Other networks, such as a user LAN in a large building or department, might need to accommodate hundreds of hosts. Network administrators need to devise the internetwork addressing scheme to accommodate the maximum number of hosts for each network. The number of hosts in each division should allow growth in the number of hosts.

To examine this process, see the example network in Figure 6-21. Each step of this process in the following sections will use this as an example. Subnetting an address block for an internetwork uses the following steps:

How To

Step 1.   Determine the total number of addresses.

Step 2.   Determine the number of networks and the number of hosts in each network.

Step 3.   Partition the address block to create a network of appropriate size for the largest subnet network.

Step 4.   Create another partition of appropriate size for the next largest network.

Step 5.   Continue to create partitions for each subsequently smaller network until all subnets have address blocks assigned.

Determine the Total Number of Hosts

First, consider the total number of hosts required by the entire corporate internetwork. You must use a block of addresses that is large enough to accommodate all devices in all the corporate networks. This includes end-user devices, servers, intermediate devices, and router interfaces.

Figure 6-21   Example Network to Subnet

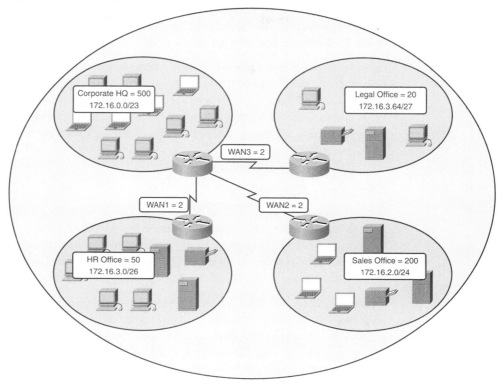

Determine the Number and Size of the Networks

For this internetwork, consider the number of networks and the number of hosts in each network. The network is subnetted to overcome issues with location, size, and control. In designing the addressing, consider the factors for grouping the hosts that we discussed previously:

- Grouping based on common geographic location

- Grouping based on hosts used for specific purposes

- Grouping based on ownership

Each WAN link is a network. You create subnets for the WAN that interconnect different geographic locations. When connecting the different locations, you use a router to account for the hardware differences between the LANs and the WAN.

Although hosts in a common geographic location typically comprise a single block of addresses, you might need to subnet this block to form additional networks at each location. You need to create subnetworks at the different locations that have hosts for common user needs. You might also have other groups of users that require many network resources, or you might have many users that require their own subnetwork. Additionally, you can have subnetworks for special hosts such as servers. Each of these factors needs to be considered in the network count. You also have to consider any special security or administrative ownership needs that require additional networks.

One useful tool in this address-planning process is a network diagram. A diagram allows you to see the networks and make a more accurate count. As an example, the corporate internetwork in Figure 6-21 needs to accommodate 800 hosts in its four locations and the WAN connections. To accommodate 800 hosts in the four company locations, you use binary arithmetic to allocate a /22 block, which leaves 10 bits for host addresses $(2^{10} - 2 = 1022)$.

Allocating Addresses

With a count of the networks and the number of hosts for each network completed, you need to start allocating addresses from your overall block of addresses. This process begins by allocating network addresses for the locations that require the most hosts and work downward to the point-to-point links. This process ensures that large enough blocks of addresses are made available to accommodate the hosts and networks for these locations.

When making the divisions and assignment of available subnets, make sure that there are adequately sized address blocks available for the larger demands. Also, plan carefully to ensure that the address blocks assigned to the subnet do not overlap. A helpful tool in this planning process is a spreadsheet. You can place the addresses in columns to visualize the allocation of the addresses. This helps prevent the duplication of address assignments. Figure 6-22 shows the use of a spreadsheet to plan address allocation.

With the major blocks of the example network allocated, you subnet any of the locations that require further dividing. In this example, you divide the corporate HQ into two networks. The subnets for this location are shown in Figure 6-23. This further division of the addresses is often called *subnetting the subnets*. As with any subnetting, you need to carefully plan the address allocation so that you have available blocks of addresses.

Figure 6-22 Subnets Planned on a Spreadsheet

Corporate Net	HQ	Sales	HR	Legal	WAN1	WAN2	WAN3	Unused
172.16.0.0/22	172.16.0.0/23	172.16.2.0/24	172.16.3.0/26	172.16.3.64/27	172.16.3.128/30	172.16.3.132/30	172.16.3.136/30	
172.16.0.1	172.16.0.1							
	172.16.1.255							
		172.16.2.0						
		172.16.2.255						
			172.16.3.0					
			172.16.3.63					
				172.16.3.64				
				172.16.3.127				
					172.16.3.128			
					172.16.3.131			
						172.16.3.132		
						172.16.3.135		
							172.16.3.136	
							172.16.3.139	
								172.16.3.140
172.16.3.255								172.16.3.255

Figure 6-23 Additional Subnetting of the HQ Location

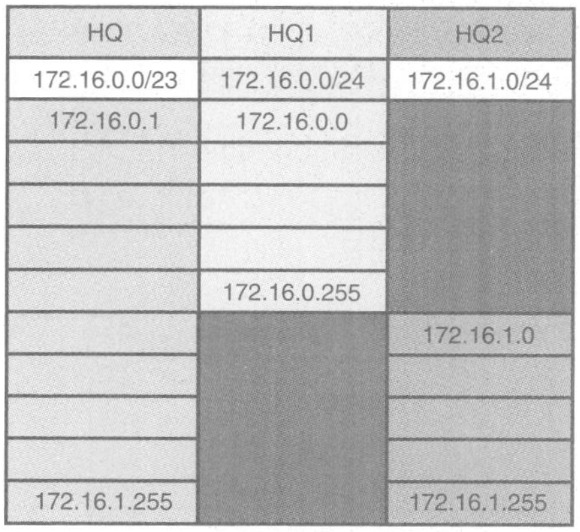

HQ	HQ1	HQ2
172.16.0.0/23	172.16.0.0/24	172.16.1.0/24
172.16.0.1	172.16.0.0	
	172.16.0.255	
		172.16.1.0
172.16.1.255		172.16.1.255

As previously presented, the creation of new, smaller networks from a given address block is done by extending the length of the prefix, that is, adding 1s to the subnet mask. Doing this allocates more bits to the network portion of the address to provide more patterns for the new subnet. For each bit you borrow, you double the number of networks you have. For example, if you use 1 bit, you have the potential to divide that block into two smaller networks.

With a single bit pattern, you can produce two unique bit patterns, 1 and 0. If you borrow 2 bits, you can provide four unique patterns to represent networks 00, 01, 10, and 11. Three bits would allow eight blocks, and so on.

Determine the Total Number of Hosts

Recall from the previous section that as you divide the address range into subnets, you lose two host addresses for each new network. These are the network address and broadcast address.

The formula for calculating the number of hosts in a network is

$$\text{Usable hosts} = 2^n - 2$$

where n is the number of bits remaining to be used for hosts.

Subnetting a Subnet

Subnetting a subnet, or using variable-length subnet mask (VLSM), was designed to maximize addressing efficiency. VLSM is a practice associated with classless addressing. When identifying the total number of hosts using traditional subnetting, you allocate the same number of addresses for each subnet. If all the subnets have the same requirements for the number of hosts, these fixed-size address blocks would be efficient. However, that is most often not the case.

For example, the topology in Figure 6-24 shows a subnet requirement of seven subnets, one for each of the four LANs and one for each of the three WANs. With the given address of 192.168.20.0, you need to borrow 3 bits from the host bits in the last octet, which provides eight subnets, to meet your subnet requirement of seven subnets.

Figure 6-24   VLSM Subnetting

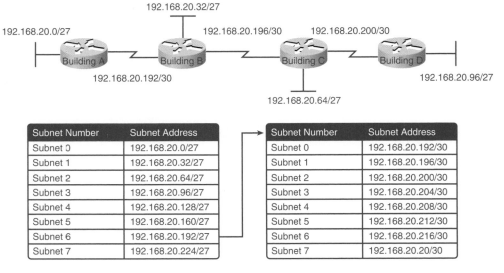

Subnet Number	Subnet Address
Subnet 0	192.168.20.0/27
Subnet 1	192.168.20.32/27
Subnet 2	192.168.20.64/27
Subnet 3	192.168.20.96/27
Subnet 4	192.168.20.128/27
Subnet 5	192.168.20.160/27
Subnet 6	192.168.20.192/27
Subnet 7	192.168.20.224/27

Subnet Number	Subnet Address
Subnet 0	192.168.20.192/30
Subnet 1	192.168.20.196/30
Subnet 2	192.168.20.200/30
Subnet 3	192.168.20.204/30
Subnet 4	192.168.20.208/30
Subnet 5	192.168.20.212/30
Subnet 6	192.168.20.216/30
Subnet 7	192.168.20.20/30

These bits are borrowed bits by changing the corresponding subnet mask bits to 1s to indicate that these bits are now being used as network bits. The last octet of the mask is then represented in binary by 11100000, which is 224. The new mask of 255.255.255.224 is represented with the /27 notation to represent a total of 27 bits for the mask.

In binary, this subnet mask is represented as 11111111.11111111.11111111.11100000. After borrowing 3 of the host bits to use as network bits, this leaves 5 host bits. These 5 bits will allow up to 30 hosts per subnet.

Although you have accomplished the task of dividing the network into an adequate number of subnets, it was done with a significant waste of unused addresses. For example, only two addresses are needed in each subnet for the WAN links. There are 28 unused addresses in each of the three WAN subnets that have been locked into these address blocks. Furthermore, this limits future growth by reducing the total number of subnets available. This inefficient use of addresses is characteristic of fixed-block sizes that is a carryover from practices with classful addressing.

Applying a standard subnetting scheme to this scenario is inefficient. In fact, this example is a good model for showing how subnetting a subnet can be used to maximize address utilization.

Getting More Subnet for Less Hosts

Recall in previous examples that the original subnets were divided to gain additional, smaller subnets to use for the WAN links. Creating smaller subnets, each subnet is able to support two hosts, which leaves the original subnets free to be allotted to other devices and prevents many addresses from being wasted.

To create these smaller subnets for the WAN links in the network in Figure 6-24, begin with 192.168.20.192. You can divide this subnet into many smaller subnets. To provide address blocks for the WANs with two addresses each, you will borrow 3 additional host bits to be used as network bits:

Address 192.168.20.192 is 11000000.10101000.00010100.11000000 in binary.

Mask 255.255.255.252 is 11111111.11111111.11111111.11111100 in binary.

This addressing plan breaks up the 192.168.20.192 /27 subnets into smaller /30 subnets to provide addresses for the WANs. Doing this reduces the number of addresses per subnet to a size appropriate for the WANs. With this addressing, you have subnets 4, 5, and 7 available for future networks, as well as several other subnets available for WANs.

Additional Subnetting Example

With Figure 6-25, you can look at addressing from another view. You will consider subnetting based on the number of hosts, including router interfaces and WAN connections. This scenario has the following requirements:

- **AtlantaHQ:** 58 host addresses
- **PerthHQ:** 26 host addresses
- **SydneyHQ:** 10 host addresses
- **CorpusHQ:** 10 host addresses
- **WAN links:** 2 host addresses (each)

Figure 6-25   VLSM Subnetting of a Network

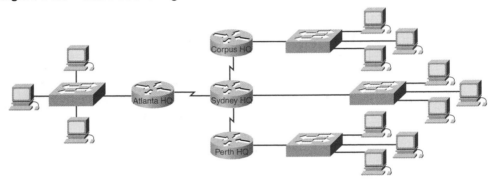

It should be clear from the diverse requirements of the networks that using a standard subnetting scheme would, indeed, be wasteful. In this internetwork, standard subnetting would lock each subnet into blocks of 60 hosts, which would mean a significant waste of potential addresses. This waste is especially evident in the PerthHQ LAN that supports 26 users and the SydneyHQ and CorpusHQ LAN routers that support only 10 users each. Therefore, with the given address block of 192.168.15.0 /24, you will begin designing an addressing scheme for the network in Figure 6-25 to meet the requirements and save potential addresses.

Assigning the AtlantaHQ LAN

When creating an appropriate addressing scheme, always begin with the largest requirement. In this case, the AtlantaHQ, with 58 users, has the largest requirement. Starting with 192.168.15.0, you will need 6 host bits to accommodate the requirement of 58 hosts. This allows 2 additional bits for the network portion. The prefix for this network would be /26 and the subnet mask would be 255.255.255.192.

You should begin by subnetting the original address block of 192.168.15.0 /24. Using the usable hosts = $2^n - 2$ formula, you calculate that 6 host bits allow 62 hosts in the subnet.

The 62 hosts would meet the required 58 hosts of the AtlantaHQ company router and provide 2 additional network bits:

Address 192.168.15.0 is 11000000.10101000.00001111.00000000 in binary.

Mask 255.255.255.192 is 11111111.11111111.11111111.**11**000000 in binary.

Borrowing 2 host bits to accommodate the AtlantaHQ LAN requires a /26 bit mask.

If the fixed-block addressing scheme were used, all the subnets would use this same /26 mask. That would provide the following subnetting scheme:

Subnet 1: 192.168.15.0 /26, host address range 1 to 62

Subnet 2: 192.168.15.64 /26, host address range 65 to 126

Subnet 3: 192.168.15.128 /26, host address range 129 to 190

Subnet 4: 192.168.15.192 /26, host address range 193 to 254

This fixed-block method would allow only four subnets and therefore not allow enough address blocks for the subnets in this internetwork.

In this subnetting scenario, you will need to use VLSM to make the size of each subnet consistent with the host requirements. Using VLSM provides an addressing scheme that directly correlates the addresses allocated to each subnet to the number of hosts required in each network.

Assigning the PerthHQ LAN

Next, you examine the requirements for the next largest subnet for the network in Figure 6-25. This is the PerthHQ LAN, requiring 26 host addresses, including the router interface. You should begin with the next available address of 192.168.15.64 to create an address block for this subnet. By borrowing 1 more bit, you are able to meet the needs of PerthHQ while limiting the wasted addresses. The borrowed bit gives you a /27 mask with the following address range:

192.168.15.64 /27, host address range 65 to 94

This block of addresses provides 30 addresses, which meets the requirement of 26 hosts and allows room for growth for this subnet.

Assigning the SydneyHQ LAN and CorpusHQ LAN

To provide the addressing for the next two largest subnets, SydneyHQ and CorpusHQ LANs, each LAN requires 10 host addresses. This subnetting requires you to borrow another bit, to further extend the mask to /28. Starting with address 192.168.15.96, you get the following address blocks:

Subnet 1: 192.168.15.96 /28, host address range 97 to 110

Subnet 2: 192.168.15.112 /28, host address range 113 to 126

These blocks provide 14 addresses for the hosts and router interfaces on each LAN.

Assigning the WANs

Finally, you need to provide subnets for the WAN links for the network in Figure 6-25. These point-to-point WAN links require only two addresses. To meet the requirement, you borrow 2 more bits to use a /30 mask. Using the next available addresses, you get the following address blocks:

Subnet 1: 192.168.15.128 /30, host address range 129 to 130

Subnet 2: 192.168.15.132 /30, host address range 133 to 134

Subnet 3: 192.168.15.136 /30, host address range 137 to 138

The results shown in your addressing scheme using VLSM display a wide array of correctly allocated address blocks. As a best practice, you begin by documenting your requirements from the largest to the smallest. By starting with the largest requirement, you can determine that a fixed-block addressing scheme will not allow efficient use of the IPv4 addresses and, as shown in this example, will not provide enough addresses.

From the allocated address block, you borrow bits to create the address ranges that would fit the topology. Using VLSM to allocate the addresses makes it possible to apply the subnetting. A summary of the addressing used for the network in Figure 6-25 is shown in Table 6-18.

Table 6-18   Subnets for the Sample Network

Name	Required Number of Addresses	Subnet Address	Address Range	Broadcast Address	Network/ Prefix
AtlantaHQ	58	192.168.15.0	.1–.62	.63	192.168.15.0 /26
PerthHQ	26	192.168.15.64	.65–.94	.95	192.168.15.64 /27
SydneyHQ	10	192.168.15.96	.97–.110	.111	192.168.15.96 /28
CorpusHQ	10	192.168.15.112	.113–.126	.127	192.168.15.112 /28
WAN1	2	192.168.15.128	.129–.130	.131	192.168.15.128 /30
WAN2	2	192.168.15.132	.133–.134	.135	192.168.15.132 /30
WAN3	2	192.168.15.136	.137–.138	.139	192.168.15.136 /30

VLSM Chart

Address planning can be accomplished using a variety of tools. One method is to use a VLSM chart to identify which blocks of addresses are available for use and which ones are already assigned. This method helps to prevent assigning addresses that have already been allocated. This chart can be used to do address planning for networks with prefixes in the /25 to /30 range. These are the most commonly used network ranges for subnetting.

Using the network from the example in Figure 6-25, you can walk through the address planning using the VLSM chart, to see its use.

Figure 6-26 shows the completed portion of a VLSM chart for planning the network in Figure 6-25. A complete chart for your use is available on the CD-ROM accompanying this book.

Figure 6-26   Subnet Planning Using a VLSM Chart

/25 (1 Subnet Bits) 2 Subnets 126 Hosts	/26 (2 Subnet Bits) 4 Subnets 62 Hosts	/27 (3 Subnet Bits) 8 Subnets 30 Hosts	/28 (4 Subnet Bits) 16 Subnets 14 Hosts	/29 (5 Subnet Bits) 32 Subnets 6 Hosts	/30 (6 Subnet Bits) 64 Subnets 2 Hosts
.0		**AtlantaHQ Block**		.0 (.1-.6)	.0 (.1-.2)
.4			.0 (.1-.14)		.4 (.5-.6)
.8				.8 (.9-.14)	.8 (.9-.10)
.12		.0 (.1-.30)			.12 (.13-.14)
.16				.16 (.17-.22)	.16 (.17-.18)
.20			.16 (.17-.30)		.20 (.21-.22)
.24				.24 (.25-.30)	.24 (.25-.26)
.28					.28 (.29-.30)
.32	.0 (.1-.62)			.32 (.33-.38)	.32 (.33-.34)
.36			.32 (.33-.46)		.36 (.37-.38)
.40				.40 (.41-.46)	.40 (.41-.42)
.44		.32 (.33-.62)			.44 (.45-.46)
.48				.48 (.49-.54)	.48 (.49-.50)
.52			.48 (.49-.62)		.52 (.53-.54)
.56				.56 (.57-.62)	.56 (.57-.58)
.60	.0				.60 (.61-.62)
.64		**PerthHQ Block**		.64 (.65-.70)	.64 (.65-.66)
.68			.64 (.65-.78)		.68 (.69-.70)
.72				.72 (.73-.78)	.72 (.73-.74)
.76		.64 (.65-.94)			.76 (.77-.78)
.80				.80 (.81-.86)	.80 (.81-.82)
.84			.80 (.81-.94)		.84 (.85-.86)
.88				.88 (.89-.94)	.88 (.89-.90)
.92	.64 (.65-.126)				.92 (.93-.94)
.96		**SydneyHQ Block**		.96 (.97-.102)	.96 (.97-.98)
.100			.96 (.97-.110)		.100 (.101-.102)
.104				.104 (.105-.110)	.104 (.105-.106)
.108		.96 (.97-.126)			.108 (.109-.110)
.112				.112 (.113-.118)	.112 (.113-.114)
.116			.112 (.113-.126)		.116 (.117-.118)
.120				.120 (.121-.126)	.120 (.121-.122)
.124		**CorpusHQ Block**			.124 (.125-.126)
.128				**WAN Blocks (3)**	.128 (.129-.130)
.132			.128 (.129-.142)	.136 (.137-.142)	.132 (.133-.134)
.136					.136 (.137-.138)
.140					.140 (.141-.142)

Choosing a Block for the AtlantaHQ LAN

As before, start with the subnet that has the largest number of hosts. In this case, it is AtlantaHQ, with 58 hosts. Following the chart header from left to right, find the header that indicates a block size of sufficient size for the 58 hosts. This is the /26 column. In this column, notice that there are four blocks of this size:

.0 /26, host address range 1 to 62

.64 /26, host address range 65 to 126

.128 /26, host address range 129 to 190

.192 /26, host address range 193 to 254

Because no addresses have been allocated, you can choose any one of these blocks. Although there might be reasons for using a different block, commonly the first available block, .0 /26, is used.

After you assign the address block, these addresses are considered used. Examining the chart in Figure 6-26, when the .0 /26 block to the AtlantaHQ is allocated, mark all the blocks that contain these addresses. These are all blocks that contain any of the addresses .1 through .62. By marking these, you can see which addresses cannot be used and which are still available.

Choosing a Block for the PerthHQ LAN

The next largest address block is the PerthHQ LAN of 26 hosts. Moving across the chart header, find the column that has the subnets of sufficient size for this LAN. Then move down the chart to the first available block with no used addresses. The section of the chart available for PerthHQ is the .64 /27 block. Although you could choose any of the available blocks, typically proceed to the first available block that satisfies the need.

The address range for this block is

.64 /27, host address range 65 to 94

In Figure 6-26, continue to mark the address blocks as they are allocated to prevent overlapping of address assignments.

Choosing Blocks for the SydneyHQ LAN and the CorpusHQ LAN

To meet the needs of the SydneyHQ LAN and CorpusHQ LAN in Figure 6-25, again locate the next available blocks. This time, move to the /28 column and move down to the .96 and .112 blocks.

These blocks are

.96 /28, host address range 97 to 110

.112 /28, host address range 113 to 126

Choosing Blocks for the WANs

The last addressing requirement is for the WAN connections between the networks. Referring again to the chart in Figure 6-26, move to the far-right column for the /30 prefix. Then move down to find the first three available blocks. The following three blocks will provide the two addresses per WAN:

.128 /30, host address range 129 to 130

.132 /30, host address range 133 to 134

.136 /30, host address range 137 to 138

In the chart, mark the addresses assigned to the WAN to indicate that the blocks containing these can no longer be assigned. Notice with the assignment of these WAN ranges that you have marked several larger blocks that cannot be assigned. Because the addresses in these blocks are also part of larger address blocks, the assignment of the larger blocks would overlap the use of these addresses.

These include

.128 /25

.128 /26

.128 /27

.128 /28

.128 /29

.136 /29

As you have seen, the use of VLSM enables you to maximize addressing while minimizing waste. The chart method shown is just one additional tool that network administrators and network technicians can use to create an addressing scheme that is less wasteful than the fixed-size block approach.

Assigning Addresses (6.5.7.1)

In this activity, you will be given a pool of addresses and masks to assign a host with an address, a subnet mask, and a gateway to allow it to communicate in a network. Use file e1-6571.pka on the CD-ROM that accompanies this book to perform this activity using Packet Tracer.

Addressing in a Tiered Internetwork (6.5.8.1)

In this activity, you will be given a topology and a list of possible IP addresses. You will assign the interfaces of a router with the appropriate IP address and subnet mask that would satisfy the host requirements of each network while leaving the minimum number of unused IP addresses possible. Use file e1-6581.pka on the CD-ROM that accompanies this book to perform this activity using Packet Tracer.

Testing the Network Layer

Ping is a utility for testing IP connectivity between hosts. Ping sends out requests for responses from a specified host address. Ping uses a Layer 3 protocol that is a part of the TCP/IP suite called Internet Control Message Protocol (ICMP). Ping uses an ICMP echo request datagram.

If the host at the specified address receives the echo request, it responds with an ICMP echo reply datagram. For each packet sent, ping measures the time required for the reply.

As each response is received, ping provides a display of the time between the ping being sent and the response being received. This is a measure of the network performance. Ping has a timeout value for the response. If a response is not received within that timeout, ping gives up and provides a message indicating that a response was not received.

After all the sending of the requests, the ping utility provides an output with the summary of the responses. This output includes the success rate and average round-trip time to the destination.

Ping 127.0.0.1: Testing the Local Stack

There are some special testing and verification cases for which you can use ping. One case is for testing the internal configuration of IP on the local host. To perform this test, you ping the special reserve address of local loopback (127.0.0.1).

A response from 127.0.0.1, as shown in Example 6-1, indicates that IP is properly installed on the host. This response comes from the network layer. This response is *not*, however, an indication that the addresses, masks, or gateways are properly configured. Nor does it indicate anything about the status of the lower layer of the network stack. This simply tests IP down through the network layer of IP. An error message is an indication that TCP/IP is not operational on the host.

Example 6-1 Successful Loopback Ping

```
C:\> ping 127.0.0.1

Pinging 127.0.0.1 with 32 bytes of data:

Reply from 127.0.0.1: bytes=32 time<1ms TTL=128
Reply from 127.0.0.1: bytes=32 time<1ms TTL=128
Reply from 127.0.0.1: bytes=32 time<1ms TTL=128
Reply from 127.0.0.1: bytes=32 time<1ms TTL=128

Ping statistics for 127.0.0.1:
    Packets: Sent = 4, Received = 4, Lost = 0 (0% loss),
Approximate round trip times in milli-seconds:
    Minimum = 0ms, Maximum = 0ms, Average = 0ms

C:\>
```

Ping Gateway: Testing Connectivity to the Local LAN

You can also use ping to test the host's ability to communicate on the local network. This is generally done by pinging the IP address of the gateway of the host. A ping to the gateway indicates that the host and the router's interface serving as that gateway are both operational on the local network.

For this test, the gateway address is most often used, because the router is normally always operational. If the gateway address does not respond, you can try the IP address of another host that you are confident is operational in the local network.

In Figure 6-27, host 10.0.0.1 tests connectivity to the gateway by pinging the address 10.0.0.254. If either the gateway or another host responds, the local hosts can successfully communicate over the local network. If the gateway does not respond but another host, such as 10.0.0.2, responds to the ping, this could indicate a problem with the router's interface serving as the gateway.

Figure 6-27   Ping of Gateway

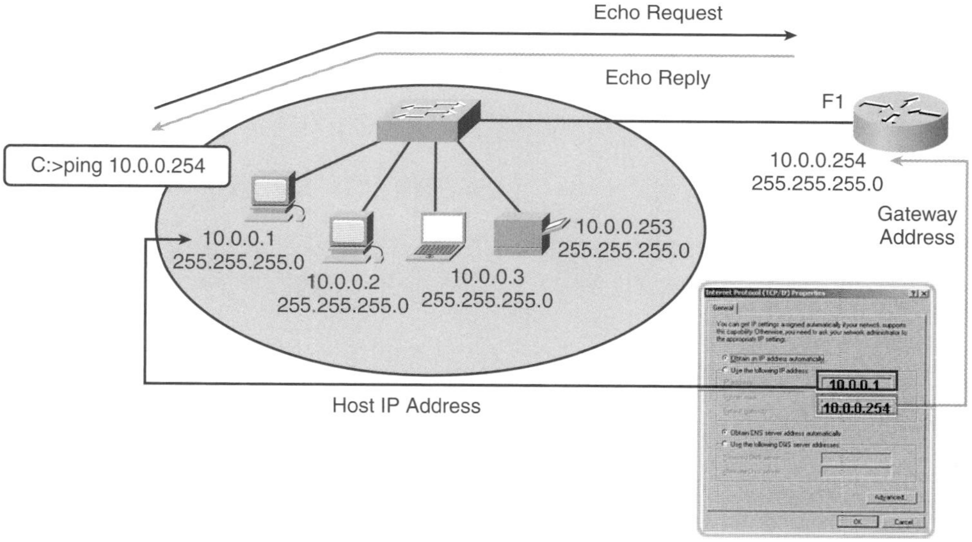

One possibility is that you have the wrong address for the gateway. Another possibility is that the router interface might be fully operational but have security applied to it that prevents it from processing or responding to ping requests. Other hosts might also have the same security restriction applied.

Ping Remote Host: Testing Connectivity to Remote LAN

You can also use ping to test the ability of the local IP host to communicate across an inter-network. The local host can ping an operational host of a remote network.

If this ping is successful, you will have verified the operation of a large piece of the inter-network. It means that you have verified your host's communication on the local network, the operation of the router serving as your gateway, and all other routers that might be in the path between your network and the network of the remote host.

Additionally, you have verified the same functionality of the remote host. In Figure 6-28, host 10.0.0.1 tests connectivity to a remote network by pinging address 10.0.1.1. A successful response from this host verifies the local host (10.0.0.1), the local network, the gateway address, the successful routing in router, the remote network, and the operation of the remote host 10.0.1.1.

Figure 6-28 Ping of Remote Host

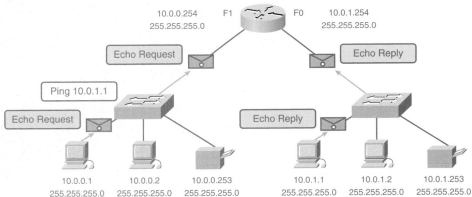

This also verifies that the remote host has the proper gateway configured. If, for any reason, the remote host (10.0.1.1) could not use its local network or gateway to communicate outside its network, no response would be received.

Remember, many network administrators limit or prohibit the entry of ICMP datagrams into the corporate network. Therefore, the lack of a ping response could be because of security restrictions and not because of nonoperational elements of the networks.

Ping (6.6.3.2)

In this activity, you will examine the behavior of ping in several common network situations. Use file e1-6632.pka on the CD-ROM that accompanies this book to perform this activity using Packet Tracer.

Traceroute (tracert): Testing the Path

Ping is used to indicate the connectivity between two hosts. Traceroute (tracert) is a utility that allows you to observe the path between these hosts. The trace generates a list of hops that were successfully reached along the path. This list can provide you with important verification and troubleshooting information.

If the data reaches the destination, the trace lists the interface on every router in the path. If the data fails at some hop along the way, you have the address of the last router that responded to the trace. This is an indication of where the problem or security restrictions are.

Round-Trip Time (RTT)

Using traceroute provides the *round-trip time (RTT)* for each hop along the path and indicates whether a hop fails to respond. The RTT is the time a packet takes to reach the remote host and for the response from the host to return. An asterisk (*) is used to indicate a lost packet.

You can use this information to locate a problematic router in the path. High response times or data losses from a particular hop indicate that the resources of the router or its connections might be stressed.

Time to Live (TTL)

Traceroute uses a function of the Time to Live (TTL) field in the Layer 3 header and ICMP Time Exceeded message. The TTL field is used to limit the number of hops that a packet can cross. When a packet enters a router, the TTL field is decremented by 1. When the TTL reaches 0, a router will not forward the packet, and the packet is dropped.

In addition to dropping the packet, the router normally sends an ICMP Time Exceeded message addressed to the originating host. This ICMP message will contain the IP address of the router that responded.

The first sequence of messages sent from traceroute will have a TTL field of 1. This causes the TTL to time out the packet at the first router. This router then responds with an ICMP message. Traceroute now has the address of the first hop.

Traceroute then progressively increments the TTL field (2, 3, 4, and so on) for each sequence of messages. This provides the trace with the address of each hop as the packets time out farther down the path. The TTL field continues to be increased until the destination is reached or it is incremented to a predefined maximum.

In Example 6-2, the tracert to www.cisco.com shows responses from the routers along the path. The local host sends a packet to the designation address of 198.133.219.2. The first response is a response from the host's default gateway, 10.20.0.94. The packet sent from the local host had a TTL = 1. When it reached this first router, the TTL was decremented to 0.

The router sends an ICMP message to indicate that the packet was dropped. The RTT indicates the amount of time required for this response. The local host sends two additional packets with a TTL = 1. For each one, the local gateway responds with a message, and an RTT is recorded.

```
Example 6-2 Trace to www.cisco.com
C:\> tracert www.cisco.com

Tracing route to www.cisco.com [198.133.219.25]
over a maximum of 30 hops:

  1    87 ms    87 ms    89 ms  sjck-access-gw2-vla30.cisco.com [10.20.0.94]
  2    89 ms    88 ms    87 ms  sjce-sbb1-gw1-gig3-7.cisco.com [171.69.14.245]
  3    88 ms    87 ms    88 ms  sjck-rbb-gw2-ten7-1.cisco.com [171.69.14.45]
  4    90 ms    87 ms    95 ms  sjck-corp-gw1-gig1-0-0.cisco.com [171.69.7.174]
  5    90 ms    88 ms    92 ms  sjce-dmzbb-gw1.cisco.com [128.107.236.38]
  6     *        *        *     Request timed out.
  7     *        *       ^C
C:\>
```

The local host then sends three more packets, this time with a TTL = 2. The gateway router decrements the TTL = 1 and forwards these packets to the next router in the route, 171.69.14.245. For each of the three packets, the TTL is decremented to 0. The 171.69.14.245 router sends an ICMP message to indicate that the packet was dropped. The RTT again indicates the amount of time required for this response.

This process of using the increasing TTL provides a map of the route a packet takes across an internetwork. When the final destination is reached, the host responds with either an ICMP Port Unreachable message or an ICMP Echo Reply message, instead of the ICMP Time Exceeded message. In the case of Example 6-2, the asterisk (*) indicates that there were no responses from the destination.

Trace and Time to Live (6.6.4.2)

In this activity, you will first investigate how traceroute (tracert) is actually built out of a series of ICMP echo requests. Then you will experiment with a routing loop, where a packet would circulate forever if not for its Time to Live field. Use file e1-6642.pka on the CD-ROM that accompanies this book to perform this activity using Packet Tracer.

ICMPv4: The Protocol Supporting Testing and Messaging

Although IPv4 is not a reliable protocol, it does allow messages to be sent in the event of certain errors. These messages are sent using services of the *Internet Control Message*

Protocol (ICMP). The purpose of these messages is to provide feedback about issues related to the processing of IP packets under certain conditions, not to make IP reliable. ICMP messages are not required and are often not allowed for security reasons.

ICMP is the messaging protocol for the TCP/IP suite. ICMP provides control and error messages and is used by the ping and traceroute utilities. Although ICMP uses the basic support of IP as if it were a higher-level protocol ICMP, it is actually a separate Layer 3 of the TCP/IP suite.

The types of ICMP messages and their meanings are extensive. The following sections introduce some of the more common messages. ICMP messages that can be sent include:

- Host confirmation
- Unreachable destination or service
- Time exceeded
- Route redirection
- Source quench

Host Confirmation

An ICMP Echo message can be used to determine whether a host is operational. The local host sends an ICMP echo request to a host. The host receiving the Echo message replies with the ICMP echo reply. This use of the ICMP Echo messages is the basis of the ping utility.

Unreachable Destination or Service

The ICMP Destination Unreachable message can be used to notify a host that the destination or service is unreachable. When a host or gateway receives a packet that it cannot deliver, it can send an ICMP Destination Unreachable packet to the host originating the packet. The Destination Unreachable packet will contain codes that indicate why the packet could not be delivered.

The Destination Unreachable codes include

- 0 = net unreachable
- 1 = host unreachable
- 2 = protocol unreachable
- 3 = port unreachable

Codes for *net unreachable* and *host unreachable* are responses from a router when it cannot forward a packet. If a router receives a packet for which it does not have a route, it can respond with an ICMP Destination Unreachable message with a code = 0, indicating net unreachable. If a router receives a packet for which it has an attached route but is unable to deliver the packet to the host on the attached network, the router can respond with an ICMP Destination Unreachable message with a code = 1, indicating that the network is known but the host is unreachable.

The codes 2 and 3 (*protocol unreachable* and *port unreachable*) are used by an end host to indicate that the TCP segment or UDP datagram contained in a packet could not be delivered to the upper-layer service.

When the end host receives a packet with a Layer 4 protocol data unit (PDU) that is to be delivered to an unavailable service, the host can respond to the source host with an ICMP Destination Unreachable message with a code = 2 or code = 3, indicating that the service is not available. The service might not be available because no daemon is providing the service or because security on the host is not allowing access to the service.

Time Exceeded

An ICMP Time Exceeded message is used by a router to indicate that a packet cannot be forwarded because the TTL field of the packet has expired. If a router receives a packet and decrements the TTL field in the packet to 0, it discards the packet. The router can also send an ICMP Time Exceeded message to the source host to inform the host of the reason the packet was dropped.

Route Redirection

A router can use the ICMP Redirect message to notify the hosts on a network that a better route is available for a particular destination. This message can only be used when the source host is on the same physical network as both gateways. If a router receives a packet for which it has a route and for which the next hop is attached to the same interface as the packet arrived, the router can send an ICMP Redirect message to the source host. This message will inform the source host of the next hop contained in a route in the routing table.

Source Quench

The ICMP Source Quench message can be used to tell the source to temporarily stop sending packets. If a router does not have enough buffer space to receive incoming packets, a router will discard the packets. If the router has to do so, it can also send an ICMP Source Quench message to source hosts for every message that it discards. A destination host can also send a Source Quench message if datagrams arrive too fast to be processed.

When a host receives an ICMP Source Quench message, it reports it to the transport layer. The source host can then use the TCP flow control mechanisms to adjust the transmission.

Note

For more information about ICMP, you can visit the following:

- RFC 792, "Internet Control Message Protocol," http://www.ietf.org/rfc/rfc0792.txt
- RFC 1122, "Requirements for Internet Hosts—Communication Layers," http://www.ietf.org/rfc/rfc1122.txt
- RFC 2003, "IP Encapsulation within IP," http://www.ietf.org/rfc/rfc2003.txt

Overview of IPv6

In the early 1990s, the Internet Engineering Task Force (IETF) grew concerned about the exhaustion of the IPv4 network addresses and began to look for a replacement for this protocol. This activity led to the development of what is now known as IPv6. This section presents a brief introduction to IPv6.

Creating expanded addressing capabilities was the initial motivation for developing this new protocol. Other issues were also considered during the development of IPv6, such as these:

- Improved packet handling
- Increased scalability and longevity
- Quality of service (QoS) mechanisms
- Integrated security

To provide these features, IPv6 offers the following:

- 128-bit hierarchical addressing to expand addressing capabilities
- Header format simplification to improve packet handling
- Improved support for extensions and options for increased scalability/longevity and improved packet handling
- Flow-labeling capabilities as QoS mechanisms
- Authentication and privacy capabilities to integrate security

IPv6 is not merely a new Layer 3 protocol; it is a new protocol suite. New protocols at various layers of the stack have been developed to support this new protocol. There is a new messaging protocol called ICMPv6 and new routing protocols. Because of the increased size of the IPv6 header shown in Figure 6-29, it also impacts the underlying network infrastructure.

Figure 6-29 IPv6 Header

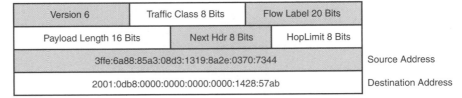

As you can see from this brief introduction, IPv6 has been designed with scalability to allow for years of internetwork growth. However, IPv6 is being implemented slowly and in select networks. Because of better tools, technologies, and address management in the past few years, IPv4 is still very widely used and is likely to remain so for some time into the future. However, IPv6 might eventually replace IPv4 as the dominant Internet protocol.

Note

To find more information about at IPv6, you can refer to the following RFCs:

- RFC 2460, "Internet Protocol version 6 (IPv6)," http://www.ietf.org/rfc/rfc2460.txt
- RFC 3513, "Internet Protocol version 6 (IPv6) Addressing Architecture," http://www.ietf.org/rfc/rfc3513.txt
- RFC 2401, "Security Architecture for the Internet Protocol," http://www.ietf.org/rfc/rfc2401.txt
- RFC 3168, "The Addition of Explicit Congestion Notification (ECN) to IP," http://www.ietf.org/rfc/rfc3168.txt
- RFC 4302, "IP Authentication Header," http://www.ietf.org/rfc/rfc4302.txt
- RFC 4443, "Internet Control Message Protocol (ICMPv6) for the Internet Protocol version 6 (IPv6) Specification," http://www.ietf.org/rfc/rfc4443.txt

Summary

IPv4 addresses are hierarchical, with network, subnetwork, and host portions. An IPv4 address can represent a complete network, a specific host, or the broadcast address of the network. Different addresses are used for unicast, multicast, and broadcast data communications.

Addressing authorities and ISPs allocate address ranges to users, who in turn can assign these addresses to their network devices statically or dynamically. The allocated address ranges can be divided into subnetworks by calculating and applying subnet masks.

Careful address planning is required to make the best use of the available address space. Size, location, use, and access requirements are all considerations in the address-planning process.

After it is implemented, an IP network needs to be tested to verify its connectivity and operational performance. Many tools such as ping and traceroute can help verify the network.

Labs

The labs available in the companion *Network Fundamentals, CCNA Exploration Labs and Study Guide* (ISBN 1-58713-203-6) provide hands-on practice with the following topics introduced in this chapter:

Lab 6-1: Ping and Traceroute (6.7.1.1)

In this lab, you will use the **ping** and **tracert** commands from a host to observe the steps of the operation of these commands in a network.

Lab 6-2: Examining ICMP Packets (6.7.2.1)

In this lab, you will use Wireshark to capture ICMP packets to observe the different ICMP codes.

Lab 6-3: IPv4 Address Subnetting Part 1 (6.7.3.1)

In this activity, you will compute major network IP address information from a given IP address.

Lab 6-4: IPv4 Address Subnetting Part 2 (6.7.4.1)

In this activity, you will compute subnet information for a given IP address and subnetwork mask.

Lab 6-5: Subnet and Router Configuration (6.7.5.1)

In this lab activity, you will design and apply an IP addressing scheme for a given topology. After cabling the network, you will then configure each device using the appropriate basic configuration commands. When the configuration is complete, the appropriate IOS commands will be used to verify that the network is working properly.

Many of the hands-on labs include Packet Tracer companion activities, where you can use Packet Tracer to complete a simulation of the lab. Look for this icon in *Network Fundamentals, CCNA Exploration Labs and Study Guide* (ISBN 1-58713-203-6) for hands-on labs that have Packet Tracer companion activities.

Check Your Understanding

Complete all the review questions listed here to test your understanding of the topics and concepts in this chapter. The appendix, "Check Your Understanding and Challenge Questions Answer Key," lists the answers.

1. Which IP addresses are network addresses? (Choose two.)

    A. 64.104.3.7 /28

    B. 192.168.12.64 /26

    C. 192.135.12.191 /26

    D. 198.18.12.16 /28

    E. 209.165.200.254 /27

    F. 220.12.12.33/27

2. A network administrator is building a network for a small business that has 22 hosts. The ISP has assigned only one Internet routable IP address. Which IP address block can the network administrator use to address the network?

    A. 10.11.12.16 /28

    B. 172.31.255.128 /27

    C. 192.168.1.0 /28

    D. 209.165.202.128 /27

3. What subnet mask would be used with the hosts in the 128.107.176.0 /22 network?

   A. 255.0.0.0

   B. 255.248.0.0

   C. 255.255.252.0

   D. 255.255.255.0

   E. 255.255.255.252

4. You have been assigned the address block 10.255.255.224 /28 to create the network addresses for point-to-point WAN links. How many of these WANs can you support with this address block?

   A. 1

   B. 4

   C. 7

   D. 14

5. What defines an IPv4 logical network?

6. Name and state the purpose of the three types of IPv4 addresses.

7. A network administrator needs to create a new network that has 14 computers and two router interfaces. What subnet mask will provide the appropriate number of IPv4 addresses for this network with minimal wasted addresses?

   A. 255.255.255.128

   B. 255.255.255.192

   C. 255.255.255.224

   D. 255.255.255.240

   E. 255.255.255.248

   F. 255.255.255.252

8. What distinguishes each of the three types of IPv4 addresses?

9. List the three forms of IPv4 communication.

10. List the purpose of having specified ranges of IPv4 addresses for public and private use.

11. A host in the south branch cannot access the server with the address 192.168.254.222 /224. While examining the host, you determine that its IPv4 address is 169.254.11.15 /16. What is the apparent problem?

   A. The host is using a link-local address.

   B. The server is using an invalid subnet mask.

   C. The host has been assigned a broadcast address.

   D. The server thinks that the host is on the logical network with the server.

12. List three reasons for planning and documenting IPv4 addresses.

13. Cite examples where network administrators should statically assign IPv4 addresses.

14. What was the primary motivation for the development of IPv6?

15. What is the purpose of the subnet mask in IPv4 addressing?

16. List factors to consider when planning an IPv4 addressing scheme.

17. What are three tests that use the ping utility to test and verify the operation of a host?

Challenge Questions and Activities

These questions and activities require a deeper application of the concepts covered in this chapter. You can find the answers in the appendix.

1. What are the reserved and special IPv4 addresses, and how are they used?

2. Why is ICMPv4 an important protocol to have operating with IPv4? What are the ICMP message types?

Packet Tracer
☐ Challenge

Look for this icon in *Network Fundamentals, CCNA Exploration Labs and Study Guide* (ISBN 1-58713-203-6) for instructions on how to perform the Packet Tracer Skills Integration Challenge for this chapter.

To Learn More

The following questions encourage you to reflect on the topics discussed in this chapter. Your instructor might ask you to research the questions and discuss your findings in class.

1. Discuss the requirements of an IPv4 addressing plan for an organization whose operations are spread over a number of locations. The organization has a number of different functional areas at most locations that require servers, printers, and mobile devices in addition to regular desktop PCs and laptops. What other address space issues would have to be considered if the organization required Internet access for its users as well as access to specific servers by its customers?

2. Discuss and consider how an organization could rearrange its current /20 IPv4 addressing plan if it needed to expand its network to have more, smaller subnetworks, each with a varying number of potential hosts.

3. Research the different ICMPv4 messages. Discuss why one message might be sent instead of another. For example, what is the difference between the Unreachable Destination or Service response, the Network Unreachable response, and the Host Unreachable response? Also, consider what type of issues can cause each particular response.

4. Using a host where you have command-line access and Internet access, use the ping and tracert utilities to test connectivity and paths to various locations. Perform these tests multiple times while observing and capturing the output for further discussion. From these, consider the reasons for the variations in paths and response time from tests to the same location. Additionally, speculate where and why the tracert responses fail to get responses.

CHAPTER 7

OSI Data Link Layer

Objectives

Upon completion of this chapter, you will able to answer the following questions:

- What is the role of data link layer protocols in data transmission?

- How does the data link layer prepare data for transmission on network media?

- How do the types of MAC methods operate?

- What are several common logical network topologies?

- How does the logical topology determine the MAC method for a type of network?

- What is the purpose of encapsulating packets into frames to facilitate media access?

- What are the purposes of the Layer 2 frame structure?

- What are generic fields of a Layer 2 frame?

- What is the role of the key frame header and trailer fields, including addressing, QoS, type of protocol, and Frame Check Sequence?

Key Terms

This chapter uses the following key terms. You can find the definitions in the Glossary.

nodes   page 245

physical network   page 245

logical network   page 245

network segment   page 245

network interface card (NIC)   page 250

Logical Link Control (LLC)   page 250

MAC   page 250

deterministic   page 253

carrier sense multiple access (CSMA)   page 253

carrier   page 253

collision   page 253

CSMA/collision avoid (CSMA/CA)   page 254

half duplex   page 255

full duplex   page 255

physical topology   page 255

logical topology   page 255

virtual circuit   page 257

token passing   page 258

cyclic redundancy check (CRC)   page 261

backoff   page 265

association identity (AID)   page 266

Address Resolution Protocol (ARP)   page 267

To support communication, the OSI model divides the functions of a data network into layers. So far in this book, you have learned about the following layers:

- The application layer provides the interface to the user.

- The transport layer is responsible for dividing and managing communications between the processes running in the two end systems.

- The network layer protocols organize communication data so that it can travel across internetworks from the originating host to a destination host.

For network layer packets to be transported from source host to destination host, they must traverse different physical networks. These physical networks can consist of different types of physical media such as copper wires, microwaves, optical fibers, and satellite links. Network layer packets do not have a way to directly access these different media.

The services defined by the OSI data link layer prepares network layer packets for transmission and controls access to the physical media. This chapter introduces the general functions of the data link layer and the protocols associated with it.

Data Link Layer: Accessing the Media

The data link layer provides a means for exchanging data over a common local media. The data link layer links the many upper-layer services responsible for packaging the data for communication between hosts with the services to transfer that data across the media.

To transfer this data across the local media, the data link layer repackages it into frames and controls the frames' access to the media. Because an indescribable number of physical media exist, a wide variety of data link layer protocols define different types of frames and different methods of controlling access to the media.

Some types of frames and data link layer services support communications for LANs; others support communications across WANs. Some frame types are used on a specific type of media; others can be used on multiple types of media.

So generalizing the functions of the data link layer is not an easy task. To learn about the data link layer, this chapter examines generalizations of the data link layer as described by the OSI model and then provides insight into different types of data link and physical technologies, including some of the logical topologies. Finally, Ethernet is presented as an example for the physical and data link layers.

Supporting and Connecting to Upper-Layer Services

The data link layer performs two basic services:

- Allows the upper layers to access the media using techniques such as framing

- Controls how data is placed onto the media and is received from the media using techniques such as media access control (MAC) and error detection

The data link layer is responsible for the exchange of frames between *nodes* (devices communicating at Layer 2) over the media of a *physical network*. This includes encapsulating the packet into a frame, placing the frame onto the media, receiving the frame from the media, and decapsulating the frame back into a packet.

Note

A physical network is different from a *logical network*. The network layer defines logical networks by the arrangement of the hierarchical addressing scheme. Physical networks represent the interconnection of devices on a common media. Sometimes, a physical network is also referred to as a *network segment*.

At the source node, the data link layer prepares communication for the media. The functions of the upper layers of the node are not aware what media the communication will use or over how many different media the communication can travel. The data link layer effectively insulates the communication processes at the higher layers from the media transitions occurring end to end. Network layer protocols need not be aware of which media the communication will use.

A network model allows each layer to function with minimal concern for the roles of the other layers. The data link layer relieves the upper layers from the responsibility of putting data on the network and receiving data from the network. This layer provides services to support the communication processes for each medium over which data is to be transmitted.

In any given exchange of network layer packets, there can be numerous data link layer and media transitions. That is, the packet can be repackaged into different frames as it passes across different media. At each hop along the path, an intermediary device, usually a router, processes the frame as follows:

1. Accepting the frame from a medium

2. Decapsulating the frame into a packet

3. Constructing a new frame appropriate for the next media

4. Forwarding the packet inside the new frame across the next segment of the physical network

At each hop, the received frame is also examined for errors. If an error is found in a received frame, the frame is discarded. If the frame is good, the data link layer directs the packet to an upper-layer protocol, in this case IPv4 or IPv6.

As an example, Figure 7-1 shows a data conversation between two distant hosts. Although the two hosts can be communicating with their peer network layer protocols (IP, for example), numerous data link layer protocols are being used to transport the IP packets over various types of LANs and WANs. The packet exchange between these two hosts requires a diversity of protocols that must exist at the data link layer. At each router, a different data link layer protocol is used for transport on a new medium.

Figure 7-1   Data Link Layer Example

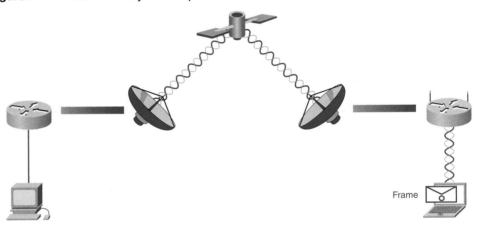

At each link between the devices shown in Figure 7-1, a different medium is used. Between the first PC and the router, an Ethernet link exists. The routers are connected through a satellite link, and the laptop is connected through a wireless link to the last router. In this example, as an IP packet travels from the PC to the laptop, it will be encapsulated into an Ethernet frame leaving the PC. At the first router, the Ethernet frame is decapsulated, processed, and then encapsulated into a new data link frame to cross the satellite link. For the final link, the packet will use a wireless data link frame from the router to the laptop.

Without the data link layer, a network layer protocol, like IP, would require provisions for connecting to every type of media that could exist along a delivery path. Moreover, IP would have to adapt every time a new network technology or medium was developed. This frequent change in the network layer standards would hamper protocol and network media innovation and development. This is a key reason for using a layered approach to networking.

Because of this isolation of the networking layers, development of a wide range of diverse data link layer protocols continues. The range of data link layer services has to include all the currently used types of media and the methods for accessing them. Because of the number of communication services provided by the data link layer, it is difficult to generalize their role and provide examples of a generic set of services. For that reason, any given protocol might or might not support all these data link layer services.

Controlling Transfer Across Local Media

Layer 2 protocols specify the encapsulation of a packet into a frame and the techniques for getting the encapsulated packet on and off each medium. The technique used for getting the frame on and off media is called the media access method or *MAC method*. For the data to be transferred across a number of different media, different media access control methods might be required during the course of a single communication. The media access control methods described by the data link layer protocols define the processes by which network devices can access the network media and transmit frames in diverse network environments.

Each network environment that packets encounter can have different characteristics. For example, one network environment can consist of many hosts contending to access the network medium on an improvised basis. Another environment might consist of a direct connection between only two devices. Another media might provide an orderly way for access.

A node that is an end device uses an adapter to make the connection to the network. For example, the device would use the appropriate network interface card (NIC) to connect to the LAN media. The adapter manages the framing and media access method.

At intermediary devices, such as routers, where the media type could change for each connected network, different physical interfaces encapsulate the packet into the appropriate frame, and a suitable MAC method is used to access each link. The router in Figure 7-2 has an Ethernet interface to connect to the LAN and a serial interface to connect to the WAN. As the router processes the frame, it will use data link layer services to receive the frame from one medium, decapsulate it to the Layer 3 protocol data unit (PDU), reencapsulate the PDU into a new frame, and place the frame on the medium of the next link of the network. In this figure, the packet is received with an encapsulation used by the LAN technology and reencapsulates the packet into a frame supported by the protocol used in the WAN.

Figure 7-2   Transfer of Frames

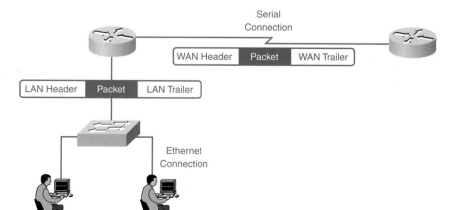

The type of frame used on an interface can be configured in the device. This is especially true in serial interfaces. For example, you can configure the encapsulation for the serial interface to use one of several WAN protocols such as High-Level Data Link Control (HDLC), Frame Relay, or PPP. PPP will be introduced later in this chapter in the section "Sample Data Link Layer Frames." All three of these protocols will be examined in later courses and their companion books.

Creating a Frame

The description of a frame is a key element of each data link layer protocol. Data link layer protocols require control information to enable the protocols to function. Control information can describe the following:

- Which nodes are in communication with each other

- When communication between individual nodes begins and ends

- If errors occurred while the nodes communicated

- Which nodes will communicate next

The encapsulation includes this control information. The protocol describes what control information is required and how that information is included in the encapsulation. Using the encapsulation described in the protocol, the data link layer prepares a packet for transport across the local media by encapsulating it with a header and a trailer to create a frame.

The data link layer frame includes the following elements:

- **Data:** The packet from the network layer

- **Header:** The control information, such as addressing, located at the beginning of the PDU

- **Trailer:** The control information added to the end of the PDU

You learn more about these frame elements later in this chapter in the section "Media Access Control: Addressing and Framing Data."

Data traveling on the media is converted into a stream of bits, or 1s and 0s. As a node receives long streams of bits, it must determine where a frame starts and stops and which bits represent the address or other control information.

Within each frame, there are a specific number of bits allocated for each control field. The receiving node uses the data link layer framing to determine the different groupings of bits contained in the stream that comprise each field. As seen in Figure 7-3, control information is inserted by the transmitting node in the header and trailer as values in different fields. This formatting gives the physical signals a structure that is decoded into packets at the destination.

Figure 7-3   Formatting for Data Transmission

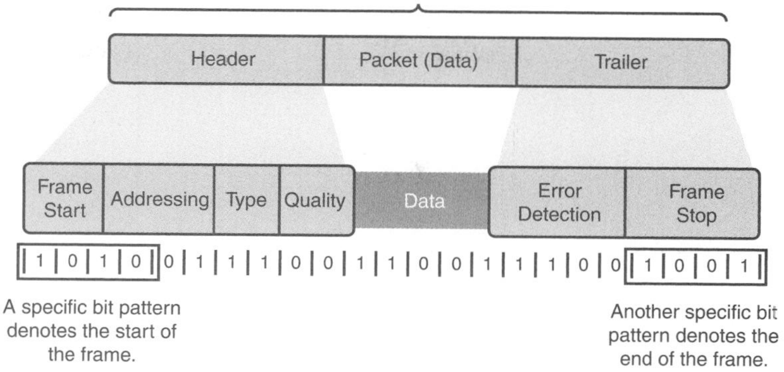

Typical field types include

- **Start and stop indicator fields:** The beginning and end limits of the frame

- **Addressing or naming fields:** The destination and/or source devices

- **Type field:** The type of PDU contained in the frame

- **Quality:** The control fields

- **Data field:** The frame payload (network layer packet)

Fields at the end of the frame form the trailer. These fields are used to detect errors and to mark the end of the frame.

Not all protocols include all these fields. The standards for a specific data link protocol define the actual frame format. Examples of some frame formats will be discussed in the section "Data Link Layer Protocols: The Frame," later in this chapter.

Connecting Upper-Layer Services to the Media

The data link layer exists as a connecting layer between the software processes of the layers above it and the hardware of physical layer below it. As shown in Figure 7-4, it has the distinction as the only layer that is implemented in software and in hardware. As such, the data link layer prepares the network layer packets for transmission across some form of media, be it copper, fiber, or the atmosphere.

Figure 7-4   Hardware and Software in the OSI Layers

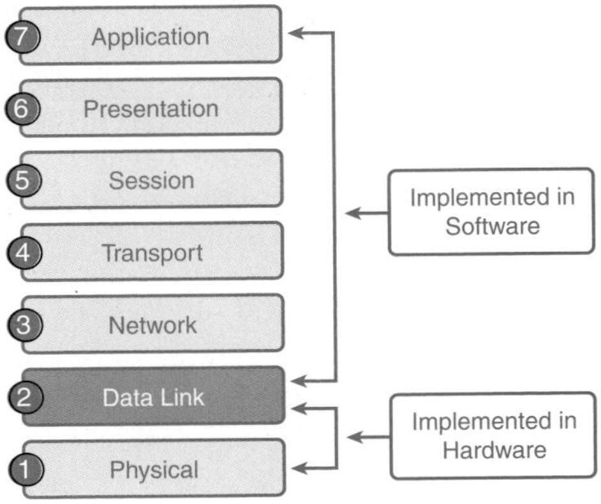

In many cases, the data link layer is embodied as a physical entity, such as an Ethernet *network interface card (NIC)*, which inserts into the system bus of a computer and makes the connection between running software processes on the computer and the physical media. The NIC does not operate solely as a physical entity. Software associated with the NIC enables the NIC to perform its intermediary functions of preparing data for transmission and encoding the data as signals to be sent on the associated media.

To support a wide variety of network functions, the data link layer is often divided into two sublayers:

- The upper sublayer defines the software processes that provide services to the network layer protocols.

- The lower sublayer defines the media access processes performed by the hardware.

Separating the data link layer into sublayers allows one type of frame defined by the upper layer to access different types of media defined by the lower layer. Such is the case in many LAN technologies, including Ethernet.

The two common LAN sublayers are as follows:

- *Logical Link Control (LLC)* places information in the frame that identifies which network layer protocol is being used for the frame. This information allows multiple Layer 3 protocols, such as IPv4, IPv6, and IPX, to utilize the same network interface and media.

- *MAC* provides data link layer addressing and delimiting of data according to the physical signaling requirements of the medium and the type of data link layer protocol in use.

Standards

Unlike the protocols of the upper layers of the TCP/IP suite, data link layer protocols are generally not defined by Requests For Comments (RFC). Although the Internet Engineering Task Force (IETF) maintains the functional protocols and services for the TCP/IP protocol suite in the upper layers, it does not define the functions and operation of that model's network access layer. The TCP/IP network access layer is the equivalent of the OSI data link and physical layers. You learn more about the physical layer in Chapter 8, "OSI Physical Layer."

The functional protocols and services at the data link layer are described by engineering organizations (such as IEEE, ANSI, and ITU) and communications companies. Engineering organizations set open standards and protocols. Communications companies can set and use proprietary protocols to take advantage of new advances in technology or market opportunities.

Data link layer services and specifications are defined by multiple standards based on a variety of technologies and media to which the protocols are applied. Some of these standards integrate both Layer 2 and Layer 1 services.

Engineering organizations that define open standards and protocols that apply to the data link layer include

- International Organization for Standardization (ISO, http://www.iso.org)

- Institute of Electrical and Electronics Engineers (IEEE, http://www.ieee.org)

- American National Standards Institute (ANSI, http://www.ansi.org)

- International Telecommunication Union (ITU, http://www.itu.org)

Unlike the upper-layer protocols, which are implemented mostly in software such as the host operating system or specific applications, data link layer processes occur in both software and hardware. The protocols at this layer are implemented within the electronics of the network adapters with which the node connects to the physical network. For example, the NIC is the device implementing the data link layer on a computer. For a laptop, a wireless PCMCIA adapter is commonly used. Each of these adapters is the hardware that complies with the Layer 2 standards and protocols.

MAC Techniques: Placing Data on the Media

Regulating the placement of data frames onto the media is known as MAC. Among the different implementations of the data link layer protocols, there are different methods of controlling access to the media. These MAC techniques define whether and how the nodes share the media.

MAC is the equivalent of traffic rules that regulate the entrance of motor vehicles onto a roadway. The absence of any MAC would be the equivalent of vehicles ignoring all other traffic and entering the road without regard to the other vehicles.

However, not all roads and entrances are the same. Traffic can enter the road by merging, by waiting for its turn at a stop sign, or by obeying signal lights. A driver follows a different set of rules for each type of entrance.

In the same way, there are different ways to regulate the placing of frames onto the media. The protocols at the data link layer define the rules for access to different media. Some MAC methods use highly controlled processes to ensure that frames are safely placed on the media. These methods are defined by sophisticated protocols, which require mechanisms that introduce overhead onto the network.

The method of MAC used depends on

- **Media sharing:** If and how the nodes share the media

- **Topology:** How the connection between the nodes appears to the data link layer

MAC for Shared Media

Some network topologies share a common medium with multiple nodes. At any one time, there can be a number of devices attempting to send and receive data using the network media. There are rules that govern how these devices share the media.

In the traffic analogy, consider a street with driveways from many buildings intersecting the street. This provides many intersections for cars to enter this street. To prevent collisions, access to this road would need to be regulated. This road infrastructure is similar to the characteristics of logical multiaccess. Multiaccess topologies provide multiple nodes to share the use of the media to transport the frames.

Any number of MAC techniques might be appropriate for this type of logical topology. The two basic MAC methods for shared media are as follows:

- **Controlled:** Each node has its own time to use the medium.

- **Contention-based:** All nodes compete for the use of the medium.

Table 7-1 lists some characteristics and examples of these two MAC techniques. The sections that follow describe the characteristics of both methods in more detail.

Table 7-1   MAC Methods for Shared Media

Method	Characteristics	Examples
Controlled access	Only one station transmits at a time. Devices wanting to transmit must wait their turn. No collisions. Some networks use token passing.	Token Ring FDDI
Contention-based access	Stations can transmit at any time. Collisions exist. Mechanisms exist to resolve contention: CSMA/CD for Ethernet networks CSMA/CA for 802.11 wireless networks	Ethernet Wireless

Controlled Access for Shared Media

When using the controlled access method, network devices take turns, in sequence, to access the medium. This method is also known as scheduled access or *deterministic*. When it is time for a device to access the media but the device does not need to access the medium, the opportunity to use the medium passes to the next device in line. When one device is placing a frame on the media, no other device can do so until the frame has arrived at the destination and has been processed by the destination.

Although controlled access is well ordered and provides predictable throughput, these methods can be inefficient because a device has to wait for its turn before it can use the medium.

Contention-Based Access for Shared Media

Contention-based methods allow any device to try to access the medium whenever it has data to send. These MAC methods are sometimes referred to as *nondeterministic*. To prevent complete chaos on the media, these methods use a *carrier sense multiple access (CSMA)* process to first detect whether the media is carrying a signal. If a *carrier* signal on the media from another node is detected, it means that another device is transmitting. When the device attempting to transmit sees that the media is busy, it will wait and try again after a short time period. If no carrier signal is detected, the device transmits its data. Ethernet and wireless networks use contention-based MAC.

It is possible that the CSMA process will fail and two devices will transmit at the same time. This is called a *collision*. If a collision occurs, the data sent by both devices will be corrupted and will need to be re-sent.

Contention-based MAC methods do not have the overhead of controlled access methods. Unlike controlled access methods, a mechanism for tracking whose turn it is to access the media is not required. However, the contention-based systems do not scale well under heavy media use. As use and the number of nodes increase, the probability of successful media access without a collision decreases. Additionally, the recovery mechanisms required to correct errors due to these collisions further diminishes the throughput.

CSMA is usually implemented in conjunction with a method for resolving the media contention. The two commonly used methods are

- CSMA/collision detect (CSMA/CD)

- CSMA/collision avoid (CSMA/CA)

The next sections describe CSMA/CD and CSMA/CA.

CSMA/Collision Detect

In CSMA/CD, the device monitors the media for the presence of a data signal. If a data signal is absent, indicating that the media is free, the device transmits the data. If signals are then detected that show another device was transmitting at the same time, all devices stop sending and try again later. Traditional forms of Ethernet use this method. CSMA/CD is covered in more detail in Chapter 9, "Ethernet."

CSMA/Collision Avoid

In *CSMA/collision avoid (CSMA/CA)*, the device examines the media for the presence of a data signal. If the media is free, the device sends a notification across the media of its intent to use it. The device then sends the data. This method is used by 802.11 wireless networking technologies.

MAC for Nonshared Media

MAC protocols for nonshared media require little or no control before placing frames onto the media. These protocols have simpler rules and procedures for MAC. Such is the case for point-to-point topologies.

In point-to-point topologies, the media interconnects just two nodes. Referring to the road analogy, a road between two buildings with no traffic access except at either end could be considered a point-to-point example. If the road has only one lane, the only traffic regulation required is to ensure that traffic flows from only one end of the road at any one time. If the road has two lanes and no other points where cars could enter the roadway, the traffic could flow in both directions at the same time, and additional regulation of traffic would not be required.

In a point-to-point topology, the nodes do not have to share the media with other hosts or determine whether a frame is destined for that node. Therefore, data link layer protocols have little to do for controlling nonshared media access.

In point-to-point connections, the data link layer has to consider whether the communication is *half duplex* or *full duplex*. Using the traffic analogy, half duplex would be a one-lane road, and full duplex would be a two-lane road.

Half-duplex communication means that the devices can both transmit and receive on the media but cannot do so simultaneously. Ethernet has established arbitration rules for resolving conflicts arising from instances when more than one station attempts to transmit at the same time.

In full-duplex communication, both devices can transmit and receive on the media at the same time. The data link layer assumes that the media is available for transmission for both nodes at any time. Therefore, there is no media arbitration necessary in the data link layer.

The details of a specific MAC technique can only be examined by studying a specific protocol. Within this book, you will study traditional Ethernet, which uses CSMA/CD. Other techniques will be covered in later courses and their companion books.

Logical Topology Versus Physical Topology

The topology of a network is the arrangement or relationship of the network devices and the interconnections between them. Network topologies can be viewed at the physical level and the logical level.

The *physical topology* is an arrangement of the nodes and the physical connections between them. The representation of how the media is used to interconnect the devices is the physical topology. These will be further discussed in Chapter 9 of this book and covered in detail in later courses and their companion books.

A *logical topology* is the way a network transfers frames from one node to the next. This arrangement consists of virtual connections between the nodes of a network independent of their physical layout. These logical signal paths are defined by data link layer protocols. The data link layer "sees" the logical topology of a network when controlling data access to the media. It is the logical topology that influences the type of network framing and MAC used.

Note

The physical or cabled topology of a network will most likely not be the same as the logical topology.

The logical topology of a network is closely related to the mechanism used to manage network access. When several entities share the same media, some mechanism must be in place to control access. Access methods are applied to networks to regulate this media access so that all stations have access.

The following logical and physical topologies typically used in networks are illustrated in Figure 7-5:

- Point-to-point

- Multiaccess

- Ring

Figure 7-5   Logical Topologies

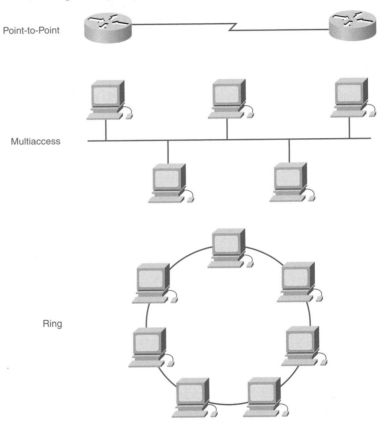

The logical implementations of these topologies and their associated MAC methods are considered in the following sections.

Point-to-Point Topology

A point-to-point topology connects two nodes directly. In data networks with point-to-point topologies, the MAC protocol can be very simple. All frames on the media can only travel to or from the two nodes. The frames are placed on the media by the node at one end and taken off the media by the node at the other end of the point-to-point circuit.

In point-to-point networks, if data can only flow in one direction at a time, it is operating as a half-duplex link. If data can successfully flow across the link from each node simultaneously, it is a full-duplex link. Data link layer protocols could provide more sophisticated MAC processes for logical point-to-point topologies, but this would only add unnecessary protocol overhead.

Instead of being directly attached, the two end nodes communicating in a point-to-point network can be logically connected through a number of intermediate devices. However, the use of these physical devices in the network does not affect the logical topology. As shown in Figure 7-6, the source and destination node can be indirectly connected to each other over some geographical distance. In some cases, the logical connection between nodes forms what is called a *virtual circuit*. A virtual circuit is a logical connection created within a network between two network devices. The two nodes on either end of the virtual circuit exchange the frames with each other. This occurs even if the frames are directed through intermediary devices. Virtual circuits are important logical communication constructs used by some Layer 2 technologies.

Figure 7-6   Logical Point-to-Point Topology

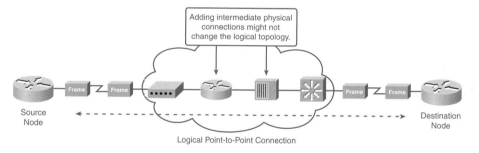

The media access method used by the data link protocol is determined by the topology, not the *physical* topology. This means that the logical point-to-point connection between two nodes might not necessarily be between two physical nodes at each end of a single physical link.

Multiaccess Topology

A logical multiaccess topology enables a number of nodes to communicate by using the same shared media. Data from only one node can be placed on the medium at any one time. Every node "sees" all the frames that are on the medium. In multiaccess topologies, the frame requires addresses to identify to which node the frame is intended. With every node receiving the frame, the only node to process the contents of the frame is the node to which the frame is addressed.

Having many nodes share access to the medium requires a data link MAC method to regulate the transmission of data and thereby reduce collisions between different signals.

The MAC methods used by logical multiaccess topologies are typically CSMA/CD or CSMA/CA. However, token-passing methods can also be used. You learn about token passing in the next section.

A number of MAC techniques are available for this type of logical topology. The data link layer protocol specifies the MAC method that will provide the appropriate balance between frame control, frame protection, and network overhead.

Ring Topology

In a logical ring topology, each node in turn receives a frame. If the frame is not addressed to the node, the node passes the frame to the next node. This allows a ring to use a controlled MAC technique called *token passing*.

Nodes in a logical ring topology remove the frame from the ring, examine the destination address of the frame, and send it on if it is not addressed for that node. All nodes around the ring between the source and destination node examine the frame.

There are multiple MAC techniques that could be used with a logical ring, depending on the level of control required. For example, only one frame at a time is usually carried by the media. If there is no data being transmitted, a signal (known as a token) can be placed on the media, and a node can only place a data frame on the media when it has the token.

Remember that the data link layer "sees" a logical ring topology. The actual physical cabling topology could be another topology.

MAC: Addressing and Framing Data

Two important functions of the MAC sublayer are the addressing and framing of data. The framing provides the control information necessary to receive the data. One very important piece of control information is the Layer 2 address.

Data Link Layer Protocols: The Frame

Remember that although there are many different data link layer protocols that describe data link layer frames, each frame type has three basic parts:

- Header
- Data
- Trailer

All data link layer protocols encapsulate the Layer 3 PDU within the data field of the frame. However, the structure of the frame and the fields contained in the header and trailer vary according to the protocol.

The data link layer protocol describes the features required for the transport of packets across different media. These features of the protocol are integrated into the encapsulation of the frame. When the frame arrives at its destination and the data link protocol takes the frame off the media, the framing information is read and discarded.

Consider the previously discussed traffic analogy. The Layer 2 protocol in use is like a fleet of vehicles. For example, we have all types of vehicles from small automobiles to large trucks. Small vehicles are easily maneuverable around crowded urban environments but do not carry many passengers or much cargo. While large trucks or buses are not maneuverable, they are well suited to carry large payloads on the highway. Similarly, features of the frames used by different data link layer protocols vary according to the transmission environment.

No one frame structure meets the needs of all data transportation across all types of media. Depending on the environment, the amount of control information needed in the frame varies to match the MAC requirements of the media and logical topology.

Framing: Role of the Header

The frame header contains the control information specified by the data link layer protocol for the specific logical topology and media used. Frame control information is unique to each type of protocol. It is used by the Layer 2 protocol to provide features demanded by the communication environment. Typical frame header fields include

- **Start of Frame field:** Indicates the beginning of the frame

- **Source and Destination address fields:** Indicate the source and destination nodes on the media

- **Priority/Quality of Service field:** Indicates a particular type of communication service for processing

- **Type field**: Indicates the upper-layer service contained in the frame

- **Logical connection control field:** Used to establish a logical connection between nodes

- **Physical link control field:** Used to establish the media link

- **Flow control field:** Used to start and stop traffic over the media

- **Congestion control field:** Indicates congestion in the media

The preceding field names are nonspecific fields listed as examples. Different data link layer protocols can use different fields from those mentioned. Because the purposes and functions of data link layer protocols are related to the specific topologies and media, you have to examine each protocol to gain a detailed understanding of its frame structure. As protocols are discussed in this book, more information about the frame structure is provided.

Addressing: Where the Frame Goes

The data link layer provides addressing that is used in transporting the frame across the shared local media. Device addresses at this layer are referred to as *physical addresses*. Data link layer addressing is contained within the frame header and specifies the frame destination node on the local network. The frame header can also contain the source address of the frame.

Unlike Layer 3 logical addresses that are hierarchical, physical addresses do not indicate on what logical network the device is located. If the device is moved to another network or subnet, it will still function with the same Layer 2 physical address.

Because the frame is used only to transport data between nodes across the local media, the data link layer address is used only for local delivery. Addresses at this layer have no meaning beyond the local network. As compared to Layer 3, where addresses in the packet header are carried from source host to destination host regardless of the number of network hops along the route, Layer 2 uses addressing to transport the frame across the local media.

If the packet in the frame must pass onto another network segment, the intermediate device, a router, will decapsulate the original frame, create a new frame for the packet, and send the new frame onto the new segment. The new frame will use source and destination addressing as necessary to transport the packet across the new media.

The need for data link layer addressing at this layer depends on the logical topology. Point-to-point topologies, with just two interconnected nodes, do not require addressing. After it is on the medium, the frame has only one place it can go.

Because ring and multiaccess topologies can connect many nodes on a common medium, addressing is required for these topologies. When a frame reaches each node in the topology, the node examines the destination address in the header to determine whether it is the destination of the frame.

Framing: Role of the Trailer

Data link layer protocols add a trailer to the end of each frame.

Typical frame trailer fields include

- **Frame Check Sequence fields:** Used for error checking of the frame contents.
- **Stop field:** Used to indicate the end of the frame. Also, can be used to increase the size of a frame to an expected fixed size or minimum size.

The trailer is used to determine whether the frame arrived without error. This process is called *error detection*. Error detection is accomplished by placing a logical or mathematical summary of the bits that comprise the frame in the trailer.

The Frame Check Sequence (FCS) field is used to determine whether errors occurred in the transmission and reception of the frame. Error detection is added at the data link layer because this is where data is transferred across the media. The media is a potentially unsafe environment for data. The signals on the media could be subject to interference, distortion, or loss that would change the bit values that those signals represent. The error-detection mechanism provided by the use of the FCS field discovers most errors caused on the media.

To ensure that the content of the received frame at the destination matches that of the frame that left the source node, a transmitting node creates a logical summary of the contents of the frame. This is known as the ***cyclic redundancy check (CRC)*** value. This value is placed in the FCS field of the frame to represent the contents of the frame.

If the CRC generated by the originating station, or far-end device, does not match the checksum calculated from the data received, an error is indicated in the frame. When the frame arrives at the destination node, the receiving node calculates its own logical summary, or CRC, of the frame. The receiving node compares the two CRC values. If the two values are the same, the frame is considered to have arrived as it was transmitted. If the CRC value in the FCS differs from the CRC calculated at the receiving node, the frame is discarded.

By comparing the CRC, changes to the frame are detected. CRC errors typically indicate noise or other transmission problems on the data link. On an Ethernet segment, CRC errors result from collisions or from a station transmitting bad data.

There is always the small possibility that a frame with a good CRC result is actually corrupt. Errors in bits can cancel each other out when the CRC is calculated. Upper-layer protocols would then be required to detect and correct this data loss.

Note

Error detections should not be confused with reliability or error correction. Reliability is the process of using error detection to determine whether there are errors in the data and to retransmit the data if necessary. Error correction is the ability to determine whether a frame contains an error and the ability to repair the error from the information sent with the frame communication.

Both error detection and error correction involve the additional bits. With error checking, these bits are only used to determine the error. With error correction, the bits are used to restore the flawed data to the original bits of data as they were transmitted. Therefore, error correction is more complex and requires more overhead than error detection.

The protocol used in the data link layer will determine whether the communication uses reliability or error correction. The FCS field is used by all data link layer protocols to detect the error, but some protocols will support error-correction codes in the FCS.

Sample Data Link Layer Frames

In a TCP/IP network, OSI Layer 2 protocols work with the Internet Protocol at OSI Layer 3. However, the actual Layer 2 protocol used depends on the logical topology of the network and the implementation of the physical layer. Given the wide range of physical media used across the range of topologies in networking, there are a correspondingly high number of Layer 2 protocols in use.

The CCNA courses and companion books cover the following protocols:

- Ethernet

- PPP

- High-Level Data Link Control (HDLC)

- Frame Relay

- ATM

Each protocol performs MAC for specified Layer 2 logical topologies. This means that a number of different network devices can act as nodes that operate at the data link layer when implementing these protocols. These devices include the network adapter or NICs on computers as well as the interfaces on routers and Layer 2 switches.

The Layer 2 protocol used for a particular network topology is determined by the technology used to implement that topology. The technology is, in turn, determined by the size of the network (in terms of the number of hosts and the geographic scope) and the services to be provided over the network. Figure 7-7 shows an example of some of these different Layer 2 frames transporting a packet across an internetwork.

Figure 7-7   Examples of Layer 2 Protocols

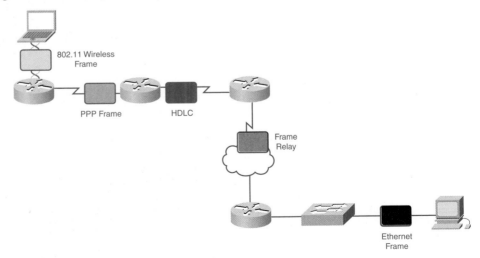

An internetwork has two types of environments: LANs and WANs. Each of these environments has different requirements for frames.

A LAN typically uses a high-bandwidth technology that is capable of supporting large numbers of hosts. A LAN's relatively small geographic area (a single building or a multi-building campus) and its high density of users make this technology cost effective.

However, using a high-bandwidth technology is usually not cost effective for WANs that cover large geographic areas (cities or multiple cities, for example). The cost of the long-distance physical links and the technology used to carry the signals over those distances typically result in lower-bandwidth capacity.

The frames moving through WANs are exposed to more detrimental environments than those of LANs. This means that the frames traveling across WANs are more likely to be damaged than those in LANs. A difference in bandwidths and environments normally results in the use of different protocols for LANs and WANs, as described in the following sections.

Ethernet Protocol for LANs

Ethernet is a family of networking technologies that are defined in the IEEE 802.2 and 802.3 standards. Ethernet standards define both the Layer 2 protocols and the Layer 1 technologies. Ethernet is the most widely used LAN technology and supports data bandwidths of 10, 100, 1000, or 10,000 Mbps.

The basic frame format and the IEEE sublayers of OSI Layers 1 and 2 remain consistent across all forms of Ethernet. However, the methods for detecting and placing data on the media vary with different implementations.

Ethernet provides unacknowledged connectionless service over a shared media using CSMA/CD as the media access method. Shared media requires that the Ethernet packet header use a data link layer address to identify the source and destination nodes. As with most LAN protocols, this address is referred to as the *MAC address* of the node. An Ethernet MAC address is 48 bits and is generally represented in hexadecimal format.

The Ethernet frame has many fields, as shown in Figure 7-8:

- **Preamble:** Used to time synchronization; this also contains a delimiter to mark the end of the timing information.

- **Destination Address:** 48-bit MAC address for the destination node.

- **Source Address:** 48-bit MAC address for the source node.

- **Type:** Value to indicate which upper-layer protocol will receive the data after the Ethernet process is complete.

- **Data or payload:** This is the PDU, typically an IPv4 packet, that is to be transported over the media.

- **Frame Check Sequence (FCS):** A CRC value used to check for damaged frames.

Figure 7-8 Ethernet Protocol

	Frame					
Field Name	Preamble	Destination	Source	Type	Data	Frame Check Sequence
Size	8 Bytes	6 Bytes	6 Bytes	2 Bytes	46–1500 Bytes	4 Bytes

Ethernet is such an important part of data networking, Chapter 9 is devoted to it. You also see it in examples throughout this series of courses.

PPP for WANs

PPP is a protocol used to deliver frames between two nodes. Unlike many data link layer protocols that are defined by electrical engineering organizations, the PPP standard is defined by RFCs. PPP was developed as a WAN protocol and remains the protocol of choice to implement many serial WANs. PPP can be used on various physical media, including twisted-pair cable, fiber-optic lines, and satellite transmission, as well as for virtual connections.

PPP uses a layered architecture. To accommodate the different types of media, PPP establishes logical connections, called *sessions*, between two nodes. The PPP session hides the underlying physical media from the upper-layer protocol. These sessions also provide PPP with a method for encapsulating multiple upper-layer protocols over a point-to-point link. Each protocol encapsulated over the link establishes its own PPP session.

PPP also allows the two nodes to negotiate the following options within the PPP session:

- **Authentication:** PPP authentication requires the nodes on each end of the PPP link to authenticate in order to establish communications over a point-to-point link.
- **Compression:** PPP compression reduces the size of a data frame transmitted over a network link. Reducing the size of the frame reduces the time required to transmit the frame across the network.
- **Multilink:** PPP multilink is the method of using multiple data links to send the frames. This allows the use of multiple physical links to support a single PPP session.

Figure 7-9 shows the following basic fields in a PPP frame:

- **Flag:** A single byte that indicates the beginning or end of a frame. The flag field consists of the binary sequence 01111110.
- **Address:** A single byte that contains the standard PPP broadcast address. PPP does not assign individual station addresses.

- **Control:** A single byte that contains the binary sequence 00000011, which calls for transmission of user data in an unsequenced frame.

- **Protocol:** Two bytes that identify the protocol encapsulated in the data field of the frame. The most up-to-date values of the protocol field are specified in the most recent Assigned Numbers RFC.

- **Data:** Zero or more bytes that contain the datagram for the protocol specified in the protocol field.

- **Frame Check Sequence (FCS):** Normally 16 bits (2 bytes). By prior agreement, consenting PPP implementations can use a 32-bit (4-byte) FCS for improved error detection.

Figure 7-9   Point-to-Point Protocol

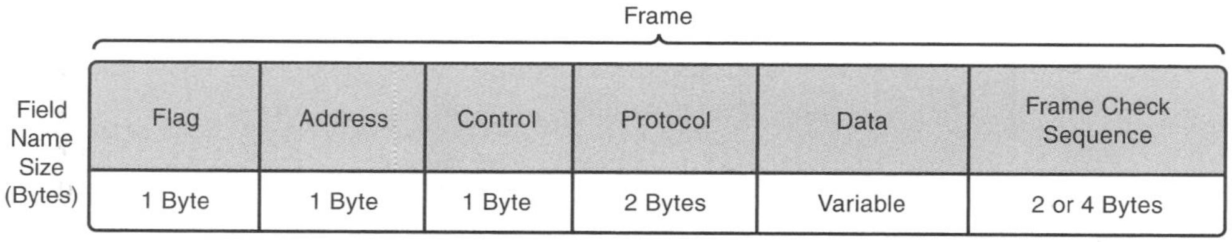

			Frame			
Field Name	Flag	Address	Control	Protocol	Data	Frame Check Sequence
Size (Bytes)	1 Byte	1 Byte	1 Byte	2 Bytes	Variable	2 or 4 Bytes

Wireless Protocol for LANs

802.11 is an extension of the IEEE 802 standards. It uses the same 802.2 LLC and 48-bit addressing scheme as other 802 LANs. However, there are many differences at the MAC sublayer and physical layer. In a wireless environment, the environment requires special considerations. There is no definable physical connectivity; therefore, external factors can interfere with data transfer, and it is difficult to control access. To meet these challenges, wireless standards have additional controls.

The standard IEEE 802.11, commonly referred to as *Wi-Fi*, is a contention-based system using a CSMA/CA media access process. CSMA/CA specifies a random *backoff* procedure for all nodes that are waiting to transmit. The most likely opportunity for medium contention is just after the medium becomes available. Making the nodes back off for a random period greatly reduces the likelihood of a collision.

802.11 networks also use data link acknowledgments to confirm that a frame is received successfully. If the sending station does not detect the acknowledgment frame, either because the original data frame or the acknowledgment was not received intact, the frame is retransmitted. This explicit acknowledgment overcomes interference and other radio-related problems.

Other services supported by 802.11 are authentication, association (connectivity to a wireless device), and privacy (encryption).

The 802.11 frame contains these fields, as shown in Figure 7-10:

- **Protocol Version:** Version of 802.11 frame in use

- **Type and Subtype:** Identifies one of three functions and subfunctions of the frame: control, data, and management

- **To DS:** Set to 1 in data frames destined for the distribution system (devices in the wireless structure)

- **From DS:** Set to 1 in data frames exiting the distribution system

- **More Fragments:** Set to 1 for frames that have another fragment

- **Retry:** Set to 1 if the frame is a retransmission of an earlier frame

- **Power Management:** Set to 1 to indicate that a node will be in power-save mode

- **More Data:** Set to 1 to indicate to a node in power-save mode that more frames are buffered for that node

- **Wired Equivalent Privacy (WEP):** Set to 1 if the frame contains WEP-encrypted information for security

- **Order:** Set to 1 in a data type frame that uses Strictly Ordered service class (does not need reordering)

- **Duration/ID:** Depending on the type of frame, represents either the time, in microseconds, required to transmit the frame or an *association identity (AID)* for the station that transmitted the frame

- **Destination Address (DA):** MAC address of the final destination node in the network

- **Source Address (SA):** MAC address of the node that initiated the frame

- **Receiver Address (RA):** MAC address that identifies the wireless device that is the immediate recipient of the frame

- **Transmitter Address (TA):** MAC address that identifies the wireless device that transmitted the frame

- **Sequence Number:** Indicates the sequence number assigned to the frame; retransmitted frames are identified by duplicate sequence numbers

- **Fragment Number:** Indicates the number for each fragment of a frame

- **Frame Body:** Contains the information being transported; for data frames, typically an IP packet

- **FCS:** Contains a 32-bit cyclic redundancy check (CRC) of the frame

Figure 7-10   802.11 Wireless LAN Protocol

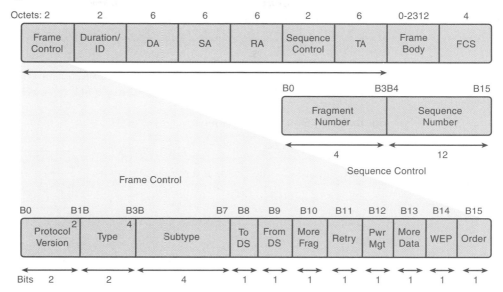

Note

PPP information can be found in RFC 1661 at the IETF website, http://www.ietf.org.

Putting It All Together: Following Data Through an Internetwork

To understand the operation of network communication, it is helpful to examine the communication process at the different layers. Examining the operation at each layer helps you understand the function of the layer as well as its interaction with the adjoining layers. In this section, you will examine a simple communication between two hosts across an internetwork. For this example, an HTTP request is depicted between a client and a server.

To focus on the data transfer process, this discussion omits many elements that can occur in a real transaction. In each step, the attention is on the major elements. Many parts of the headers are ignored, for example.

This example also demonstrates the use of some technologies that have not yet been explained. This section will help provide a framework to understand these technologies.

This example assumes that all routing tables are converged and *Address Resolution Protocol (ARP)* tables are complete. Additionally, this example assumes that a TCP session is already established between the client and server. It is also assumed that the Domain Name System (DNS) lookup for the WWW server is already cached at the client.

In the WAN connection between the two routers, the PPP physical circuit and PPP session have been established.

In Figure 7-11, a user on a LAN wants to access a web page stored on a server that is located on a remote network. The user starts by activating a link on a web page.

Figure 7-11   Source Host Request

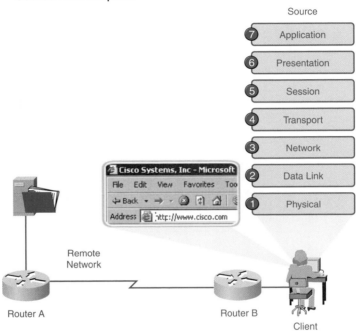

The browser initiates an HTTP GET request. The application layer adds the Layer 7 header to identify the application and data type.

The transport layer identifies the upper-layer service as a World Wide Web (WWW) client. The transport layer then associates this service with TCP and assigns the port numbers. It uses a randomly selected source port that is associated with this established session (12345). The destination port (80) is associated with a World Wide Web service.

TCP also sends an acknowledgment number that tells the World Wide Web server the sequence number of the next TCP segment it expects to receive. The sequence number will indicate where this segment is placed in the series of related segments. Flags are also set as appropriate to an established session.

At the network layer, an IP packet is constructed to identify the source and destination hosts. For the destination address, the client host uses the IP address associated with the

World Wide Web server host name that is cached in the host table. It uses its own IPv4 address as the source address. The network layer also identifies the upper-layer protocol encapsulated in this packet as a TCP segment.

The data link layer refers to the Address Resolution Protocol (ARP) cache to determine the MAC address that is associated with the interface of Router B, which is specified as the default gateway. It then uses this address to build an Ethernet II frame, shown in Figure 7-12, to transport the IPv4 packet across the local media. The MAC address of the laptop is used as the source MAC address, and the MAC address of the Fa0/0 interface of Router B is used as the destination MAC address in the frame.

Figure 7-12   Source Host Encapsulation

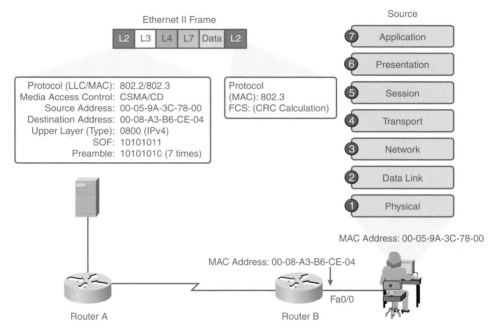

The frame also indicates the upper-layer protocol of IPv4 with a value of 0800 in the Type field. The frame begins with a Preamble and Start of Frame (SOF) indicator and ends with a cyclic redundancy check (CRC) in the frame check sequence at the end of the frame for the error detection.

It then uses CSMA/CD to control the placing of the frame onto the media. The physical layer begins encoding the frame onto the media, bit by bit. The segment between Router A and the server is a 10BASE-T segment; therefore, the bits are encoded using Manchester Differential encoding. Router B buffers the bits as they are received.

In Figure 7-13, Router B examines the bits in the Preamble and SOF, looking for the two consecutive 1 bits that indicate the beginning of the frame. Router B then begins buffering the bits as part of the reconstructed frame. When the entire frame is received, Router B generates a CRC of the frame. It then compares this to the FCS at the end of the frame to determine that the frame was received intact.

Figure 7-13   Router B Decapsulation and Encapsulation

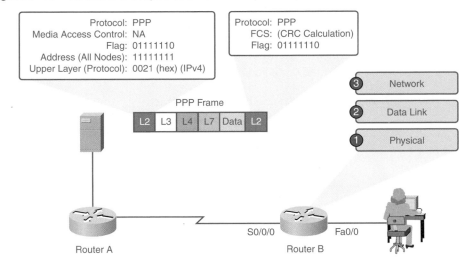

When the frame is confirmed as a good frame, the destination MAC address in the frame is compared to the MAC address of the interface (Fa0/0). Because it matches, the encapsulation is removed and the packet is pushed up to the network layer.

At the network layer, the destination IPv4 address of the packet is compared against the routes in the routing table. A match is found that is associated with a next hop out interface S0/0/0. The packet inside Router B is then passed to the circuitry for the S0/0/0 interface.

Router B creates a PPP frame to transport the packet across the WAN. In the PPP header, a flag of 01111110 binary is added to indicate the start of the frame. Following that, an address field of 11111111 is added, which is equivalent to a broadcast (it means "send to all stations"). Because PPP is point-to-point and is used as a direct link between two nodes, this field has no real meaning. Also included is a Protocol field with a value of 0021 (hex) to indicate that an IPv4 packet is encapsulated. The frame trailer ends with a CRC in the FCS for the error detection. A Flag value of 01111110 binary indicates the end of a PPP frame.

With the circuit and PPP session already established between the routers, the physical layer begins encoding the frame onto the WAN media, bit by bit. The receiving router (Router A) buffers the bits as they are received. The type of bit representation and encoding is dependent on the type of WAN technology being used.

In Figure 7-14, Router A examines the bits in the flag to identify the beginning of the frame. Router A then begins buffering the bits as part of the reconstructed frame. When the entire frame is received, as indicated by the flag in the trailer, Router A generates a CRC of the frame. It then compares this to the FCS at the end of the frame to determine that the frame was received intact.

Figure 7-14   Router A Decapsulation and Encapsulation

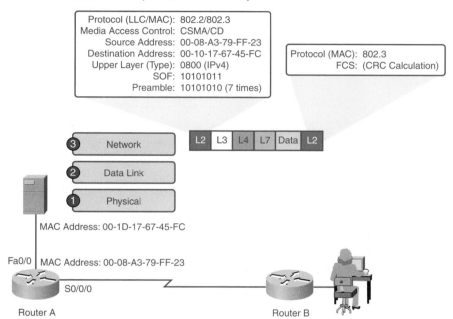

When the frame is confirmed as a good frame, the encapsulation is removed and the packet is pushed up to the network layer of Router A.

At the network layer, the destination IPv4 address of the packet is compared against the routes in the routing table. A match is found that is directly connected to interface Fa0/0. The packet inside Router A is then passed to the circuitry for the Fa0/0 interface.

The data link layer refers to the ARP cache of Router A to determine the MAC address that is associated with the interface of the web server. It then uses this MAC address to build an Ethernet II frame to transport the IPv4 packet across the local media to the server. The MAC address of the Fa0/0 interface of Router A is used as the source MAC address, and the MAC address of the server is used as the destination MAC address in the frame.

The frame also indicates the upper-layer protocol of IPv4 with a value of 0800 in the Type field. The frame begins with a Preamble and Start of Frame (SOF) indicator and ends with a CRC in the FCS at the end of the frame for the error detection.

It then uses CSMA/CD to control the placing of the frame onto the media. The physical layer begins encoding the frame onto the media, bit by bit. The segment between Router A and the server is a 100BASE-T segment; therefore, the bits are encoded using 4B/5B encoding. The server buffers the bits as they are received.

In Figure 7-15, the web server examines the bits in the Preamble and SOF, looking for the two consecutive 1 bits that indicate the beginning of the frame. The server then begins buffering the bits as part of the reconstructed frame. When it has received the entire frame, the server generates a CRC of the frame. It then compares this to the FCS at the end of the frame to determine that the frame was received intact.

Figure 7-15   Web Server Frame Reception and Decapsulation

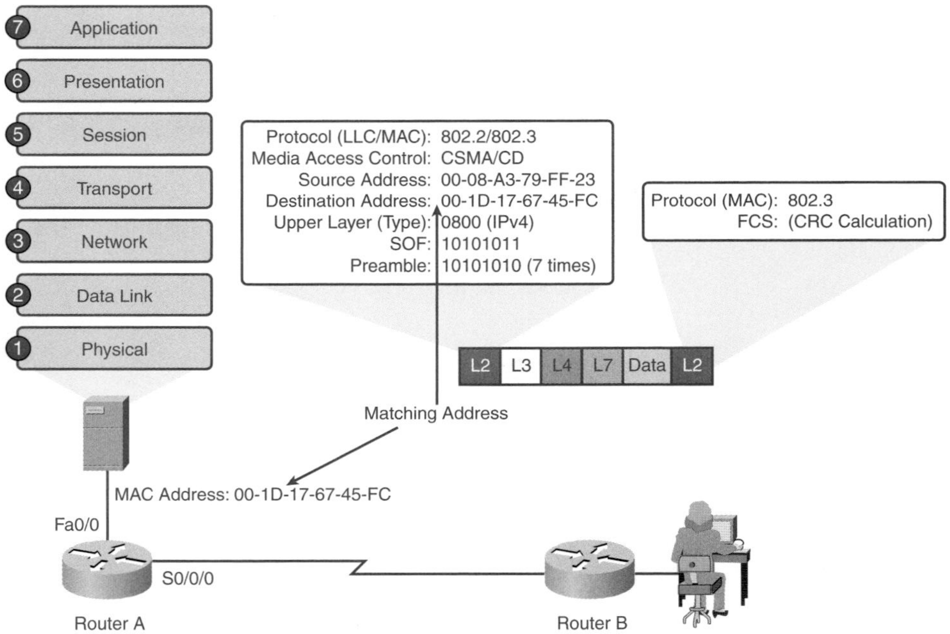

When the frame is confirmed as a good frame, the destination MAC address in the frame is compared to the MAC address of the NIC in the server. Because it matches, the encapsulation is removed and the packet is pushed up to the network layer.

At the network layer, the destination IPv4 address of the packet is examined to identify the destination host. Because this address matches its own IPv4 address, the packet is processed by the server. The network layer identifies the upper-layer protocol as TCP and directs the contained segment to the TCP service at the transport layer.

At the transport layer of the server, the TCP segment is examined to determine the session to which the data contained in the segment belongs. This is done by examining the source and destination ports. The unique source and destination port identifies an existing session to the web server service.

The sequence number is used to place this segment in the proper order to be sent upward to the application layer. At the application layer, the HTTP GET request is delivered to the web server service (httpd). The service can then formulate a response to the request.

Packet Tracer
☐ Activity

Packet Tracing Across an Internetwork (7.4.1.3)

In this activity, you can examine in further detail the sample communication between two hosts presented in this section. Use file e1-7413.pka on the CD-ROM that accompanies this book to perform this activity using Packet Tracer.

Packet Tracer
☐ Activity

Investigate the Layer 2 Frame Headers (7.5.1.1)

In this activity, you can explore some of the most common Layer 2 encapsulations. Use file e1-7511.pka on the CD-ROM that accompanies this book to perform this activity using Packet Tracer.

Summary

The OSI data link layer prepares network layer packets for placement onto the physical media that transports data.

The wide range of data communications media requires a correspondingly wide range of data link protocols to control data access to these media.

Media access can be orderly and controlled, or it can be contention based. The logical topology and physical medium help determine the media access method.

The data link layer prepares the data for placement on the media by encapsulating the Layer 3 packet into a frame. A frame has header and trailer fields that include data link source and destination addresses, QoS, type of protocol, and Frame Check Sequence values.

Labs

The labs available in the companion *Network Fundamentals, CCNA Exploration Labs and Study Guide* (ISBN 1-58713-203-6) provide hands-on practice with the following topics introduced in this chapter:

Lab 7-1: Frame Examination (7.5.2.1)

In this lab, you will use Wireshark to capture and analyze Ethernet II frame header fields.

Many of the hands-on labs include Packet Tracer companion activities, where you can use Packet Tracer to complete a simulation of the lab. Look for this icon in *Network Fundamentals, CCNA Exploration Labs and Study Guide* (ISBN 1-58713-203-6) for hands-on labs that have Packet Tracer companion activities.

Check Your Understanding

Complete all the review questions listed here to test your understanding of the topics and concepts in this chapter. The appendix, "Check Your Understanding and Challenge Questions Answer Key," lists the answers.

1. How does the data link layer prepare packets for transmission?

2. Describe four general data link layer media access methods. Suggest data communications environments in which these access methods can be appropriately implemented.

3. Describe the features of a logical ring topology.

4. Name five Layer 2 protocols.

5. List five header field types in data link frames.

6. If a node receives a frame and the calculated CRC does not match the CRC in the FCS, what action will the node take?

    A. Drop the frame

    B. Reconstruct the frame from the CRC

    C. Forward the frame as it is to the next host

    D. Disable the interface on which the frame arrives

7. Which of the following protocols are typically used in WANs? (Choose two.)

    A. 802.11

    B. Ethernet

    C. HDLC

    D. PPP

8. What are the contents of the data field in a frame?

    A. 64 bytes

    B. The network layer PDU

    C. The Layer 2 source address

    D. The data directly from the application that generated the data

9. Which of the following is a characteristic of contention-based MAC?

    A. Used on nonshared media.

    B. Nodes compete for the use of the medium.

    C. Leaves MAC to the upper layer.

    D. Each node has a specific time to use the medium.

10. Which of the following are common data link sublayers used in LANs? (Choose two.)

    A. Protocol data unit

    B. Logic Link Control

    C. MAC

    D. Network interface card

    E. Carrier access multiaccess

11. Which of the following describes a virtual circuit?

    A. Is an error-detection technique

    B. Provides an encapsulation technique

    C. Is used only with point-to-point physical topologies

    D. Establishes a logical connection between two network devices

12. Name three basic parts that are common to all data link layer frames.

13. Which of the following functions does the data link layer perform?

   A. Provides user interfaces

   B. Ensures end-to-end delivery of data between hosts

   C. Connects the network software to the network hardware

   D. Establishes and maintains sessions between applications

14. Which of the following is true about the logical topology of a network?

   A. Is always multiaccess

   B. Provides the physical addressing

   C. Is determined by how the nodes in the network are connected

   D. Influences the type of MAC used in the network

Challenge Questions and Activities

These questions and activities require a deeper application of the concepts covered in this chapter. You can find the answers in the appendix.

1. Explain the purpose of the Frame Check Sequence field in a data link frame trailer.

2. How do data link layer addresses differ from network layer addresses?

3. Compare and contrast the logical point-to-point and logical multiaccess topologies.

4. Describe the issues in a router when it is interconnecting interfaces of different speeds, such as connecting an Ethernet network to a WAN on a serial interface.

5. Discuss the purpose of including a source address in the frame header. Could just one Layer 2 address be used? If so, how? Are there any data link layer protocols that use a single address?

6. Discuss the possible effect on throughput if a communication is operating in full duplex. Compare full duplex to multiaccess and half duplex.

7. Describe how the router can use different frame formats to forward an IP packet.

Packet Tracer
☐ Challenge

Look for this icon in *Network Fundamentals, CCNA Exploration Labs and Study Guide* (ISBN 1-58713-203-6) for instructions on how to perform the Packet Tracer Skills Integration Challenge for this chapter.

To Learn More

The following questions encourage you to reflect on the topics discussed in this chapter. Your instructor might ask you to research the questions and discuss your findings in class.

1. How did the widespread adoption of the OSI model change the development of network technologies? How does today's data communications environment differ from that of 20 years ago because of the adoption of the model?

2. Discuss and compare carrier sense multiaccess data link media access protocol features and operation with those of deterministic media access protocols.

3. Discuss and consider the issues that the developers of a new physical data communications medium have to resolve to ensure interoperability with the existing upper-layer TCP/IP protocols.

4. Research and discuss different data link layer protocols. Classify these protocols by different usage and then consider the similar characteristics within each classification.

5. Research and discuss error-detection and error-correction methods. Consider differences, including the amount of overhead required.

CHAPTER 8

OSI Physical Layer

Objectives

Upon completion of this chapter, you will able to answer the following questions:

- What role do the physical layer protocols and services play in supporting communication across data networks?

- What is the purpose of physical layer signaling and encoding used in networks?

- How do signals represent bits as a frame as data is transported across the local media?

- What are the basic characteristics of copper, fiber, and wireless network media?

- What are common implementations of copper, fiber, and wireless media in networks?

Key Terms

This chapter uses the following key terms. You can find the definitions in the Glossary.

physical medium   page 280

signal   page 280

encode   page 280

bit time   page 285

nonreturn to zero (NRZ)   page 286

Manchester encoding   page 286

code group   page 288

4B/5B   page 289

kilobits   page 290

megabits   page 290

throughput   page 291

goodput   page 291

attenuation   page 294

noise   page 294

unshielded twisted-pair (UTP) cable   page 294

RJ-45   page 295

pinout   page 296

straight-through cable   page 297

crossover cable   page 297

rollover cable   page 297

coaxial cable   page 297

coax   page 297

hybrid fiber-coax (HFC)   page 298

shielded twisted-pair (STP) cable   page 298

fiber-optic cable   page 299

Optical Time Domain Reflectometer (OTDR)   page 306

Previous chapters describe the process of encapsulating application data with different layers of control information as it descends the steps of the OSI model. This chapter explores the functions of the physical layer (Layer 1) and the standards and protocols that manage the transmission of data across the local medium.

Physical Layer: Communication Signals

The following sections introduce the purpose, operation, and fundamental principles associated with the physical layer. These sections also introduce the electrical and communications engineering organizations that define physical layer specifications.

Purpose of the Physical Layer

The role of the OSI physical layer is to encode the binary digits that represent data link layer frames into signals and to transmit and receive these signals across the physical media—copper wires, optical fiber, and wireless—that connect network devices. The data-link frame that comes down to the physical layer contains a string of bits representing application, presentation, session, and transport and network information. These bits are arranged in the logical order required by the specific protocols and applications that use them. These bits must travel over a *physical medium* such as copper cable or a glass fiber-optic cable, or wirelessly through the air. The physical medium is capable of conducting a *signal* in the form of voltage, light, or radio waves from one device to another. It is possible that the media will be shared by traffic from many protocols and subjected to physical distortions along the way. Part of the physical layer design is to minimize these effects of overhead and interference.

To prepare a data-link frame for the journey across the medium, the physical layer *encodes* the logical frame with patterns of data that will make it recognizable to the device that will pick it up on the other end of the medium. The device can be a router that will forward the frame or the destination device.

The delivery of frames across the local media requires the following physical layer elements:

- The physical media and associated connectors
- A representation of bits on the media
- Encoding of data and control information
- Transmitter and receiver circuitry on the network devices

After the signals traverse the medium, they are decoded to their original bit representations of data and given to the data link layer as a complete frame.

Figure 8-1 demonstrates the full encapsulation process and the transmitting of encoded binary bits across the OSI Layer 1 medium to the destination. The squared line across the bottom represents encoded signals.

Figure 8-1   Physical Layer Encoding

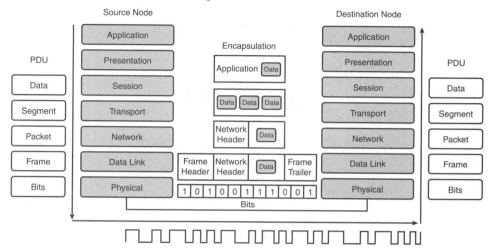

Physical Layer Operation

Each medium has unique signaling used to represent the bits in the data-link frames, but because IP is media independent, the frames remain unchanged as they cross to the next device. Table 8-1 lists the key media types and the signal type used for each.

Table 8-1   Signal Types for Each of the Media at the Physical Layer

Media	Signal Type
Copper cable	Patterns of electrical pulses
Fiber-optic cable	Patterns of light pulses
Wireless	Patterns of radio transmissions

When the physical layer puts a frame out onto media, it generates a set patterns of bits, or signal pattern, that can be understood by the receiving device. They are organized so that the device will be able to understand when a frame begins and when it ends. Without the signal pattern, the receiving device will not know when the frame ends, and the transmission will fail. While the data link layer identifies a frame, many OSI Layer 1 technologies require the adding of signals at the beginning and the end of frames.

To mark the beginning and end of frames, the transmitting device uses a bit pattern that is unique and is only used to identify the start or end of frames. As mentioned earlier, each physical media has different requirements for signaling, and they will be the topic of later sections in this chapter.

Physical Layer Standards

The physical layer performs functions very different from the other OSI layers. The upper layers perform logical functions carried out by instructions in software. The upper OSI layers were designed by software engineers and computer scientists who designed the services and protocols in the TCP/IP suite as part of the Internet Engineering Task Force (IETF).

By contrast, the physical layer, along with some similar technologies in the data link layer, defines hardware specifications, including electronic circuitry, media, and connectors. Instead of software engineers, the physical layer specifications were defined by electrical and communications engineering organizations. The following are some of the key organizations:

- The International Organization for Standardization (ISO)

- The Institute of Electrical and Electronics Engineers (IEEE)

- The American National Standards Institute (ANSI)

- The International Telecommunication Union (ITU)

- The Electronics Industry Alliance/Telecommunications Industry Association (EIA/TIA)

- National telecommunications authorities such as the Federal Communications Commission (FCC) in the United States

Figure 8-2 highlights the difference between the physical layer and the other layers of the OSI model.

Figure 8-2   Hardware and Software in the OSI Model

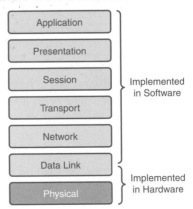

The engineers who designed the specifications of the physical layer had to consider several different media standards to complete a transmission. For example, how will the signal behave on different media types? What types of media are likely to be both effective and practical? What media properties will enhance or detract from the quality of the signal? Further, what kind of signal patterns will work most efficiently on the various media? What are the limits of the media? How do different media interconnect? These and many other questions were dealt with by isolating the standards of the physical layer into four areas:

- Physical and electrical properties of the media

- Mechanical properties (materials, dimensions, and pinouts) of the connectors

- Bit representation by the signals (encoding)

- Definition of control information signals

Manufacturers can look to the standards set in these four areas and competitively design cables, connectors, and media access devices such as network interface cards (NIC). The standardization of these components has allowed competition to thrive and, by making devices more affordable, has contributed to the growth in the use of networks.

Physical Layer Fundamental Principles

Communication at the physical layer is a process involving physical components that carry encoded data sent out as a signal appropriate to the medium. The following three components of Layer 1 communication are key to understanding how the physical layer functions:

- Physical components

- Encoding

- Signaling

There is some parallel between human communication and the processes of the physical layer. In a simplified communication model, when a person wants to communicate an idea to another, she processes an abstract thought into words, which are then encoded into speech sounds and sent out through the medium of air. At the other end, the receiver interprets the signal of sound, recognizes patterns in the sound that denote words, and then processes the meaning of the words into the original idea.

Exploring the analogy further, humans can be media independent when communicating by using a medium other than sound signals through the air. Gestures are conveyed in light, and written letters are conveyed by ink and paper. Each of these media has a unique way of ordering bits of communication into recognizable patterns indicating when messages begin and end.

This is also true of communication at the physical layer. Physical components carry the message in a reliable and consistent manner so that the receiver gets the message as it was sent.

Encoding is another major function of the physical layer. The bits in the encapsulated data link layer frame need to be grouped, or encoded, into patterns recognized by Layer 1 devices. After transmission, the receiving Layer 1 device decodes patterns and hands the frame up to the data link layer.

Another function of encoding is control information. Just as human speech uses pauses to indicate the start and end of sentences, the physical layer inserts a control code to indicate the beginning and end of frames. The control code is a specific pattern of 1s and 0s added to each end of the encoded frame. You learn more about encoding later in this chapter in the section "Encoding: Grouping Bits."

After the frame and control information are encoded into a string of binary digits, the bits are converted into a signal that will carry the pattern to the destination. Signaling is another key function of the physical layer. The process of signaling involves determining how to represent the binary bit on a specific medium. For example, if the medium is copper, the signal will be in the form of positive and negative patterns of voltage.

Figure 8-3 displays the process of a Layer 2 frame being encoded, converted to a signal, and then put onto the physical medium.

Figure 8-3   Physical Layer Processes

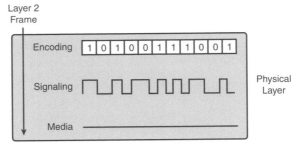

The processes of encoding and signaling complete the preparation of data for transport. The physical layer sends these bits out one at a time onto the medium as a signal, and those signals get picked up and decoded at the receiving end. There are several possible methods used to represent the binary digits as a signal, which are explored in the next section.

Physical Signaling and Encoding: Representing Bits

When computers communicate, the message they are sending is mathematical logic in the form of binary code. One task of the physical layer is to take the logical message and convert it into patterns of physical energy, a signal that can represent the binary code as it travels the physical medium.

Signaling Bits for the Media

There are several different methods of representing these binary digits on physical media as a signal. Each method finds a way to convert a pulse of energy into a defined amount of time known as a *bit time*. Bit time is the time it takes for a NIC at OSI Layer 2 to generate 1 bit of data and send it out to the media as a signal. The signal will exist somewhere within the bit time and indicate the value of the bit to the receiver. The type of signal within the bit time depends on the method of signaling used.

The amount of real time a bit time consumes depends on the speed of the NIC. Faster NICs produce shorter bit times. It is essential that the bits are read in order, and because the bit time can vary between different devices, there must be synchronization between the sending and the receiving units. Synchronization means that both sending and receiving units agree on the timing of the signals. Synchronization of the signals assures that the bits will be in order and can be properly interpreted by the receiving NIC. In local-area networks, each device keeps its own clock, and some signal methods include predictable transitions in the signal to provide synchronization.

Different signaling methods vary in the way they represent bits in the bit time. Three possible variations of a signal that can represent encoded bits are

- Amplitude

- Frequency

- Phase

For example, amplitude is a measure of the variation of the signal cycle. The peak level of amplitude can represent a binary 1, and a lesser level of amplitude can denote a binary 0. Figure 8-4 demonstrates how each of these three characteristics can change within one bit time.

Figure 8-4   Signal Methods

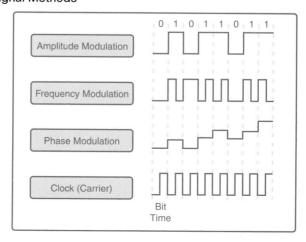

Different signal methods have different advantages and performance standards, but it is essential that all devices on the network use the same method so that the messages from sending devices can be read by the receiving devices. Signaling methods can be very complex, and an in-depth study of them is beyond the scope of this book, but a closer look at two methods—nonreturn to zero (NRZ) and Manchester encoding—provides a fundamental understanding of their function in the physical layer.

Nonreturn to Zero

The signaling method known as *nonreturn to zero (NRZ)* samples the voltage level on the medium during a bit time. The method defines which voltage levels represent 1 and 0, with a low voltage being 0 and a higher voltage representing a 1. The actual amount of voltage in the bit time can vary by standard.

NRZ, as its name implies, has no constant zero voltage, so additional signaling is sometimes necessary for synchronization with other devices. This additional signal requirement limits the efficiency of NRZ and increases the risk of distortion if any common electromagnetic interference is present. This inefficiency relegates NRZ to use on lower-speed links. Figure 8-5 depicts an NRZ signal representing both 1 and 0.

Figure 8-5   NRZ Encoding

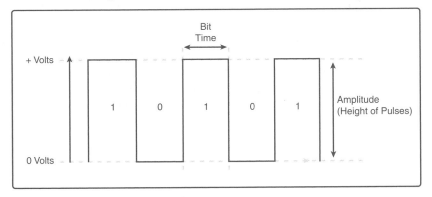

Manchester Encoding

Manchester encoding is a signaling method that looks for a change in voltage in the middle of a bit time. A voltage change from low to high within the bit time represents a 1. Conversely, a voltage drop within the bit time from a high to a low voltage represents a 0. When there are repeating bit values, meaning consecutive 1s or 0s, a transition will occur at the edge of the bit time, so a repeated rise or fall will occur in the middle of the bit time.

Figure 8-6 demonstrates the Manchester encoding method of voltage changes in the middle of a bit times as well as a repeating bit transition at the edge of the bit time.

Figure 8-6   Manchester Encoding

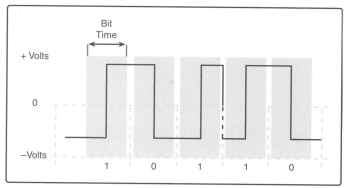

Manchester encoding is the signaling standard for 10BASE-T Ethernet (10 megabits per second). Higher-speed links require other standards.

Encoding: Grouping Bits

The physical media in a network can be a busy place crowded with signals from several devices going to several destinations. Without a system to identify messages, communication would be much more difficult. Imagine a room full of busy people doing business with cell phones set to the same ring tone. When a call comes in for one person, they all stop work and try to answer their own phone, but only one person actually gets a call. This is a frustrating waste of time for busy people, so they look for a solution to the problem of constant interruptions. An easy solution would be for each cell phone user to create a unique ring tone. That way people can ignore all the calls that are for other people and only take the time to answer calls with their own ring.

Encoding signals by grouping bits solves the same problem in a network. With so many electrical signals traveling up and down data lines, there is a need for a method of making a unique physical layer signal so that the receiving device knows which signals are important and require attention. The process of adding signal patterns to identify important signal transmissions is the solution used at the physical layer. Like a unique ring tone in the waiting room example, a signal pattern lets devices work more efficiently by allowing them to ignore unimportant signals on the media and pay attention only to important signals.

Before each frame is transmitted at Layer 1 as a signal, it is encoded with signal patterns that announce to the receiving device when the frame starts and stops and which part of the frame has data to be passed to OSI Layer 2. Figure 8-7 shows how a signal is isolated and recognized from all the busy chatter on the media.

Figure 8-7   Signal Patterns

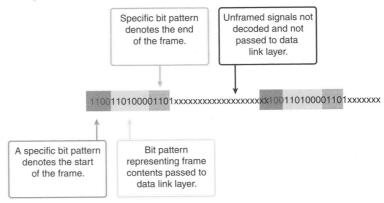

Signal patterns are just one special use for encoding at the physical layer. Code groups, another method of encoding, can improve network efficiency and signal reliability.

Code groups become more important at high data speeds, where networks become more error prone. A *code group* is a symbol that is a predefined small group of bits that represents a larger group of data bits. Code grouping is part of the encoding process and happens before the signal is put on the media.

Figure 8-8 demonstrates how bits can be represented by symbols before being encoded as a signal on a medium.

Figure 8-8   Code Groups

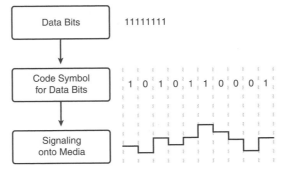

Code groups can help prevent several reliability problems that commonly arise with the use of higher-speed networks. Code groups improve performance on higher-speed networks in the following four areas:

- Reducing bit level error

- Limiting the effective energy transmitted into the media

- Helping to distinguish data bits from control bits

- Providing better media error detection

By design, code groups ensure several transitions between 1 and 0. As mentioned earlier, these transitions can be used for synchronization, which provides more reliable bit time sampling. Without code groups, these transitions might not occur often enough to ensure quality synchronization and result in bit errors.

The balancing of 1s and 0s in the signal can also help reduce error rates by preventing components from overheating. Some signal methods represent binary 1 as the presence of energy, for example, laser light or voltage, and binary 0 as an absence of energy. At higher speeds, too many consecutive 1s can generate heat that can degrade a signal or damage sensitive optical equipment, resulting in bit rate errors.

Because code group symbols are known patterns, they can improve error detection. If a string of too many consecutive 1s or 0s occurs in the transmission, an error can be assumed because code groups avoid consecutive patterns.

Encoding can help a receiving device distinguish frames and data in a transmission. Code groups can enhance the distinctions in a signal by using three different types of symbols:

- **Data symbols:** The data sent down from the physical layer

- **Control symbols:** The Layer 1 patterns denoting the beginning and end of frames

- **Invalid symbols:** Bit patterns not allowed on the media that can indicate a frame error

An example of a code group is the relatively simple *4B/5B* group. In this technique, 4 bits are grouped into a symbol containing 5 bits. While this might seem like it is generating more processing overhead and extra bits, remember that the extra bit can serve as a synchronization and control mechanism.

Figure 8-9 contains examples of the 4B/5B symbols.

Figure 8-9   4B/5B Code Group

Data Codes		Control and Invalid Codes	
45 Code	**16 Symbol**	**45 Code**	**16 Symbol**
0000	11110	Idle	11111
0001	01001	start of stream	11000
0010	10100	start of stream	10001
0011	10101	end of stream	01101
0100	01010	end of stream	00111
0101	01011	transmit error	01111
0110	01110	invalid	00000
0111	01111	invalid	00001
1000	10010	invalid	00010
1001	10011	invalid	00011
1010	10110	invalid	00100
1011	10111	invalid	00101
1100	11010	invalid	00110
1101	11011	invalid	01000
1110	11100	invalid	10000
1111	11101	invalid	11001

Note that patterns in the symbols used for data ensure a balance of 1s and 0s. Also note there are specific symbols that indicate the start and stop of certain data streams, which enhances efficiency.

Data-Carrying Capacity

Each physical layer medium carries data at a different speed. There are three different ways to analyze the transfer speed of data on a medium:

- Theoretically as bandwidth

- Practically as throughput

- Qualitatively as goodput

Although each of these items measures a different aspect of data transfer, all three are measured by the same standard of bits per second.

Bandwidth is the capacity of a medium to carry data in a given amount of time. The standard measure for bandwidth is in bits per second (bps). As the technologies have improved over the years, it has become more practical to refer to bandwidth in *kilobits*, or thousands of bits per second (kbps), and *megabits*, or millions of bits per second (Mbps). The bandwidth measurement takes into account the physical properties of the medium and the signaling method applied to it. Table 8-2 lists the four most common units of measure for bandwidth along with the mathematical equivalence for each.

Table 8-2   Bandwidth Units of Measure

Units of Bandwidth	Abbreviation	Equivalence
Bits per second	bps	1 bps = Base unit
Kilobits per second	kbps	1 kbps = 1000 bps = 10^3 bps
Megabits per second	Mbps	1 Mbps = 1,000,000 bps = 10^6 bps
Gigabits per second	Gbps	1 Gbps = 1,000,000,000 bps = 10^9 bps
Terabits per second	Tbps	1 Tbps = 1,000,000,000,000 bps = 10^{12} bps

Throughput is the actual transfer rate of data over the medium in a period of time. Bandwidth is the capacity for moving data, but attaining that capacity is rare because of factors such as interference and errors. It is useful to plan networks around expected throughput and the actual rate of speed rather than theoretical bandwidth. Throughput, like bandwidth, is measured in bits per second.

Many factors influence throughput, including the following:

- The amount of traffic
- The type of traffic
- The number of network devices encountered on the network being measured

In a multiaccess topology such as Ethernet, nodes are competing for media access and its use. Therefore, the throughput of each node is degraded as usage of the media increases.

In an internetwork or network with multiple segments, throughput cannot be faster than the slowest link of the path from source to destination. Even if all or most of the segments have high bandwidth, it will take only one segment in the path with low throughput to create a bottleneck to the throughput of the entire network.

Goodput is the transfer rate of actual usable data bits. Goodput is the data throughput less the protocol overhead bits, error corrections, and retransmission requests. The difference between goodput and throughput can vary greatly depending on the quality of network connections and devices.

Unlike throughput, which measures the transfer of bits and not the transfer of usable data, goodput accounts for bits devoted to protocol overhead. Goodput is throughput minus traffic overhead for establishing sessions, acknowledgments, and encapsulation.

As an example, consider two hosts on a LAN transferring a file. The bandwidth of the LAN is 100 Mbps. Because of the sharing and media overhead, the throughput between the computers is only 60 Mbps. With the overhead of the encapsulation process of the TCP/IP stack, the actual rate of the data received by the destination computer, goodput, is only 40 Mbps.

Figure 8-10 depicts the difference between throughput and goodput. In this example, throughput measures network performance and goodput measures the transfer rate of application layer data.

Figure 8-10   Throughput and Goodput

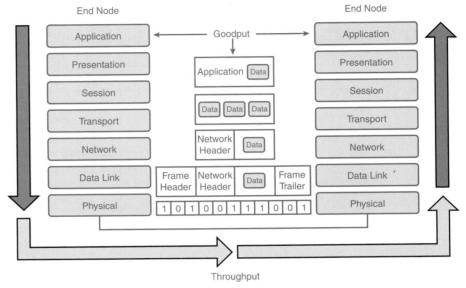

Physical Media: Connecting Communication

The physical layer is concerned with network media and signaling. This layer produces the representation and groupings of bits as voltages, radio frequencies, or light pulses. Various standards organizations have contributed to the definition of the physical, electrical, and mechanical properties of the media available for different data communications. These specifications guarantee that cables and connectors will function as anticipated with different data link layer implementations.

Types of Physical Media

The physical layer defines the performance standards for the physical components of a network such as copper and fiber cables and the connectors used on them. The physical layer also defines how bits are presented in the form of voltage, light pulses, and radio signals. The design of the physical layer differs from the design of upper layers in that it deals with the physics and electrical properties of the media rather than the logical processes.

This section explores copper, fiber, and wireless media. Table 8-3 lists several different Ethernet standards for copper and fiber-optic media.

Table 8-3   Ethernet Media

	Media	Maximum Segment Length	Topology	Connector
10BASE-T	EIA/TIA Category 3, 4, or 5 UTP, four-pair	100 m (328 feet)	Star	ISO 8877
100BASE-TX	EIA/TIA Category 5 UTP, two-pair	100 m (328 feet)	Star	—
100BASE-FX	5.0/62.5-micron multimode fiber	2 km (6562 feet)	Star	ISO 8877 (RJ-45)
100BASE-CX	STP	25 m (82 feet)	Star	ISO 8877 (RJ-45)
1000BASE-T	EIA/TIA Category 5 (or greater) UTP, four-pair	100 m (328 feet)	Star	—
1000BASE-SX	5.0/62.5-micron multimode fiber	Up to 550 m (1804 feet), depending on fiber used	Star	—
1000BASE-LX	5.0/62.5-micron multimode fiber or 9-micron	550-m multimode fiber, 10-km single-mode fiber	Star	—
1000BASE-ZX	Single-mode fiber	Approx. 70 km	Star	—
10GBASE-ZR	Single-mode fiber	Up to 80 km	Star	—

Copper Media

The most pervasive media in use for data transfer in local networks is copper. Copper cable standards and technologies have evolved over the past few decades, but copper remains the most common medium for connecting network devices. Copper connects hosts to devices such as routers, switches, and hubs within a LAN. Copper media has standards defined for each of the following

- Type of copper cabling used

- Bandwidth of the communication

- Type of connectors used

- Pinout and color codes of connections to the media

- Maximum distance of the media

Copper is an effective medium because it conducts electrical signals very well, but it has its limitations. Data travels on copper cables as small pulses of electrical voltage. The voltage is quite low and easily distorted by outside interference and signal attenuation. *Attenuation* is the loss of energy in a signal as it travels longer distances. The timing and voltage values of these signals are susceptible to interference or *noise* from outside the communications system. These unwanted signals can distort and corrupt the data signals being carried by copper media. Radio waves and electromagnetic devices, such as fluorescent lights, electric motors, and other devices, are potential sources of noise.

The advances in copper cable design have improved data transfer rates by reducing the effects of noise and signal attenuation on the wire. But improving the cable design is only part of a solution to interference. Architects designing new buildings can locate network devices away from building systems that generate electromagnetic interference. Cable installers can use quality cabling practices to enhance reliability at the physical layer, and choosing the proper cable type for the intended environment ensures the best possible performance.

There are different types of copper cable designed to meet the specific needs of different networks. The most common is unshielded twisted-pair (UTP) cabling, as it is used in Ethernet LANs. Others are coaxial cable and shielded twisted-pair cables. The features of each type are described in the following sections.

Unshielded Twisted-Pair (UTP) Cable

The most common copper network media is *unshielded twisted-pair (UTP) cable*. UTP in Ethernet consists of eight wires twisted into four color-coded pairs and then wound inside a cable jacket. The colored pairs identify the wires for proper connection at the terminals. Figure 8-11 depicts the twisted-wire pairs inside the cable jacket.

Figure 8-11   Unshielded Twisted-Pair (UTP) Cable

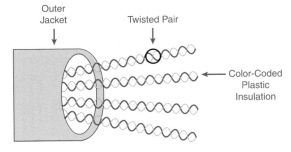

The twisting of pairs in UTP cable is part of the cable engineering design. When wires carry electrical current, they can create an electromagnetic field that can cause interference on other wires in the cable. Because each wire in the pair carries current in the opposite direction, keeping them close together with twisting will cause the magnetic fields on the wire pair to cancel each other. This magnetic interference from wires within the cable is called *crosstalk*. The rate of twisting in each pair of wires is different so that each pair self-cancels and reduces crosstalk to a minimum.

Computer equipment manufactures build equipment to industry standards so that different systems can interoperate. It is important that these standards apply to the installation of cables and connectors in LANs. The previously mentioned TIA/EIA engineering groups in the telecommunications industry define the following standards for UTP cable installations:

- Cable types

- Cable lengths

- Connectors

- Cable termination

- Methods of testing cable

It is essential that the physical layer cable installations and connections closely follow industry standards. Poor cabling is a very common culprit in poor network performance.

There are several categories of UTP cable. Each category indicates a level of bandwidth performance as defined by the IEEE. Important cable category changes were from Category 3 (Cat 3) to Category 5 (Cat 5), where UTP cable improvements allowed 100-megabit transmissions. In 1999, the Cat 5 standard improved to Cat 5e, which enabled full-duplex Fast Ethernet gigabit transmission over UTP cable.

In 2002, Category 6 (Cat 6) was defined. Cat 6 cable offers stricter manufacturing and termination standards that allow higher performance and less crosstalk. Cat5e is still acceptable for most LANs, but Cat 6 is the current recommended standard for gigabit connections and in new installations, as it will more readily allow future growth in LAN performance. Like all cable category upgrades, Cat 6 remains backward compatible with previous-generation cable categories.

The most common UTP cable connector in LAN devices is an *RJ-45* connector. Most computers accessing a network through cable use an RJ-45 connector plugged into the computer network interface card at one end and a hub or switch device at the other. An RJ-45 connector is commonly mistaken for a telephone jack, but an RJ-45 jack is larger and has a different cable termination. Figure 8-12 depicts RJ-45 connectors terminating a UTP cable.

Figure 8-12 RJ-45 Connector

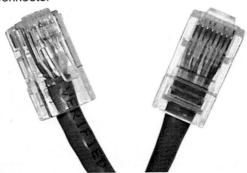

The cable wires inserted into the RJ-45 connector are not always ordered in the same way. The required order of the wires in the connector, called the *pinout*, varies according to where the cable fits in the network. The order of the wires in the pinouts is defined by TIA/EIA standards 568A and 568B. Each device connection requires a specific cable pinout to ensure that signals transmitted on a wire at one end arrive on the correct "receive" circuit at the other end of the cable.

Figure 8-13 shows the color patterns for TIA/EIA 568A and 568B pinouts. As you can see in the figure, the difference between 568A and 568B is simply the switched position of wire pair 2 and wire pair 3.

Figure 8-13   568A and 568B Pinouts on an RJ-45 Connector

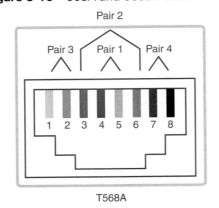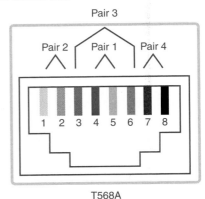

At one time, different geographic areas adapted 568A and others 568B. One is not necessarily better than the other, but the important thing is to use the same standard throughout the network.

Three UTP cable types are described in this book. Table 8-4 lists the specifications and purpose of each cable.

Table 8-4   UTP Cable Types

Cable Type	TIA/EIA Standard	Cable Use
Straight-through cable	Both ends the same, either 568A or 568B.	Connects a network host to a hub or switch.
Crossover cable	One end 568A, and the other 568B. It does not matter which end goes to which device.	Directly connects like devices, such as two hosts, two switches, or two routers. Also used to directly connect a host to a router.
Rollover cable (also known as a "Cisco" cable)	Cisco-proprietary.	Connects a workstation serial port to a Cisco device console port.

These cable types are not interchangeable, and it is a common mistake to use the wrong wire for the intended purpose. Using a crossover or straight-through cable in the wrong place will cross the send and receive signals, and no connection will be established. This common mistake will not usually damage the device, but the connection will not work without the proper cable type installed. When installing cables, checking cable types should be one of the first steps if a device fails to connect.

The following steps are a quick way to determine whether your cable is a straight-through or crossover cable.

Step 1.   Hold both cable ends next to each other with the copper ends pointing away and the insertion lock tabs on the bottom.

Step 2.   Look closely at the color patterns in the cable. If the color pattern matches, it is probably a straight-through. To verify that the cable is properly constructed, check to see whether the patterns match a 568A or 568B pinout pattern.

Step 3.   If the patterns do not match, determine whether the first and third pairs are switched. If so, it is likely a crossover cable. To verify the crossed pairs, check to see that one end is a 568A pattern and the other is a 568B pattern.

Step 4.   If the color pattern is reversed, it is a rollover cable.

Other Copper Cable Types

One of the first types of copper cable used in LANs was coaxial cable. *Coaxial cable*, also known as *coax*, has a single, coated copper wire center and an outer metal mesh that acts as both a grounding circuit and an electromagnetic shield to reduce interference. The outer layer is the plastic cable jacket. The use of coax has migrated from LAN media, where it was once common but now is a legacy technology, to uses in wireless implementations connecting antennas to wireless devices.

Figure 8-14 depicts the structure of coaxial cable.

Figure 8-14   Coaxial Cable

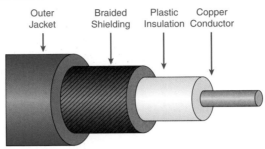

For decades, coax has carried high-frequency radio and television signals over wire. The "cable" in cable TV is coax, and its use in TV is evolving from a one-way broadcast system to a two-way communication medium using new coax technologies known as *hybrid fiber-coax (HFC)*. HFC combines the electrical properties of coax and the bandwidth and distance benefits of fiber-optic cable.

Coax cable connects to a host's NIC and other devices with a barrel connector. Some of the connectors have special terminators to help control the electrical interference on the line.

Figure 8-15 depicts the examples of coaxial cable connectors.

Figure 8-15   Coaxial Cable Connectors

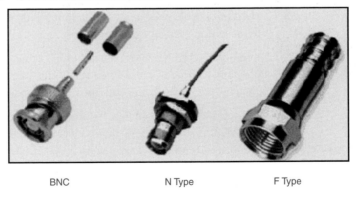

Shielded twisted-pair (STP) cable is a LAN technology that has become less commonly used in recent years. STP cable was a standard in the IBM Token Ring network technology, but its use has faded as Token Ring networks have been replaced with other Ethernet technologies.

STP cable combines two methods of noise reduction by twisting the pairs of wire inside the cable to reduce interference and then shielding the cable in a wire mesh. STP can still be useful in installations where electromagnetic interference (EMI) is an issue, but STP cable is much more expensive than other available cable, so its use is quite limited at this time. Figure 8-16 depicts the structure of STP cable.

Figure 8-16   Shielded Twisted-Pair (STP) Cable

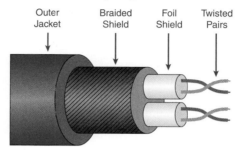

Copper Media Safety

Because copper carries electrical current, there is an inherent risk in using it. The cable standards and local building codes address these issues with wiring closet and cable length specifications, but there is still risk from defective devices sending out electrical charges to other devices and, occasionally, their users.

Another potential danger is overextending cable runs between buildings and floors within buildings. It is possible for an excessively long cable run to connect two areas with different earth grounds, causing a short that can endanger a user. Copper runs between buildings are also more susceptible to the effects of lightning, which can render network devices unusable. Using fiber or wireless between buildings and between floors in one building can minimize these hazards.

The materials used to manufacture some cables can be a fire hazard. Some buildings have a common space for air ducts and cable runs, and should fire reach the cables, they could emit toxic fumes. Many building codes require specially constructed cable for cable runs in air duct areas.

Fiber Media

At the physical layer, diverse technologies can perform the same function of data transfer. Fiber-optic cable is very different from copper, yet both effectively carry data over networks.

Whereas copper uses electrical voltage to represent data on the wire, *fiber-optic cable* uses light pulses conducted through special glass conductors to carry data. The cable is engineered to be as pure as possible and to allow reliable light signals to traverse the medium. Like copper media, the standards and performance levels of fiber are constantly improving.

Fiber has some advantages over copper, but there are also some challenges when installing fiber in a network. For example, fiber has greater bandwidth and can run much farther than cable without needing a signal enhanced, but the higher cost of fiber-optic cable and connectors, along with special training required for installing fiber, limits its feasibility to special uses. Fiber cable also requires more special handling than copper cable.

Fiber is an answer to the safety issues of long copper runs mentioned in the previous section. Because fiber does not carry voltage and current, it is immune to the earth ground and lightning concerns. Because it is safer and can carry data much farther than copper, fiber-optic cable is usually considered the best choice for backbone connections between floors and wiring closets in large buildings and for connections between buildings on a campus.

Fiber-optic cable starts with a core strand of glass or special plastic on which the light signal travels. Around the glass is *cladding*, a special material that reflects escaping light into the core. Outer layers protect and strengthen the vulnerable center core from moisture and damage. Figure 8-17 depicts a cutout of a fiber-optic cable.

Figure 8-17   Fiber-Optic Cable

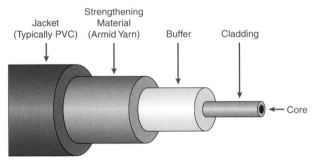

Fiber-optic cable can carry light in only one direction, so fiber cables usually include a pair of fiber cores. This allows full-duplex transmission, which is the transmitting and receiving of data simultaneously on one cable.

The light carried on fiber cables is generated by either a laser or a light emitting diode (LED) that converts the data to light pulses. The lasers used in fiber-optic cables can be intense and can damage the human eye, so great care is required when troubleshooting or installing the cable.

At the receiving end, devices called *photodiodes* interpret the light signal, decode the bit pattern, and send it up to the data link layer.

There are two basic types of fiber-optic cable: single-mode and multimode. Figure 8-18 displays single-mode and multimode cables.

Figure 8-18   Single-Mode and Multimode Fiber-Optic Cable

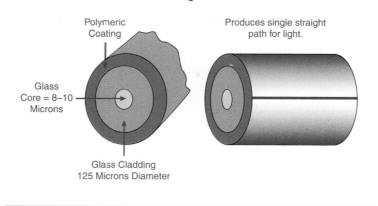

Table 8-5 describes the differences between single-mode and multimode fiber-optic cable.

Table 8-5   Single-Mode and Multimode Fiber-Optic Cable

Single-Mode	Multimode
Small glass core: 8–10 microns	Larger core: 50+ microns, can be glass or plastic
Less dispersion of light	Greater dispersion (loss of light)
Longer distance: Up to about 100 km	Shorter distance: Up to 2 km
Uses lasers as light source	Uses LEDs as light source on shorter runs

Dispersion of the light signal means that it separates as it travels. Because the cladding helps contain the intense laser light in the smaller glass core, the single-mode fiber can carry data greater distances. The dispersion rate is greater in multimode fiber, so the signal does not travel as far.

Fiber-optics are economical on longer, high-speed, point-to-point backbone runs, but they are not currently well suited for local connections between hosts and other network devices.

Wireless Media

A third distinct physical layer technology is wireless. Wireless media carry electromagnetic radio signals that represent the binary data of the data-link frame. Wireless technologies transmit and receive signals through the medium of the open atmosphere, which frees users from having to connect to a copper or fiber cable connection.

Open areas are best for wireless connections. Within buildings, interference occurs from physical objects such as walls, metal air ducts, and floors and machinery. The wireless signal is also subject to degradation from small appliances, microwave ovens, fluorescent lighting, and household wireless devices like phones and Bluetooth devices.

Although wireless has advantages, there are some disadvantages to its use. A wireless connection is usually slower than a cable connection, and because the medium is open to anyone with a wireless receiver, it is more susceptible to security breaches than other media.

The IEEE and telecommunications industry standards for wireless data communications cover both the data link and physical layers. Following are four common data communications standards that apply to wireless media:

- **Standard IEEE 802.11:** Commonly referred to as *Wi-Fi*, 802.11 is a wireless LAN (WLAN) technology that uses a contention or nondeterministic system with a carrier sense multiple access/collision avoid (CSMA/CA) media access process.

- **Standard IEEE 802.15: Wireless Personal-Area Network (WPAN):** Commonly known as Bluetooth, 802.15 uses a device-pairing process to communicate over distances from 1 to 100 meters.

- **Standard IEEE 802.16:** Commonly known as *WiMAX (Worldwide Interoperability for Microwave Access)*, 802.16 uses a point-to-multipoint topology to provide wireless broadband access.

- **Global System for Mobile Communication (GSM):** Includes physical layer specifications that enable the implementation of the Layer 2 General Packet Radio Service (GPRS) protocol to provide data transfer over mobile cellular telephony networks.

Other wireless technologies, such as satellite communications, provide data network connectivity for locations without another means of connection. Protocols including GPRS enable data to be transferred between earth stations and satellite links.

In each of these examples, physical layer specifications are applied to areas that include data–to–radio signal encoding, frequency and power of transmission, signal reception and decoding requirements, and antenna design and construction.

Wireless LAN

A common wireless data implementation is enabling devices to wirelessly connect through a LAN. In general, a wireless LAN requires the following network devices:

- **Wireless access point (AP):** Concentrates the wireless signals from users and connects, usually through a copper cable, to the existing copper-based network infrastructure such as Ethernet

- **Wireless NIC adapter:** Provides wireless communication capability to each network host

As the technology has developed, a number of WLAN Ethernet-based standards have emerged. Care needs to be taken in purchasing wireless devices to ensure compatibility and interoperability.

Table 8-6 describes four of the basic 802.11 standards in use. Within each standard, the physical layer specifications pertain to the radio signal, the encoding of data, and the frequency and power of the transmission signals.

Table 8-6   802.11 Wireless LAN Standards

IEEE Standard	Description
IEEE 802.11a	- Operates in the 5-GHz frequency band - Speeds of up to 54 Mbps - Small coverage area - Not interoperable with the 802.11b and 802.11g standards
IEEE 802.11b	- Operates in the 2.4-GHz frequency band - Speeds of up to 11 Mbps - Longer range and better able to penetrate building structures than devices based on 802.11a
IEEE 802.11g	- Operates in the 2.4-GHz frequency band - Speeds of up to 54 Mbps - Same radio frequency and range as 802.11b but with the bandwidth of 802.11a
IEEE 802.11n	- Standard is currently in draft form - Proposed 2.4-GHz or 5-GHz - Expected data rates are 100 Mbps to 210 Mbps, with a distance range of up to 70 meters

The cost savings and ease of access are the major benefits of wireless LANS, with network security being the major caveat.

Packet Tracer
☐ Activity

Simple Wireless LAN Model (8.3.7.4)

In this activity, you can explore a wireless router connected to an Internet service provider (ISP) in a setup typical of a home or small business. You are encouraged to build your own models as well, possibly incorporating such wireless devices. Use file e1-8374.pka on the CD-ROM that accompanies this book to perform this activity using Packet Tracer.

Media Connectors

Just as a chain is only as strong as its weakest link, so is a network only as strong as its weakest connection. A user can easily have six cable connectors between the NIC and the hub or switch in the wiring closet: two on the cable from the PC to the wall outlet, two on the wall outlet to a patch panel, and two more between the patch panel and the switch. It is common for all these connectors to be hand-wired during a network installation.

Each time copper cabling is terminated, there is the possibility of signal loss and the introduction of noise to the communication circuit. Ethernet workplace cabling specifications stipulate the cabling necessary to connect a computer to an active network intermediary device. When terminated improperly, each cable is a potential source of physical layer performance degradation. It is essential that all copper media terminations be of high quality to ensure optimum performance with current and future network technologies. Figure 8-19 depicts two RJ-45 terminations, one poorly wired with untwisted cables and the other properly wired with no exposed or untwisted wire pairs.

Figure 8-19   RJ-45 Terminations

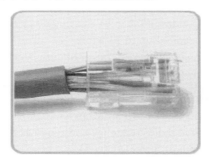 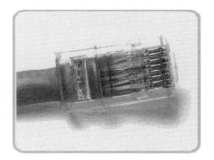

Bad connector—
Wires are untwisted for
too great a length.

Good connector—
Wires are untwisted to the
extent necessary to
attach the connector.

Each media type—copper, fiber-optic, and wireless—has its own type of connectors, and all the connectors have defined standards to describe the manufacturing minimums and the installation requirements.

As seen earlier, connectors that might look the same can have differing pinouts. For example, without close examination of the wire pattern in the cable ends, it is impossible to tell whether an unshielded twisted-pair cable is a straight-through, crossover, rollover, or some other special-use cable.

Many of the commonly used cables are available manufactured with machine-tested connections and common lengths. It might be cheaper to buy standard patch cables pre-made than to pay a technician on site to make them, but the individual cable runs and punch-down blocks still need the skilled touch of human hands. Figure 8-20 depicts front and back images of copper cable wall sockets and punch blocks that connect wall jacks to equipment in the wiring closet.

Figure 8-20   Copper Cable Sockets and Punch Blocks

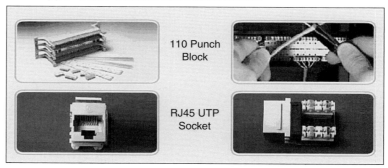

Fiber-optic cabling is much more specialized than copper cable, and installing or repairing fiber requires special training and equipment. Three common fiber repair problems are as follows:

- Misalignment
- End gaps where fibers do not completely touch
- Poorly finished ends causing poor clarity

When terminating fiber-optic cable, it is important to have the ends properly aligned, fused, and polished so that signaling remains strong and dispersion is at a minimum.

Fiber-optic links can be given a basic test with a flashlight shining in one end and looking for light at the other. If the light is visible, the fiber is not broken. But there can be flaws in the line that a flashlight will not reveal, so for detailed analysis of a cable, including locations of faults in the cable, it is best to use a special fiber-optic test device called an *Optical Time Domain Reflectometer (OTDR)*.

Fiber-optic connectors come in a variety of types. Straight Tip (ST) for multimode and the Subscriber Connector (SC) for single-mode are two of the most common types in use. The Lucent Connector is gaining popularity and can adapt to both single-mode and multimode cables.

Summary

This chapter covered the details of how the physical layer functions as part of the OSI communication model. OSI Layer 1 takes data link layer frames and encodes the data bits into signals that travel copper, fiber-optic, or wireless media to the next device, where they are decoded and sent back up to the data link layer. Physical layer encoding and signaling methods can include symbols, like 4B/5B, to represent code groups. These can improve the reliability of communication by adding bit patterns recognized by receiving devices.

Copper cable, fiber-optic cable, and wireless media have varying performance benefits and costs that determine their use in a network's infrastructure. One performance measure is bandwidth, which, when measured with throughput and goodput, is a key factor in determining a network's performance.

Physical layer equipment standards describe the physical, electrical, and mechanical characteristics of the physical media and the connectors used to connect media to devices. These standards are under constant review and are updated as new technologies become available.

Labs

The labs available in the companion *Network Fundamentals, CCNA Exploration Labs and Study Guide* (ISBN 1-58713-203-6) provide hands-on practice with the following topics introduced in this chapter:

Lab 8-1: Media Connectors (8.4.1.1)

Effective network troubleshooting requires the ability to visually distinguish between straight-through and crossover UTP cables and to test for correct and faulty cable terminations.

This lab provides the opportunity to practice physically examining and testing UTP cables.

Packet Tracer
☐ Challenge

Many of the hands-on labs include Packet Tracer companion activities, where you can use Packet Tracer to complete a simulation of the lab. Look for this icon in *Network Fundamentals, CCNA Exploration Labs and Study Guide* (ISBN 1-58713-203-6) for hands-on labs that have Packet Tracer companion activities.

Check Your Understanding

Complete all the review questions listed here to test your understanding of the topics and concepts in this chapter. The appendix, "Check Your Understanding and Challenge Questions Answer Key," lists the answers.

1. Copper cable and fiber-optic cable are examples of _____, which is used to carry the communication signal.

2. What is the purpose of encoding?

   A. To identify the start and stop bits in a frame

   B. To denote the physical layer's connectors of computers in relation to the way they connect to network media

   C. To control the way frames are placed on the media at the data link layer

   D. To represent the data bits by using different voltages, light patterns, or electromagnetic waves as they are placed onto the physical media

3. What two signaling methods use voltage to encode bits?

4. What best describes the purpose of the physical layer?

   A. Ensures reliable transmission of data across a physical link

   B. Determines connectivity and path selection between two end systems

   C. Establishes the physical addressing, networking topology, and media access

   D. Defines the functional specifications for links between end systems and the electrical, optical, and radio signals

5. What is the most common UTP connector type?

6. Through what process does UTP cable help to avoid crosstalk?

   A. Shielding of cable

   B. Twisting of pairs

   C. Grounding the endpoints

   D. Cladding in cable

7. What is the required order of wires in a connector called?

8. What are the advantages of using fiber-optic cable over copper cable? (Choose three.)

   A. Copper is more expensive

   B. Immunity to electromagnetic interference

   C. Careful cable handling

   D. Longer maximum cable length

   E. Efficient electrical current transfer

   F. Greater bandwidth potential

9. The physical media most susceptible to security breaches is _____.

10. What is the purpose of cladding in fiber-optic cables?

   A. Cable grounding

   B. Noise cancellation

   C. Prevention of light loss

   D. EMI protection

11. Which two of the following are true about straight-through cables?

   A. They work in Cisco console ports.

   B. They can be either 568A or 568B.

   C. They can connect a host to a switch.

   D. They can connect two switches.

12. A _____ cable is also known as a Cisco cable because it is generally used as a connection to Cisco equipment.

13. Which of the following measures the actual data transfer rate over a medium?

   A. Bandwidth

   B. Output

   C. Throughput

   D. Goodput

14. Which of the following is NOT true?

   A. 1 Gbps = 1,000,000,000 bits per second

   B. 1 kbps = 1000 bits per second

   C. 1 Mbps = 100,000 bits per second

   D. 1 Tbps = 1,000,000,000,000 bits per second

15. What is synchronization?

   A. Keeping the correct time of day on all network machines

   B. The timing mechanism devices use when transmitting data

   C. Devices processing bits to the data link layer at the same speed

   D. Constant bit times throughout the network

16. What is true about "bit time"?

    A. It is the time it takes to encapsulate application data into a bit segment.

    B. It is the time it takes for a NIC to move a bit from the data link layer to the Layer 1 media.

    C. IEEE standards require it to be the same on all NICs.

    D. It is the time it takes for a byte to traverse the copper or fiber cable.

Challenge Questions and Activities

These questions and activities require a deeper application of the concepts covered in this chapter. You can find the answers in the appendix.

1. A user has a peer-to-peer network with two directly connected hosts. To add a third host, the user installs a hub and adds two straight-through cables so that each computer has its own connection to the hub. What will be the result of this network upgrade?

    A. All three hosts will link to the hub.

    B. Two hosts will link to the hub.

    C. One host will link to the hub.

    D. None of the hosts will link to the hub.

2. A network administrator for a small wood products manufacturing company has throughput issues in the A wing of her building. The network devices are the same for all wings, and all appear to be performing normally, but the throughput has become consistently significantly lower in the A wing. Sales orders are up, and the machines on the production floor are working to full capacity. The administrator is under pressure to get throughput up to acceptable speed. In researching the problem, she determines the following list of facts. Which three of them are most likely to be contributing factors to the poor network performance?

    A. The A wing has the largest number of hosts connected to the network.

    B. The janitor buffs the floor of that wing at 4:00 p.m. Wednesdays. The other wings are buffed at night.

    C. Some employees in the A wing have added refrigerators and microwave ovens close to their workstations.

    D. The A wing has had a computer network for three years; the other wings have had a network for four years.

    E. Hosts in the A wing are located next to the manufacturing shop.

    F. The A wing has Cat 5 cable throughout, while the other wings have wireless and Cat 5.

To Learn More

The following questions encourage you to reflect on the topics discussed in this chapter. Your instructor might ask you to research the questions and discuss your findings in class.

1. Discuss how copper media, optical fiber, and wireless media could be used to provide network access at your academy. Review what networking media are used now and what could be used in the future.

2. Discuss the factors that might limit the widespread adoption of wireless networks despite the obvious benefits of this technology. How might these limitations be overcome?

Objectives

Upon completion of this chapter, you will be able to answer the following questions:

- How did Ethernet evolve?

- What are the purposes of the fields of the Ethernet frame?

- What are the functions and characteristics of the media access control method used by Ethernet protocol?

- What are the physical and data link layer features of Ethernet?

- How are Ethernet hubs and switches different?

- What is the purpose of Address Resolution Protocol (ARP), and how does it operate?

Key Terms

This chapter uses the following key terms. You can find the definitions in the Glossary.

delimiter   page 318

Gigabit Ethernet   page 319

metropolitan-area network (MAN)   page 319

Thicknet   page 320

Thinnet   page 320

hub   page 321

Fast Ethernet   page 322

Voice over IP (VoIP)   page 323

virtual local-area network (VLAN)   page 324

Pad   page 325

Organizational Unique Identifier (OUI)   page 326

burned-in address (BIA)   page 327

read-only memory (ROM)   page 327

random-access memory (RAM)   page 327

universally administered address (UAA)   page 327

locally administered address (LAA)   page 327

forwarding   page 327

host group   page 333

carrier sense multiple access collision detect (CSMA/CD)   page 334

jam signal   page 336

collision domain   page 337

extended star   page 337

latency   page 338

asynchronous   page 339

synchronous   page 339

slot time   page 340

interframe spacing   page 341

runt frames page 342

Ethernet PHY page 342

pulse amplitude modulation (PAM) page 345

selective forwarding page 351

store and forward page 352

MAC table page 352

switch table page 352

transparent bridging page 352

bridge table page 352

bridge page 352

bridging page 352

flooding page 354

filtering page 354

ARP table page 355

ARP cache page 355

proxy ARP page 358

ARP spoofing page 361

ARP poisoning page 361

Thus far, each chapter has focused on the different functions of each layer of the OSI and TCP/IP protocol models and described how protocols are used to support network communication. The organizations that define standards for these upper-layer protocols are different from the organizations that define the functions of Ethernet.

The Internet Engineering Task Force (IETF) maintains the functional protocols and services for the TCP/IP protocol suite in the upper layers. However, the functional protocols and services at the OSI data link layer and physical layer are described by various engineering organizations (IEEE, ANSI, ITU, and so on) or by private companies (proprietary protocols).

Because Ethernet is composed of standards at these lower layers, it can best be understood in reference to the OSI model. The OSI model separates the data link layer functionalities of addressing, framing, and accessing the media from the physical layer standards of the media. Ethernet standards define both the Layer 2 protocols and the Layer 1 technologies. Although Ethernet specifications support different media, bandwidths, and other Layer 1 and 2 variations, the basic frame format and address scheme is the same for all varieties of Ethernet.

This chapter examines the characteristics and operation of Ethernet as it has evolved from a shared media, contention-based data communications technology to today's high-bandwidth, full-duplex technology. Ethernet is now the predominant LAN technology in the world.

Overview of Ethernet

The Ethernet is a family of local-area network (LAN) products described by the IEEE standards. There have been many technologies that have challenged the dominance. However, Ethernet standards have evolved to continue meeting the needs of LANs.

Ethernet has undergone changes in the type of media used and the available speed of Ethernet. The following sections introduce the development of Ethernet and the different Ethernet standards and implementations.

Ethernet: Standards and Implementation

Compared to many other computer and networking technologies, Ethernet has endured for a long time. The first LAN was the original version of Ethernet. Robert Metcalfe and his coworkers at Xerox designed it more than 30 years ago. The first Ethernet standard was published in 1980 by a consortium of Digital Equipment Corporation, Intel, and Xerox (DIX). Metcalfe wanted Ethernet to be a shared standard from which everyone could benefit, and therefore it was released as an open standard. The first products that were developed from the Ethernet standard were sold in the early 1980s.

In 1985, the IEEE standards committee for local and metropolitan networks published standards for LANs. These standards start with the number 802. The standard for Ethernet is 802.3. The IEEE wanted to make sure that its standards were compatible with those of the ISO and the Open Systems Interconnection (OSI) model. To ensure compatibility, the IEEE 802.3 standards had to address the needs of Layer 1 (the physical layer) and the lower portion of Layer 2 (the data link layer) of the OSI model. As a result, some small modifications to the original Ethernet standard were made in 802.3. For example, the standard allowed Gigabit Ethernet frames to have a variable-length nondata extension field added to frames that are shorter than the minimum length.

Ethernet: Layer 1 and Layer 2

The OSI model provides a reference to which Ethernet can be related. However, as shown in Figure 9-1, the 802.3 protocols are actually implemented in the lower half of the data link layer, which is known as the Media Access Control (MAC) sublayer, and the physical layer only.

Figure 9-1   Ethernet: Data Link Layer and Physical Layer Protocols

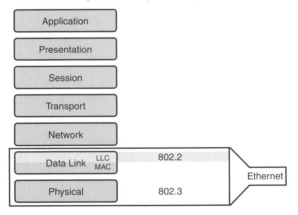

Note

You can access the IEEE 802.3 standard documents at http://standards.ieee.org/getieee802/802.3.html.

Ethernet defines these Layer 1 elements:

- Signals

- Bit streams that travel on the media

- Physical components that put signals on media

- Various topologies

Ethernet Layer 1 performs a key role in the communication that takes place between devices. However, communications between hosts also require the functions of Layer 2. Ethernet at the data link layer addresses these requirements:

- Provides an interface to the upper-layer protocols

- Provides an address to identify devices

- Uses frames to organize bits into meaningful groups

- Controls the transmission of data from sources

Ethernet uses data-link sublayers to define these functions further. The functions described in the OSI model for the data link layer are assigned to the Logical Link Control (LLC) and MAC sublayers. The use of these sublayers contributes significantly to compatibility between diverse end devices.

The MAC sublayer is concerned with the physical components that are used to communicate the information and prepare the data for transmission over the media. The LLC sublayer remains relatively independent of the physical equipment that is used for the communication process.

Logical Link Control: Connecting to the Upper Layers

For Ethernet, the IEEE 802.2 standard describes the LLC sublayer functions, and the 802.3 standard describes the MAC sublayer and the physical layer functions. LLC manages the communication between the networking software at upper layers and the lower layers, typically the hardware. These two sets of standards, 802.2 and 802.3, describe the functions of Ethernet. The LLC sublayer takes the network layer protocol data unit (PDU), which is typically an IPv4 packet, and adds control information to deliver the packet to the destination node. Layer 2 communicates with the upper layers through the functions of LLC.

LLC is implemented in software, and its implementation is independent of the physical equipment. In a computer, the LLC can be considered the driver software for the network interface card (NIC). The NIC driver is a program that interacts directly with the hardware on the NIC to pass the data between the media and the MAC sublayer.

Note

You can access some of the 802.2 standards and LLC information at the IEEE website:

- http://standards.ieee.org/getieee802/download/802.2-1998.pdf
- http://standards.ieee.org/regauth/llc/llctutorial.html

MAC: Getting Data to the Media

The lower Ethernet sublayer of the data link layer is the MAC sublayer. It is implemented by hardware, typically in the computer NIC.

The Ethernet MAC sublayer has two primary responsibilities:

- Data encapsulation

- MAC

These two data link layer processes have evolved differently through the different versions of Ethernet. Although the data encapsulation at the MAC sublayer has remained virtually unchanged, the MAC varies with different physical layer implementations. The following section will explore these two functions.

Data Encapsulation

Data encapsulation at the data link layer is the process of creating and adding headers and trailers to the network layer PDUs. Data encapsulation provides three primary functions:

- Frame delimiting

- Addressing

- Error detection

The data encapsulation process includes frame assembly before transmission and frame parsing upon reception of a frame. In forming the frame, the MAC sublayer adds a header and trailer to the Layer 3 PDU. The use of frames aids in the interpretation of bits at the receiving node. Grouping bits for transmission as they are placed on the media makes it easier for the receiving node to determine which bits comprise a single piece of usable information.

The framing process provides important *delimiters* that are used to identify a group of bits that make up a frame. This process provides synchronization between the transmitting and receiving nodes. These delimiters indicate the start and end of the frame. All bits between these two delimiters are a part of the same frame.

The encapsulation process also provides data link layer addressing. Each Ethernet header added in the frame contains the physical address (MAC address) that indicates to which node the frame should be delivered. The Ethernet header also contains a source MAC address that indicates the physical address of the node that originated the frame onto the LAN.

An additional function of data encapsulation is error detection. Each Ethernet frame contains a trailer with a cyclic redundancy check (CRC) of the frame contents. After reception of a frame, the receiving node creates a CRC from the bits in the frame to compare to the CRC value in the frame trailer. If these two CRC calculations match, the frame can be trusted as being received without error. The trusted frame will then be processed. A frame received with bad, nonmatching CRCs will be discarded.

MAC

The MAC sublayer controls the placement of frames on the media and the removal of frames from the media. As its name implies, it manages how and when the nodes gain access to the media. This includes the initiation of frame transmission and recovery from transmission failure because of collisions.

The logical topology used in a LAN technology affects the type of MAC required. The traditional underlying logical topology of Ethernet is a multiaccess bus. This means that all the nodes (devices) in that network segment share the medium. This further means that all the nodes in that segment receive all the frames transmitted by any node on that segment. Because all the nodes receive all the frames, each node needs to determine whether a frame is to be accepted and processed by that node. This requires examining the addressing in the frame provided by the MAC address.

Ethernet provides a method for determining how the nodes share access to the media. The MAC method for historic and legacy Ethernet networks is carrier sense multiple access collision detect (CSMA/CD). This method is described later in the "CSMA/CD: The Process" section of this chapter.

Current implementations of Ethernet typically employ LAN switches that can provide a point-to-point logical topology. In these networks, the traditional MAC method of CSMA/CD is not required. The implementation of Ethernet using switches will also be described later in this chapter.

Physical Implementations of Ethernet

Most of the traffic on the Internet originates and ends with Ethernet connections. Since its inception in the 1970s, Ethernet has evolved to meet the increased demand for high-speed LANs. When optical fiber media was introduced, Ethernet adapted to this new technology to take advantage of the superior bandwidth and low error rate that fiber offers. Today, the same data-link protocols that transported data at 3 Mbps can carry data at 10 Gbps. The introduction of *Gigabit Ethernet* has extended the original LAN technology to distances that make Ethernet a *metropolitan-area network (MAN)* and WAN standard.

Ethernet is successful because of the following factors:

- Simplicity and ease of maintenance
- Ability to incorporate new technologies
- Reliability
- Low cost of installation and upgrade

As a technology associated with the physical layer, Ethernet supports a broad range of media and connector specifications. Ethernet protocols specify numerous encoding and decoding schemes that enable frame bits to be carried as signals across these different media.

In today's networks, Ethernet uses unshielded twisted-pair (UTP) copper cables and optical fiber to interconnect network devices through intermediary devices such as hubs and switches. With all the various media types that Ethernet supports, the Ethernet frame structure remains consistent across all its physical implementations. It is for this reason that it has evolved to meet today's networking requirements.

Ethernet: Communication Through the LAN

The foundation for Ethernet technology was established in 1970 with a program called Alohanet. Alohanet was a digital radio network designed to transmit information over a shared radio frequency between the Hawaiian Islands. Alohanet required all stations to follow a protocol in which an unacknowledged transmission required retransmitting after a short period of waiting. From these concepts, the techniques for using a shared medium were later applied to wired LAN technology in the form of Ethernet.

In the following sections, the different generations of Ethernet will be presented. These include historic Ethernet, legacy Ethernet, current Ethernet, and developing Ethernet implementations.

Historic Ethernet

The original design of Ethernet accommodated multiple interconnected computers on a shared bus topology. The first versions of Ethernet used coaxial cable to connect computers in a bus topology. Each computer directly connected to the backbone. These versions of Ethernet incorporated the CSMA/CD media access method. CSMA/CD managed the problems that result when multiple devices attempt to communicate over a shared physical medium. These early versions of Ethernet were known as *Thicknet* (10BASE5) and *Thinnet* (10BASE2).

10BASE5, or Thicknet, used a thick coaxial cable that allowed cabling distances of up to 500 meters before the signal required a repeater. 10BASE2, or Thinnet, used a thin coaxial cable that was smaller in diameter and more flexible than Thicknet and allowed cabling distances of 185 meters. The original thick coaxial and thin coaxial physical media were replaced by early categories of UTP cables. Compared to the coaxial cables, the UTP cables were easier to work with, lighter, and less expensive.

The early implementations of Ethernet were deployed in a low-bandwidth LAN environment where access to the shared media was managed by CSMA, and later CSMA/CD. As shown in Figure 9-2, in addition to being a logical bus topology at the data link layer, Ethernet used a physical bus topology. This topology became more problematic as LANs grew larger and LAN services made increasing demands on the infrastructure. These demands lead to the next generation of Ethernet.

Figure 9-2   Historic Ethernet: Physical and Logical Bus Topology

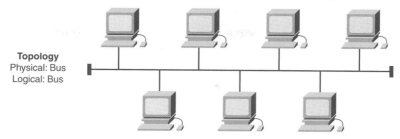

Topology
Physical: Bus
Logical: Bus

The Ethernet networks used in the past used a shared and contention-based media. With changes in technology, most Ethernet networks now being implemented use dedicated links between devices without media contention.

Legacy Ethernet

With the change of the Ethernet media to UTP, the next generation of Ethernet emerged. 10BASE-T networks used this physical topology with a *hub* as the central point of the network segment. As shown in Figure 9-3, the new physical topology was a star. However, these networks shared media as a logical bus. Hubs form a central point of a physical network segment to concentrate connections. In other words, they take a group of nodes and allow the network to see them as a single unit. As the signals representing the bits of a frame arrive at one port, they are copied to the other ports so that all the segments on the LAN receive the frame. Because of the shared media, only one station could successfully transmit at a time. This type of connection is described as a half-duplex communication.

Figure 9-3   Legacy Ethernet: Physical Star and Logical Bus

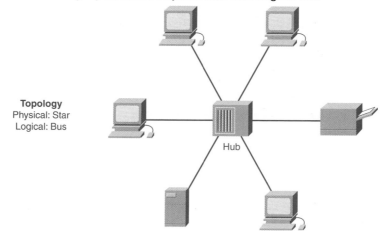

Topology
Physical: Star
Logical: Bus

Hub

In shared media, all the nodes share the availability of the media and have to contend for access to the media. This media contention used the same CSMA/CD MAC as the previous generation of Ethernet networks. The devices on a segment also shared the available bandwidth of the media.

With the wide acceptance of personal computers and the reduced cost of networking media, the development of Ethernet networks coincided with a rapid upsurge in the use of computer networks. This brought about an increased number of devices on the network segments and the need for more throughput and reliability.

As more devices were added to these legacy Ethernet networks, these devices not only had less available bandwidth, but the amount of frame collisions also increased significantly. During periods of low communications activity, the few collisions that occur are managed by the CSMA/CD MAC, with little or no impact on performance. As the number of devices and subsequent data traffic increases, the rise in collisions can have a significant impact on the user experience.

Using the hub in this physical star topology increased network reliability over the early Ethernet networks by allowing any single cable to fail without disrupting the entire network. However, the network segments remained as a logical bus. The repeating of the frame to all other ports did not solve the issue of collisions.

The performance and reliability of Ethernet were vastly improved with the implementation of LAN switches. Additionally, the media speed of 10 Mbps began to be inadequate for many LAN needs.

Current Ethernet

To meet the growing demand of data networks, new technologies were developed to enhance the performance of Ethernet. Two major developments were the increase in Ethernet bandwidth from 10 Mbps to 100 Mbps and the introduction of the LAN switch. These two developments occurred at about the same time to form the foundation for the current implementations of Ethernet.

A tenfold increase in media speed was a major transformation in networks. This innovation was a major turning point in Ethernet's acceptance as the de facto LAN standard. These 100-Mbps networks are referred to as *Fast Ethernet*. In many cases, the upgrade to Fast Ethernet did not require the replacement of existing network cables.

LAN performance also significantly increased with the introduction of switches to replace hubs in Ethernet-based networks. Unlike hubs, switches allow each node connected to them to have the full bandwidth of the media and remove contention for the media. Switches do this by controlling the flow of data by isolating each port and sending a frame only to its proper destination (if the destination is known) rather than sending every frame to every device. By reducing the number of devices receiving each frame, the switch minimizes the possibility of collisions and eliminates the overhead of MAC. This and the later introduction of full-duplex communications, having a connection that can carry both transmitted and received signals at the same time, have enabled the development of 1-Gbps Ethernet and beyond. As shown in Figure 9-4, the current implementation of Ethernet uses physical star topology and a logical point-to-point topology.

Figure 9-4   Current Ethernet Implementation

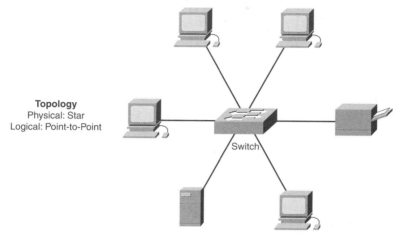

Topology
Physical: Star
Logical: Point-to-Point

Switch

Moving to 1 Gbps and Beyond

The increased performance of LANs created a new generation of computing with the network as the platform for their design. Computer hardware, operating systems, and applications are now designed with reliance on LANs. These applications that cross network links on a daily basis tax even the most robust Fast Ethernet networks. For example, the increasing use of *Voice over IP (VoIP)* and multimedia services requires connections that are faster than 100-Mbps Ethernet. These demands required the development of higher-throughput networks.

This led to the development of Gigabit Ethernet. Gigabit Ethernet describes Ethernet implementations that provide bandwidth of 1000 Mbps (1 Gbps) or greater. This capacity has been built on UTP with the full-duplex capability and fiber-optic media technologies of earlier Ethernet. The increase in network performance is significant when potential throughput increases from 100 Mbps to 1 Gbps and above.

Upgrading to 1-Gbps Ethernet does not always mean that the existing network infrastructure of cables and switches has to be completely replaced. Some of the equipment and cabling in modern, well-designed and well-installed networks can be capable of working at the higher speeds with only minimal upgrading. This capability has the benefit of reducing the total cost of ownership of the network.

The increased cabling distances enabled by the use of fiber-optic cable in Ethernet-based networks have resulted in a blurring of the distinction between LANs and WANs. Ethernet was initially limited to LAN cable systems within single buildings and then extended to between buildings. It can now be applied across a city in a MAN.

Ethernet Frame

Like all data link layer standards, the Ethernet protocol describes the frame formats. The ability to migrate the original implementation of Ethernet to current and future Ethernet implementations is based on the practically unchanged structure of the Layer 2 frame. Physical media and MAC continually evolved, but the Ethernet frame header and trailer have essentially remained constant through the many generations of Ethernet.

Knowing the purpose of the fields in the Ethernet frame is important in understanding the operation of Ethernet. Two of the most important of these fields are the source and destination MAC addresses. Because MAC addresses are expressed in hexadecimal, you need to understand this numbering system. Additionally, you should understand the differences in Layer 2 and Layer 3 addresses. The following sections present these topics.

Frame: Encapsulating the Packet

The Ethernet frame structure adds headers and trailers around the Layer 3 PDU to encapsulate the sent message. Both the Ethernet header and trailer have several sections of information used by the Ethernet protocol. Each section of the frame is called a *field*. There are two styles of Ethernet framing: IEEE 802.3 (original) and the revised IEEE 802.3 (Ethernet).

The differences between framing styles are minimal. The most significant difference between the IEEE 802.3 (original) and the revised IEEE 802.3 is the addition of a Start Frame Delimiter (SFD) and a small change to the Type field to include the Length.

The original Ethernet standard defined the minimum frame size as 64 bytes and the maximum as 1518 bytes. This includes all bytes from the Destination MAC Address field through the Frame Check Sequence (FCS) field. The Preamble and Start Frame Delimiter fields are not included when describing the size of a frame.

The IEEE 802.3ac standard, released in 1998, extended the maximum allowable frame size to 1522 bytes. The frame size increased to accommodate a technology used in switched networks called *virtual local-area network (VLAN)*. VLAN will be presented in the "LAN Switching and Wireless" course of the Exploration curriculum.

If the size of a received frame is less than the minimum or greater than the maximum, the frame is considered corrupt. A receiving device drops any corrupt frames. These frames are likely the result of collisions or other unwanted signals.

Figure 9-5 shows the following Ethernet frame fields:

- **Preamble and Start Frame Delimiter:** The Preamble (7 bytes) and Start Frame Delimiter (SFD) (1 byte) fields synchronize the sending and receiving devices. These first 8 bytes of the frame get the attention of the receiving nodes. Essentially, the first few bytes tell the receivers to get ready to receive a new frame.

- **Destination Address:** The Destination MAC Address field (6 bytes) is the identifier for the intended recipient node. As previously presented, this Layer 2 address assists devices in determining whether a frame is intended for them. The device compares its MAC address to this address in the frame. If there is a match, the device accepts the frame. Switches also use this address to determine out which interface to forward the frame.

- **Source Address:** The Source MAC Address field (6 bytes) identifies the originating NIC or interface of the frame. Switches also use this address to add to entries in their lookup tables.

- **Length/Type:** The Length/Type field (2 bytes) defines the exact length of the data field of the frame. This is used later as part of the CRC process to ensure that the message was received properly. This can be either a length or a type value. However, only one or the other can be used in a given implementation. If the purpose of the field is to designate a type, the Type field describes which upper-layer protocol is encapsulated in the frame. In the early IEEE versions, the field labeled Length/Type was only listed as Length and only listed as Type in the DIX version. These two uses of the field were officially combined in a later IEEE version because both uses were common.

  Ethernet II incorporated the Type field into the current 802.3 frame definition. Ethernet II is the Ethernet frame format used in TCP/IP networks. When a node receives a frame, it must examine the Length/Type field to determine which higher-layer protocol is present. If the two-octet value is equal to or greater than 0x0600 hexadecimal or 1536 decimal, the contents of the Data field are decoded according to the protocol indicated.

- **Data and Pad:** The Data and Pad fields (46–1500 bytes) contain the encapsulated data from a higher layer, which is a generic Layer 3 PDU, or more commonly, an IPv4 packet. All frames must be at least 64 bytes long. If the encapsulated packet is small, the *Pad* increases the size of the frame to this minimum size.

- **Frame Check Sequence (FCS):** The Frame Check Sequence (FCS) field (4 bytes) is used to detect errors in a frame. It uses a CRC. The sending device includes the results of a CRC in the FCS field of the frame. The receiving device receives the frame and generates a CRC from the frame contents. If the calculations match, no error has occurred. Calculations that do not match are an indication that the data has changed. Therefore, the frame is dropped. A change in the data could be the result of a disruption of the electrical signals that represent the bits.

Figure 9-5   Ethernet Frame

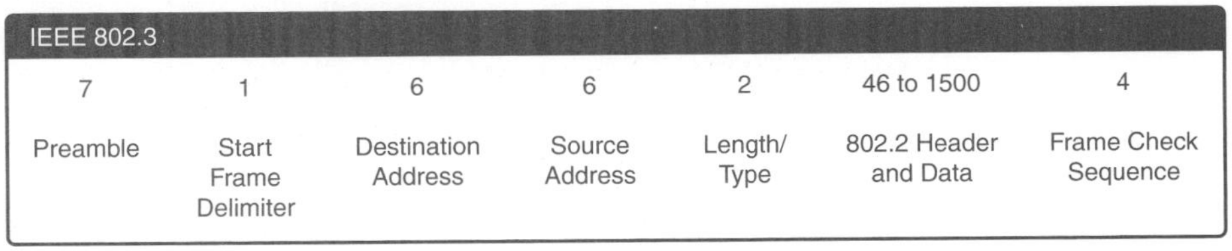

IEEE 802.3						
7	1	6	6	2	46 to 1500	4
Preamble	Start Frame Delimiter	Destination Address	Source Address	Length/ Type	802.2 Header and Data	Frame Check Sequence

Ethernet MAC Address

As presented previously in the section "Historic Ethernet," past versions of Ethernet implemented a logical bus topology. Every network device received all the frames from the shared media. This creates a problem of how to determine whether the received frame is intended for the node.

Layer 2 addressing solves this issue. Each device is identified with a MAC address, and each frame contains a destination MAC address. A unique MAC address identifies the source and destination device within an Ethernet network. Regardless of the variety of Ethernet used, the naming convention provided a method for device identification at a lower level of the OSI model.

As you will recall, MAC addressing is added as part of a Layer 2 PDU. An Ethernet MAC address is a 48-bit binary value expressed as 12 hexadecimal digits. The next sections examine this MAC structure and describe how they are used to identify network devices.

MAC Address Structure

The MAC address is used by the NIC to determine whether a message should be passed to the upper layers for processing. The MAC addresses are assigned based on IEEE-enforced rules for vendors to ensure globally unique addresses for each Ethernet device. As shown in Figure 9-6, these rules, established by IEEE, require any vendor that sells Ethernet devices to register with IEEE. The IEEE assigns the vendor a 3-byte code, called the *Organizational Unique Identifier (OUI)*.

Figure 9-6   Ethernet MAC Address Structure

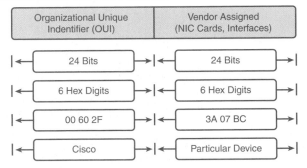

IEEE requires a vendor to follow two simple rules:

- All MAC addresses assigned to a NIC or other Ethernet device must use that vendor's assigned OUI as the first 3 bytes.

- All MAC addresses with the same OUI must be assigned a unique value (vendor code or serial number) in the last 3 bytes.

The MAC address is often referred to as a ***burned-in address (BIA)*** because it is burned into ***read-only memory (ROM)*** on the NIC. This means that the address is encoded into the ROM chip permanently and cannot be changed by software. However, when the computer starts up, the NIC copies the address into ***random-access memory (RAM)***, where it is used as the identifier for this node. When you are examining frames, it is the address in RAM that is used as the source address to compare with the destination address.

The BIA is also sometimes called a ***universally administered address (UAA)***. In place of using the UAA, a device can be configured with a ***locally administered address (LAA)***. The LAA can be convenient for network management because you can configure a device to use a specific MAC value. This means that you can replace a NIC or use a substitute device without changing the address used by the network to access the station.

This allows you to have a device with a new NIC or a replacement device to satisfy any network security rules based on the MAC address. One such case is replacing a local device that is connected to an Internet service provider (ISP) that identifies or authenticates the client by the MAC address. An LAA can be used to allow a replacement device to appear to be the original device to the ISP.

Another situation where you can choose to use an LAA is when a LAN switch is using security to allow only devices to connect that have specific MAC addresses. In this case, a configured LAA can allow the MAC address of a device to meet the MAC requirements of the security on the switch.

Note

You can access information about MAC addresses at the IEEE website, http://standards.ieee.org/regauth/groupmac/tutorial.html.

Network Devices

When the source device is *forwarding* the message on an Ethernet shared network segment, the frame header contains the destination MAC address. Each NIC on a network segment views the information in each frame header to see whether the MAC address matches its physical address. If there is no match, the device discards the frame. When the frame reaches a device where the MAC of the NIC matches the destination MAC in the frame header, the NIC passes the frame up the OSI layers, where the decapsulation process takes place.

MAC addresses are assigned to workstations, servers, printers, switches, routers, or any other device that must originate or receive data on the network. All devices connected to an

Ethernet LAN have 48-bit MAC addresses for each LAN interface. However, when you examine the MAC addresses, they are represented by the operating system in hexadecimal format. Different operating systems or software might represent the MAC address in different hexadecimal formats, such as the following:

- 00-05-9A-3C-78-00

- 00:05:9A:3C:78:00

- 0005.9A3C.7800

Hexadecimal Numbering and Addressing

Hexadecimal ("hex") is a convenient way to represent binary values. Just as decimal is a base 10 numbering system and binary is base 2, hexadecimal is a base 16 system.

The base 16 numbering system uses the numbers 0 to 9 and the letters A to F. Table 9-1 shows the equivalent decimal, binary, and hexadecimal values for binary 0000 to 1111. It is easier to express a value as a single hexadecimal digit than as 4 bits.

Table 9-1   Hexadecimal Digits

Decimal	Binary	Hexadecimal
0	0000	0
1	0001	1
2	0010	2
3	0011	3
4	0100	4
5	0101	5
6	0110	6
7	0111	7
8	1000	8
9	1001	9
10	1010	A
11	1011	B
12	1100	C
13	1101	D
14	1110	E
15	1111	F

Understanding the relationship of bytes to hexadecimal values and learning how to do hexadecimal conversion are presented in the following sections. Additionally, you will learn how to view the MAC address on a Windows-based computer.

Understanding Bytes

Given that 8 bits (a byte) is a common binary grouping, binary 00000000 to 11111111 represent the hexadecimal range 00 to FF. Leading 0s are always displayed to complete the 8-bit representation. For example, the binary value 0000 1010 represents 0A in hexadecimal.

Representing Hexadecimal Values

It is important to distinguish hexadecimal values from decimal values. For example, the digits 73 could be decimal or hexadecimal. Hexadecimal is usually represented in text as a subscript 16. However, because subscript text is not recognized in command-line or programming environments, the technical representation of hexadecimal is preceded with 0x (zero X). Therefore, the previous hexadecimal examples would be shown as 0x0A and 0x73, respectively. Less common, a value can be followed by an H, for example, 73H.

Hexadecimal is used to represent Ethernet MAC addresses and IPv6 addresses. In the course labs, you have seen hexadecimal used in the Packets Byte pane of Wireshark, where it represents the binary values within frames and packets.

Hexadecimal Conversions

Number conversions between decimal and hexadecimal values are straightforward, but quickly dividing or multiplying by 16 is not always convenient. If such conversions are required, it is usually easier to convert the decimal or hexadecimal value to binary and then to convert the binary value to either decimal or hexadecimal as appropriate. With practice, it is possible to recognize the binary bit patterns that match the decimal and hexadecimal values.

In the conversion of binary to hexadecimal, you only need to convert 4-bit binary numbers. These positions represent these quantities:

$$2^3 \quad 2^2 \quad 2^1 \quad 2^0$$

$$8 \quad 4 \quad 2 \quad 1$$

As with binary-to-decimal conversion, the quantity that position represents is added to the total if the digit is a 1, and 0 is added if the digit is a 0.

As an example, binary 10101000 is converted to 0xA8 by converting each 4 bits at a time.

The first 4-bit sequence, 1010, is converted as follows:

$1 * 8 = 8$

$0 * 4 = 0$

$1 * 2 = 2$

$0 * 1 = 0$

$8 + 0 + 2 + 0 = 10$, or A in hexadecimal

The lower 4 bits, 1000, are then converted as follows:

$1 * 8 = 8$

$0 * 4 = 0$

$0 * 2 = 0$

$0 * 1 = 0$

$8 + 0 + 0 + 0 = 8$, or 8 in hexadecimal

So, the byte 10101000 is represented as A8 in hexadecimal (0xA8).

Viewing the MAC Address

To examine the MAC address of your computer, use the **ipconfig /all** or **ifconfig** command. In Example 9-1, notice the MAC address of this computer shown as the physical address. If you have access, you might want to try this on your own computer.

Example 9-1 Viewing the MAC Address of a Computer

```
C:\> ipconfig /all

Windows IP Configuration
        Host Name . . . . . . . . . . . . : mark-wxp2
        Primary Dns Suffix  . . . . . . . : amer.cisco.com
        Node Type . . . . . . . . . . . . : Hybrid
        IP Routing Enabled. . . . . . . . : No
        WINS Proxy Enabled. . . . . . . . : No
        DNS Suffix Search List. . . . . . : cisco.com


Ethernet adapter Wireless Network Connection:
        Connection-specific DNS Suffix  . : cisco.com
        Description . . . . . . . . . . . : Cisco/Wireless PCM350
        Physical Address. . . . . . . . . : 00-0A-BA-47-E6-12
        Dhcp Enabled. . . . . . . . . . . : No
        IP Address. . . . . . . . . . . . : 192.168.254.9
        Subnet Mask . . . . . . . . . . . : 255.255.255.0
        Default Gateway . . . . . . . . . : 192.168.254.1
        DNS Servers . . . . . . . . . . . : 192.168.254.196
                                            192.168.254.162
C:\>
```

Note

You can view information about the registered OUI codes at the IANA website, http://www.iana.org/assignments/ethernet-numbers.

Another Layer of Addressing

In network operations, there are different types of addresses. The purpose of these addresses can often be confusing. This is especially true in understanding the differences in Layer 2 and Layer 3 addresses. After all, they both identify end devices. However, the addresses are used for different purposes. This section will compare the purposes of Layer 2 and Layer 3 addresses. These purposes are as follows:

- The data link layer address enables the packet to be carried by the local media across each segment.

- The network layer address enables the packet to be forwarded toward its destination.

Data Link Layer

OSI data link layer (Layer 2) physical addressing, implemented as an Ethernet MAC address, is used to transport the frame across the local media. Although they provide unique addresses for the devices, physical addresses are nonhierarchical. MAC addresses are associated with a particular device, regardless of its location or the network to which it is connected.

These Layer 2 addresses have no meaning outside the local network media. A Layer 3 packet might have to traverse a number of different data-link technologies in LANs and WANs before it reaches its destination. A source device therefore has no knowledge of the technology used in intermediate and destination networks or of their Layer 2 addressing and frame structures.

Network Layer

Network layer (Layer 3) addresses, such as IPv4 addresses, provide logical addressing that is used to carry the packet from source host to the final destination host. However, as the packet is framed by the different data link layer protocols along the way, the Layer 2 address it receives each time applies only to that local portion of the journey and its media.

Ethernet Unicast, Multicast, and Broadcast

In Ethernet, different MAC addresses are used for Layer 2 unicast, multicast, and broadcast communications. These addresses are discussed in the following sections.

Unicast

A unicast MAC address is the unique address used when a frame is sent from a single transmitting device to a single destination device.

In the example shown in Figure 9-7, a source host with IP address 192.168.1.5 requests a web page from the server at IP address 192.168.1.200. For a unicast packet to be sent and received, a destination IP address must be in the IP packet header. A corresponding destination MAC address must also be present in the Ethernet frame header. The IP address and the MAC address are used to deliver data to one specific destination host.

Figure 9-7   Unicast Communication

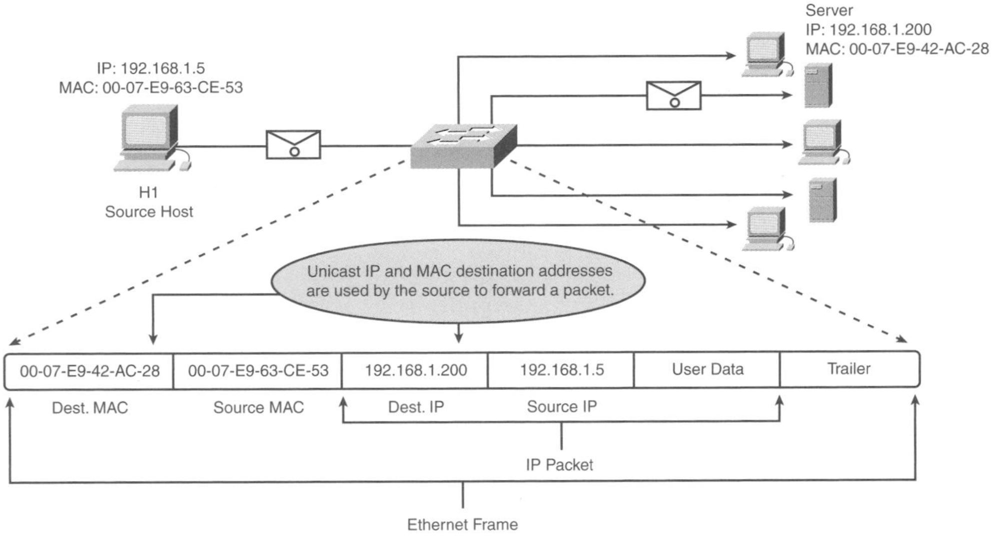

Broadcast

Broadcast at Layer 2 uses a special address that allows all nodes to accept and process the frame. On Ethernet networks, the broadcast MAC address is 48 1s, which is displayed as hexadecimal FF-FF-FF-FF-FF-FF.

With a broadcast at Layer 3, the packet also uses a destination IP address that has all 1s in the host portion. This numbering in the address means that all hosts on that local network (broadcast domain) process the packet within the received frame. In many cases, a Layer 3 broadcast also uses a Layer 2 broadcast address in the frame. This happens when an application or service needs to communicate with all the hosts on the network.

In some cases, a data link layer broadcast does not always contain a Layer 3 broadcast address. This occurs when an application or service needs to communicate with a host whose Layer 3 address is known but the MAC address is not known. As an example,

Address Resolution Protocol (ARP) uses a broadcast at Layer 2 to discover the MAC address of the host addressed in the IP packet header. How ARP uses broadcasts to map Layer 2 to Layer 3 addresses is discussed in the "Address Resolution Protocol (ARP)" section, later in this chapter.

As shown in Figure 9-8, a broadcast IP address for a network contains a corresponding broadcast MAC address in the Ethernet frame.

Figure 9-8   Broadcast Communication

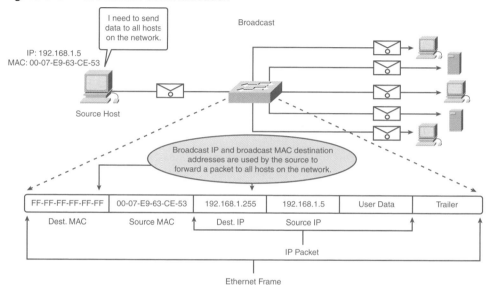

Multicast

Recall that multicast addresses allow a source device to send a packet to a group of devices. Hosts that belong to a multicast group are assigned a multicast group IP address. The range of IPv4 multicast addresses is 224.0.0.0 to 239.255.255.255. Because multicast addresses represent a group of hosts (sometimes called a *host group*), they can only be used as the destination of a packet. The source will always have an IPv4 unicast address.

When a host wants to participate in a multicast group, it uses an application or service to subscribe to the multicast group. This allows Layer 3 to process packets to this address. As with the unicast and broadcast addresses, the multicast IPv4 address requires a corresponding multicast MAC address to actually deliver frames on a local network.

For these multicast packets to reach Layer 3 to be processed by the receiving host, the device must first accept the frame containing this packet. This requires a multicast MAC address corresponding to the subscribed multicast group to be configured on the device. The multicast MAC address is a special value that begins with 01-00-5E in hexadecimal. The value ends by converting the lower 23 bits of the IP multicast group address into the remaining six hexadecimal characters of the Ethernet address. The remaining bit in the MAC address is always 0.

To have a NIC process a frame with a specific multicast address, this address must be stored in the RAM of the NIC in a similar way that the LAA is. This MAC address, along with the BIA and the MAC broadcast address, can then be compared to the destination MAC address in each incoming frame.

Note

You can access more information on multicast communication at

- http://www.cisco.com/en/US/docs/app_ntwk_services/waas/acns/v51/configuration/central/guide/51ipmul.html
- http://www.cisco.com/univercd/cc/td/doc/cisintwk/ito_doc/ipmulti.htm

Ethernet MAC

The MAC method used in Ethernet varies depending on the type of implementation. Legacy Ethernet used shared media and required a method to manage the device's access to the media. This method is carrier sense multiple access collision detect (CSMA/CD).

In most current implementations of Ethernet, switches are used to provide dedicated media for the individual devices. In these LANs, CSMA/CD is not required.

MAC in Ethernet

In a shared media environment, all devices have guaranteed access to the medium, but they have no prioritized claim on it. If more than one device transmits simultaneously, the physical signals collide and the network must recover for communication to continue. In shared media Ethernet, collisions are the cost that Ethernet pays to get the low overhead associated with each transmission.

CSMA/CD: The Process

Historically, Ethernet used *carrier sense multiple access collision detect (CSMA/CD)* to detect and handle collisions and manage the resumption of communications. Because all devices using a shared logical bus Ethernet segment send their messages on the same media, CSMA is used to detect the electrical activity on the cable. A device can determine when it can transmit when it does not detect that any other computer is sending a signal.

The following sections examine the following steps in the CSMA/CD process:

- Listen before sending

- Detecting a collision

- Jam signal and random backoff

How the use of hubs affects collisions is also explored.

Listen Before Sending

In the CSMA/CD access method, a device that has a frame to send must listen before transmitting the frame. If a device detects a signal from another device, it will wait for a specified amount of time before attempting to transmit. Computer C in Figure 9-9 detects a signal on the media from another device and waits to transmit. If the computer had not detected traffic, it would transmit its frame.

Figure 9-9   Detecting Media Signal

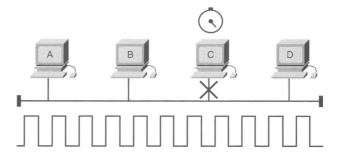

Detecting a Collision

If a device does not detect the signal from a second device, the first device can also start to transmit. The media now has two devices transmitting their signals at the same time. In Figure 9-10, computers A and D transmit at the same time, creating a collision on the shared media. Their messages will propagate across the media until they encounter each other. At that point, the signals mix, a collision occurs, and the message is destroyed. Although the messages are corrupted, the jumble of remaining signals continues to propagate across the media. While this transmission is occurring, the device continues to listen to the media to determine whether a collision occurs. If the frame is sent without a collision being detected, the device returns to its listening mode.

Figure 9-10 Multiple Devices Transmitting

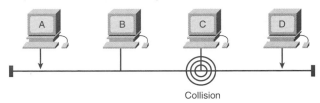

Collision

Jam Signal and Random Backoff

If a collision occurs, the transmitting devices that detect the collision will continue to transmit for a specific period to ensure that all devices on the network detect the collision. This is called the *jam signal*. This jamming signal is used to notify the other devices of a collision so that they will invoke a backoff algorithm. The backoff algorithm causes all devices to stop transmitting for a random amount of time, which allows the collision signals to subside and the media to stabilize.

In Figure 9-11, the hosts detecting the collision transmit a jam signal. After the jam signal, all the devices that see the collision have random backoff timers.

Figure 9-11 Sending Jam Signals

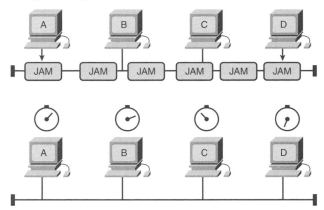

After the backoff delay has expired on a device, the device goes back into the "listening before transmit" mode. A random backoff period ensures that the devices that were involved in the collision do not try to send their traffic again at the same time, which would cause the entire process to repeat. However, this also means that a third device might transmit before either of the two involved in the original collision have a chance to retransmit.

Hubs and Collision Domains

Given that collisions will occur occasionally in any shared media topology, even when employing CSMA/CD, you need to identify the conditions that can result in an increase in collisions. Some of these conditions include the following:

- More devices connected to the network

- More frequent access to the network media

- Increased cable distances between devices

Recall that hubs were created as intermediary network devices that enable more nodes to connect to the shared media. Also known as a multiport repeater, a hub retransmits received data signals to all connected devices, except the one from which it received the signals. Hubs do not perform higher-level network functions such as directing data based on addresses or filtering of data.

Hubs and repeaters extend the distance that cabling in Ethernet can reach. Because hubs operate at the physical layer, dealing only with the signals on the media, collisions can occur between the devices they connect and within the hubs themselves. Further, using hubs to provide network access to more users reduces the performance for each user because the fixed bandwidth of the media has to be shared between more and more devices.

The connected devices that access a common media through a hub or series of connected hubs make up what is known as a *collision domain*. A collision domain is also referred to as a *network segment*. Hubs and repeaters therefore have the effect of increasing the size of the collision domain.

As shown in Figure 9-12, the interconnection of hubs forms a physical topology that creates an *extended star*. The extended star can create a greatly expanded collision domain.

An increased number of collisions reduces the network's efficiency and effectiveness until the collisions become a nuisance to the user. Although CSMA/CD is a MAC method, it was designed to manage limited numbers of devices on networks with light network usage. When collision domains grow too large, the overhead involved with managing the collisions greatly hampers network communication. Therefore, other mechanisms are required when large numbers of users require access and when more active network access is needed. You will see in the section "Ethernet: Using Switches," later in this chapter, that using switches in place of hubs can begin to alleviate this problem.

Observing the Effects of Collisions in a Shared Media Network (9.4.2.3)

In this Packet Tracer Activity, you will build large collision domains to view the effects of collisions on data transmission and network operation. Use file e1-9423.pka on the CD-ROM that accompanies this book to perform this activity using Packet Tracer.

Figure 9-12 Extended Star with Hubs

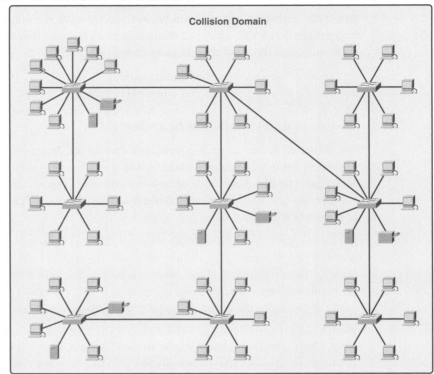

Ethernet Timing

At higher transmission rates, the time for a signal to be on the media decreases. These faster physical layer implementations of Ethernet introduce complexities to the management of collisions.

Latency

As discussed, each device that wants to transmit must first "listen" to the media to check for traffic. If no traffic exists, the station will begin to transmit immediately. The electrical signal that is transmitted takes a certain amount of time, or *latency*, to propagate (travel) down the cable. Each hub or repeater in the signal's path adds latency as it forwards the bits from one port to the next.

This accumulated delay increases the likelihood that collisions will occur because a listening node might transition into transmitting while the hub or repeater is processing the message. Because the signal had not reached this node while it was listening, the media appeared available the device. This condition often results in collisions.

Timing and Synchronization

In half-duplex mode, if a collision has not occurred, the sending device will transmit 64 bits of timing synchronization information, which is known as the Preamble. The sending device will then transmit the complete frame.

Ethernet implementations with throughput speeds of 10 Mbps and slower are *asynchronous*. An asynchronous communication in this context means that each receiving device will use the 8 bytes of timing information to synchronize the receive circuit to the incoming data and then discard the 8 bytes.

Ethernet implementations with throughput speeds of 100 Mbps and faster are *synchronous*. Synchronous communication in this context means that the timing information in the header is not required. However, for compatibility reasons, the Preamble and Start Frame Delimiter (SFD) fields are still present. These higher-speed Ethernet implementations use signaling methods that include a method of synchronizing the transmit and receive clocks between the two nodes. This allows each bit to be synchronized.

Bit Time

For each different media speed, a period of time is required for a bit to be placed and sensed on the media. This period of time is referred to as *the bit time*. On 10-Mbps Ethernet, 1 bit at the MAC sublayer requires 100 nanoseconds (ns) to transmit. At 100 Mbps, that same bit requires 10 ns to transmit. At 1000 Mbps, only 1 ns is available to transmit a bit. As a rough estimate, 20.3 centimeters (8 inches) per nanosecond is often used for calculating the propagation delay on a UTP cable. The result is that for 100 meters of UTP cable, it takes just under five bit times for a 10BASE-T signal to travel the length of the cable.

The bit times for common Ethernet speeds are shown in Table 9-2.

Table 9-2   Ethernet Bit Times

Ethernet Speed	Bit Time (ns)
10 Mbps	100
100 Mbps	10
1 Gbps	1
10 Gbps	0.1

For CSMA/CD Ethernet to operate, a sending device must become aware of a collision before it has completed the transmission of a minimum-sized frame. At 100 Mbps, the device timing is barely able to accommodate 100-meter cables. At 1000 Mbps, special adjustments are required because nearly an entire minimum-sized frame would be transmitted before the first bit reached the end of the first 100 meters of UTP cable. For this reason, half-duplex mode is not permitted in 10-Gigabit Ethernet on UTP.

These timing considerations have to be applied to the interframe spacing and *backoff times* to ensure that when a device transmits its next frame, the risk of a collision is minimized. Interframe spacing and backoff times are discussed in the section "Interframe Spacing and Backoff," later in this chapter.

Slot Time

In half-duplex Ethernet, where data can only travel in one direction at once, *slot time* becomes an important parameter in determining how many devices can share a network. Slot time for a network is the maximum time required to detect a collision. This is equal to twice the time it takes a signal to travel between the two most-distant stations on the network. This ensures that all devices start to receive a frame before the transmitting NIC has finished sending it.

Slot time is used to establish the following:

- The minimum size of an Ethernet frame
- A limit on the maximum size of a network's segments

These two factors are interrelated. The slot time ensures that if a collision is going to occur, it will be detected within the transmission time of a minimum-size frame. A longer minimum frame length allows longer slot times and larger collision diameters. A shorter minimum frame length creates shorter slot times and smaller collision diameters.

When determining the standard for a slot time, it is a trade-off between the need to reduce the impact of collision recovery (backoff and retransmission times) and the need for network distances to be large enough to accommodate reasonable network sizes. The compromise was to choose a maximum network diameter and then to set the minimum frame length long enough to ensure detection of all worst-case collisions.

The standards ensure that the minimum transmission time for a frame must be at least one slot time, and the time required for collisions to propagate to all stations on the network must be less than one slot time. The slot time for 10- and 100-Mbps Ethernet is 512 bit times, or 64 octets. Slot time for 1000-Mbps Ethernet is 4096 bit times, or 512 octets. These slot times are shown in Table 9-3.

Table 9-3   Ethernet Slot Times

Ethernet Speed	Slot Time
10 Mbps	512 bit times
100 Mbps	512 bit times
1 Gbps	4096 bit times
10 Gbps	— (Shared media not supported)

These slot times ensure that a station cannot finish transmission of a frame before detecting that a collision has occurred. If a collision is going to occur, it will be detected within the first 64 bytes (512 bits) and 512 bytes (4096 bits) for Gigabit Ethernet of the frame transmission. By only detecting collisions during the minimum frame sizes, the handling of frame retransmissions following a collision is simplified.

This slot time includes the time it takes the signal to travel through cables and hubs. The slot time is used to define the standard for the maximum lengths of network cables and the number of hubs used in a shared Ethernet segment. If a shared Ethernet segment is created longer than the standards, it will allow slot times that are too long. These longer slot times will create late collisions. Late collisions are the collisions that arrive too late in the frame transmission to be detected and managed by CSMA/CD functions. The frame being transmitted will be dropped, requiring that application software detect its loss and initiate a retransmission.

Interframe Spacing and Backoff

After a node has transmitted, a delay needs to occur before the next transmission. These delays give the signals on the media time to dissipate. This quiet time is necessary whether or not the frame was successfully placed on the media. The delay after successful frame transmission is called *interframe spacing*. The delay after a collision is a *backoff*.

Interframe Spacing

The Ethernet standards require a minimum spacing between two noncolliding frames. This gives the media time to stabilize after the transmission of the previous frame and time for the devices to process the frame. *Interframe spacing* is the time measured from the last bit of the FCS field of one frame to the first bit of the Preamble of the next frame.

After a frame has been sent, all devices on a 10-Mbps Ethernet network are required to wait a minimum of 96 bit times (9.6 microseconds) before any device can transmit its next frame. On faster versions of Ethernet, the spacing remains the same at 96 bit times, but the interframe spacing time period is correspondingly shorter.

Synchronization delays between devices can result in the loss of some of the frame Preamble bits. This, in turn, can cause a minor reduction of the interframe spacing when hubs and repeaters regenerate the full 64 bits of timing information (the Preamble and SFD) at the start of every frame forwarded. If shared media is used on higher-speed Ethernet, some time-sensitive devices could potentially fail to recognize individual frames, resulting in communication failure.

Jam Signal Length

As you will recall, Ethernet allows all devices on a shared segment to compete for transmitting time. In the event that two devices transmit simultaneously, the network CSMA/CD attempts to resolve the issue. As soon as a collision is detected, the sending devices transmit a 32-bit "jam" signal that will enforce the collision. This ensures that all devices in the LAN detect the collision.

It is important that the jam signal not be detected as a valid frame; otherwise, the collision would not be identified. The most commonly observed data pattern for a jam signal is simply a repeating 1, 0, 1, 0 pattern, the same as the Preamble. The corrupted, partially transmitted messages are often referred to as collision fragments, or *runt frames*. Normal collisions are less than 64 octets in length and therefore fail both the minimum length and the FCS tests, making them easy to identify.

Backoff Timing

After a collision occurs and all devices allow the cable to become idle (each waits the full interframe spacing), the devices whose transmissions collided must wait an additional and potentially progressively longer period of time before attempting to retransmit the collided frame. The waiting period is intentionally designed to be random so that two stations do not delay for the same amount of time before retransmitting, which would result in more collisions. This is accomplished in part by expanding the interval from which the random retransmission time is selected on each retransmission attempt. The waiting period is measured in increments of the parameter slot time.

If media congestion results in the MAC sublayer being unable to send the frame after 16 attempts, it gives up and generates an error to the network layer. Such an occurrence is rare in a properly operating network and would happen only under extremely heavy network loads or when a physical problem exists on the network.

The methods described in this section allowed Ethernet to provide greater service in a shared media topology based on the use of hubs. In the section "Ethernet: Using Switches," later in this chapter, you will see how, with the use of switches, the need for CSMA/CD starts to diminish or, in some cases, is removed.

Ethernet Physical Layer

The differences between standard Ethernet, Fast Ethernet, Gigabit Ethernet, and 10-Gigabit Ethernet occur at the physical layer, often referred to as the *Ethernet PHY*.

Ethernet is covered by the IEEE 802.3 standards. Four data rates are currently defined for operation over optical fiber and twisted-pair cables:

- **10 Mbps:** 10BASE-T Ethernet
- **100 Mbps:** Fast Ethernet

- **1000 Mbps:** Gigabit Ethernet

- **10 Gbps:** 10-Gigabit Ethernet

While there are many different implementations of Ethernet at these various data rates, only the more common ones will be presented here. Table 9-4 shows some of the Ethernet PHY characteristics.

Table 9-4   Selected Ethernet PHY Characteristics

Ethernet Type	Bandwidth	Cable Type	Maximum Distance (meters)
10BASE5	10 Mbps	Thick coax	500
10BASE2	10 Mbps	Thin coax	185
10BASE-T	10 Mbps	Cat3/Cat5 UTP	100
100BASE-TX	100 Mbps	Cat5 UTP	100
100BASE-FX	100 Mbps	Multimode/single-mode fiber	400/2000
1000BASE-T	1 Gbps	Cat5e UTP	100
1000BASE-TX	1 Gbps	Cat6 UTP	100
1000BASE-SX	1 Gbps	Multimode fiber	550
1000BASE-LX	1 Gbps	Single-mode fiber	2000
10GBASE-T	10 Gbps	Cat6a/Cat7 UTP	100
10GBASE-LX4	10 Gbps	Multimode fiber	300
10GBASE-LX4	10 Gbps	Single-mode fiber	10,000

The portion of Ethernet that operates on the physical layer will be discussed in the following sections, beginning with 10BASE-T and continuing to 10-Gbps varieties.

10- and 100-Mbps Ethernet

The principal 10-Mbps implementations of Ethernet include

- 10BASE5 using Thicknet coaxial cable

- 10BASE2 using Thinnet coaxial cable

- 10BASE-T using Cat3/Cat5 unshielded twisted-pair cable

The early implementations of Ethernet, 10BASE5 and 10BASE2, used coaxial cable in a physical bus. These implementations are no longer used and are not supported by the newer 802.3 standards.

10-Mbps Ethernet: 10BASE-T

10-Mbps Ethernet is considered to be legacy Ethernet and uses a physical star topology. Ethernet 10BASE-T links can be up to 100 meters in length before requiring a hub or repeater. 10BASE-T uses Manchester encoding over two unshielded twisted-pair cables.

10BASE-T uses two pairs of a four-pair cable and is terminated at each end with an 8-pin RJ-45 connector. The pair connected to pins 1 and 2 is used for transmitting, and the pair connected to pins 3 and 6 is used for receiving. The early implementations of 10BASE-T used Cat3 cabling. However, Cat5 or later cabling is typically used today.

10BASE-T is generally not chosen for new LAN installations. However, there are still many 10BASE-T Ethernet networks in existence today. The replacement of hubs with switches in 10BASE-T networks has greatly increased the throughput available to these networks and has given legacy Ethernet greater longevity. The 10BASE-T links connected to a switch can support either half-duplex or full-duplex operation.

100-Mbps: Fast Ethernet

In the mid to late 1990s, several new 802.3 standards were established to describe methods for transmitting data over Ethernet media at 100 Mbps. These standards used different encoding requirements for achieving these higher data rates. 100-Mbps Ethernet, also known as Fast Ethernet, can be implemented using twisted-pair copper wire or fiber media. The most popular implementations of 100-Mbps Ethernet are

- 100BASE-TX using Cat5 or later UTP

- 100BASE-FX using fiber-optic cable

Because the higher-frequency signals used in Fast Ethernet are more susceptible to noise, two separate encoding steps are used by 100-Mbps Ethernet to enhance signal integrity.

100BASE-TX

100BASE-TX was designed to support transmission over two pairs of Category 5 UTP copper wire. The 100BASE-TX implementation uses the same two pairs and pinouts of UTP as 10BASE-T. However, 100BASE-TX requires Category 5 or later UTP. The 4B/5B encoding is used for 100BASE-T Ethernet.

As with 10BASE-T, 100BASE-TX is connected as a physical star. However, unlike 10BASE-T, 100BASE-TX networks typically use a switch at the center of the star instead of a hub. At about the same time that 100BASE-TX technologies became mainstream, LAN switches were also being widely deployed. These concurrent developments led to their natural combination in the design of 100BASE-TX networks.

100BASE-FX

The 100BASE-FX standard uses the same signaling procedure as 100BASE-TX, but over optical fiber media rather than UTP copper. Although the encoding, decoding, and clock recovery procedures are the same for both media, the signal transmission is different: electrical pulses in copper and light pulses in optical fiber. 100BASE-FX uses low-cost fiber interface connectors (commonly called duplex SC connectors).

Fiber implementations are point-to-point connections; that is, they are used to interconnect two devices. These connections can be between two computers, between a computer and a switch, or between two switches.

1000-Mbps Ethernet

The development of Gigabit Ethernet standards resulted in specifications for UTP copper, single-mode fiber, and multimode fiber. On Gigabit Ethernet networks, bits occur in a fraction of the time that they take on 100-Mbps networks and 10-Mbps networks. With signals occurring in less time, the bits become more susceptible to noise, and therefore timing is critical. The question of performance is based on how fast the network adapter or interface can change voltage levels and how well that voltage change can be detected reliably 100 meters away, at the receiving NIC or interface.

At these higher speeds, encoding and decoding data are more complex. Gigabit Ethernet uses two separate encoding steps. Data transmission is more efficient when codes are used to represent the binary bit stream. Encoding the data enables synchronization, efficient usage of bandwidth, and improved signal-to-noise ratio characteristics.

1000BASE-T Ethernet

1000BASE-T Ethernet provides full-duplex transmission using all four pairs in Category 5 or later UTP cable. Gigabit Ethernet over copper wire enables an increase from 100 Mbps per wire pair to 125 Mbps per wire pair, or 500 Mbps for the four pairs. Each wire pair signals in full duplex, doubling the 500 Mbps to 1000 Mbps.

1000BASE-T uses 4D-PAM5 line encoding to obtain 1 Gbps data throughput. This encoding scheme enables the transmission signals over four wire pairs simultaneously. It translates an 8-bit byte of data into a simultaneous transmission of four code symbols (4D), which are sent over the media, one on each pair, as 5-level *pulse amplitude modulation (PAM5)* signals. This means that every symbol corresponds to 2 bits of data. Because the information travels simultaneously across the four paths, the circuitry has to divide frames at the transmitter and reassemble them at the receiver.

1000BASE-T allows the transmission and reception of data in both directions—on the same wire and at the same time. This traffic flow creates permanent collisions on the wire pairs. These collisions result in complex voltage patterns. The hybrid circuits detecting the signals use sophisticated techniques such as echo cancellation, Layer 1 forward error correction (FEC), and prudent selection of voltage levels. Using these techniques, the system achieves the 1-Gbps throughput.

To help with synchronization, the physical layer encapsulates each frame with start-of-stream and end-of-stream delimiters. Loop timing is maintained by continuous streams of special codes called IDLE symbols sent on each wire pair during the interframe spacing.

Unlike most digital signals, where there are usually a couple of discrete voltage levels, 1000BASE-T uses many voltage levels. In idle periods, nine voltage levels are found on the cable. During data transmission periods, up to 17 voltage levels are found on the cable. With this large number of states, combined with the effects of noise, the signal on the wire looks more analog than digital. Like analog, the system is more susceptible to noise because of cable and termination problems.

1000BASE-SX and 1000BASE-LX Ethernet Using Fiber-Optics

The fiber versions of Gigabit Ethernet—1000BASE-SX and 1000BASE-LX—offer the following advantages over UTP:

- Noise immunity
- Small physical size
- Increased unrepeated distances
- Bandwidth

All 1000BASE-SX and 1000BASE-LX versions support full-duplex binary transmission at 1250 Mbps over two strands of optical fiber. The transmission coding is based on the 8B/10B encoding scheme. Because of the overhead of this encoding, the data transfer rate is still 1000 Mbps.

Each data frame is encapsulated at the physical layer before transmission, and link synchronization is maintained by sending a continuous stream of IDLE symbols during the interframe spacing.

The principal differences among the 1000BASE-SX and 1000BASE-LX fiber versions are the link media, connectors, and wavelength of the optical signal.

Ethernet: Future Options

The IEEE 802.3ae standard was adapted to include 10-Gbps, full-duplex transmission over fiber-optic cable. The 802.3ae standard and the 802.3 standards for the original Ethernet are very similar. 10-Gigabit Ethernet (10GbE) is evolving for use not only in LANs but also in

WANs and MANs. Because the frame format and other Ethernet Layer 2 specifications are compatible with previous standards, 10GbE can provide increased bandwidth to individual networks that is interoperable with the existing network infrastructure.

10-Gbps Ethernet compares to other varieties of Ethernet in the following ways:

- The frame format is the same, allowing interoperability among all varieties of legacy, Fast, Gigabit, and 10-Gigabit Ethernet, with no reframing or protocol conversions necessary.

- The bit time is now 0.1 ns. All other time variables scale accordingly.

- Because only full-duplex fiber connections are used, there is no media contention, and CSMA/CD is not necessary.

- The IEEE 802.3 sublayers within OSI Layers 1 and 2 are mostly preserved, with a few additions to accommodate 40-km fiber links and interoperability with other fiber technologies.

With 10-Gbps Ethernet, flexible, efficient, reliable, and relatively low-cost end-to-end Ethernet networks become possible. Although 1-Gigabit Ethernet is now widely available and 10-Gigabit products are becoming more available, the IEEE and the 10-Gigabit Ethernet Alliance are working on 40-, 100-, and even 160-Gbps standards. The technologies that are adopted will depend on a number of factors, including the rate of maturation of the technologies and standards, the rate of adoption in the market, and the cost of emerging products.

Hubs and Switches

The previous sections presented shared media implementations of Ethernet. These topologies are based on the use of hubs at the center of the network segment. The following sections also describe how switches greatly enhance the performance of the Ethernet network.

Legacy Ethernet: Using Hubs

Legacy Ethernet uses shared media and contention-based MAC. Legacy Ethernet uses hubs to interconnect nodes on the LAN segment. Hubs do not perform traffic filtering. Instead, the hub forwards all the bits to every device connected to the hub. This forces all the devices in the LAN to share the bandwidth of the media.

Additionally, this legacy Ethernet implementation often results in high levels of collisions on the LAN. Because of these performance issues, this type of Ethernet LAN has limited use in networks today. Ethernet implementations using hubs are now typically used only in small LANs or in LANs with low bandwidth requirements.

Sharing media among devices creates significant issues as the network grows. These issues include the following:

- Lack of scalability
- Increased latency
- More network failure
- More collisions

Limited Scalability

In a hub-based Ethernet network, there is a limit to the amount of bandwidth that devices can share. With each device added to the shared media, the average bandwidth available to each device decreases. With each increase in the number of devices on the media, performance is further degraded.

Increased Latency

Network latency is the amount of time it takes a signal to reach all destinations on the media. Each node in a hub-based network has to wait for an opportunity to transmit in order to avoid collisions. Latency can increase significantly as the distance between nodes is extended. Latency is also affected by a delay of the signal across the media as well as the delay added by the processing of the signals through hubs and repeaters. Increasing the length of media or the number of hubs and repeaters connected to a segment results in increased latency. With greater latency, it is more likely that nodes will not receive initial signals, thereby increasing the collisions present in the network.

More Network Failures

Because legacy Ethernet shares the media, any device in the network could potentially cause problems for other devices. If any device connected to the hub generates detrimental traffic, the communication for all devices on the media could be impeded. This harmful traffic could be because of incorrect speed or full-duplex settings on a NIC.

More Collisions

According to CSMA/CD, a node should not send a packet unless the network is clear of traffic. If two nodes send packets at the same time, a collision occurs and the packets are lost. Then both nodes send a jam signal, wait for a random amount of time, and retransmit their packets. Any part of the network where packets from two or more nodes can interfere with each other is considered a collision domain. A network with a larger number of nodes on the same segment has a larger collision domain and typically has more traffic. As the amount of traffic in the network increases, the likelihood of collisions increases.

Ethernet: Using Switches

Switches provide an alternative to the contention-based environment of legacy Ethernet. In the past few years, switches have quickly become a fundamental part of most networks. Switches allow the segmentation of the LAN into separate collision domains. Each port of the switch represents a separate collision domain and provides the full media bandwidth to the node or nodes connected on that port. With fewer nodes in each collision domain, there is an increase in the average bandwidth available to each node, and collisions are reduced.

A LAN can have a centralized switch connecting to hubs that still provide the connectivity to nodes. On the other hand, a LAN might have all nodes connected directly to a switch. In a LAN where a hub is connected to a switch port, as shown in Figure 9-13, there is still shared bandwidth, which can result in collisions within the shared environment of the hub. However, the switch will isolate the segment and limit collisions to traffic between the ports of the hubs.

Figure 9-13 shows two collision domains, one for each shared media segment connected to a switch port.

Figure 9-13   Switch Connecting Shared Segments with Hubs

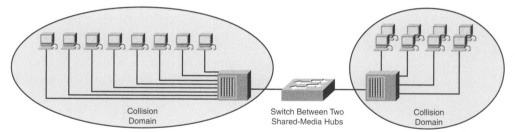

Nodes Are Connected Directly

In a LAN where all nodes are connected directly to the switch, as shown in Figure 9-14, the throughput of the network increases dramatically. With each computer connected to a separate port on the switch, each is in a separate collision domain and has its own dedicated segment. The three primary reasons for this increase are these:

- Dedicated bandwidth to each port
- Collision-free environment
- Full-duplex operation

Figure 9-14   Switch with Directly Connected Nodes

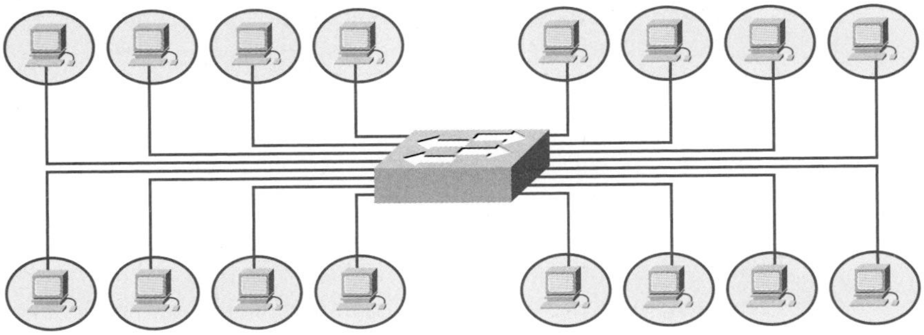

These physical star topologies are essentially point-to-point links.

Dedicated Bandwidth

With switches, each device effectively has a dedicated point-to-point connection between the device and the switch, without media contention. Each node has the full media bandwidth available in the connection between the node and the switch.

As an example, compare two 100-Mbps LANs, each with 10 nodes. In network segment A, the 10 nodes are connected to a hub. Each node shares the available 100-Mbps bandwidth. This provides an average of 10 Mbps to each node. In network segment B, the 10 nodes are connected to a switch. In this segment, all 10 nodes have the full 100-Mbps bandwidth available to them.

Even in this small network example, the increase in bandwidth is significant. As the number of nodes increases, the discrepancy between the available bandwidth in the two implementations increases significantly.

Collision-Free Environment

A dedicated point-to-point connection to a switch also removes any media contention between devices, allowing a node to operate with few or no collisions. In a moderately sized legacy Ethernet network using hubs, approximately 40 to 50 percent of the bandwidth is consumed by collision recovery. In a switched Ethernet network—where there are virtually no collisions—the overhead devoted to collision recovery is virtually eliminated. This provides the switched network with significantly better throughput rates.

Full-Duplex Operation

Switching also allows a network to operate as a full-duplex Ethernet environment. Before switching existed, Ethernet was half duplex only. This meant that at any given time, a node could either transmit or receive. With full duplex enabled in a switched Ethernet network, the devices connected directly to the switch ports can transmit and receive simultaneously, at the full media bandwidth.

The connection between the device and the switch is collision-free. This arrangement effectively doubles the transmission rate when compared to half duplex. For example, if the speed of the network is 100 Mbps, each node can transmit a frame at 100 Mbps and, at the same time, receive a frame at 100 Mbps.

Using Switches Instead of Hubs

Most modern Ethernets use switches to connect the end devices and operate full duplex. Because switches provide so much greater throughput than hubs and increase performance so dramatically, it is fair to ask: Why not use switches in every Ethernet LAN? You might still encounter hubs in a LAN for three reasons:

- **Availability:** LAN switches were not developed until the early 1990s and were not readily available until the mid-1990s. Early Ethernet networks used UTP hubs, and many of them remain in operation to this day.

- **Economics:** Initially, switches were rather expensive. As the price of switches has dropped, the use of hubs has decreased and cost is becoming less of a factor in deployment decisions.

- **Requirements:** The early LAN networks were simple networks designed to exchange files and share printers. For many locations, the early networks have evolved into the converged networks of today, resulting in a substantial need for increased bandwidth available to individual users. In some circumstances, however, a shared media hub will still suffice, and these products remain on the market.

The next section explores the basic operation of switches and explains how a switch achieves the enhanced performance. The "LAN Switching and Wireless" course in the Exploration curriculum will present more details and additional technologies related to switching.

From Hubs to Switches (9.6.2.3)

In this Packet Tracer activity, a model is provided to compare the collisions found in hub-based networks to the collision-free behavior of switches. Use file e1-9623.pka on the CD-ROM that accompanies this book to perform this activity using Packet Tracer.

Switches: Selective Forwarding

Ethernet switches selectively forward individual frames from a receiving port to the port where the destination node is connected. This *selective forwarding* process can be thought of as establishing a momentary point-to-point connection between the transmitting and receiving nodes. During this instant, the two nodes have a full bandwidth connection between them and represent a logical point-to-point connection. The connection is made only long enough to forward a single frame.

In the switched implementation of Ethernet, the destination address takes on an additional role. The destination MAC address is used to complete the momentary point-to-point connection. In addition to being used by the receiving node to determine whether the frame is for that node, the destination MAC address is also used by the switch to determine to which port the frame should be forwarded. This outgoing port is then used as the other connection for the momentary point-to-point connection.

To be technically accurate, this temporary connection is not made between the two nodes simultaneously. In essence, this makes two point-to-point connections: one between the source host and the switch and another connection between the destination host and the switch. In fact, any node operating in full-duplex mode can transmit anytime it has a frame, without regard to the availability of the receiving node. This is because a LAN switch will buffer an incoming frame and then forward it to the proper port when that port is idle. This process is referred to as *store and forward*.

With store-and-forward switching, the switch receives the entire frame, checks the FCS for errors, and forwards the frame to the appropriate port for the destination node. Because the nodes do not have to wait for the media to be idle, the nodes can send and receive at full media speed without losses because of collisions or the overhead associated with managing collisions.

Forwarding Based on the Destination MAC Address

The switch maintains a table, called a *MAC table*, that maps destination MAC addresses with the ports used to connect to each node. For each incoming frame, the destination MAC address in the frame header is compared to the list of addresses in the MAC table. If a match is found, the port number in the table that is paired with the MAC address is used as the exit port for the frame.

The MAC table can be referred to by many different names. It is often called the *switch table*. Because switching was derived from an older technology called *transparent bridging*, the table is sometimes called the *bridge table*. For this reason, many processes performed by LAN switches can contain *bridge* or *bridging* in their names.

A bridge is a device used more commonly in the early days of LANs to connect, or bridge, two physical network segments. Switches can be used to perform this operation as well as to allow end-device connectivity to the LAN. Many other technologies have been developed around LAN switching. Many of these technologies will be presented in a later course. One place where bridges are prevalent is in wireless networks. Wireless bridges are used to interconnect two wireless network segments. Therefore, you can find both terms, *switching* and *bridging*, in use by the networking industry.

The transmission of a frame from computer A to computer C through a switch is represented in Figure 9-15. Computer A sends a frame with a destination MAC address of 0C. The switch receives the frame and examines the MAC table to determine on which port the node with the MAC 0C is connected. Because it found a match, the switch will forward the frame out port 6 to computer C. A copy of this frame was not forwarded out the other switch ports.

Figure 9-15   Switch Forwarding Based on MAC Address

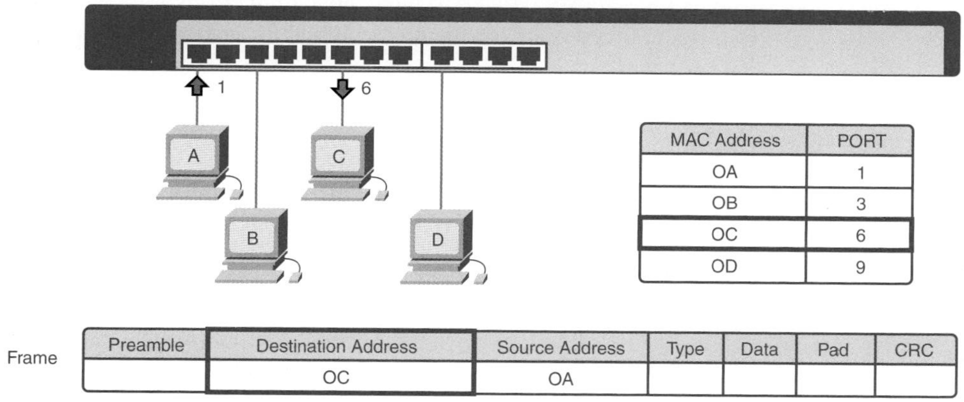

Switch Operation

To accomplish their purpose, Ethernet LAN switches use five basic operations:

- Learning

- Aging

- Flooding

- Selective forwarding

- Filtering

The following sections describe the basic principles of each operation.

Learning

The MAC table must be populated with MAC addresses and their corresponding ports. The learning process allows these mappings to be dynamically acquired during normal operation.

As each frame enters the switch, the switch examines the source MAC address. Using a lookup procedure, the switch determines whether the table already contains an entry for that MAC address. If no entry exists, the switch creates a new entry in the MAC table using the source MAC address and pairs the address with the port on which the entry arrived. The switch can now use this mapping to forward frames to this node.

Aging

The entries in the MAC table acquired by the learning process are time stamped. This time-stamp is used as a means for removing old entries in the MAC table. After an entry is made in the MAC table, a procedure begins a countdown, using the timestamp as the beginning value. After the value reaches 0, the entry in the table is aged out and is removed from the MAC table. The age timer can be reset to the beginning value when the switch next receives a frame from that node on the same port. Resetting the timer will prevent a MAC entry from being removed. As an example, an age timer might be set to 300 seconds. If another frame is not received from the node within 300 seconds, this entry will be removed from the MAC table.

Flooding

If the switch does not have a MAC address entry in its MAC table that matches the destina-tion MAC address of a received frame, the switch will flood the frame. *Flooding* involves sending a frame to all ports except the port on which the frame arrived. The switch does not forward the frame to the port on which it arrived because any destination on that segment will have already received the frame. Flooding is also used for frames sent to the broadcast MAC address.

Selective Forwarding

Selective forwarding is the process of examining the destination MAC address of a frame and forwarding it out the appropriate port. This is the central function of the switch. When a frame from a node arrives at the switch for which the switch has already learned the MAC address, this address is matched to an entry in the MAC table, and the frame is forwarded to the corresponding port. Instead of flooding the frame to all ports, the switch sends the frame to the destination node through its nominated port. This action is called *forwarding*.

Filtering

In some cases, a frame is not forwarded. This process is called frame *filtering*. One use of filtering has already been described: A switch does not forward a frame to the same port on which it arrived. A switch will also drop a corrupt frame. If a frame fails a CRC check, the frame is dropped. An additional reason for filtering a frame is security. A switch has securi-ty settings for blocking frames to or from selective MAC addresses or specific ports.

Switch Operation (9.6.4.2)

In this Packet Tracer activity, you will have the opportunity to visualize and experiment with the behavior of switches in a network. Use file e1-9642.pka on the CD-ROM that accompanies this book to perform this activity using Packet Tracer.

Address Resolution Protocol (ARP)

Address Resolution Protocol (ARP) provides two basic functions:

- Resolving IPv4 addresses to MAC addresses
- Maintaining a cache of mappings

Resolving IPv4 Addresses to MAC Addresses

For an Ethernet frame to be placed on the LAN media, it must have a destination MAC address. In a transmitting device, when an IPv4 packet is sent to the data link layer to be encapsulated into a frame, the device must identify the data link layer address that is mapped to the destination IPv4 address. To find this MAC address, the node refers to a table in its RAM memory called the *ARP table* or the *ARP cache*.

Each entry, or row, of the ARP table has a pair of values: an IP address and a MAC address. The relationship between the two values in the row is a *map*. A map allows the node to locate an IP address in the table and discover the corresponding MAC address. The ARP table caches the mapping for the devices on the local LAN.

To begin the process, a transmitting node attempts to locate in the ARP table the MAC address mapped to an IPv4 destination. If this map is cached in the table, the node uses the MAC address as the destination MAC in the frame that encapsulates the IPv4 packet. The frame is then encoded onto the networking media.

In Figure 9-16, computer A needs to send data to computer C (10.10.0.3). To do this, the IPv4 packet containing the data must be encapsulated in a frame and sent to the MAC address of computer C. Computer A does not have an entry in its ARP cache for 10.10.0.3. So, it constructs an ARP query and broadcasts it onto the network segment. Because the query was sent as a Layer 2 broadcast, all nodes on the network segments accept the frame. After examining the IPv4 address in the ARP query, only computer C determines that this address matches the host address. So, only computer C responds to the ARP request.

Figure 9-16   Resolving MAC Address for Host on Local Network

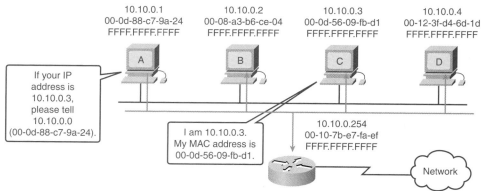

When computer A receives the ARP reply, it can create an entry in the ARP cache and can now create frames to send packets to host C.

Maintaining a Cache of Mappings

There are a number of different ARP processes required to provide the IP address to MAC addresses, such as these:

- Adding entries to the ARP table
- Getting the map for a frame
- Mapping destinations outside the local network
- Removing addressing mappings from the ARP table

The following sections describe these operations.

Adding Entries to the ARP Table

The ARP table is maintained dynamically. There are two ways that a device can gather MAC addresses. One way is to monitor the traffic that occurs on the local network segment. As a node receives frames from the media, it can record the source IP and MAC address as a mapping in the ARP table. As frames are transmitted on the network, the device populates the ARP table with address pairs.

Another way a device can get an address pair is to broadcast an ARP request. ARP sends a Layer 2 broadcast to all devices on the Ethernet LAN. The frame contains an ARP request packet with the IPv4 address of the destination host. The node receiving the frame that identifies the IP address as its own responds by sending an ARP reply packet back to the sender as a unicast frame. This response is then used to make a new entry in the ARP table.

These dynamic entries in the ARP table are timestamped in much the same way that MAC table entries are timestamped in switches. If a device does not receive a frame from a particular device by the time the timestamp expires, the entry for this device is removed from the ARP table.

Additionally, static map entries can be entered in an ARP table, but this is rarely done. Static ARP table entries do not expire over time. Therefore, they must be manually removed.

Getting the Map for a Frame

What does a node do when it needs to create a frame and the ARP cache does not contain a map of an IP address to a destination MAC address? When ARP receives a request to map an IPv4 address to a MAC address, it looks for the cached map in its ARP table. If an entry is not found, the encapsulation of the IPv4 packet fails and the Layer 2 processes notify ARP that they need a map.

The ARP processes then send out an ARP request packet to discover the MAC address of the destination device on the local network. If a device receiving the request has been configured with the destination IPv4 address in the ARP request, that device responds with an ARP reply. When the ARP reply is received, the map is created in the ARP table. Packets for that IPv4 address can now be encapsulated in frames in the host.

If no device responds to the ARP request, the packet is dropped because a frame cannot be created. This encapsulation failure is reported to the upper layers of the device. If the device is an intermediary device, like a router, the upper layers can choose to respond to the source host with an error in an ICMPv4 packet.

Mapping Destinations Outside the Local Network

Frames do not traverse a router into another network. Therefore, frames must be delivered to a node on the local network segment. If the destination IPv4 host is on the local network, the frame will use the MAC address of this device as the destination MAC address to carry the packet.

If the destination IPv4 host is not on the local network, the source node needs to deliver the frame to the router interface that is the gateway or next hop used to reach that destination. To do this, the IPv4 packets addressed to hosts on other networks will be carried on the local network in a frame using the MAC address of the gateway as the destination address.

The IPv4 address gateway router interface is stored in the IPv4 configuration of the hosts. When a host creates a packet for a destination, it compares the destination IPv4 address and its own IPv4 address to determine whether the two IP addresses are located on the same Layer 3 network. If the receiving host is not on the same network, the source host uses the ARP process to determine the MAC address for the router interface serving as the gateway. In the event that the gateway entry is not in the table, the normal ARP process will send an ARP request to retrieve the MAC address associated with the IP address of the router interface.

In Figure 9-17, computer A needs to send a packet to a host 172.16.0.10. Computer A first determines that the destination is outside the local network. Because the destination device is outside of the local network, the computer needs to create a frame to the default gateway to transport the frame across the local network.

Figure 9-17 Resolving MAC Address for Host Outside the Local Network

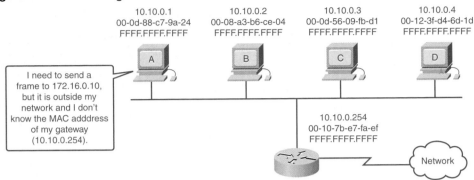

After examining the ARP cache for the IPv4 address of the gateway, no entry is found. So, computer A has to now use ARP to get the MAC address of the default gateway. The ARP request uses a Layer 2 broadcast address (ff-ff-ff-ff-ff-ff) as the destination address in the frame and a query for IPv4 address 10.10.0.254 (default gateway address). The gateway will respond with its MAC address of 00-10-7b-e7-fa-ef. Computer A can create a frame with a destination MAC address of 00-10-7b-e7-fa-ef to carry the IPv4 packet across the local network.

When the frame arrives at the router, it is decapsulated by the router to examine the destination IPv4 address. The router then examines the routing table to determine an appropriate route to forward the packet to 172.16.0.10. When that route is identified, the Layer 3 next-hop address of that route is used to determine the Layer 2 address to create a new frame. This new frame will be an appropriate type to transport this packet across the media connected to the interface out which the packet needs to be forwarded.

Another protocol that can assist the delivery packets outside the local network is *proxy ARP*. This is used in circumstances under which a host might send an ARP request seeking to map an IPv4 address outside of the range of the local network. In these cases, the device sends ARP requests for IPv4 addresses that are not on the local network instead of requesting the MAC address associated with the IPv4 address of the gateway. To provide a MAC address for these hosts, a router interface can use a proxy ARP to respond on behalf of these remote hosts. This means that the ARP cache of the requesting device will contain the MAC address of the gateway mapped to any IPv4 addresses not on the local network. Using proxy ARP, a router interface acts as if it is the host with the IPv4 address requested by the ARP request. By "faking" its identity, the router accepts responsibility for routing packets to the "real" destination.

One such use of this process is when an older implementation of IPv4 cannot determine whether the destination host is on the same logical network as the source. In these implementations, ARP always sends ARP requests for the destination IPv4 address. If proxy ARP is disabled on the router interface, these hosts cannot communicate outside of the local network. By default, Cisco routers have proxy ARP enabled on LAN interfaces.

Another case where a proxy ARP is used is when a host believes that it is directly connected to the same logical network as the destination host. This generally occurs when a host is configured with an improper mask.

As shown in Figure 9-18, host A has been improperly configured with a /16 subnet mask. This host believes that it is directly connected to the 172.16.0.0 /16 network instead of to the 172.16.10.0 /24 subnet.

Figure 9-18   Proxy ARP

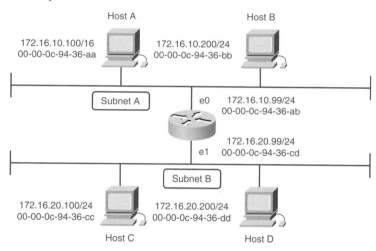

When attempts are made to communicate with any IPv4 host in the range of 172.16.0.1 to 172.16.255.254, host A will send an ARP request for that IPv4 address. The router can use a proxy ARP to respond to requests for the IPv4 address of host C (172.16.20.100) and host D (172.16.20.200). Host A will subsequently have entries for these addresses mapped to the MAC address of the e0 interface of the router (00-00-0c-94-36-ab).

Yet another use for a proxy ARP is when a host is not configured with a default gateway. Proxy ARP can help devices on a network reach remote subnets without the need to configure routing or a default gateway.

Note

For more information on proxy ARP, access the document "Proxy ARP" at the following Cisco page: http://www.cisco.com/warp/public/105/5.html.

Removing Address Mappings

Each device uses ARP cache timers to remove ARP entries that have not been used for a specified period of time. The times differ depending on the device and its operating system. For example, some Windows operating systems store ARP cache entries for 2 minutes. If the entry is used again during that time, the ARP timer for that entry is extended to 10 minutes.

Commands can also be used to manually remove all or some of the entries in the ARP table. After an entry has been removed, the process for sending an ARP request and receiving an ARP reply must occur again to enter the map in the ARP table.

In a Windows operating system, use the **arp** command to view and to clear the contents of a computer's ARP cache. Note that this command, despite its name, does not invoke the execution of the services from Address Resolution Protocol. The command is merely used to display, add, or remove the entries of the ARP table. ARP service is integrated within the IPv4 protocol and implemented by the device. Its operation is transparent to both upper-layer applications and users.

Note

ARP is a protocol of the IPv4 protocol suite. Other network layer protocols provide their own methods of resolving Layer 3 addresses to Layer 2 addresses on a LAN. For example, in IPv6 LANs, the Neighbor Discovery Protocol is used to translate 128-bit IPv6 addresses into 48-bit hardware addresses.

ARP Broadcast Issues

Because ARP uses broadcast, it presents the same issues as other broadcast communication. Broadcasts affect network performance and represent security risks.

Overhead on the Media

As a broadcast frame, an ARP request is received and processed by every device on the local network. On a typical business network, these broadcasts would probably have minimal impact on network performance. However, if a large number of devices were to be powered up and all start accessing network services at the same time, there could be some reduction in performance for a short period of time. For example, if all students in a lab logged in to classroom computers and attempted to access the Internet at the same time, there could be delays. However, after the devices send out the initial ARP broadcasts and have learned the necessary MAC addresses, any impact on the network will be minimized.

Security

In some cases, the use of ARP can lead to a potential security risk. *ARP spoofing*, or *ARP poisoning*, is a technique used by an attacker to inject the wrong MAC address association into a network by issuing fake ARP requests. An attacker forges the MAC address of a device, and then frames can be sent to the wrong destination.

Manually configuring static ARP associations is one way to prevent ARP spoofing. Authorized MAC addresses can be configured on some network devices to restrict network access to only those devices listed.

Summary

Ethernet is an effective and widely used TCP/IP network access protocol. Its common frame structure has been implemented across a range of media technologies, both copper and fiber, making it the most common LAN protocol in use today.

As an implementation of the IEEE 802.2/3 standards, the Ethernet frame provides MAC addressing and error checking. Being a shared media technology, early Ethernet had to apply a CSMA/CD mechanism to manage the use of the media by multiple devices. Replacing hubs with switches in the local network has reduced the probability of frame collisions in half-duplex links. Current and future versions, however, inherently operate as full-duplex communications links and do not need to manage media contention to the same detail.

The Layer 2 addressing provided by Ethernet supports unicast, multicast, and broadcast communications. Ethernet uses the Address Resolution Protocol to determine the MAC addresses of destinations and map them against known network layer addresses.

Labs

The labs available in the companion *Network Fundamentals, CCNA Exploration Labs and Study Guide* (ISBN 1-58713-203-6) provide hands-on practice with the following topics introduced in this chapter:

Lab 9-1: Address Resolution Protocol (ARP) (9.8.1.1)

This lab introduces the Windows arp utility to examine and change ARP cache entries on a host computer. You will then use Wireshark to capture and analyze ARP exchanges between network devices.

Lab 9-2: Cisco Switch MAC Table Examination (9.8.2.1)

In this lab, you will connect to a switch through a Telnet session, log in, and use the required operating system commands to examine the stored MAC addresses and their association to switch ports.

Lab 9-3: Intermediary Device as an End Device (9.8.3.1)

This lab uses Wireshark to capture and analyze frames to determine which network nodes originated them. A Telnet session between a host computer and switch is then captured and analyzed for frame content.

Packet Tracer
☐ Companion

Many of the hands-on labs include Packet Tracer companion activities, where you can use Packet Tracer to complete a simulation of the lab. Look for this icon in *Network Fundamentals, CCNA Exploration Labs and Study Guide* (ISBN 1-58713-203-6) for hands-on labs that have Packet Tracer companion activities.

Check Your Understanding

Complete all the review questions listed here to test your understanding of the topics and concepts in this chapter. The appendix, "Check Your Understanding and Challenge Questions Answer Key," lists the answers.

1. Name the two data link sublayers, and list their purposes.

2. Which of the following describes a limitation of legacy Ethernet technologies?

   A. Poor scalability

   B. Expensive media

   C. No collisions

   D. Frame format incompatible with current Ethernet

3. Which field of an Ethernet frame is used for error detection?

   A. Type

   B. Preamble

   C. Frame Check Sequence

   D. Destination MAC Address

4. How many bits are in an Ethernet MAC address?

   A. 12

   B. 32

   C. 48

   D. 256

5. Why are Layer 2 MAC addresses necessary?

6. Which of the following addresses is used as a destination address for an Ethernet broadcast frame?

   A. 0.0.0.0

   B. 255.255.255.255

   C. FF-FF-FF-FF-FF-FF

   D. 0C-FA-94-24-EF-00

7. What is the purpose of the jam signal in CSMA/CD?

   A. To allow the media to recover

   B. To make sure that all sending nodes see the collision

   C. To notify other nodes that a node is about to send

   D. To identify the length of a frame

8. Describe an Ethernet collision domain.

9. What Ethernet characteristic is shared by historic Ethernet and legacy Ethernet?

   A. Same cable type

   B. Same segment lengths

   C. Same logical topology

   D. Same installation cost

10. Which of the following describes a connection to a switch port?

    A. Isolates broadcasts

    B. Is a separate collision domain

    C. Uses the MAC address of the switch port as the destination

    D. Regenerates every bit that arrives out every port on the switch

11. What is the stage of operation of an Ethernet switch that creates MAC table entries?

    A. Aging

    B. Filtering

    C. Flooding

    D. Learning

12. If a frame arrives at a switch that contains a source MAC address that is not listed in the MAC table, what process will occur?

    A. Aging

    B. Filtering

    C. Flooding

    D. Learning

13. When does a network host need to broadcast an ARP request?

14. If a frame arrives at a switch that contains a destination MAC address that is not listed in the MAC table, what process will occur?

  A. Aging

  B. Filtering

  C. Flooding

  D. Learning

15. Why are higher-speed Ethernet implementations more susceptible to noise?

  A. More collisions

  B. Shorter bit times

  C. Full-duplex operation

  D. UTP cables are required instead of fiber

Challenge Questions and Activities

These questions and activities require a deeper application of the concepts covered in this chapter. You can find the answers in the appendix.

  1. Discuss why Ethernet has maintained the same frame format and what might have resulted from changing the frame format.

  2. Discuss the reasons why using LAN switches improves the security of a network.

Packet Tracer
☐ Challenge

Look for this icon in *Network Fundamentals, CCNA Exploration Labs and Study Guide* [ISBN 1-58713-203-6] for instructions on how to perform the Packet Tracer Skills Integration Challenge for this chapter.

To Learn More

The following questions encourage you to reflect on the topics discussed in this chapter. Your instructor might ask you to research the questions and discuss your findings in class.

  1. Discuss the move of Ethernet from a LAN technology to also becoming a metropolitan- and wide-area technology. What has made this possible?

  2. Initially used only for data communications networks, Ethernet is now also being applied in real-time industrial control networking. Discuss the physical and operational challenges that Ethernet has to overcome to be fully applied in this area.

CHAPTER 10

Planning and Cabling Networks

Objectives

Upon completion of this chapter, you will be able to answer the following questions:

- What basic network media is required to make a LAN connection?

- What are the types of connections used for intermediate and end-device connectivity in a LAN?

- What are the pinout configurations for straight-through and crossover cables?

- What are the different cabling types, standards, and ports used in WAN connections?

- What is the role of device connections management when using Cisco equipment?

- How do you design an addressing scheme for an internetwork and assign ranges for hosts, network devices, and the router interface?

- Why is network design so important?

Key Terms

This chapter uses the following key terms. You can find the definitions in the Glossary.

fiber-optics   page 369

electromagnetic interference (EMI)   page 380

radio frequency interference (RFI)   page 380

media-dependent interface (MDI)   page 381

media-dependent interface, crossover (MDIX)
  page 381

channel service unit/data service unit (CSU/DSU)
  page 381

Winchester connector   page 385

data communications equipment (DCE)   page 386

data terminal equipment (DTE)   page 386

terminal emulator   page 400

console port   page 401

Before using an IP phone, accessing instant messaging, or conducting any number of other interactions over a data network, you must connect end devices and intermediary devices through cable or wireless connections to form a functioning network. This network will support your communication in the human network.

Up to this point in the course, you have considered the services that a data network can provide to the human network, examined the features of each layer of the OSI model and the operations of TCP/IP protocols, and looked in detail at Ethernet, a universal LAN technology. The next step is to learn how to assemble these elements into a functioning network.

In this chapter, you will examine various media and the distinct roles they play with the devices that they connect. You will identify the cables needed to make successful LAN and WAN connections and learn how to use device management connections.

The selection of devices and the design of a network addressing scheme will be presented and then applied in the networking labs.

LANs: Making the Physical Connection

Three of the main networking devices that make up a LAN are the router, switch, and hub. The following sections look at the many aspects of physically connecting the different devices that make up a LAN. There are several considerations that must be examined to best determine what device needs to be used where in the LAN, and these sections explore the different possibilities.

Choosing the Appropriate LAN Device

Each LAN will have a router as its gateway connecting the LAN to other networks. Inside the LAN will be one or more hubs or switches to connect the end devices to the LAN.

For this book, the choice of which router to deploy is determined by the Ethernet interfaces that match the technology of the switches at the center of the LAN. It is important to note that routers offer many services and features to the LAN. These services and features are covered in the more advanced courses and their companion books.

Internetwork Devices

Routers are the primary devices used to interconnect networks. Each port on a router connects to a different network and routes packets between the networks. Routers have the ability to break up broadcast domains and collision domains.

Routers are also used to interconnect networks that use different technologies. They can have both LAN and WAN interfaces.

The LAN interfaces of the router allow routers to connect to the LAN media. This is usually through untwisted-pair (UTP) cabling, but modules can be added using *fiber-optics*. Depending on the series or model of router, there can be multiple interface types for connecting LAN and WAN cabling. An example of internetwork connections with a router is shown in Figure 10-1.

Figure 10-1   Internetwork Connections with a Router

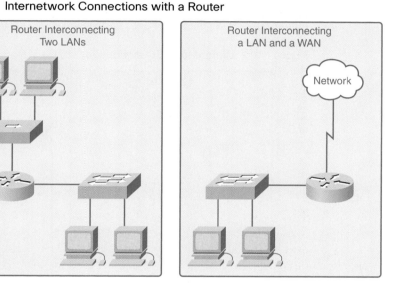

Intranetwork Devices

To create a LAN, you need to select the appropriate devices to connect the end device to the network. The two most common devices used are hubs and switches.

A hub receives a signal, regenerates it, and sends the signal over all ports. The use of hubs creates a logical bus. This means that the LAN uses multiaccess media. The ports use a shared bandwidth approach and often have reduced performance in the LAN because of collisions and recovery. Although multiple hubs can be interconnected, they remain a single collision domain.

Hubs are less expensive than switches. A hub is typically chosen as an intermediary device within a very small LAN, in a LAN that has low throughput requirements, or when finances are limited.

A switch receives a frame and regenerates each bit of the frame on to the appropriate destination port. You can use a switch to segment a network into multiple collision domains. Unlike the hub, a switch reduces the collisions on a LAN. Each port on the switch creates a separate collision domain. This creates a point-to-point logical topology to the device on each port. Additionally, a switch provides dedicated bandwidth on each port, which can increase LAN performance. A LAN switch can also be used to interconnect network segments of different speeds.

In general, switches are chosen for connecting devices to a LAN. Although a switch is more expensive than a hub, its enhanced performance and reliability make it cost effective. There is a range of switches available with a variety of features that enable the interconnection of multiple computers in a typical enterprise LAN setting.

Figure 10-2 shows the use of hubs and switches in a small LAN.

Figure 10-2   Intranetwork Connections

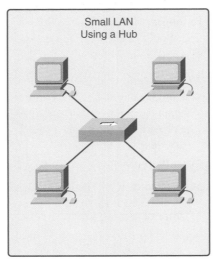
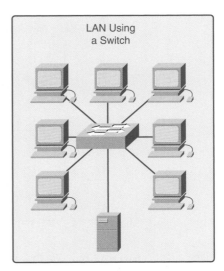

Device Selection Factors

To meet user requirements, a LAN needs to be planned and designed. Planning ensures that all requirements, cost factors, and deployment options are given due consideration.

When selecting a device for a particular LAN, you need to consider a number of factors, including the following:

- Cost

- Speed and types of ports/interfaces

- Scalability

- Manageability

- Additional features and services

The next sections describe factors to consider when choosing switches and routers.

Choosing a Switch

Although you need to consider many factors when selecting a switch, this section explores two: cost and interface characteristics.

The cost of a switch is determined by its capacity and features. The switch capacity includes the number and types of ports available and the switching speed. Other factors that impact the cost are its network management capabilities, embedded security technologies, and optional advanced switching technologies.

Using a simple cost-per-port calculation, it might appear initially that the best option is to deploy one large switch at a central location. However, this apparent cost savings can be offset by the expense from the longer cable lengths required to connect every device on the LAN to one switch. This option should be compared to the cost of deploying a number of smaller switches connected by a few long cables to a central switch.

Another cost consideration is how much to invest in redundancy. The operation of the entire physical network is affected if a single central switch experiences problems. The goal of redundant systems is to allow the physical network to continue its operation even if one device fails. Redundancy can be provided in a number of ways. You can provide a secondary central switch to operate concurrently with the primary central switch. You can also provide additional cabling to provide multiple interconnections between the switches.

Figure 10-3 shows the concept of redundancy in LAN switch selection.

Figure 10-3   Redundancy in Determining LAN Switch Selection

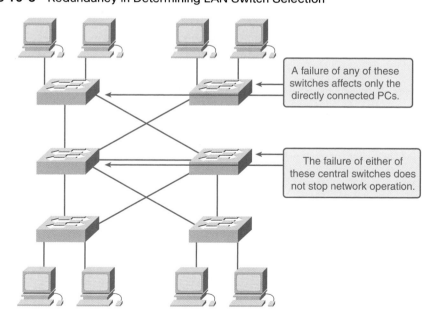

A failure of any of these switches affects only the directly connected PCs.

The failure of either of these central switches does not stop network operation.

Two Central Switches
with Redundancy

The need for speed is ever-present in a LAN environment. Newer computers with built-in 10/100/1000-Mbps network interface cards (NIC) are available. Choosing Layer 2 devices that can accommodate increased speeds allows the network to evolve without replacing the central devices.

When choosing a switch, select that offers the following criteria:

- **Sufficient ports:** Know how many ports you need for the network today, and consider how soon you will require additional ports.

- **A mixture of UTP speeds:** Consider how many ports will need 1-Gbps capability and how many ports only require 10/100-Mbps bandwidths.

- **UTP and fiber ports:** Consider carefully how many UTP ports will be needed and how many fiber ports will be needed.

Figure 10-4 depicts the different port speeds, types, and expandability considerations. It shows two different requirements at the top of the figure. One LAN requires just different port speeds, 10 Mbps and 100 Mbps. The other LAN requires both different speeds and different media. It requires both copper media (for the 10-Mbps and 100-Mbps speeds), and in this scenario, a fiber media (for the 1000-Mbps speed). Three different switch types are also shown as possible solutions.

Figure 10-4 Factors Determining LAN Switch Selection, Port Speeds, Types, and Expandability

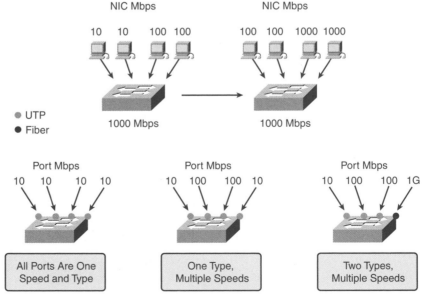

Choosing a Router

When selecting a router, you need to match the characteristics of the router to its purpose. Similar to the switch, cost and interface types and speeds must be considered. Additional factors for choosing a router include these:

- Expandability
- Media
- Operating system features

Networking devices, such as routers and switches, come in both fixed and modular physical configurations. Fixed configurations have a specific number and type of ports or interfaces. Modular devices have expansion slots that provide the flexibility to add new modules as requirements evolve. Most modular devices come with a basic number of fixed ports as well as expansion slots.

Because you can use routers for connecting different numbers and types of networks, you must take care to select the appropriate modules and interfaces for the specific media. Additional modules, such as fiber-optics, can increase the costs, so the media used to connect to the router should be supported without needing to purchase additional modules.

Depending on the version of the operating system, the router can support certain features and services such as the following:

- Security
- Quality of service (QoS)
- Voice over IP (VoIP)
- Routing multiple Layer 3 protocols
- Special services such as Network Address Translation (NAT) and DHCP

Figure 10-5 shows a variety of Cisco routers.

Figure 10-5   Cisco Routers

Device Interconnections

In the following sections, you look at the different cable standards and requirements. You also explore the making of LAN and WAN connections.

LAN and WAN: Getting Connected

When planning the installation of LAN cabling, you need to consider four physical areas:

- Work area
- Telecommunications room, also known as the distribution facility
- Horizontal cabling, also known as distribution cabling
- Backbone cabling, also known as vertical cabling

Figure 10-6 displays the interconnectivity between the LAN cabling areas.

Figure 10-6   LAN Cabling Areas

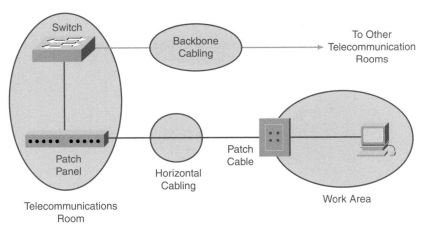

When looking at the interconnectivity between the LAN cabling areas, there a few requirements, such as type of media, cable lengths, costs, the actual work areas, and bandwidth. The following sections look at these requirements and the different solutions.

Work Areas

The *work areas* are the locations devoted to the end devices used by individual users. Each work area has a minimum of two jacks that can be used to connect an individual device to the network. A patch cable or patch cord is an electrical cable, used to connect ("patch in") one electronic device to another for signal routing. Patch cords are usually produced in many different colors so as to be easily distinguishable, and are relatively short, usually no longer than six feet. You use patch cables to connect individual devices to these wall jacks. The EIA/TIA standard specifies that the UTP patch cords used to connect devices to the wall jacks have a maximum length of 10 meters.

Straight-through cable is the most common patch cable used in the work area. This type of cable is used to connect end devices, such as computers, to a network. When a hub or switch is placed in the work area, a crossover cable is typically used to connect the device to the wall jack.

Telecommunications Room

The *telecommunications room* is where connections to intermediary devices take place. These rooms contain the intermediary devices—hubs, switches, routers, and data service units (DSU)—that tie the network together. These devices provide the transitions between the backbone cabling and the horizontal cabling.

Inside the telecommunications room, patch cords make connections between the patch panels, where the horizontal cables terminate, and the intermediary devices. Patch cables also interconnect these intermediary devices.

The EIA/TIA standards specify two different types of UTP patch cables. One type is a patch cord, with a length of up to 5 meters, which is used to interconnect equipment and patch panels in the telecommunications room. Another type of patch cable can be up to 5 meters in length and is used to connect devices to a termination point on the wall.

Telecommunications rooms often serve dual purposes. In addition to housing connections to intermediary devices, the telecommunications room contains the servers used by the network in many organizations.

Horizontal Cabling

Horizontal cabling refers to the cables connecting the telecommunication rooms with the work areas. The length of a cable from a termination point in the telecommunication room to the termination at the work area outlet must not exceed 90 meters. This 90-meter maximum horizontal cabling distance is referred to as the *permanent link* because it is installed in the building structure. The horizontal media runs from a patch panel in the telecommunications room to a wall jack in each work area. Connections to the devices are made with patch cables.

Backbone Cabling

Backbone cabling refers to the cabling used to connect the telecommunication rooms to the equipment rooms, where the servers are often located. Backbone cabling also interconnects multiple telecommunications rooms throughout the facility. Backbone cabling is also used to interconnect LANs between buildings. These cables are sometimes routed outside the building to the WAN connection or Internet service provider (ISP).

Backbones, or vertical cabling, are used for aggregated traffic, such as traffic to and from the Internet and access to corporate resources at a remote location. A large portion of the traffic from the various work areas will use the backbone cabling to access resources outside the area or facility. Therefore, backbones typically require high-bandwidth media such as fiber-optic cabling.

Types of Media

Choosing the cables necessary to make a successful LAN or WAN connection requires consideration of the different media types. As you recall, many different physical layer implementations support multiple media types:

- UTP (Category 5, 5e, 6, and 7)
- Fiber-optics
- Wireless

Figure 10-7 shows some different media types.

Figure 10-7   Media Types

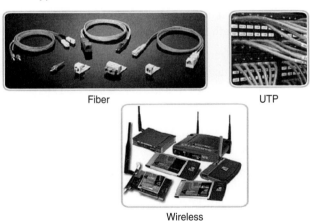

Fiber   UTP

Wireless

Each media type has its advantages and disadvantages. Consider the following factors:

- **Cable length:** The cable needs to span across a room or from building to building.

- **Cost:** The budget might allow using a more expensive media type.

- **Bandwidth:** The technology used with the media provides adequate bandwidth.

- **Ease of installation:** The implementation team has the ability to install the cable, or a vendor is required.

- **Susceptible to electromagnetic interference/radio frequency interference (EMI/RFI):** The local environment can interfere with the signal.

The following sections describe each of these factors in more detail.

Cable Length

The total length of cable required to connect a device includes all cables from the end devices in the work area to the intermediary device in the telecommunication room (usually a switch). This includes cable from the devices to the wall plug; cable through the building from the wall plug to the cross-connecting point, or patch panel; and cable from the patch panel to the switch. If the switches are located in telecommunication rooms on different floors in a building or in different buildings, the cable between these points counts as part of the total cable length.

For UTP installations, the ANSI/TIA/EIA-568-B standard specifies that the total combined length of cable spanning the four areas previously listed is limited to a distance of 100 meters per channel. This standard specifies that there can be up to 5 meters of patch cable for interconnecting patch panels. There can be up to 5 meters of cable from the cable termination point on the wall to the telephone or computer.

Attenuation is reduction of the strength of a signal as it moves down a medium. The longer the medium, the more attenuation will affect the signal. At some point, the signal will not be detectable. Cabling distance is a significant factor in data signal performance. Signal attenuation and exposure to possible interference increase with cable length.

For example, when using UTP cabling for Ethernet, the horizontal (or fixed) cabling length needs to stay within the recommended maximum distance of 90 meters to avoid attenuation of the signal. Fiber-optic cables can provide a greater cabling distance—up to 500 meters to a few kilometers, depending on the technology. However, fiber-optic cable can also suffer from attenuation when these limits are reached.

Cost

The cost associated with LAN cabling can vary from one media type to another, and the decision makers might not realize the impact on the budget. In a perfect setting, the budget would allow fiber-optic cabling to every device in the LAN. Although fiber provides greater bandwidth than UTP, the material and installation costs are significantly higher. In practice, this level of performance is not usually required and is not a reasonable expectation in most environments. Network designers must match the performance needs of the users with the cost of the equipment and cabling to achieve the best cost/performance ratio.

Bandwidth

The devices in a network have different bandwidth requirements. When selecting the media for individual connections, carefully consider the bandwidth requirements.

For example, a server generally has a need for more bandwidth than a computer dedicated to a single user. For a server connection, consider media that will provide high bandwidth and can grow to meet increased bandwidth requirements and newer technologies. A fiber cable can be a logical choice for a server connection.

Currently, the technology used in fiber-optic media offers the greatest bandwidth available among the choices for LAN media. Given the seemingly unlimited bandwidth available in fiber cables, much greater speeds for LANs are expected. Wireless is also supporting huge increases (currently the IEEE 802.11n protocol is looking at 248 Mbps) in bandwidth, but it has limitations in distance and power consumption.

Table 10-1 shows the relationship between the media standards, cable length, and bandwidth.

Table 10-1   Media Standards, Cable Length, and Bandwidth

Ethernet Type	Bandwidth	Cable Type	Maximum Distance
10BASE-T	10 Mbps	Cat3/Cat5 UTP	100 m
100BASE-TX	100 Mbps	Cat5 UTP	100 m
100BASE-TX	200 Mbps	Cat5 UTP	100 m
100BASE-FX	100 Mbps	Multimode fiber	400 m
100BASE-FX	200 Mbps	Multimode fiber	2 km
1000BASE-T	1 Gbps	Cat5e UTP	100 m
1000BASE-TX	1 Gbps	Cat6 UTP	100 m
1000BASE-SX	1 Gbps	Multimode fiber	550 m
1000BASE-LX	1 Gbps	Single-mode fiber	2 km
10GBASE-T	10 Gbps	Cat6a/Cat7 UTP	100 m
10GBASE-LX4	10 Gbps	Multimode fiber	300 m
10GBASE-LX4	10 Gbps	Single-mode fiber	10 km

Ease of Installation

The ease of cable installation varies according to cable types and building architecture. Access to floor or roof spaces, and the physical size and properties of the cable, influences how easily a cable can be installed in various buildings. Cables in buildings are typically installed in raceways.

As shown in Figure 10-8, a *raceway* is an enclosure or tube that protects the cable. A raceway also keeps cabling neat and easy to thread.

Figure 10-8   Cable Raceway

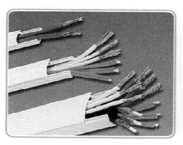

UTP Cable Raceway   Fiber Cable Raceway

UTP cable is relatively lightweight and flexible and has a small diameter, which allows it to fit into small spaces. The connectors, RJ-45 plugs, are relatively easy to install and are a standard for all Ethernet devices.

Many fiber-optic cables contain a thin glass fiber. This creates issues for the bend radius of the cable. Crimps or sharp bends can break the fiber. The termination of the cable connectors (Straight Tip [ST], Subscriber Connector [SC], Mechanical Transfer Registered Jack [MT-RJ]) is significantly more difficult to install and requires special equipment.

Wireless networks require cabling, at some point, to connect devices such as access points to the wired LAN. Because there are fewer cables required in a wireless network, wireless is often easier to install than UTP or fiber cable. However, a wireless LAN requires more careful planning and testing. For example, wireless LANs operate using radio frequencies and transmit data on different channels within the frequency range, so care must be taken to not have like frequency channels overlap themselves. Wireless LANs, unlike wired LANs, have bandwidth that diminishes the farther away from a wireless access point you are; this phenomenon requires additional planning and testing to ensure required coverage. Also, there are many external factors, such as other radio frequency devices and building construction, that can affect its operation.

Electromagnetic Interference (EMI) and Radio Frequency Interference (RFI)

Electromagnetic interference (EMI) and *radio frequency interference (RFI)* must be taken into consideration when choosing a media type for a LAN. EMI/RFI in an industrial environment can significantly impact data communications if the wrong cable is used.

Electrical machines, lighting, and other communications devices, including computers and radio equipment, can produce interference. As an example, consider an installation where devices in two separate buildings are interconnected. The media used to interconnect these buildings will be exposed to the possibility of lightning strikes. Additionally, a great distance might separate these two buildings. For this installation, fiber cable is the best choice.

Wireless is the medium most susceptible to RFI. Before using wireless technology, potential sources of interference must be identified and, if possible, minimized.

Making LAN Connections

UTP cabling connections are specified by the EIA/TIA.

The RJ-45 connector is the male component crimped on the end of the cable. When viewed from the front, as shown in Figure 10-9, the pins are numbered from 8 to 1. When viewed from above with the opening gate/pins facing you, the pins are numbered 1 through 8, from left to right. This orientation is important to remember when identifying a cable.

Figure 10-9 RJ-45 T568A and T568B Termination

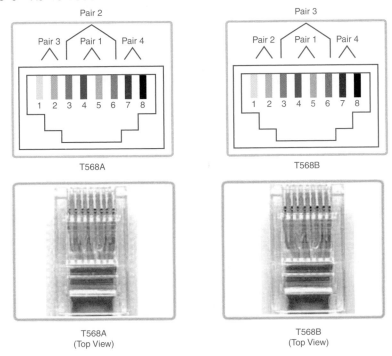

Using the EIA/TIA T568A and T568B termination standards, several patch cables can be built. Depending on the type of interface the cable connects to (MDI or MDIX; see the next section), you would need either a straight-through or a crossover cable. The next few sections discuss these in detail.

Types of Interfaces

In an Ethernet LAN, devices use one of two types of UTP interfaces: *media-dependent interface (MDI)* or *media-dependent interface, crossover (MDIX)*.

The MDI uses the normal Ethernet pinout. Pins 1 and 2 are used for transmitting, and pins 3 and 6 are used for receiving. Devices such as computers, servers, or routers have MDI connections.

The devices that provide LAN connectivity—usually hubs or switches—typically use MDIX connections. The MDIX cables swap the transmit pairs internally. This swapping allows the end devices to be connected to the hub or switch using a straight-through cable.

Typically, when connecting different types of devices (an MDI and an MDIX), use a straight-through cable. When connecting the same type of device (MDI to MDI, or MDIX to MDIX), use a crossover cable.

Many devices allow the UTP Ethernet port to be set to MDI or MDIX. This can be done in one of three ways, depending on the features of the device:

- On some devices, ports can have a mechanism that electrically swaps the transmit and receive pairs. The port can be changed from MDI to MDIX by engaging the mechanism.

- As part of the configuration, some devices allow selecting whether a port functions as MDI or as MDIX.

- Many newer devices have an automatic crossover feature. This feature allows the device to detect the required cable type and configures the interfaces accordingly. On some devices, this autodetection is performed by default. Other devices require an interface configuration command for enabling MDIX autodetection.

Straight-Through UTP Cables

A straight-through cable has connectors on each end that are terminated the same in accordance with either the T568A or T568B standard. Figure 10-10 shows the pinout for a straight-through cable.

Figure 10-10 Straight-Through Cable

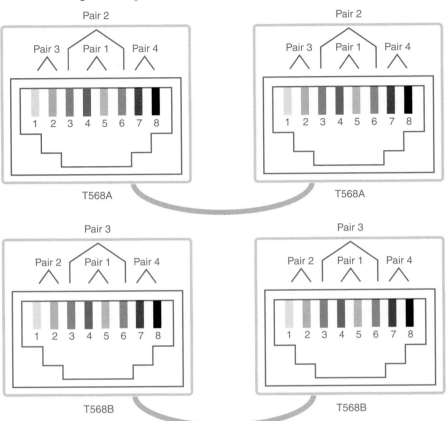

Identifying the cable standard used allows you to determine whether you have the right cable for the job. More importantly, it is a common practice to use the same color codes throughout the LAN for consistency in documentation.

Use straight-through cables for the following connections:

- Switch to router Ethernet port
- Computer to switch
- Computer to hub

Crossover UTP Cables

For two devices to communicate through a cable that directly connects them, the transmit terminal of one device needs to be connected to the receive terminal of the other device. The cable must be terminated so that the transmit pin, Tx, taking the signal from device A at one end, is wired to the receive pin, Rx, on device B. Similarly, device B's Tx pin must be connected to device A's Rx pin. If the Tx pin on a device is numbered 1 and the Rx pin is numbered 2, the cable connects pin 1 at one end with pin 2 at the other end. These "crossed over" pin connections give this type of cable its name, crossover.

To achieve this type of connection with a UTP cable, one end must be terminated as EIA/TIA T568A pinout and the other end terminated with T568B pinout. Figure 10-11 shows the pinout of a crossover cable. The figure uses TP0, TP1, TP2, and TP3 to depict pin/pair assignments.

Figure 10-11 Crossover Cable

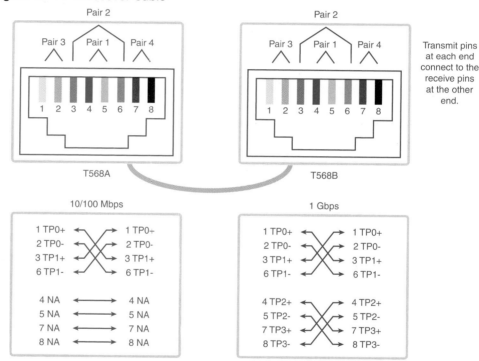

To summarize, crossover cables directly connect the following devices on a LAN:

- Switch to switch

- Switch to hub

- Hub to hub

- Router to router Ethernet port connection

- Computer to computer

- Computer to router Ethernet port

Figure 10-12 shows the correct UTP cable type for the different network connections.

Figure 10-12 Network with Straight-Through and Crossover Cables

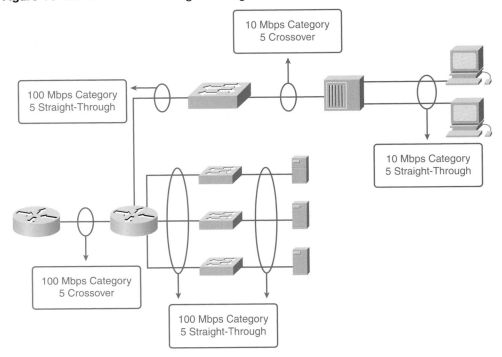

Making WAN Connections

By definition, WAN links can span extremely long distances. These distances can range across the globe as they provide the communication links that we use to manage e-mail accounts, view web pages, or conduct a teleconference session with a client.

Wide-area connections between networks take a number of forms, including these:

- Phone line RJ-11 connectors for dialup or digital subscriber line (DSL) connections

- 60-pin serial connections

In the course labs, you might be using Cisco routers with one of two types of physical serial cables. Both cables use a large Winchester 15-pin connector on the network end. This end of the cable is used as a V.35 connection to a physical layer device such as a *channel service unit/data service unit* (CSU/DSU).

The first cable type has a male DB-60 connector on the Cisco end and a male *Winchester connector* on the network end. The second type is a more compact version of this cable and has a Smart Serial connector on the Cisco device end. You must be able to identify the two different types to connect successfully to the router. Figure 10-13 shows these connectors.

Figure 10-13 Types of WAN Connections

Router: Male Smart Serial   Network: Male Winchester Block Type

Figure 10-14 shows the use of serial WAN connections.

Figure 10-14 Types of WAN Connections: Serial

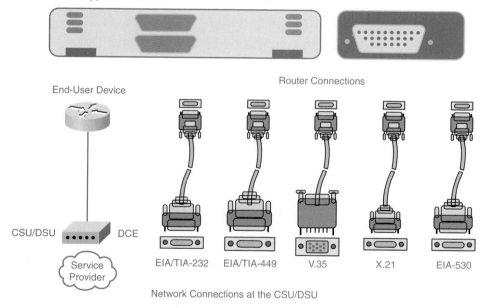

Figure 10-15 shows the type of WAN connection used for a DSL connection.

Figure 10-15 Types of WAN Connections: DSL

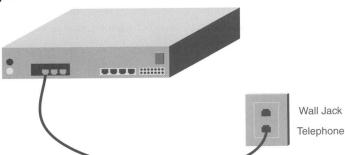

Wall Jack

Telephone

The next two sections look at the type of devices that interconnect two LANs through a WAN connection. You also look at the difference between these connections in a lab situation versus an operational connection.

Data Communications Equipment and Data Terminal Equipment

The following terms describe the types of devices that maintain the link between a sending and a receiving device:

- *Data communications equipment (DCE)*: A device that supplies the clocking services to another device. Typically, this device is at the WAN access provider end of the link.

- *Data terminal equipment (DTE)*: A device that receives clocking services from another device and adjusts accordingly. Typically, this device is at the WAN customer or user end of the link.

If a serial connection is made directly to a service provider or to a device that provides signal clocking such as a channel service unit/data service unit (CSU/DSU), the router is considered to be data terminal equipment (DTE) and will use a DTE serial cable, as shown in Figure 10-16.

Figure 10-16 Serial DCE and DTE WAN Connections

DTE   DCE   DCE   DTE

Be aware that there will be occasions, especially in labs associated with this course, when the local router is required to provide the clock rate, because the routers in the lab will be connected back to back and will therefore use data communications equipment (DCE) cable.

DCEs and DTEs are used in WAN connections. The communication through a WAN connection is maintained by providing a clock rate that is acceptable to both the sending and the receiving device. In most cases, the telco or ISP provides the clocking service that synchronizes the transmitted signal.

For example, if a device connected through a WAN link is sending its signal at 1.544 Mbps, each receiving device must use a clock, sending out a sample signal every 1/1,544,000 of a second. The timing in this case is extremely short. The devices must be able to very quickly synchronize to the signal that is sent and received.

The DCE device assigns a clock rate to the DTE router, in effect, setting the timing for the DTE router. This allows that router to adjust the speed of its communication operations, thereby synchronizing with the devices connected to it.

Setting Up WAN Connections in the Lab

When making WAN connections between two routers in a lab environment, connect two routers with a serial cable to simulate a point-to-point WAN link. In this case, decide which router is going to be the one in control of clocking. Routers are DTE devices by default, but they can be configured to act as DCE devices, and as such, they have to provide the clocking.

The V.35-compliant cables are available in DTE and DCE versions. To create a point-to-point serial connection between two routers, join a DTE and DCE cable. Each cable comes with a connector that mates with its complementary type. These connectors are configured so that you cannot join two DCE or two DTE cables by mistake.

Figure 10-17 shows how the DTE and DCE cables connect to form a crossover cable.

Figure 10-17 Serial DCE and DTE Rx and Tx Crossover

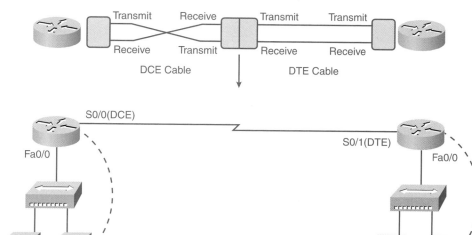

Connecting Devices with Different Media Types (10.2.3.4)

In this activity, you will practice important networking lab skills by making interconnections in Packet Tracer. Use file e1-10234.pka on the CD-ROM that accompanies this book to perform this activity using Packet Tracer.

Developing an Addressing Scheme

In the following sections, you look at how to determine the number of hosts and networks you require. You also learn about designing the address standard for your internetwork.

How Many Hosts in the Network?

To develop an addressing scheme for a network, start by determining the total number of hosts. Consider every device that will require an IP address, now and in the future.

The end devices requiring an IP address include these:

- User computers
- Administrator computers
- Servers
- Other end devices such as printers, IP phones, and IP cameras

Network devices requiring an IP address include these:

- Router LAN interfaces
- Router WAN (serial) interfaces

Network devices requiring an IP address for management include these:

- Switches
- Wireless access points

Other devices on a network can require an IP address. Add them to this list and estimate how many addresses will be needed to account for growth in the network as more devices are added.

When the total number of hosts—current and future—has been determined, consider the range of addresses available and where they fit within the given network address. Remember, you learned in Chapter 6, "Addressing the Network: IPv4," these addresses could be private IP addresses or allocated public addresses.

Next, determine whether all hosts will be part of the same network or whether the network as a whole will be divided into separate subnets.

Recall that the number of hosts on one network or subnet is calculated using the following formula:

$2^n - 2$

In this formula, n is the number of bits available as host bits. Recall also that you subtract two addresses because the network address and the network broadcast address cannot be assigned to hosts.

How Many Networks?

There are many reasons to divide a network into subnets, including the following:

- **Manage broadcast traffic:** Broadcasts can be controlled because one large broadcast domain is divided into a number of smaller domains. Not every host in the system receives every broadcast.

- **Different network requirements:** If different groups of users require specific network or computing facilities, it is easier to manage these requirements if those users who share requirements are all together on one subnet.

- **Security:** Different levels of network security can be implemented based on network addresses. This enables the management of access to different network and data services.

After you make a decision about how many networks you need, you need to be able to identify which network you are referencing. The next two sections describe this process.

Counting the Subnets

Each subnet, as a physical network segment, requires a router interface as the gateway for that subnet. In addition, each connection between routers is a separate subnet.

Figure 10-18 shows five different subnets in a network.

The number of subnets on one network is also calculated using the formula 2^n, where n is the number of bits "borrowed" from the given IP network address available to create subnets.

Figure 10-18 Five Subnets

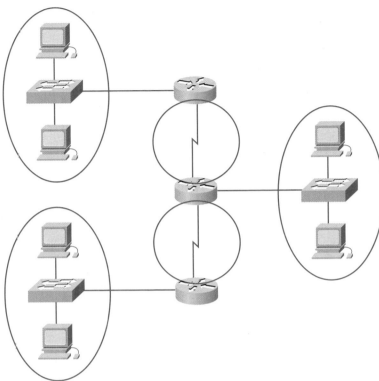

Subnet Masks

Having determined the required number of hosts and subnets, the next step is to apply one subnet mask for the entire network and then calculate the following values:

- A unique subnet and subnet mask for each physical segment

- A range of usable host addresses for each subnet

Designing the Address Standard for Your Internetwork

To assist in troubleshooting and expedite adding new hosts to the network, use addresses that fit a common pattern across all subnets. Group devices according to types, and allocate them to a logical block of addresses within the address range of the network.

Some of the different categories for hosts are as follows:

- General users

- Special users

- Network resources
- Router LAN interfaces
- Router WAN links
- Management access

For example, when allocating an IP address to a router interface that is the gateway for a LAN, it is common practice to use the first (lowest) or last (highest) address within the subnet range. This consistent approach aids in configuration and troubleshooting.

Similarly, when assigning addresses to devices that manage other devices, using a consistent pattern within a subnet makes these addresses easily recognizable.

In addition, remember to document your IP addressing scheme electronically and on paper. This will be an important aid in troubleshooting and evolving the network.

Calculating the Subnets

You will now look at how to calculate the subnets using two possible cases.

Calculating Addresses: Case 1

This section uses the sample topology shown in Figure 10-19 to practice allocating addresses to hosts. By starting with a given IP address and prefix (subnet mask) 172.16.0.0 255.255.252.0 assigned by the network administrator, you can begin creating your network documentation.

Figure 10-19 Network Topology

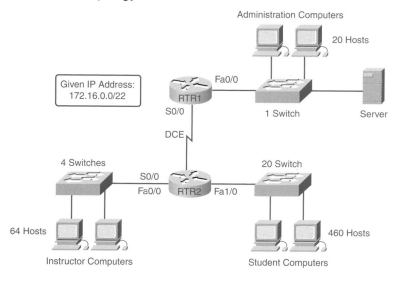

Hosts are divided into groups: the student LAN, instructor LAN, administrator LAN, and WAN. The number of hosts for the student group follows:

- **Student computers:** 460
- **Router (LAN gateway):** 1
- **Switches (management):** 20
- **Total for student subnetwork:** 481

The instructor LAN requires the following hosts:

- **Instructor computers:** 64
- **Router (LAN gateway):** 1
- **Switches (management):** 4
- **Total for instructor subnetwork:** 69

The administrator LAN requires the following hosts:

- **Administrator computers:** 20
- **Server:** 1
- **Router (LAN gateway):** 1
- **Switch (management):** 1
- **Total for administration subnetwork:** 23

The WAN requires the following:

- **Router-to-router WAN:** 2
- **Total for WAN:** 2

Allocation Methods

There are two methods available for allocating addresses to an internetwork. You can use variable-length subnet masking (VLSM), where you assign the prefix and host bits to each network based on the number of hosts in that network. Or, you can use a non-VLSM approach, where all subnets use the same prefix length and the same number of host bits. This network example demonstrates both approaches.

Calculating and Assigning Addresses Without VLSM

When using the non-VLSM method of assigning addresses, all subnets have the same number of addresses assigned to them. To provide each network with an adequate number of addresses, base the number of addresses for all networks on the addressing requirements for the largest network.

In case 1, the student LAN is the largest network, requiring 481 addresses. Use this formula to calculate the number of hosts:

Usable hosts = $2^n - 2$

Use 9 as the value for n because 9 is the first power of 2 that is over 481. Borrowing 9 bits for the host portion yields this calculation:

$2^9 = 512$

$512 - 2 = 510$ usable host addresses

This meets the current requirement for at least 481 addresses, with a small allowance for growth. This also leaves 23 network bits (32 total bits − 9 host bits).

Because there are four networks in the internetwork, you will need four blocks of 512 addresses each, for a total of 2048 addresses. You will use the address block 172.16.0.0 /23, which provides addresses in the range from 172.16.0.0 to 172.16.7.255.

The address calculations for the networks are as follows.

In binary, address 172.16.0.0 is

10101100.00010000.00000000.00000000

The mask 255.255.254.0 is 23 bits in binary:

11111111.11111111.11111110.00000000

This mask will provide the four address ranges shown in Figure 10-20.

Figure 10-20 Addresses Without VLSM

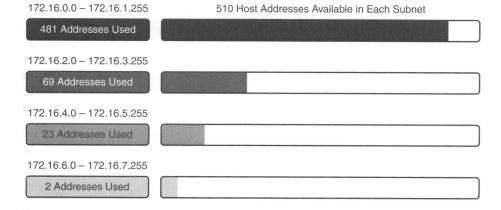

For the student network block, the values would be 172.16.0.1 to 172.16.1.254, with a broadcast address of 172.16.1.255.

The administrator network requires a total of 66 addresses. The remaining addresses in this block of 512 addresses will go unused. The values for the administrator network are 172.16.2.1 to 172.16.3.254, with a broadcast address of 172.16.3.255.

Assigning the 172.16.4.0 /23 block to the instructor LAN assigns an address range of 172.16.4.1 to 172.16.5.254, with a broadcast address of 172.16.5.255. Only 23 of the 512 addresses will actually be used in the instructor LAN.

The WAN has a point-to-point connection between the two routers. This network only requires two IPv4 addresses for the routers on this serial link. Figure 10-20 shows that assigning this address block to the WAN link wastes 508 addresses.

You can use VLSM in this internetwork to save addressing space, but using VLSM requires more planning. The next section demonstrates the planning associated with the use of VLSM.

Table 10-2 shows these four different networks and their IP address ranges.

Table 10-2   Networks Without VLSM Address Ranges for Subnets

Network	Subnet Address	Host Address Range	Broadcast Address
Student	172.16.0.0/23	172.16.0.1–172.16.1.254	172.16.1.255
Instructor	172.16.2.0/23	172.16.2.1–172.16.2.254	172.16.2.255
Administrator	172.16.4.0/23	172.16.4.1–172.16.4.254	172.16.4.255
WAN	172.16.6.0/23	172.16.6.1–172.16.6.254	172.16.6.255

Calculating and Assigning Addresses with VLSM

For the VLSM assignment, you can allocate a much smaller block of addresses to each network, as appropriate, as shown in Figure 10-21.

The address block 172.16.0.0/22 (subnet mask 255.255.252.0) has been assigned to this internetwork as a whole. Ten bits will be used to define host addresses and subnetworks. This yields a total of 1024 IPv4 local addresses in the range of 172.16.0.0 to 172.16.3.0.

The largest subnetwork is the student LAN, which requires 460 addresses.

Using the formula usable hosts = 2^{n-2}, borrowing 9 bits for the host portion gives $512 - 2 = 510$ usable host addresses. This meets the current requirement, with a small allowance for growth.

Figure 10-21 Addresses with VLSM

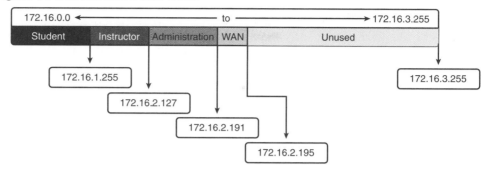

Using 9 bits for hosts leaves 1 bit that can be used locally to define the subnet address. Using the lowest available address gives you a subnet address of 172.16.0.0 /23.

In binary, the address 172.16.0.0 is

10101100.00010000.00000000.00000000

The mask 255.255.254.0 is 23 bits in binary:

11111111.11111111.11111110.00000000

In the student network, the IPv4 host range would be 172.16.0.1 through 172.16.1.254, with a broadcast address of 172.16.1.255.

Because the student LAN has been assigned these addresses, they are not available for assignment to the remaining subnets: instructor LAN, administrator LAN, and WAN. The addresses still to be assigned are in the range of 172.16.2.0 to 172.16.3.255.

The next largest network is the instructor LAN. This network requires at least 66 addresses. Using 6 in the power of 2 formula, 2^6-2, only provides 62 usable addresses. You must use an address block using 7 host bits. The calculation 2^7-2 will yield a block of 126 addresses. This leaves 25 bits to assign to the network address. The next available block of this size is the 172.16.2.0 /25 network.

In binary, the address 172.16.2.0 is

10101100.00010000.0000010.00000000

The mask 255.255.255.128 is 25 bits in binary:

11111111.11111111.1111111.10000000

This provides an IPv4 host range of 172.16.2.1 to 172.16.2.126, with a broadcast address of 172.16.2.127.

From the original address block of 172.16.0.0 /22, you allocated addresses 172.16.0.0 to 172.16.2.127. The remaining addresses to be allocated are 172.16.2.128 to 172.16.3.255.

For the administrator LAN, you need to accommodate 23 hosts. This will require the use of 6 host bits using the calculation 2^6–2. The next available block of addresses that can accommodate these hosts is the 172.16.2.128 /26 block.

In binary, address 172.16.2.128 is

10101100.00010000.0000010.10000000

The mask 255.255.255.192 is 26 bits in binary:

11111111.11111111.1111111.11000000

This provides an IPv4 host range of 172.16.2.129 to 172.16.2.190, with a broadcast address of 172.16.2.191. This yields 62 unique IPv4 addresses for the administrator LAN.

The last segment is the WAN connection, requiring two host addresses. Only 2 host bits will accommodate the WAN links: 2^2–2=2.

This leaves 8 bits to define the local subnet address. The next available address block is 172.16.2.192 /30.

In binary, address 172.16.2.192 is

10101100.00010000.0000010.11000000

The mask 255.255.255.252 is 30 bits in binary:

11111111.11111111.1111111.11111100

This provides an IPv4 host range of 172.16.2.193 to 172.16.2.194, with a broadcast address of 172.16.2.195.

This completes the allocation of addresses using VLSM for case 1. If an adjustment is necessary to accommodate future growth, addresses in the range of 172.16.2.196 to 172.16.3.255 are still available.

Table 10-3 shows these four different networks and their IP address ranges.

Table 10-3   Networks with VLSM Address Ranges for Subnets

Network	Subnet Address	Host Address Range	Broadcast Address
Student	172.16.0.0/23	172.16.0.1–172.16.1.254	172.16.1.255
Instructor	172.16.2.0/25	172.16.2.1–172.16.2.126	172.16.2.127
Admin	172.16.2.128/26	172.16.2.129–172.16.2.190	172.16.2.191
WAN	172.16.2.192/30	172.16.2.193–172.16.2.194	172.16.2.195
Unused	—	172.16.2.197–172.16.3.254	—

Calculating Addresses: Case 2

In case 2, the challenge is to subnet the internetwork shown in Figure 10-22 while limiting the number of wasted hosts and subnets. Figure 10-22 shows five different subnets, each with different host requirements. The given IP address is 192.168.1.0/24.

Figure 10-22 Calculating Addresses for Host Requirements

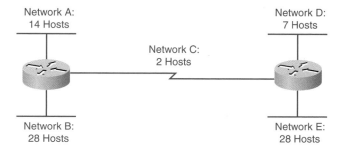

The following are the host requirements:

- **Network A:** 14 hosts
- **Network B:** 28 hosts
- **Network C:** 2 hosts
- **Network D:** 7 hosts
- **Network E:** 28 hosts

As in case 1, begin the process by subnetting for the largest host requirement first. In this case, the largest requirements are for network B and network E, each with 28 hosts.

Apply the formula usable hosts = 2^n-2. For networks B and E, 5 bits are borrowed from the host portion and the calculation is $2^5=32-2$. Only 30 usable host addresses are available because of the two reserved addresses. Borrowing 5 bits meets the requirement but gives little room for growth.

So you might consider borrowing 6 bits for subnets, leaving 2 bits for the hosts. This allows eight subnets with 62 hosts each.

Allocate addresses for networks B and E first:

- **Network B will use subnet 0:** 192.168.1.0/27, host address range 1 to 30
- **Network E will use Subnet 1:** 192.168.1.32/27, host address range 33 to 62

The next largest host requirement is network A, followed by network D.

Borrowing another bit and subnetting the network address 192.168.1.64 yields a host range as follows:

- **Network A will use subnet 0:** 192.168.1.64/28, host address range 65 to 78
- **Network D will use subnet 1:** 192.168.1.80/28, host address range 81 to 94

This allocation supports 14 hosts on each subnet and satisfies the requirement.

Network C has only two hosts. Two bits are borrowed to meet this requirement. Starting from 192.168.1.96 and borrowing 2 more bits results in subnet 192.168.1.96/30. Network C will use subnet 1: 192.168.1.96/30, host address range 97 to 98.

In case 2, you have met all requirements without wasting many potential subnets and available addresses. In this case, bits were borrowed from addresses that had already been subnetted. As you will recall from a previous section, this method is known as *VLSM*.

Device Interconnections

Most network devices, such as routers and switches, have between two and four different interfaces on them to connect to. The following sections look at each, describe the characteristics of each, and examine how each is interconnected.

Device Interfaces

It is important to understand that Cisco devices, routers, and switches have several types of interfaces associated with them. You have worked with these interfaces in the labs. These interfaces, also commonly called ports, are where cables are connected to the device. Figure 10-23 shows the following sample interfaces:

- FastEthernet interface
- Serial interface
- Console interface
- Auxiliary interface

Figure 10-23 Sample Device Interfaces

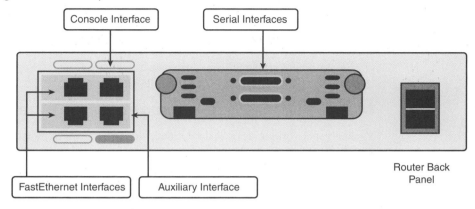

The next sections describe each of these interface types.

Ethernet Interface

The Ethernet interface is used for connecting cables that terminate with LAN devices such as computers and switches. This interface can also be used to connect routers to each other.

Several conventions for naming Ethernet interfaces are popular, including AUI (older Cisco devices using a transceiver), Ethernet, FastEthernet, and Fa 0/0. The name used depends on the type and model of the device.

Serial Interface

Serial WAN interfaces are used for connecting WAN devices to the CSU/DSU. Serial interfaces between routers will also be used in the labs as part of various courses. For lab purposes, you will make a back-to-back connection between two routers using serial cables and set a clock rate on one of the interfaces.

You might also need to configure other data link and physical layer parameters on a router. To establish communication with a router through a console on a remote WAN, a WAN interface is assigned a Layer 3 address (IPv4 address).

Console Interface

The console interface is the primary interface for initial configuration of a Cisco router or switch. It is also an important means of troubleshooting. It is important to note that with physical access to the router console interface, an unauthorized person can interrupt or compromise network traffic. Physical security of network devices is extremely important.

Auxiliary Interface

The auxiliary (AUX) interface is used for remote management of the router. Typically, a modem is connected to the AUX interface for dialup access. From a security standpoint, enabling the option to connect remotely to a network device carries with it the responsibility of maintaining vigilant device management.

Making the Device Management Connection

Typically, networking devices do not have their own displays, keyboards, or input devices such as trackballs and mice. Accessing a network device for configuration, verification, or troubleshooting is made through a connection between the device and a computer, as shown in Figure 10-24. To enable this connection, the computer runs a program called a *terminal emulator*.

Figure 10-24 Device Management Connection

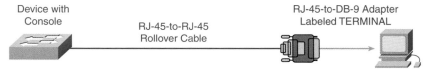

The following points apply to the use of a terminal emulator:

- The PCs require an RJ-45 to DB-9 or RJ-45 to DB-25 adapter.

- COM port settings are 9600 bps, 8 data bits, no parity, 1 stop bit, and no flow control.

- This connection provides something called out-of-band console access.

- An AUX switch port can be used for a modem-connected console.

A terminal emulator is a software program that allows one computer to access the functions on another device. It allows a person to use the display and keyboard on one computer to operate another device, as if the keyboard and display were directly connected to the other device. The cable connection between the computer running the terminal emulation program and the device is often made through the serial interface on the PCs.

To connect to a router or switch for device management using terminal emulation, follow these steps:

Step 1.   Connect a computer to the console port using the console cable.

Step 2.   Configure a terminal emulator with the proper settings.

Step 3.   Log in to the router using the terminal emulator software.

Step 1: Using the Console Cable

Connect a computer to the *console port* using the console cable. The console cable, supplied with each Cisco router and switch, has a DB-9 connector on one end and an RJ-45 connector on the other end. (Older Cisco devices came supplied with an RJ-45–to–DB-9 adapter. This adapter is used with a rollover cable that has an RJ-45 connector at each end.)

The connection to the console is made by plugging the DB-9 connector into an available EIA/TIA 232 serial port on the computer. It is important to remember that if there is more than one serial port, note which port number is being used for the console connection. After the serial connection to the computer is made, connect the RJ-45 end of the cable directly into the console interface on the router.

Many newer computers do not have an EIA/TIA 232 serial interface. If your computer has only a USB interface, use a USB-to-serial conversion cable to access the console port. Connect the conversion cable to a USB port on the computer, and then connect the console cable or RJ-45–to–DB-9 adapter to this cable.

Step 2: Configuring a Terminal Emulator

With the devices directly connected through cable, configure a terminal emulator with the proper settings. The exact instructions for configuring a terminal emulator will depend on the particular emulator. This course will usually use HyperTerminal because most varieties of Windows have it. This program can be found by choosing **Start** > **All Programs** > **Accessories** > **Communications**. Select **HyperTerminal**.

Open HyperTerminal, confirm the number of the chosen serial port, and then configure the port with these settings:

- **Bits per second:** 9600
- **Data bits:** 8
- **Parity:** None
- **Stop bits:** 1
- **Flow control:** None

Step 3: Logging In Using the Terminal Emulator

Log in to the router using the terminal emulator software. If all settings and cable connections are done properly, you can access the router by pressing Enter.

Summary

This chapter discussed the planning and design processes that contribute to the installation of a successful, operating network.

The various LAN and WAN media types and their associated cables and connectors were considered so that the most appropriate interconnection decisions can be made.

Determining the number of hosts and subnets in a network required now—and simultaneously planning for future growth—ensures that data communications are available at the best combination of cost and performance.

Similarly, a well-planned and consistently implemented addressing scheme is an important factor in ensuring that networks work well with provisions to scale as needed. Such addressing schemes also facilitate easy configuration and troubleshooting.

Terminal access to routers and switches is a means to configure addresses and network features on these devices.

Labs

The labs available in the companion *Network Fundamentals, CCNA Exploration Labs and Study Guide* (ISBN 1-58713-203-6) provide hands-on practice with the following topics introduced in this chapter:

Lab 10-1: How Many Networks? (10.3.2.2)

In this lab, you will determine the number of networks in a given topology and design an appropriate addressing scheme. After assigning subnets to the networks, you will examine the usage of the available address space.

Lab 10-2: Creating a Small Lab Topology (10.6.1.1)

In this lab, you will create a small network that requires connecting network devices, configuring host computers for basic network connectivity, and verifying that connectivity.

Lab 10-3: Establishing a Console Session with HyperTerminal (10.6.2.1)

Cisco routers and switches are configured using the device IOS. The command-line interface (CLI) of the IOS is accessed through a terminal that can be emulated on computers.

This lab introduces two Windows-based terminal emulation programs, HyperTerminal and TeraTerm. These programs can be used to connect a computer's serial (COM) port to the console port of the Cisco device running IOS.

Lab 10-4: Establishing a Console Session with Minicom (10.6.3.1)

This lab introduces the Linux-based terminal emulation program Minicom, which can be used to connect a computer's serial port to the console port of the Cisco device running IOS.

Many of the hands-on labs include Packet Tracer companion activities, where you can use Packet Tracer to complete a simulation of the lab. Look for this icon in the Network Fundamentals, CCNA Exploration Labs and Study Guide (ISBN 1-58713-203-6) for hands-on labs that have Packet Tracer companion activities.

Check Your Understanding

Complete all the review questions listed here to test your understanding of the topics and concepts in this chapter. The appendix, "Check Your Understanding and Challenge Questions Answer Key," lists the answers.

1. Which function is a unique responsibility of the DCE devices shown in Figure 10-25?

Figure 10-25 DCE Devices

A. Transmission of data

B. Reception of data

C. Clocking for the synchronous link

D. Noise cancellation in transmitted data

2. You have been given the 178.5.0.0/16 network and are assigned to create as many possible subnets with at least 100 hosts. What subnet mask will you use?

A. 255.255.255.128

B. 255.255.255.192

C. 255.255.255.0

D. 255.255.254.0

3. What would be the most efficient subnet mask to use if you needed as many subnets as possible with 32 hosts each?

   A. 255.255.255.240

   B. 255.255.255.0

   C. 255.255.255.224

   D. 255.255.255.192

4. What is the valid host range for the subnet 154.65.128.0 255.255.248.0?

   A. 154.65.128.1–154.65.128.255

   B. 154.65.128.1–154.65.135.254

   C. 154.65.120.1–154.65.135.255

   D. 154.65.0.0–154.65.255.254

5. 100BASE-FX uses fiber cabling and supports full duplex up to a distance of _____ meters?

   A. 100

   B. 1000

   C. 200

   D. 2000

6. True or false: A T568A cabling code states that pin 1 and pin 2 would be a green pair of wires.

7. List where a straight-through UTP cable would be used in connecting network devices.

8. List where a crossover UTP cable would be used in connecting network devices.

9. Describe the purposes of and differences between DCE and DTE WAN serial cables and devices.

10. List criteria that should be considered when selecting a switch for a LAN.

11. Give examples of the different types of hosts and network devices that require IP addresses.

12. List three reasons for subnetting a network.

13. List the five factors to consider when selecting the type of physical media to deploy in the LAN.

Challenge Questions and Activities

These questions require a deeper application of the concepts covered in this chapter and are similar to the style of questions you might see on a CCNA certification exam.

1. Which addresses are valid host IP addresses, given the subnet mask 255.255.255.248? (Choose three.)

    A. 192.168.200.87

    B. 194.10.10.104

    C. 223.168.210.100

    D. 220.100.100.154

    E. 200.152.2.160

    F. 196.123.142.190

2. Host A in Figure 10-26 is assigned the IP address 10.118.197.55/20. How many more network devices can be added to this same subnetwork?

Figure 10-26   Small Network

    A. 253

    B. 509

    C. 1021

    D. 2045

    E. 4093

3. The devices in Figure 10-27 have been configured with a static IP address from the network 192.168.102.0. All hosts can communicate with each other but cannot communicate with the server. What is causing this problem?

Figure 10-27   Larger Network

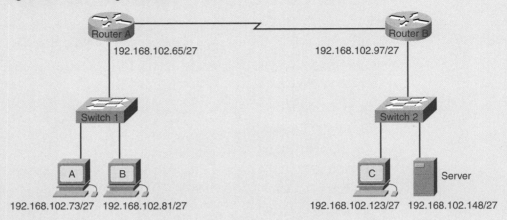

A. The IP address assigned to the server is outside the subnet.

B. The IP address assigned to the server is a broadcast address.

C. The IP address assigned to the server is a network address.

D. The switch that the server is connected to has not been assigned an IP address.

E. The route connected to the 192.168.102.96 network is configured for the 192.168.102.64 network.

4. A contractor is installing cable for a new hospital network. The cable specifications require that the network be protected from EMI and have a supported bandwidth of 1000 Mbps. Which cable type would meet both specifications?

A. Thinnet coaxial cable

B. Thicknet coaxial cable

C. Category 5 UTP cable

D. Category 5 STP cable

E. Fiber-optic cable

5. Which two items are required for initial configuration of Cisco routers?

A. Crossover cable

B. Rollover cable

C. RJ-15–to–DB-9 adapter

D. Terminal emulation software

E. Router VTY port

6. List four types of interfaces found on Cisco routers and switches, and give the function of each.

Packet Tracer
☐ Challenge

Look for this icon in Network Fundamentals, CCNA Exploration Labs and Study Guide (ISBN 1-58713-203-6) for instructions on how to perform the Packet Tracer Skills Integration Challenge for this chapter.

To Learn More

Structured cabling skills are crucial for any networking professional. Structured cabling creates a physical topology where telecommunications cabling is organized into hierarchical termination and interconnection structures according to standards. The word *telecommunications* is used to express the necessity of dealing with electrical power wires, telephone wires, and cable television coaxial cable in addition to copper and optical networking media.

Structured cabling is an OSI Layer 1 issue. Without Layer 1 connectivity, the Layer 2 switching and Layer 3 routing process that makes data transfer across large networks possible cannot occur. Especially for people new to the networking work force, many of the day-to-day jobs deal with structured cabling.

Many different standards are used to define the rules of structured cabling. These standards vary around the world. Three standards of central importance in structured cabling are ANSI TIA/EIA-568-B, ISO/IEC 11801, and IEEE 802.x.

The supplement, titled Exploration Supplement Structured Cabling.pdf on the companion CD-ROM, provides the opportunity to complete a structured cabling case study. This can be done on paper only or as part of a hands-on structured cabling installation project.

CHAPTER 11

Configuring and Testing Your Network

Objectives

Upon completion of this chapter, you will be able to answer the following questions:

- What is the role of the IOS?

- What is the purpose of a configuration file?

- What are the classes of devices that have the IOS embedded?

- What are the factors contributing to the set of IOS commands available to a device?

- What are the IOS modes of operation?

- What are the basic IOS commands?

- How are the basic **show** commands used and why?

Key Terms

This chapter uses the following key terms. You can find the definitions in the Glossary.

flash   page 410

virtual teletype interface (vty)   page 412

Secure Shell (SSH)   page 412

nonvolatile RAM (NVRAM)   page 414

global configuration mode   page 415

user executive (EXEC) mode   page 416

keywords   page 418

arguments   page 418

strong passwords   page 432

network baseline   page 458

ping sweep   page 462

In this chapter, you will examine the process for connecting and configuring computers, switches, and routers into an Ethernet LAN. You will learn the basic configuration procedures for Cisco network devices. These procedures require the use of the Cisco Internetwork Operating System (IOS) and the related configuration files for intermediary devices.

An understanding of the configuration process using the IOS is essential for network administrators and network technicians. The labs that appear in *Network Fundamentals, CCNA Exploration Labs and Study Guide* (ISBN 1-58713-203-6) will familiarize you with common practices used to configure and monitor Cisco devices.

Configuring Cisco Devices: IOS Basics

Similar to a personal computer, a router or switch cannot function without an operating system. Without an operating system, the hardware has no capabilities. Cisco IOS is the system software in Cisco devices. It is the core technology that extends across most of the Cisco product line. The Cisco IOS is used for most Cisco devices regardless of the size and type of the device. It is used for routers, LAN switches, small wireless access points, large routers with dozens of interfaces, and many other devices.

The following sections define a Cisco IOS and look at numerous methods of accessing the IOS and the different configuration files. When working with the configuration files, you will need to be familiar with not only the IOS modes but also the basic IOS command structure and the command-line interface (CLI) used to modify the configuration files.

Cisco IOS

The Cisco IOS provides devices with the following network services:

- Basic routing and switching functions
- Reliable and secure access to networked resources
- Network scalability

The IOS operational details vary on different internetworking devices, depending on the purpose of the device and feature set.

The services provided by the Cisco IOS are generally accessed using a CLI. The features accessible through the CLI vary based on the version of the IOS and the type of device.

The IOS file itself is several megabytes in size and is stored in a semipermanent memory area called *flash*. Flash memory provides nonvolatile storage. This means that the contents of the memory are not lost when the device loses power. Even though the contents are not lost, they can be changed or overwritten if needed.

Using flash memory allows the IOS to be upgraded to newer versions or to have new features added. In many router architectures, the IOS is copied into RAM when the device is powered on, and the IOS runs from RAM when the device is operating. This function increases the performance of the device.

Access Methods

You can access the CLI environment in several ways. The most common methods are

- Console

- Telnet or SSH

- AUX port

The different connections are shown in Figure 11-1.

Figure 11-1   Accessing the Cisco IOS on a Device

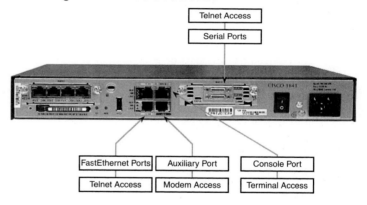

Console

The CLI can be accessed through a console session, also known as the *CTY line*. A console uses a low-speed serial connection to directly connect a computer or terminal to the console port on the router or switch.

The console port is a management port that provides out-of-band access to a router. The console port is accessible even if no networking services have been configured on the device. The console port is often used to access a device when the networking services have not been started or have failed.

Examples of console use include the following:

- The initial configuration of the network device

- Disaster recovery procedures and troubleshooting where remote access is not possible

- Password recovery procedures

When a router is first placed into service, networking parameters have not yet been configured. Therefore, the router cannot communicate through a network. To prepare for the initial startup and configuration, a computer running terminal emulation software is connected to the console port of the device. Configuration commands for setting up the router can be entered on the connected computer.

During operation, if a router cannot be accessed remotely, a connection to the console can enable a computer to determine the status of the device. By default, the console conveys the device startup, debugging, and error messages.

For many IOS devices, console access does not require any form of security, by default. However, the console should be configured with passwords to prevent unauthorized device access. In the event that a password is lost, there is a special set of procedures for bypassing the password and accessing the device. The device should be located in a locked room or equipment rack to prevent unauthorized physical access.

Telnet and SSH

A method for remotely accessing a CLI session is to telnet to the router. Unlike the console connection, Telnet sessions require active networking services on the device. The network device must have at least one active interface configured with a Layer 3 address, such as an IPv4 address. Cisco IOS devices include a Telnet server process that launches when the device is started. The IOS also contains a Telnet client.

A host with a Telnet client can access the *virtual teletype interface (vty)* sessions running on the Cisco device. A vty session is a CLI created in a router for a Telnet session. For security reasons, the IOS requires that the Telnet session use a password, as a minimum authentication method. The methods for establishing logins and passwords will be discussed in the section "Limiting Device Access: Configuring Password and Banners," later in this chapter.

The *Secure Shell (SSH)* protocol is a more secure method for remote device access. This protocol provides the structure for a remote login similar to Telnet, except that it utilizes more secure network services.

SSH provides stronger password authentication than Telnet and uses encryption when transporting session data. The SSH session encrypts all communications between the client and the IOS device. This keeps the user ID, password, and details of the management session private. As a best practice, always use SSH in place of Telnet whenever possible.

Most newer versions of the IOS contain an SSH server. In some devices, this service is enabled by default. Other devices require the SSH server to be enabled.

IOS devices also include an SSH client that can be used to establish SSH sessions with other devices. Similarly, you can use a remote computer with an SSH client to start a secure CLI session. SSH client software is not provided by default on all computer operating systems. You might need to acquire, install, and configure SSH client software for your computer.

AUX Port

Another way to establish a CLI session remotely is through a telephone dialup connection using a modem connected to the router auxiliary (AUX) port. Similar to the console connection, this method does not require networking services to be configured or available on the device.

The AUX port can also be used locally, like the console port, with a direct connection to a computer running a terminal emulation program. The console port is required for the configuration of the router, but not all routers have an AUX port. The console port is also preferred over the AUX port for troubleshooting because it displays router startup, debugging, and error messages by default.

Generally, the only time the AUX port is used locally instead of the console port is when there are problems using the console port, such as when certain console parameters are unknown.

Configuration Files

Network devices depend on two types of software for their operation: operating system and configuration. Like the operating system in any computer, the operating system facilitates the basic operation of the device hardware components.

Configuration files contain the Cisco IOS Software commands used to customize the functionality of a Cisco device. Commands are parsed (translated and executed) by the Cisco IOS Software when the system is booted (from the startup-config file) or when commands are entered in the CLI while in configuration mode. Figure 11-2 shows the relationship between the configuration files.

Figure 11-2 Configuration Files

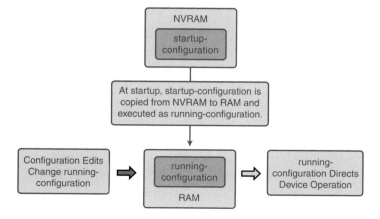

A network administrator creates a configuration that defines the desired functionality of a Cisco device. The configuration file is typically a few hundred to a few thousand bytes in size.

A Cisco network device contains two configuration files:

- **The running configuration file:** Used during the current operation of the device
- **The startup configuration file:** Used as the backup configuration and loaded when the device is started

A configuration file can be stored remotely on a server as a backup.

Startup Configuration File

The startup configuration file (startup-config) is used during system startup to configure the device. The startup configuration file or startup-config file is stored in *nonvolatile RAM (NVRAM)*. Because NVRAM is nonvolatile, when the Cisco device is turned off, the file remains intact. The startup-config files are loaded into RAM each time the router is started or reloaded. After the configuration file is loaded into RAM, it is considered the running configuration or running-config.

Running Configuration

After it is in RAM, the running configuration (running-config) is used to operate the network device. The running configuration is modified when the network administrator performs device configuration. Changes to the running configuration will immediately affect the operation of the Cisco device. After making any changes, the administrator has the option of saving those changes to the startup-config file so that they will be used the next time the device restarts.

Because the running configuration file is in RAM, it is lost if the power to the device is turned off or if the device is restarted. Changes made to the running-config file will also be lost if they are not saved to the startup-config file before the device is powered down.

Introducing Cisco IOS Modes

The Cisco IOS is designed as a modal operating system. The term *modal* describes a system where there are different modes of operation, each having its own domain of operation. The CLI uses a hierarchical structure for the modes.

From top to bottom, the major modes are as follows:

- **User executive mode:** A mode that is very limited in scope, allowing basically only "viewing" types of IOS commands.
- **Privileged executive mode:** A mode similar to the "root" in UNIX, or "administrator" in Windows, allowing users logged on in the privileged executive mode access to the entire IOS command structure.

- *Global configuration mode*: Commands executed in this mode apply to the entire router.

- **Other specific configuration modes:** Commands executed while in the router mode, for example, would apply only to that particular routing process.

Each mode is used to accomplish particular tasks and has a specific set of commands that are available when in that mode. For example, to configure a router interface, the user must enter interface configuration mode. All configurations that are entered in interface configuration mode apply only to that interface.

Table 11-1 summarizes the primary modes.

Table 11-1   IOS Primary Modes

Mode	Description	Prompts
User EXEC mode	Limited examination of router. Remote access.	Router>
Privileged EXEX mode	Detailed examination of router. Debugging and testing. File manipulation. Remote access.	Router#
Global configuration mode	Global configuration commands.	Router (config)#
Other configuration modes	Specific service or interface configurations.	Router (config-mode)#

Some commands are available to all users, in all modes; others can be executed only after entering the mode in which that command is available. Each mode is distinguished with a distinctive prompt, and only commands that are appropriate for that mode are allowed.

The hierarchal modal structure can be configured to provide security. Different authentication can be required for each hierarchal mode. This controls the level of access that network personnel can be granted.

The following are the two primary modes of operation:

- User EXEC

- Privileged EXEC

As a security feature, the Cisco IOS Software separates the EXEC sessions into two access modes. These two primary access modes are used within the Cisco CLI hierarchical structure. Each mode has similar commands. However, the privileged EXEC mode has a higher level of authority in what it allows to be executed.

Before describing the user EXEC and privileged EXEC modes in more detail, the following section introduces you to command prompts.

Command Prompts

When using the CLI, the mode is identified by the command-line prompt that is unique to that mode. The prompt is composed of the words and symbols on the line to the left of the entry area. The word *prompt* is used because the system is prompting you to make an entry.

By default, every prompt begins with the device name. Following the name, the remainder of the prompt indicates the mode. For example, the following default prompt indicates the global configuration mode on a router:

```
Router(config)#
```

As commands are used and modes are changed, the prompt changes to reflect the current context. For example, the following shows the **ping** command executed at the user EXEC level:

```
Router> ping 192.168.10.5s
```

The following shows a CLI command that will result in the contents of the file running-config being displayed on the terminal:

```
Router# show running-config
```

The following shows a CLI command, executed at the privileged EXEC level that will allow you to enter commands that will change the running-config file:

```
Router# config terminal
```

The following shows a CLI command that will take you to the specific interface configuration mode:

```
Router(config)# Interface FastEthernet 0/1
```

The following shows a CLI command that will apply an IP address and a subnet mask to a specific interface:

```
Router(config-if)# ip address 192.168.10.1 255.255.255.0
```

User Executive Mode

The *user executive (EXEC) mode* has limited capabilities but is useful for some basic operations. The user EXEC mode is at the top of the modal hierarchical structure. This mode is the first entrance into the CLI of an IOS router.

The user EXEC mode allows only a limited number of basic monitoring commands. This is often referred to as *view-only mode*. The user EXEC level does not allow the execution of any commands that might change the configuration of the device.

By default, there is no authentication required to access the user EXEC mode from the console. It is a good practice to ensure that authentication is configured during the initial configuration.

The user EXEC mode is identified by the CLI prompt that ends with the > symbol, as follows:

```
Switch>
```

Privileged EXEC Mode

The execution of configuration and management commands requires that the network administrator use the privileged EXEC mode or a specific mode farther down the hierarchy.

The privileged EXEC mode can be identified by the prompt ending with the # symbol, as follows:

```
Switch#
```

By default, privileged EXEC does not require authentication. It is a good practice to ensure that authentication is configured.

Global configuration mode and all other more specific configuration modes can be reached only from the privileged EXEC mode.

Moving Between the User EXEC and Privileged EXEC Modes

The enable and disable commands are used to change the CLI between the user EXEC mode and the privileged EXEC mode, respectively.

To access the privileged EXEC mode, use the **enable** command. The privileged EXEC mode is sometimes called the enable mode.

The syntax for entering the **enable** command is

```
Router> enable
```

This command is executed without the need for an argument or keyword. When you press Enter, the router prompt changes to

```
Router#
```

The # at the end of the prompt indicates that the router is now in privileged EXEC mode.

If password authentication has been configured for the privileged EXEC mode, the IOS will ask you to enter the password, as shown in the following example:

```
Router> enable

Password:
Router#
```

The **disable** command is used to return from the privileged EXEC to the user EXEC mode, as follows:

```
Router# disable

Router>
```

Basic IOS Command Structure

Each IOS command has a specific format or syntax and is executed at the appropriate prompt. The commands are not case sensitive. The general syntax for a command is the command followed by any appropriate keywords and arguments.

The *keywords* and *arguments* provide additional functionality and describe specific parameters to the command interpreter. For example, the **show** command is used to display information about the device, and it has various keywords that you can use to define the particular output you want to see. For example, in the following syntax, the **show** command is followed by the keyword **running-config**. The keyword specifies that the running configuration is to be displayed as the output:

```
Switch# show running-config
```

A command might require one or more arguments. Unlike a keyword, an argument is generally not a predefined word. An argument is a value or variable defined by the user. As an example, when applying a description to an interface with the description command, enter a line such as the following:

```
Switch(config-if)# description MainHQ Office Switch
```

The command is **description**. The argument is **MainHQ Office Switch**. The user defines the argument. For this command, the argument can be any text string of up to 80 characters.

After entering each complete command, including any keywords and arguments, press Enter to submit the command to the command interpreter. Prompt commands are followed by a space and then the keyword or arguments. Figure 11-3 shows the basic IOS command structure.

Figure 11-3   Basic IOS Command Structure

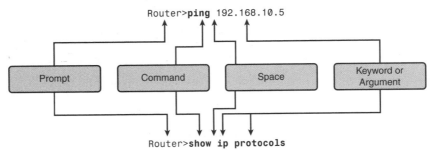

IOS Conventions

The following examples demonstrate conventions for documenting IOS commands. Table 11-2 shows some IOS conventions.

Table 11-2   IOS Conventions

Convention	Description
Boldface	Boldface text indicates commands and keywords that are entered literally as shown.
Italics	Italic text indicates arguments where the user supplies values.
[X]	Square brackets enclose an optional element (keyword or argument).
|	A vertical line indicates a choice within an optional or required set of keywords or arguments.
[X | Y]	Square brackets enclosing keywords or arguments separated by a vertical line indicate an optional choice.
{X | Y}	Braces enclosing keywords or arguments separated by a vertical line indicate a required choice.

The italicized value, in this case the correct IP address, is a value that the person configuring the router must provide.

The **ping** command uses the following format:

```
Router> ping IP address
```

With the argument in place, the syntax is written as follows:

```
Router> ping 10.10.10.5
```

The command is **ping**, and the argument is the IP address.

Similarly, the syntax for entering the **traceroute** command is as follows:

```
Switch> traceroute IP address
```

With the argument in place, the syntax is written as follows:

```
Switch> traceroute 192.168.254.254
```

The command is **traceroute**, and the argument is the IP address.

Commands are used to execute an action, and the keywords are used to identify where or how to execute the command.

Another example is the use of the **description** command, as follows:

```
Router(config-if)# description string
```

With the argument in place, the syntax is written as follows:

```
Switch(config-if)# description Interface to Building a LAN
```

The command is **description**, and the argument applied to the interface is the text string **Interface to Building a LAN**. The description is basically a remark that will be displayed in the configuration file and helps with documenting the network and in troubleshooting.

Using CLI Help

The IOS has several forms of help available:

- Context-sensitive help
- Command syntax check
- Hot keys and shortcuts

The next sections describe each of these help features.

Context-Sensitive Help

The context-sensitive help provides a list of commands and the arguments associated with those commands within the context of the current mode. To access context-sensitive help, enter a question mark (**?**) at any prompt. There is an immediate response without the need to press Enter.

One use of context-sensitive help is to get a list of available commands. You can use this list when you are unsure of the name for a command or when you want to see whether the IOS supports a particular command in a particular mode. For example, to list the commands available at the user EXEC level, type a question mark at the Router> prompt, as follows:

```
Router> ?
```

Another use of context-sensitive help is to display a list of commands or keywords that start with a specific character or characters. If you enter a question mark immediately (without a space) after entering a character sequence, the IOS will display a list of commands or keywords for this context that start with the characters that were entered. For example, enter **sh?** to get a list of commands that begin with the character sequence sh.

A final type of context-sensitive help is used to determine which options, keywords, or arguments are matched with a specific command. When entering a command, enter a space followed by a **?** to determine what can or should be entered next.

In Example 11-1, using the **clock** command provides you with a closer look at the CLI command help that is available.

```
Example 11-1    clock Command
Router# cl?

clear   clock
Router# clock ? set Set the time and date
Router# clock set
Router#clock set ?

  hh:mm:ss current time
Router# clock set 19:50:00
Router# clock set 19:50:00 ?

<1-31> Day of the month
MONTH Month of the year
Router# clock set 19:50:00 25 6
Router# clock set 19:50:00 25 June
Router#clock set 19:50:00 25 June ?

<1993-2035> Year
Router# clock set 19:50:00 25 June 2007

Cisco#
```

Command Syntax Check

When a command is submitted by pressing Enter, the command-line interpreter parses the command from left to right to determine what action is being requested. If the interpreter understands the command, the requested action is executed and the CLI returns to the appropriate prompt. However, if the interpreter cannot understand the command being entered, it will provide feedback describing what is wrong with the command.

The following are the three different types of error messages:

- Ambiguous command
- Incomplete command
- Incorrect command (invalid input)

The IOS returns an ambiguous error message to indicate that there were not enough characters entered for the command interpreter to recognize the command, as follows:

```
Switch# c

%Ambiguous command: 'c'
```

The IOS returns an incomplete error message, indicating that required keywords or arguments were left off the end of the command, as follows:

```
Switch# clock set

%Incomplete command
Switch# clock set 19:50:00

%Incomplete command
```

The IOS returns a caret symbol (^) to indicate where the command interpreter cannot decipher the command, as follows:

```
Switch# clock set 19:50:00 25 6

%Invalid input detected at  ¦^¦ marker.
```

Table 11-3 shows the command syntax check help.

Table 11-3   Command Syntax Check Help

Error Message	Meaning	Examples	How to Get Help
%Ambiguous command: 'command'	Not enough characters were entered for the IOS to recognize the command.	Switch# c %Ambiguous command: 'c'	Reenter the command followed by a question mark (**?**) with no space between the command and the question mark. The possible keywords that you can enter with the command are displayed.
%Incomplete command	Not all the required keywords or arguments were entered.	Switch# **clock set** %Incomplete command	Reenter the command followed by a question mark (**?**) with a space after last word. The required keywords or arguments are displayed.
%Invalid input detected at ¦^¦marker	Command was entered incorrectly. The error occurred where the caret mark (^) appears.	Switch# **clock set 19:50:00 25 6** ¦^¦ %Invalid input detected at ¦^¦ marker	Reenter the command followed by a question mark (**?**) in a place indicated by the ¦^¦ mark. It might also need to have the last keyword(s) or argument(s) deleted.

Hot Keys and Shortcuts

The IOS CLI provides hot keys and shortcuts that make configuring, monitoring, and troubleshooting easier. Table 11-4 shows most of the shortcuts. The table is broken into three sections. The first section shows the CLI editing shortcuts. The second section shows shortcuts to use when you get the —More— prompt on your terminal. (When a command returns more output than can be displayed on a single screen, the —More— prompt appears at the bottom of the screen.) The last section shows the control keys you can use to break out of a series of commands.

Table 11-4   Hot Keys and Shortcuts

CLI Line Editing

Shortcut	Description
Tab	Completes a partial command name entry.
Backspace	Erases the character to the left of the cursor.
Ctrl-D	Erases the character at the cursor.
Ctrl-K	Erases all characters from the cursor to the end of the command line.
Esc D	Erases all characters from the cursor to the end of the word.
Ctrl-U or Ctrl-X	Erases all characters from the cursor to the beginning of the command line.
Ctrl-W	Erases the word to the left of the cursor.
Ctrl-A	Moves the cursor to the beginning of the command line.
Left-arrow key or Ctrl-B	Moves the cursor one character to the left.
Esc F	Moves the cursor forward one word to the right.
Right-arrow key or Ctrl-F	Moves the cursor one character to the right.
Ctrl-E	Moves the cursor to the end of command line.
Up-arrow key or Ctrl-P	Recalls command in the history buffer, beginning with the most recent commands.
Ctrl-R, Ctrl-I, or Ctrl-L	Redisplays the system prompt and command line after a console message is received.

Table 11-4   Hot Keys and Shortcuts   *(continued)*

At the —More— Prompt

Shortcut	Description
Enter key	Displays the next line.
Spacebar	Displays the next screen.
Any other alphanumeric key	Returns to the EXEC prompt.

Break Keys

Shortcut	Description
Ctrl-C	When in any configuration mode, ends the configuration mode and returns to privileged EXEC mode. When in setup mode, aborts to the command prompt.
Ctrl-Z	When in any configuration mode, ends the configuration mode and returns to privileged EXEC mode.
Ctrl-Shift-6	All-purpose break sequence. Used to abort DNS lookups, traceroutes, pings.

Note

Delete, the key to erase to the right of the cursor, is not recognized by terminal emulation programs.

To use control shortcuts, press and hold the Ctrl key and then press the specified letter key. For escape sequences, press and release the Esc key and then press the letter key.

The following sections describe the shortcuts that you will find extremely useful.

Tab

Tab is used to complete the remainder of abbreviated commands and parameters. When enough of the command or keyword has been entered to appear unique, press the Tab key, and the CLI will display the rest of the command or keyword.

This is a good technique to use when you are learning because it allows you to see the full word used for the command or keyword.

Ctrl-R

Press Ctrl-R to redisplay the line. For example, you might find that the IOS is returning a message to the CLI just as you are typing a line. You can press Ctrl-R to refresh the line and avoid having to retype it.

In this example, a message regarding a failed interface is returned in the middle of a command:

```
Switch# show mac-

16w4d: %LINK-5-CHANGED: Interface FastEthernet0/10, changed state to down
16w4d: %LINEPROTO-5-UPDOWN: Line protocol on Interface FastEthernet0/10, changed
    state to down
```

To redisplay the line that you were typing, press Ctrl-R:

```
Switch# show mac
```

Ctrl-Z

To leave a configuration mode and return to privileged EXEC mode, press Ctrl-Z. Because the IOS has a hierarchal mode structure, you might find yourself several levels down. Rather than exit each mode individually, press Ctrl-Z to return directly to the privileged EXEC prompt at the top level.

Up- and Down-Arrow Keys

The Cisco IOS Software buffers several past commands and characters so that entries can be recalled. The buffer is useful for reentering commands without retyping. Key sequences are available to scroll through these buffered commands. Use the up-arrow key (Ctrl-P) to display the previously entered commands. Each time this key is pressed, the next successively older command will be displayed. Use the down-arrow key (Ctrl-N) to scroll forward through the history to display the more recent commands.

Ctrl-Shift-6 x

When an IOS process is initiated from the CLI, such as a ping or traceroute, the command runs until it is complete or is interrupted. While the process is running, the CLI is unresponsive. To interrupt the output and interact with the CLI, press Ctrl-Shift-6 and then the x key.

Ctrl-C

Pressing Ctrl-C interrupts the entry of a command and exits the configuration mode. This is useful when entering a command you might decide that you want to cancel and exits the configuration mode.

Abbreviated Commands or Keywords

Commands and keywords can be abbreviated to the minimum number of characters that identifies a unique selection. For example, the **configure** command can be abbreviated to **conf** because **configure** is the only command that begins with conf. An abbreviation of con will not work because more than one command begins with con. Keywords can also be abbreviated.

As another example, the **show interfaces** command can be abbreviated like this:

```
Router# show interfaces
Router# show int
```

You can abbreviate both the command and the keywords, as follows:

```
Router# sh int
```

IOS Examination Commands

To verify and troubleshoot network operation, you must examine the operation of the devices. The basic examination command is the **show** command.

The **show** command has many different variations. As you develop more skill with the IOS, you will learn to use and interpret the output of the **show** commands. Use the **show ?** command to get a list of available commands in a given context, or mode.

Figure 11-4 indicates how the typical **show** command can provide information about the configuration, operation, and status of parts of a Cisco router. The figure breaks the different **show** commands into (a) if they are applicable to the IOS (stored in RAM), (b) if they apply to the backup configuration file stored in NVRAM, or (c) if they apply to flash or specific interfaces.

Figure 11-4   Information Provided by the **show** Command

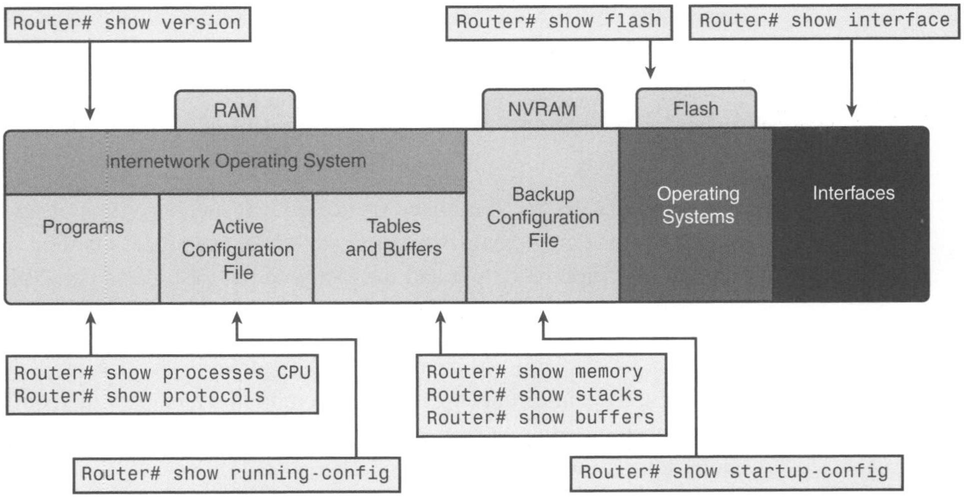

Some **show** commands are as follows:

- **show arp:** Displays the ARP table of the device.

- **show mac-address-table:** (switch only) Displays the MAC table of a switch.

- **show startup-config:** Displays the saved configuration located in NVRAM.

- **show running-config:** Displays the contents of the currently running configuration file or the configuration for a specific interface, or map class information.

- **show ip interfaces:** Displays IPv4 statistics for all interfaces on a router. To view the statistics for a specific interface, enter the **show ip interfaces** command followed by the specific interface slot/port number. Another important format of this command is **show ip interface brief**. This is useful to get a quick summary of the interfaces and their operational state, as shown in Example 11-2.

Example 11-2 Output of the **show IP interface brief** Command

```
Router# show ip interface brief

Interface IP-Address OK? Method Status Protocol
FastEthernet0/0 172.16.255.254 YES manual up up
FastEthernet0/1 unassigned YES unset down down
Serial0/0/0 10.10.10.5 YES manual up up
Serial0/0/1 unassigned YES unset down down
```

The next sections describe the following commonly used **show** commands:

- **show interfaces**

- **show version**

show interfaces Command

The **show interfaces** command displays statistics for all interfaces on the device. To view the statistics for a specific interface, enter the **show interfaces** command followed by the specific interface slot/port number, as follows:

```
Router# show interfaces serial 0/1
```

show version Command

The **show version** command displays information about the currently loaded software version, along with hardware and device information. The information shown from this command includes the following:

- **Software version:** IOS Software version (stored in flash)

- **Bootstrap version:** Bootstrap version (stored in boot ROM)

- **System up-time:** Time since last reboot

- **System restart information:** Method of restart (for example, power cycle or crash)

- **Software image name:** IOS filename stored in flash

- **Router type and processor type:** Model number and processor type

- **Memory type and allocation (Shared/Main):** Main processor RAM and shared packet I/O buffering

- **Software features:** Supported protocols and feature sets

- **Hardware interfaces:** Interfaces available on router

- **Configuration register:** Sets bootup specifications, console speed, and related parameters

Examine Common IOS show Commands (11.1.6.3)

In this activity, you will use Packet Tracer to examine common IOS **show** commands. Use file e1-11163.pka on the CD-ROM that accompanies this book to perform this activity using Packet Tracer.

IOS Configuration Modes

The primary configuration mode is called global configuration or global config. From global config, CLI configuration changes are made that affect the operation of the device as a whole.

You also use the global config mode as a precursor to accessing specific configuration modes. The following CLI command is used to take the device from privileged EXEC mode to the global configuration mode and to allow entry of configuration commands from a terminal:

```
Router# configure terminal
```

After the command is executed, the prompt changes to show that the router is in global configuration mode.

```
Router(config)#
```

From the global config mode, there are many different configuration modes that can be entered. Each of these modes allows the configuration of a particular part or function of the IOS device. The following list shows a few of them:

- **Interface mode:** Configure one of the network interfaces (Fa0/0, S0/0/0, and so on)

- **Line mode:** Configure one of the lines, physical or virtual (console, AUX, VTY, and so on)

- **Router mode:** Configure the parameters for one of the routing protocols

To exit a specific configuration mode and return to global configuration mode, enter **exit** at a prompt. To leave configuration mode completely and return to privileged EXEC mode, enter **end** or use press Ctrl-Z.

After a change has been made from the global mode, it is good practice to save it to the startup configuration file stored in NVRAM. This prevents changes from being lost because of a power failure or a deliberate restart. The command to save the running configuration to the startup configuration file is as follows:

```
Router# copy running-config startup-config
```

Packet Tracer
☐ Activity

IOS Configuration Modes (11.1.7.2)

In this activity, you will use Packet Tracer to practice accessing IOS configuration modes. Use file e1-11172.pka on the CD-ROM that accompanies this book to perform this activity using Packet Tracer.

Applying a Basic Configuration Using Cisco IOS

You are now ready to examine some of the basic Cisco IOS commands used to create configuration files on both Cisco routers and switches. The following sections provide you with the knowledge to apply device names to Cisco devices, manage access with the use of passwords and banners, manage configuration files, and configure device interfaces.

Naming Devices

The host name is used in CLI prompts. If the host name is not explicitly configured, a router uses the factory-assigned default host name "Router." A switch has a factory-assigned default host name of "Switch." Imagine if an internetwork had several routers that were all named with the default name Router. This would create considerable confusion during network configuration and maintenance.

When accessing a remote device using Telnet or SSH, it is important to have confirmation that an attachment has been made to the proper device. If all devices were left with their default names, you could not identify that the proper device is connected.

By choosing and documenting names wisely, it is easier to remember, discuss, and identify network devices. Naming devices in a consistent and useful way requires the establishment of a naming convention that spans the company or, at least, the location. It is a good practice to create the naming convention at the same time as the addressing scheme to allow continuity within the organization.

When you are naming devices, names should follow these conventions:

- Start with a letter
- Not contain a space
- End with a letter or digit

- Have characters of only letters, digits, and dashes

- Be 63 characters or fewer

The host names used in the device IOS preserve capitalization and lowercase characters. Therefore, it allows you to capitalize a name as you ordinarily would. This contrasts with most Internet naming schemes, where uppercase and lowercase characters are treated identically. RFC 1178, "Choosing a Name for Your Computer," provides rules that you can use as a reference for device naming. As part of the device configuration, a unique host name should be configured for each device.

Figure 11-5 shows an example of three routers connected in a network spanning three different cities (Atlanta, Phoenix, and Corpus).

Figure 11-5   Configuring Device Names

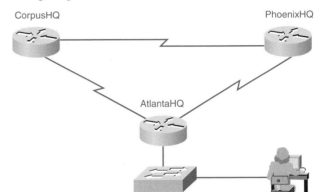

To create a naming convention for routers, take into consideration the location and the purpose of the devices. Ask yourself questions such as these: Will these routers be part of the headquarters for an organization? Does each router have a different purpose? For example, is the Atlanta router a primary junction point in the network, or is it one junction in a chain?

In this example, each router is a branch headquarters for each city. The names are AtlantaHQ, PhoenixHQ, and CorpusHQ. Had each router been a junction in a successive chain, the names could be AtlantaJunction1, PhoenixJunction2, and CorpusJunction3. In the network documentation, include these names and the reasons for choosing them to ensure continuity in the naming convention as devices are added.

After the naming convention has been identified, the next step is to apply the names to the router using the CLI. This example walks you through the naming of the Atlanta router.

From the privileged EXEC mode, access the global configuration mode by entering the **configure terminal** command:

```
Router# configure terminal
```

After the command is executed, the prompt will change to the following:

```
Router(config)#
```

In global mode, enter the host name:

```
Router(config)# hostname AtlantaHQ
```

After the command is executed, the prompt will change as follows:

```
AtlantaHQ(config)#
```

Notice that the host name appears in the prompt. To exit global mode, use the **exit** command.

Always make sure that your documentation is updated each time a device is added or modified. Identify devices in the documentation by their location, purpose, and address.

To negate the effects of a command, preface the command with the **no** keyword.

For example, to remove the name of a device, use the following:

```
AtlantaHQ(config)# no hostname

Router(config)#
```

Notice that the **no hostname** command caused the router to revert to the default host name of Router.

Configuring Host Names on Routers and Switches (11.2.1.3)

Packet Tracer
☐ Activity

In this activity, you will use Packet Tracer to configure host names on routers and switches. Use file e1-11213.pka on the CD-ROM that accompanies this book to perform this activity using Packet Tracer.

Limiting Device Access: Configuring Passwords and Banners

Physically limiting access to network devices with closets and locked racks is a good practice; however, passwords are the primary defense against unauthorized access to network devices. Every device should have locally configured passwords to limit access.

The IOS uses hierarchical modes to help with device security. As part of this security enforcement, the IOS can accept several passwords to allow different access privileges to the device.

The passwords introduced here are

- **Console password:** Limits device access using the console connection

- **Enable password:** Limits access to the privileged EXEC mode

- **Enable secret password:** Encrypted; limits access to the privileged EXEC mode

- **VTY password:** Limits device access using Telnet

As good practice, use different authentication passwords for each of these levels of access. Although logging in with multiple and different passwords is inconvenient, it is a necessary precaution to properly protect the network infrastructure from unauthorized access.

Additionally, use *strong passwords* that are not easily guessed. The use of weak or easily guessed passwords continues to be a security issue in many facets of the business world.

Consider these key points when choosing passwords:

- Use passwords that are more than eight characters in length.

- Use a combination of uppercase and lowercase and/or numeric sequences in passwords.

- Avoid using the same password for all devices.

- Avoid using common words such as password or administrator, because these are easily guessed.

Note

In most of the labs, you will use simple passwords such as cisco or class. These passwords are considered weak and easily guessable and should be avoided in a production environment. We only use these passwords for convenience in a classroom setting.

As shown in Figure 11-6, when prompted for a password, the device will not echo the password as it is being entered. In other words, the password characters will not appear when you type. This is done for security purposes; many passwords are gathered by prying eyes.

Figure 11-6   Limiting Device Access: Configuring Console Passwords

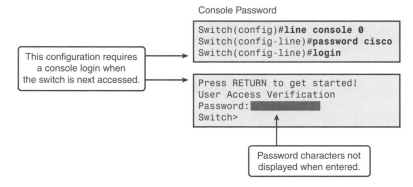

Console Password

The console port of a Cisco IOS device has special privileges. The console port of network devices must be secured, at a minimum, by requiring the user to supply a strong password. This reduces the chance of unauthorized personnel physically plugging a cable into the device and gaining device access.

The following commands are used in global configuration mode to set a password for the console line:

```
Switch(config)# line console 0
Switch(config-line)# password password
Switch(config-line)# login
```

From global configuration mode, the command **line console 0** is used to enter line configuration mode for the console. The 0 is used to represent the first (and in most cases only) console interface for a router.

The second command, **password** *password*, specifies a password on a line.

The **login** command configures the router to require authentication upon login. When login is enabled and a password set, there will be a prompt to enter a password.

After these three commands are executed, a password prompt will appear each time a user attempts to gain access to the console port.

Enable and Enable Secret Passwords

The **enable password** command or the **enable secret** command provides additional security. Either of these commands can be used to establish authentication before accessing privileged EXEC (enable) mode.

Always use the **enable secret** command, not the older **enable password** command, if possible. The **enable secret** command provides greater security because the password is encrypted. The **enable password** command can be used only if **enable secret** has not yet been set.

The **enable password** command would be used if the device uses an older copy of the Cisco IOS Software that does not recognize the **enable secret** command.

The following commands are used to set the passwords:

```
Router(config)# enable password password
Router(config)# enable secret password
```

Note

If no **enable password** or **enable secret password** is set, the IOS prevents privileged EXEC access from a Telnet session.

Without an **enable password** set, a Telnet session appears as follows:

```
Switch> enable

% No password set
Switch>
```

VTY Password

The vty lines allow access to a router through Telnet. By default, many Cisco devices support five vty lines that are numbered 0 to 4. A password needs to be set for all available vty lines. The same password can be set for all connections. However, it is often desirable to set a unique password for one line to provide a fallback for administrative entry to the device if the other connections are in use.

The following commands are used to set a password on vty lines:

```
Router(config)# line vty 0 4
Router(config-line)# password password
Router(config-line)# login
```

By default, the IOS includes the **login** command on the vty lines. This prevents Telnet access to the device without first requiring authentication. If, by mistake, the **no login** command is set, which removes the requirement for authentication, unauthorized persons could connect to the line using Telnet. This would be a major security risk.

Encrypting Password Display

Another useful command prevents passwords from showing up as plain text when viewing the configuration files. This is the **service password-encryption** command.

This command causes the encryption of passwords to occur when a password is configured. The **service password-encryption** command applies weak encryption to all unencrypted passwords. This encryption does not apply to passwords as they are sent over media, only in the configuration. The purpose of this command is to keep unauthorized individuals from viewing passwords in the configuration file.

If you execute the **show running-config** or **show startup-config** command prior to the **service password-encryption** command being executed, the unencrypted passwords are visible in the configuration output. The **service password-encryption** can then be executed and the encryption will be applied to the passwords. After the encryption has been applied, removing the encryption service does not reverse the encryption.

Banner Messages

Although requiring passwords is one way to keep unauthorized personnel out of a network, it is vital to provide a method for declaring that only authorized personnel should attempt to gain entry into the device. To do this, add a banner to the device output.

Banners can be an important part of the legal process in the event that someone is prosecuted for breaking into a device. Some legal systems do not allow prosecution, or even the monitoring of users, unless a notification is visible.

The exact content or wording of a banner depends on the local laws and corporate policies. Here are some examples of information to include in a banner:

- "Use of the device is specifically for authorized personnel."

- "Activity can be monitored."

- "Legal action will be pursued for any unauthorized use."

Because banners can be seen by anyone who attempts to log in, the message must be worded very carefully. When a banner is utilized, it should never welcome someone to the router. If a person disrupts the network after gaining unauthorized entry, proving liability will be difficult if there is the appearance of an invitation.

The banner should detail that only authorized personnel are allowed to access the device. The banner can include scheduled system shutdowns and other information that affects all network users.

The IOS provides multiple types of banners. One common banner is the message of the day (MOTD). It is often used for legal notification because it is displayed to all connected terminals.

The **banner motd** command requires the use of delimiters to identify the content of the banner message. The **banner motd** command is followed by a space and a delimiting character. Then, one or more lines of text are entered to represent the banner message. A second occurrence of the delimiting character denotes the end of the message. The delimiting character can be any character, as long as it does not occur in the message. For this reason, symbols such as # are often used.

To configure an MOTD, from global configuration mode, enter the **banner motd** command:

```
Switch(config)# banner motd # message #
```

When the command is executed, the banner will be displayed on all subsequent attempts to access the device until the banner is removed.

IOS Commands for Setting Passwords and Banners (11.2.2.4)

Packet Tracer
☐ Activity

In this activity, you will use Packet Tracer to configure host names on routers and switches. Use file e1-11224.pka on the CD-ROM that accompanies this book to perform this activity using Packet Tracer.

Managing Configuration Files

Modifying a running configuration affects the operation of the device immediately. The following sections explore some commands designed to manage the configuration files. For example, after making changes to a configuration, consider these possible options:

- Make the changed configuration the new startup configuration.
- Return the device to its original configuration.
- Back up configurations offline.
- Remove all configuration from the device.
- Back up configurations with text capture (HyperTerminal or TeraTerm).
- Restore text configurations.

Making the Changed Configuration the New Startup Configuration

Remember, because the running configuration is stored in RAM, it is temporarily active while the Cisco device is running (powered on). If power to the router is lost or if the router is restarted, all configuration changes will be lost unless they have been saved. Saving the running configuration to the startup configuration file in NVRAM preserves the changes as the new startup configuration.

Before committing to the changes, use the appropriate **show** commands to verify the device operation The **show running-config** command can be used to see a running configuration file.

When the changes are verified to be correct, use the **copy running-config startup-config** command at the privileged EXEC mode prompt, as follows:

```
Switch# copy running-config startup-config
```

After the command is executed, the running configuration file replaces the startup configuration file.

Returning the Device to Its Original Configuration

If the changes made to the running configuration do not have the desired effect, it might become necessary to restore the device to its previous configuration. Assuming that you have not overwritten the startup configuration with the changes, you can replace the running configuration with the startup configuration. This is best done by restarting the device using the **reload** command at the privileged EXEC mode prompt.

When initiating a reload, the IOS will detect that the running config has changes that were not saved to the startup configuration. A prompt will appear to ask whether to save the changes made. To discard the changes, enter **n** or **no**.

An additional prompt will appear to confirm the reload. To confirm, press Enter. Pressing any other key will abort the process, as shown in Example 11-3.

Example 11-3   reload Command

```
Router# reload

System configuration has been modified. Save? [yes/no]: n
Proceed with reload? [confirm]
*Apr 13 01:34:15.758: %SYS-5-RELOAD: Reload requested by console. Reload Reason:
  Reload Command.
System Bootstrap, Version 12.3(8r)T8, RELEASE SOFTWARE (fc1)
Technical Support: http://www.cisco.com/techsupport
Copyright  2004 by cisco Systems, Inc.
PLD version 0x10
GIO ASIC version 0x127
c1841 processor with 131072 Kbytes of main memory
Main memory is configured to 64 bit mode with parity disabled
```

Backing Up Configurations Offline

Configuration files should be stored as backup files in the event of a problem. Configuration files can be stored on a TFTP server, a CD, a USB memory stick, or a floppy disk stored in a safe place. A configuration file should also be included in the network documentation.

Backup Configuration on TFTP Server means to save the running configuration or the startup configuration to a TFTP server. Use either the **copy running-config tftp** or the **startup-config tftp** command and follow these steps:

Step 1.   Enter the **copy running-config tftp** command.

Step 2.   Enter the IP address of the TFTP server where the configuration file will be stored.

Step 3.   Enter the name to assign to the configuration file.

Step 4.   Answer **yes** to confirm each choice.

Example 11-4 shows the steps listed.

Example 11-4   Copy to TFTP Server

```
Router# copy running-config tftp

Remote host []? 131.108.2.155
Name of configuration file to write [Tokyo-config]?tokyo.w
Write file tokyo.2 to 131.108.2.155? [confirm]y
Writing tokyo.2 !!!!!! [OK]
```

Removing All Configurations

If undesired changes are saved to the startup configuration, it might be necessary to clear all the configurations. This requires erasing the startup configuration and restarting the device.

The startup configuration is removed by using the **erase startup-config command**. To erase the startup configuration file, use **erase NVRAM:startup-config** or **erase startup-config** at the privileged EXEC mode prompt:

```
Router# erase startup-config
```

When the command is issued, the router will prompt you for confirmation:

```
Erasing the nvram filesystem will remove all configuration files! Continue?
    [confirm]
```

Confirm is the default response. To confirm and erase the startup configuration file, press Enter. Pressing any other key will abort the process.

> **Caution**
>
> Exercise care when using the **erase** command. This command can be used to erase any file in the device. Improper use of the command can erase the IOS itself or another critical file.

After removing the startup configuration from NVRAM, reload the device to remove the current running configuration file from RAM. The device will then load the default startup configuration that was originally shipped with the device into the running configuration.

Backing Up Configurations with Text Capture (HyperTerminal or TeraTerm)

Configuration files can be saved or archived to a text document. This sequence of steps ensures that a working copy of the configuration files is available for editing or reuse later.

When using HyperTerminal, follow these steps:

How To

Step 1. Choose **Transfer > Capture Text**.

Step 2. Choose the location.

Step 3. Click **Start** to begin capturing text.

Step 4. When the capture has been started, execute the **show running-config** or **show startup-config** command at the privileged EXEC prompt. Text displayed in the terminal window will be placed into the chosen file.

Step 5. View the output to verify that it was not corrupted.

Figure 11-7 provides an example of this process.

Figure 11-7 Saving to a Text File in HyperTerminal

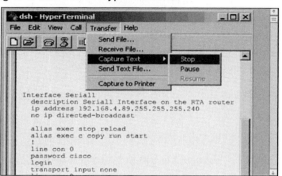

Configuration files can be saved or archived to a text document using TeraTerm. Follow these steps:

Step 1. Choose **File** > **Log**.

Step 2. Choose the location. TeraTerm will begin capturing text.

Step 3. After the capture has been started, execute the **show running-config** or **show startup-config** command at the privileged EXEC prompt. Text displayed in the terminal window will be placed into the chosen file.

Step 4. When the capture is complete, click **Close** in the TeraTerm: Log window.

Step 5. View the output to verify that it was not corrupted.

Figure 11-8 provides an example of this process.

Figure 11-8 Saving to a Text File in TeraTerm

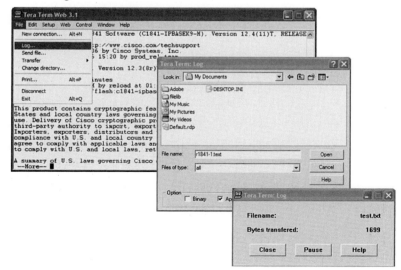

Restoring Text Configurations

A configuration file can be copied from storage to a device. When copied to the terminal, the IOS executes each line of the configuration text as a command. This means that the file will require editing to ensure that encrypted passwords are in plain text and that noncommand text such as "—More—" and IOS messages are removed.

Further, at the CLI, the device must be set at the global configuration mode to receive the commands from the text file being copied.

When using HyperTerminal, follow these steps:

Step 1.   Locate the file to be copied to the device and open the text document.

Step 2.   Copy all the text.

Step 3.   Choose **Edit** > **Paste to Host**.

When using TeraTerm, follow these steps:

Step 1.   Choose **File** > **Send File**.

Step 2.   Locate the file to be copied to the device and click Open.

Step 3.   TeraTerm will paste the file into the device.

The text in the file will be applied as commands in the CLI and become the running configuration on the device. This is a convenient method for manually configuring a router.

Use Packet Tracer to Practice IOS Configuration Management (11.2.3.5)

In this activity, you will use Packet Tracer to practice IOS configuration management. Use file e1-11235.pka on the CD-ROM that accompanies this book to perform this activity using Packet Tracer.

Configuring Interfaces

Throughout this chapter, you have learned about commands that are generic to IOS devices. Some configurations are specific to a type of device. One such configuration is the configuration of interfaces on a router.

Most intermediary network devices have an IP address for the purpose of device management. Some devices, such as switches and wireless access points, can operate without having an IP address.

Because the purpose of a router is to interconnect different networks, each interface on a router has its own unique IPv4 address. The address assigned to each interface is part of the network address range of the network segment connected to that interface.

You can configure many parameters on router interfaces. The following sections discuss the most basic interface commands.

Enabling the Interface

By default, interfaces are disabled. To enable an interface, enter the **no shutdown** command from interface configuration mode. If an interface needs to be disabled for maintenance or troubleshooting, use the **shutdown** command.

Configuring Router Ethernet Interfaces

Router Ethernet interfaces are used as the gateways for the end devices on the LANs directly connected to the router. Each Ethernet interface must have an IP address and subnet mask to route IP packets.

To configure an Ethernet interface, follow these steps:

Step 1.   Enter global configuration mode.

Step 2.   Enter interface configuration mode.

Step 3.   Specify the interface address and subnet mask.

Step 4.   Enable the interface.

Configure the Ethernet IP address using the following commands:

```
Router(config)# interface FastEthernet 0/0
Router(config-if)# ip address ip_address netmask
Router(config-if)# no shutdown
```

Configuring Router Serial Interfaces

Serial interfaces are used to connect WANs to routers at a remote site or ISP. To configure a serial interface, follow these steps:

Step 1.   Enter global configuration mode.

Step 2.   Enter interface configuration mode.

Step 3.   Specify the interface address and subnet mask.

Step 4.   Set the clock rate if a DCE cable is connected. Skip this step if a DTE cable is connected.

Step 5.   Enable the interface.

Each connected serial interface must have an IP address and subnet mask to route IP packets. Configure the IP address with the following commands:

```
Router(config)# interface Serial 0/0/0
Router(config-if)# ip address ip_address netmask
```

Serial interfaces require a clock signal to control the timing of the communications. In most environments, a DCE device such as a channel service unit/data service unit (CSU/DSU) will provide the clock. By default, Cisco routers are DTE devices, but they can be configured as DCE devices.

On serial links that are directly interconnected, as in the lab environment for this course, one side must operate as DCE to provide a clocking signal. The clock is enabled and the speed is specified with the **clock rate** command. Some bit rates might not be available on certain serial interfaces. This depends on the capacity of each interface. In the lab, if a clock rate needs to be set on an interface identified as DCE, use the **clock rate 56000** command.

The commands that are used to set a clock rate and enable a serial interface are these:

```
Router(config)# interface Serial 0/0/0
Router(config-if)# clock rate 56000
Router(config-if)# no shutdown
```

After you make configuration changes to the router, remember to use the **show** commands to verify the accuracy of the changes and then save the changed configuration as the startup configuration.

Describing Interfaces

As the host name helps to identify the device on a network, an interface description indicates the purpose of the interface. A description of what an interface does or where it is connected should be part of the configuration of each interface. This description can be useful for troubleshooting.

The interface description will appear in the output of these commands: **show startup-config**, **show running-config**, and **show interfaces**.

The following description provides valuable information about the purpose of the interface:

This interface is the gateway for the administration LAN.

A description can assist in determining the devices or locations connected to the interface. Here is another example:

Interface F0/0 is connected to the main switch in the administration building.

When support personnel can easily identify the purpose of an interface or connected device, they can more easily understand the scope of a problem, and this can lead to reaching a resolution sooner.

Circuit and contact information can also be embedded in the interface description. The following description for a serial interface provides the information the network administrator might need before deciding to test a WAN circuit. This description indicates where the circuit terminates, the circuit ID, and the phone number of the company supplying the circuit:

FR to GAD1 circuit ID:AA.HCGN.556460 DLCI 511 - support# 555.1212

To create a description, use the **description** command. This example shows the commands used to create a description for a Fast Ethernet interface:

```
HQ-switch1# configure terminal
HQ-switch1(config)# interface fa0/0
HQ-switch1(config-if)# description Connects to main switch in Building A
```

After the description is applied to the interface, use the **show interfaces** command to verify that the description is correct.

Configuring a Switch Interface

A LAN switch is an intermediary device that interconnects segments within a network. Therefore, the physical interfaces on the switch do not have IP addresses. Unlike a router, where the physical interfaces are connected to different networks, a physical interface on a switch connects devices within a network.

Switch interfaces are enabled by default. As shown in Example 11-5, you can assign descriptions but do not have to enable the interface.

Example 11-5   Switch Interface Descriptions

```
Switch# configure terminal
Switch(config)# interface FastEthernet 0/0
Switch(config-if)# description To TAM switch
Switch(config-if)# exit
Switch(config)# hostname Flour_Bluff
Flour_Bluff(config)# exit
Flour_Bluff#
```

To be able to manage a switch, assign addresses to the device. With an IP address assigned to the switch, it acts like a host device. After the address is assigned, you access the switch with Telnet, SSH, or web services.

The address for a switch is assigned to a virtual interface represented as a virtual LAN (VLAN) interface. In most cases, this is interface VLAN 1. In Example 11-6, you assign an IP address to the VLAN 1 interface. Like the physical interfaces of a router, you also must enable this interface with the **no shutdown** command.

Example 11-6   Switch Interface: VLAN1

```
Switch# configure terminal
Enter configuration commands, one per line. End with CNTL/Z.
Switch(config)# interface vlan 1
Switch(config-if)# ip address 192.168.1.2 255.255.255.0
Switch(config-if)# no shutdown
Switch(config-if)# exit
Switch(config)# ip default-gateway 192.168.1.1
Switch(config)# exit
Switch#
```

Like any other host, the switch needs a gateway address defined to communicate outside of the local network. As shown in Example 11-6, we assign this gateway with the **ip default-gateway** command.

Configuring Interfaces (11.2.4.5)

In this activity, you will use Packet Tracer to practice the IOS commands to configure interfaces. Use file e1-11245.pka on the CD-ROM that accompanies this book to perform this activity using Packet Tracer.

Verifying Connectivity

Now that you know a little about basic router and switch configuration, how do you go about testing the network connectivity? The following sections explore that topic. You will explore the ping utility, look at the interfaces and the default gateway, and become introduced to the trace utility.

Test the Stack

To verify connectivity, the first step is to test the TCP/IP stack. You want to make sure that the protocol you are using to connect to the network is working. The following sections discuss the methods to accomplish that.

Using ping in a Testing Sequence

Using the **ping** command is an effective way to test connectivity. The test is often referred to as testing the protocol stack, because the **ping** command moves from Layer 3 of the OSI model to Layer 2 and then Layer 1. **ping** uses Internet Control Message Protocol (ICMP) to check for connectivity.

In this section, you will use the router IOS **ping** command in a planned sequence of steps to establish valid connections, starting with the individual device and then extending to the LAN and, finally, to remote networks. By using the **ping** command in this ordered sequence, you can isolate problems. The **ping** command will not always pinpoint the nature of the problem, but it can help to identify the source of the problem, an important first step in troubleshooting a network failure.

The **ping** command provides a method for checking the protocol stack and IPv4 address configuration on a host. There are additional tools that can provide more information than **ping**, such as Telnet or trace, which will be discussed in more detail later in this chapter.

A ping from the IOS will yield one of several indications for each ICMP echo that was sent. The most common indicators are

- **! (exclamation mark):** Indicates receipt of an ICMP echo reply. The ! (exclamation mark) indicates that the ping completed successfully and verifies Layer 3 connectivity.

- **. (period):** Indicates a "timeout" while waiting for a reply.

    The . (period) can indicate problems in the communication. It can indicate that a connectivity problem occurred somewhere along the path. It can also indicate that a router along the path did not have a route to the destination and did not send an ICMP Destination Unreachable message. It can also indicate that ping was blocked by device security.

- **U:** An ICMP Unreachable message was received. The U indicates that a router along the path did not have a route to the destination address and responded with an ICMP Unreachable message.

Testing the Loopback

As a first step in the testing sequence, the **ping** command is used to verify the internal IP configuration on the local host. This test is accomplished by using the **ping** command on a reserved address called the loopback address (127.0.0.1). This verifies the proper operation of the protocol stack from the network layer to the physical layer—and back—without actually putting a signal on the media.

Ping commands are entered at the command line, as shown in Example 11-7.

```
Example 11-7   Ping Loopback Output
C:\> ping 127.0.0.1

Reply from 127.0.0.1: bytes=32 time<1ms TTL=128
Reply from 127.0.0.1: bytes=32 time<1ms TTL=128
Reply from 127.0.0.1: bytes=32 time<1ms TTL=128
Reply from 127.0.0.1: bytes=32 time<1ms TTL=128
Ping statistics for 127.0.0.1:
Packets: Sent = 4, Received = 4, Lost = 0 (0% loss),
Approximate round trip times in milli-seconds:
Minimum = 0ms, Maximum = 0ms, Average = 0ms
```

The result indicates that four test packets were sent—each 32 bytes in size—and were returned from host 127.0.0.1 in a time of less than 1 ms TTL (Time to Live), and defines the number of hops that the ping packet has remaining before it will be dropped.

Testing the Protocol Stack (11.3.1.2)

In this activity, you will use the IOS **ping** command in Packet Tracer to determine whether the state of the IP connection is operational. Use file e1-11312.pka on the CD-ROM that accompanies this book to perform this activity using Packet Tracer.

Testing the Interface

In the same way that you use commands and utilities to verify a host configuration, you need to learn commands to verify the interfaces of intermediary devices. The IOS provides commands to verify the operation of router and switch interfaces.

The following sections examine ways to verify router and switch configuration and router and switch connectivity in the network.

Verifying the Router Interfaces

One of the most used commands is the **show ip interface brief** command. This command provides a more abbreviated output than the **show ip interface** command. The **show ip interface brief** command provides a summary of the key information for all the interfaces.

Looking at Figure 11-9 and the output shown in Example 11-8, you can see that this output shows all interfaces attached on the router; the IP address, if any, assigned to each interface; and the operational status of the interface.

Figure 11-9   Interface Testing

192.168.254.1   192.168.254.250   Fa0/0   S0/0/0

Example 11-8   show ip interface brief Command

```
Router1# show ip interface brief

Interface          IP-Address        OK?  Method  Status                  Protocol
FastEthernet0/0    192.168.254.254   YES  NVRAM   up                      up
FastEthernet0/1/0  unassigned        YES  unset   down                    down
Serial0/0/0        172.16.0.254      YES  NVRAM   up                      up
Serial0/0/1        unassigned        YES  unset   administratively down   down
```

Looking at the line for the FastEthernet0/0 interface, you see that the IP address is 192.168.254.254. Looking at the last two columns, you can see the Layer 1 and Layer 2 status of the interface. The up in the Status column shows that this interface is operational at Layer 1. The up in the Protocol column indicates that the Layer 2 protocol is operational.

In Figure 11-9, also notice that the Serial 0/0/1 interface has not been enabled. This is indicated by administratively down in the Status column. This interface can be enabled with the **no shutdown** command.

Testing Router Connectivity

As with an end device, you can verify the Layer 3 connectivity with the **ping** and **traceroute** commands. In Example 11-9 and Example 11-10, you can see the sample outputs from a ping to a host in the local LAN and a trace to a remote host across the WAN.

Example 11-9   ping Command

```
Router1# ping 192.168.254.1


Type escape sequence to abort.
Sending 5, 100-byte ICMP Echos to 192.168.254.1, timeout is 2 seconds:
!!!!!
Success rate is 100 percent {5/5}, round-trip min/avg/max = 1/2/4 ms
```

Example 11-10 traceroute Command

```
Router1# traceroute 192.168.0.1


Type escape sequence to abort.
Tracing the route to 192.168.0.1
1 172.16.0.253 8 msec  4 msec  8 msec
2 10.0.0.254 16 msec  16 msec  8 msec
3 192.168.0.1 16 msec  *  20 msec
```

Verifying the Switch Interfaces

Examining Example 11-11, the **show ip interface brief** command is used to verify the condition of the switch interfaces. As you learned earlier, the IP address for the switch is applied to a VLAN interface. In this case, the Vlan1 interface is assigned an IP address of 192.168.254.250. You can also see that this interface has been enabled and is operational.

Example 11-11 show ip interface brief Command

```
Switch1# show ip interface brief

Interface          IP-Address         OK?    Method    Status    Protocol
Vlan1              192.168.254.250    YES    manual    up        up
FastEthernet0/1    unassigned         YES    unset     down      down
FastEthernet0/2    unassigned         YES    unset     up        up
FastEthernet0/3    unassigned         YES    unset     up        up
<output omitted>
```

Examining the FastEthernet0/1 interface, you can see that this interface is down. This indicates that no device is connected to the interface or the network interface of the device that is connected is not operational.

In contrast, the outputs for the FastEthernet0/2 and FastEthernet0/3 interfaces are operational. This is indicated by both the Status and Protocol being shown as up.

Testing Switch Connectivity

Like other hosts, the switch can test its Layer 3 connectivity with the **ping** and **traceroute** commands. Example 11-12 and Example 11-13 also show a ping to the local host and a trace to a remote host.

Example 11-12 ping Command on a Switch

```
Switch1# ping 192.168.254.1

Type escape sequence to abort.
Sending 5, 100-byte ICMP Echos to 192.168.254.1, timeout is 2 seconds:
!!!!!
Success rate is 100 percent {5/5}, round-trip min/avg/max = 1/2/4 ms
```

Example 11-13 traceroute Command on a Switch

```
Switch1# traceroute 192.168.0.1
Type escape sequence to abort.
Tracing the route to 192.168.0.1
1 192.168.254.254 4 msec 2 msec 3 msec
2 172.16.0.253 8 msec 4 msec 8 msec
3 10.0.0.254 16 msec 16 msec 8 msec
4 192.168.0.1 16 msec * 20 msec
```

Keep in mind the following important points:

- An IP address is not required for a switch to perform its job of frame forwarding.
- The switch requires a default gateway to communicate outside its local network.

The IP address and default gateway are needed for the switch to be accessed remotely for administrative purposes and for troubleshooting.

The next step in the testing sequence is to verify that the NIC address is bound to the IPv4 address and that the NIC is ready to transmit signals across the media.

In Example 11-14, assume that the IPv4 address assigned to a NIC is 10.0.0.5.

Example 11-14 ping command on a Local NIC

```
C:\> ping 10.0.0.5

Reply from 10.0.0.5: bytes=32 time<1ms TTL=128
Reply from 10.0.0.5: bytes=32 time<1ms TTL=128
Reply from 10.0.0.5: bytes=32 time<1ms TTL=128
Reply from 10.0.0.5: bytes=32 time<1ms TTL=128
Ping statistics for 10.0.0.5:
Packets: Sent = 4, Received = 4, Lost = 0 (0% loss),
Approximate round trip times in milli-seconds:
Minimum = 0ms, Maximum = 0ms, Average = 0ms
```

This test verifies that the NIC driver and most of the NIC hardware are working properly. It also verifies that the IP address is properly bound to the NIC, without actually putting a signal on the media.

If this test fails, there are probably issues with the NIC hardware and software driver that can require reinstallation of either or both. This procedure is dependent on the type of host and its operating system.

Use the ping Command to Test Interface Responses (11.3.2.3)

In this activity, you will use the **ping** command in Packet Tracer to test interface responses. Use file e1-11323.pka on the CD-ROM that accompanies this book to perform this activity using Packet Tracer.

Testing the Local Network

The next test in the sequence is to test hosts on the local LAN. Successfully pinging hosts verifies that both the local host (the router, in this case) and the remote host are configured correctly. This test is conducted by pinging each host one by one on the LAN. Figure 11-10 shows an example.

If a host responds with a Destination Unreachable message, note which address was not successful and continue to ping the other hosts on the LAN.

Another failure message is Request Timed Out. This indicates that no response was made to the ping attempt in the default time period, indicating that network latency can be an issue.

To examine network latency, the IOS offers an "extended" mode of the **ping** command. This mode is entered by typing **ping** in privileged EXEC mode at the CLI prompt without a destination IP address. A series of prompts are then presented, as shown in Example 11-15. Pressing Enter accepts the indicated default values.

Figure 11-10 Testing the Local Network

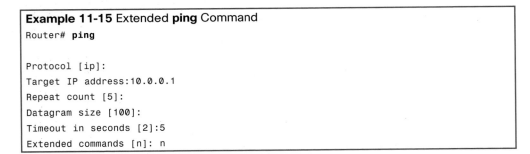

Example 11-15 Extended **ping** Command

```
Router# ping

Protocol [ip]:
Target IP address:10.0.0.1
Repeat count [5]:
Datagram size [100]:
Timeout in seconds [2]:5
Extended commands [n]: n
```

By entering a longer timeout period than the default of 2 seconds, you can test for possible latency issues. If the ping test is successful with a longer value, a connection exists between the hosts, but latency can be an issue on the network.

Note that entering **y** to the "Extended commands" prompt provides more options that are useful in troubleshooting. You will explore these options in the lab and Packet Tracer activities.

Test Connectivity to a Host on a Local Network (11.3.3.2)

In this activity, you will use the **ping** command in Packet Tracer to determine whether a router can actively communicate across the local network. Use file e1-11332.pka on the CD-ROM that accompanies this book to perform this activity using Packet Tracer.

Testing Gateway and Remote Connectivity

The next step in the testing sequence is to use the **ping** command to verify that a local host can connect with a gateway address. This is extremely important because the gateway is the host's entry and exit to the wider network. If the **ping** command returns a successful response, connectivity to the gateway is verified.

To begin, choose a station as the source device, in this case, 10.0.0.1, as shown in Figure 11-11. Use the **ping** command to reach the gateway address, in this case, 10.0.0.254.

```
c:\> ping 10.0.0.254
```

Figure 11-11 Testing Gateway and Remote Connectivity

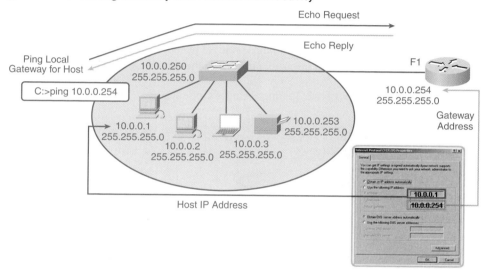

The gateway IPv4 address should be readily available in the network documentation, but if it is not available, use the **ipconfig** command to discover the gateway IP address.

If the gateway test fails, back up one step in the sequence and test another host in the local LAN to verify that the problem is not the source host. Then verify the gateway address with the network administrator to ensure that the proper address is being tested.

Testing Route Next Hop

In a router, use the IOS to test the next hop of the individual routes. As you learned, each route has the next hop listed in the routing table. To determine the next hop, examine the routing table from the output of the **show ip route** command. Frames carrying packets that are directed to the destination network listed in the routing table are sent to the device that represents the next hop. If the next hop is not accessible, the packet will be dropped. To test the next hop, determine the appropriate route to the destination and try to ping the default gateway or appropriate next hop for that route in the routing table. A failed ping indicates that there might be a configuration or hardware problem. However, the ping can also be prohibited by security in the device.

If all devices are configured properly, check the physical cabling to ensure that it is secure and properly connected. Keep an accurate record of what attempts have been made to verify connectivity. This will assist in solving this problem and, perhaps, future problems.

Testing Remote Hosts

After verification of the local LAN and gateway is complete, testing can proceed to remote devices, which is the next step in the testing sequence.

Figure 11-12 depicts a sample network topology. There are three hosts within a LAN, a router (acting as the gateway) that is connected to another router (acting as the gateway for a remote LAN), and three remote hosts. The verification tests should begin within the local network and progress outward to the remote devices.

Figure 11-12 Testing Remote Connectivity

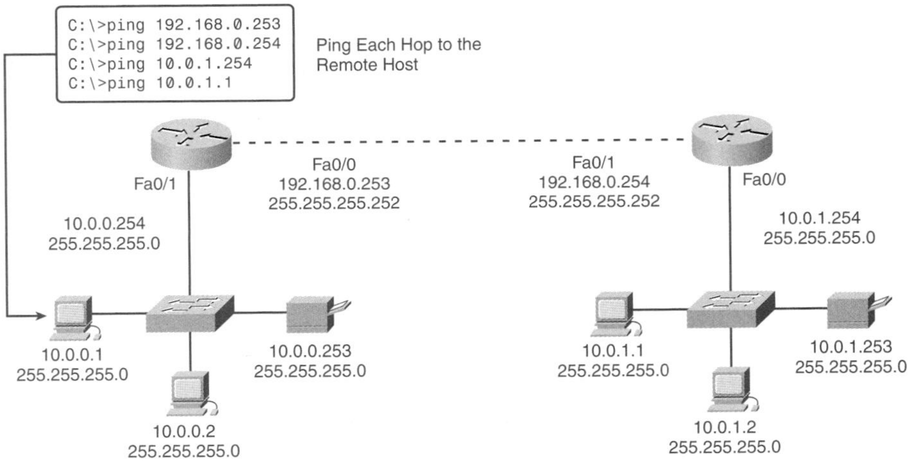

Begin by testing the outside interface of a router that is directly connected to a remote network. In this case, the **ping** command is testing the connection to 192.168.0.253, the outside interface of the local network gateway router.

If the **ping** command is successful, connectivity to the outside interface is verified. Next, ping the outside IP address of the remote router, in this case, 192.168.0.254. If successful, connectivity to the remote router is verified. If there is a failure, try to isolate the problem. Retest until there is a valid connection to a device, and double-check all addresses.

The **ping** command will not always help with identifying the underlying cause to a problem, but it can isolate problems and give direction to the troubleshooting process. Document every test, the devices involved, and the results.

Checking for Router Remote Connectivity

A router forms a connection between networks by forwarding packets between them. To forward packets between any two networks, the router must be able to communicate with both the source and the destination networks. The router will need routes to both networks in its routing table.

To test the communication to the remote network, you can ping a known host on this remote network. If you cannot successfully ping the host on the remote network from a router, you should first check the routing table for an appropriate route to the remote network. It might be that the router uses the default route to reach a destination. If there is no route to reach this network, you will need to identify why the route does not exist. As always, you also must rule out that the ping is not administratively prohibited.

Verify Communication Across the Network (11.3.4.3)

In this activity, you will use the **ping** command in Packet Tracer to verify that a local host can communicate across the internetwork to a given remote host and identify several conditions that might cause the test to fail. Use file e1-11343.pka on the CD-ROM that accompanies this book to perform this activity using Packet Tracer.

Tracing and Interpreting Trace Results

The next step in the testing sequence is to perform a trace. A trace returns a list of hops as a packet is routed through a network. The form of the command depends on where the command is issued. When performing the trace from a Windows computer, use **tracert**. When performing the trace from a router CLI, use **traceroute**.

Ping and Trace

Ping and trace can be used together to diagnose a problem. Assume that a successful connection has been established between host 1 and Router A, as shown in Figure 11-13 and Example 11-16.

Figure 11-13 Testing the Path to a Remote Host

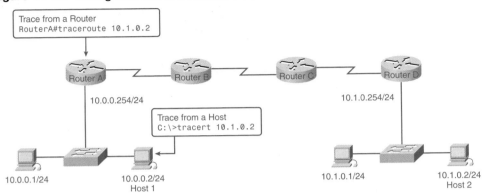

Example 11-16 Ping Failure

```
C:\> ping 10.1.0.2

Pinging 10.1.0.2 with 32 bytes of data:
Request timed out.
Request timed out.
Request timed out.
Request timed out.
Ping statistics for 10.1.0.2:
Packets: Sent = 4, Received = 0, Lost = 4 (100% loss)
```

The ping test failed. This is a test of communication beyond the local network to a remote device. Because the local gateway responded but the host beyond did not, the problem appears to be somewhere beyond the local network. A next step is to isolate the problem to a particular network beyond the local network. The trace commands can show the path of the last successful communication.

Trace to a Remote Host

Like **ping** commands, **trace** commands are entered at the command line and take an IP address as the argument. Assuming that the command will be issued from a Windows computer, use the **tracert** form, as shown in Example 11-17.

Example 11-17 Trace to Host

```
C:\> tracert 10.1.0.2

Tracing route to 10.1.0.2 over a maximum of 30 hops
1  2 ms  2 ms  2 ms  10.0.0.254
2  *  *  *  Request timed out.
3  *  *  *  Request timed out.
4  ^C
```

The only successful response was from the gateway on Router A. Trace requests to the next hop timed out, meaning that the next hop did not respond. The trace results indicate that the failure is therefore in the internetwork beyond the LAN.

Testing Sequence: Putting It All Together

As a review, we walk through the testing sequence in another scenario using Figure 11-14.

Figure 11-14 Testing the Path to a Remote Host

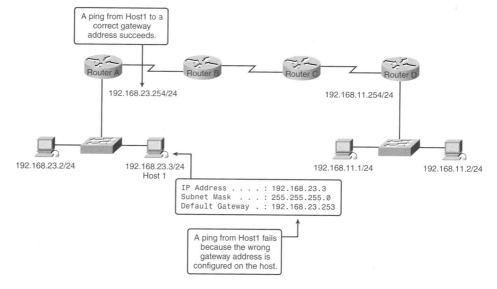

Example 11-18 shows a successful local loopback test.

Example 11-18 Test 1: Local Loopback—Successful

```
C:\> ping 127.0.0.1

Pinging 127.0.0.1 with 32 bytes of data:
Reply from 127.0.0.1: bytes=32 time<1ms TTL=128
Reply from 127.0.0.1: bytes=32 time<1ms TTL=128
Reply from 127.0.0.1: bytes=32 time<1ms TTL=128
Reply from 127.0.0.1: bytes=32 time<1ms TTL=128
Ping statistics for 127.0.0.1:
    Packets: Sent = 4, Received = 4, Lost = 0 (0% loss),
Approximate round trip times in milli-seconds:
    Minimum = 0ms, Maximum = 0ms, Average = 0ms
```

Host 1 has the IP stack properly configured.

Example 11-19 shows a successful local NIC test.

Example 11-19 Test 2: Local NIC—Successful

```
C:\> ping 192.168.23.3

Pinging 192.168.23.3 with 32 bytes of data:
Reply from 192.168.23.3: bytes=32 time<1ms TTL=128
Reply from 192.168.23.3: bytes=32 time<1ms TTL=128
Reply from 192.168.23.3: bytes=32 time<1ms TTL=128
Reply from 192.168.23.3: bytes=32 time<1ms TTL=128
Ping statistics for 192.168.23.3:
    Packets: Sent = 4, Received = 4, Lost = 0 (0% loss),Approximate round trip times
    in milli-seconds:
    Minimum = 0ms, Maximum = 0ms, Average = 0ms
```

The IP address is properly assigned to the NIC, and the electronics in the NIC respond to the IP address.

The third test shows a successful local gateway ping, as shown in Example 11-20.

Example 11-20 Test 3: Ping Local Gateway—Successful

```
C:\> ping 192.168.23.254

Pinging 192.168.23.254 with 32 bytes of data:
Reply from 192.168.23.254: bytes=32 time<1ms TTL=128
Reply from 192.168.23.254: bytes=32 time<1ms TTL=128
Reply from 192.168.23.254: bytes=32 time<1ms TTL=128
Reply from 192.168.23.254: bytes=32 time<1ms TTL=128
Ping statistics for 192.168.23.254:
    Packets: Sent = 4, Received = 4, Lost = 0 (0% loss),
    Approximate round trip times in milli-seconds:
    Minimum = 0ms, Maximum = 0ms, Average = 0ms
```

The default gateway is operational. This also verifies the operation of the local network.

Example 11-21 shows a failed remote host ping.

Example 11-21 Test 4: Ping Remote Host—Failure

```
C:\> ping 192.168.11.1

Pinging 192.168.11.1 with 32 bytes of data:
Request timed out.
Request timed out.
Request timed out.
Request timed out.
Ping statistics for 192.168.11.1:
    Packets: Sent = 4, Received = 0, Lost = 4 (100% loss)
```

This is a test of the communication beyond the local network. Because the gateway responded but the host beyond did not, the problem appears to be somewhere beyond the local network.

Example 11-22 shows a traceroute to a remote host.

Example 11-22 Test 5: Traceroute to Remote Host—Failure at First Hop

```
C:\> tracert 192.168.11.1

Tracing route to 192.168.11.1 over a maximum of 30 hops
  1 * * * Request timed out.
  2 * * * Request timed out.
  3 ^C
```

There appear to be conflicting results. The default gateway responds, indicating that there is communication between host 1 and the gateway. On the other hand, the gateway does not appear to be responding to traceroute. One explanation is that the local host is not configured properly to use 192.168.23.254 as the default gateway. To confirm this, examine the configuration of host 1, as shown in Example 11-23.

Example 11-23 Test 6: Examine Host Configuration for Proper Local Gateway—
                Incorrect

```
C:\> ipconfig

Windows IP Configuration
Ethernet adapter Local Area Connection:
        IP Address. . . . . . . . . . . . : 192.168.23. 3
        Subnet Mask . . . . . . . . . . : 255.255.255.0
        Default Gateway . . . . . . . : 192.168.23.253
```

From the output of the **ipconfig** command, you can determine that the gateway is not properly configured on the host. This explains the false indication that the problem was in the internetwork beyond the local network. Even though the address 192.168.23.254 responded, this was not the address configured in host 1 as the gateway.

Unable to build a frame, host 1 drops the packet. In this case, there is no response indicated from the trace to the remote host.

Packet Tracer
☐ Activity

Test Host Connectivity with Ping (11.3.5.3)

In this activity, you will use the various **ping** commands to identify network connectivity problems. Use file e1-11353.pka on the CD-ROM that accompanies this book to perform this activity using Packet Tracer.

Packet Tracer
☐ **Activity**

Test Host Connectivity with Traceroute (11.3.5.4)

In this activity, you will use the **tracert** and **traceroute** commands to observe a path used across an internetwork. Use file e1-11354.pka on the CD-ROM that accompanies this book to perform this activity using Packet Tracer.

Monitoring and Documenting Networks

Now that you have learned how to configure a basic network and how to verify connectivity, the following sections present the steps involved in monitoring and documenting the network.

Basic Network Baselines

One of the most effective tools for monitoring and troubleshooting network performance is to establish a *network baseline*. A baseline is a process for studying the network at regular intervals to ensure that it is working as designed. It is more than a single report detailing the health of the network at a certain point in time. Creating an effective network performance baseline is accomplished over a period of time. Measuring performance at varying times and loads will assist in creating a better picture of overall network performance.

The output derived from network commands can contribute data to the network baseline.

One method for starting a baseline is to copy and paste the results from an executed **ping**, **trace**, or other relevant command into a text file. These text files can be time stamped with the date and saved to an archive for later retrieval.

An effective use of the stored information is to compare the results over time. Among items to consider are error messages and the response times from host to host. If there is a considerable increase in response times, there can be a latency issue to address.

The importance of creating documentation cannot be emphasized enough. Verification of host-to-host connectivity, latency issues, and resolutions of identified problems can assist a network administrator in keeping a network running as efficiently as possible.

Corporate networks should have extensive baselines, more extensive than we can describe in this book. Professional-grade software tools are available for storing and maintaining baseline information.

Host Capture

One common method for capturing baseline information is to copy the output from the command-line window and paste it into a text file. To capture the results of the **ping** command, begin by executing a command at the command line similar to this one. Substitute a valid IP address on your network.

```
C:\> ping 10.66.254.159
```

The reply will follow the command.

With the output still in the command window, follow these steps:

How To

Step 1.   Right-click in the command prompt window, and then choose **Select All**.

Step 2.   Press Ctrl-C to copy the output.

Step 3.   Open a text editor.

Step 4.   Press Ctrl-V to paste the text.

Step 5.   Save the text file with the date and time as part of the filename.

Run the same test over a period of days and save the data each time. An examination of the files will begin to reveal patterns in network performance and provide the baseline for future troubleshooting.

When selecting text from the command window, right-click and choose **Select All** to copy all the text in the window. Use the **Mark** command to select a portion of the text.

IOS Capture

Capturing **ping** command output can also be completed from the IOS prompt. The following steps describe how to capture the output and save it to a text file.

When using HyperTerminal for access, the steps are as follows:

Step 1.   Choose **Transfer** > **Capture Text**.

Step 2.   Click **Browse** to locate or type the name of the saving file.

Step 3.   Click **Start** to begin capturing text.

Step 4.   Execute the **ping** command in the user EXEC mode or at the privileged EXEC prompt. The router will place the text displayed on the terminal in the location chosen.

Step 5.   View the output to verify that it was not corrupted.

Step 6.   Choose **Transfer** > **Capture Text** and then click **Stop Capture**.

Data generated using either the computer prompt or the router prompt can contribute to the baseline. For additional information on baselines, use the following URL:

http://www.cisco.com/warp/public/126/HAS_baseline.html#why

Capturing and Interpreting Trace Information

As previously discussed, trace can be used to trace the steps, or hops, between hosts. If the request reaches the intended destination, the output shows every router that the packet traverses. This output can be captured and used in the same way that ping output is used.

Sometimes the security settings at the destination network will prevent the trace from reaching the final destination. However, you can still capture a baseline of the hops along the path.

Recall that the form for using trace from a Windows host is **tracert**. Example 11-24 shows a sample output of a trace from your computer to www.cisco.com.

Example 11-24 tracert Sample Output

```
C:\> tracert..www.cisco.com


Tracing route to WWW.CISCO.COM
1    1 ms      <1 ms     < 1 ms     192.168.0.1
2    20 ms     20 ms     20 ms      nexthop.wa.ii.net [203.59.14.16]
3    20 ms     19 ms     20 ms      gi2-4.per-qvl-bdr1.ii.net [2003.215.4.32]
4    79 ms     78 ms     78 ms      gi0-14-0-0.syd-ult-core1.ii.net [203.215.20.2]
5    79 ms     81 ms     79 ms      202.139.19.33
6    227 ms    228 ms    227 ms     203.0208.148.17
7    227 ms    227 ms    227 ms     203.208.149.34
8    225 ms    225 ms    226 ms     208.30.205.145
9    236 ms    249 ms    233 ms     s1-bb23-ana-8-0-0.sprintlink.net [144.232.9.23]
10   241 ms    244 ms    240 ms     s1-bb25-sj-9-0.sprintlink.net[144.232.20.159]
11   238 ms    238 ms    239 ms     s1-gw8-sj-10-0.spritlink.net [144.232.3.114]
12   238 ms    239 ms    240 ms     144.228.44.14
13   240 ms    242 ms    248 ms     sjce-dmzbb-gw1.cisco.com [128.107.239.89]
```

The steps for saving the trace output are identical to the steps for saving ping output: Select the text from the command window and paste it into a text file.

The data from a trace can be added to the data from the **ping** commands to provide a combined picture of network performance. For example, if the speed of a **ping** command decreases over time, compare the **tracert** output for the same time period. Examining the response times in a hop-by-hop comparison can reveal a particular point of longer response time. This delay can be because of congestion at that hop creating a bottleneck in the network.

Another case might show that the hop pathway to the destination can vary over time as the routers select different best paths for the trace packets. These variations can show patterns that could be useful in scheduling large transfers between sites.

Capturing the **traceroute** output can also be done from the router prompt. The following steps show how to capture the output and save it to a file.

Recall that the form of trace for the router CLI is **traceroute**.

When using HyperTerminal, follow these steps:

Step 1.   Choose **Transfer > Capture Text**.

Step 2.   Click **Browse** to locate or type the name of the saving file.

Step 3.   Click **Start** to begin capturing text.

Step 4.   Execute the **traceroute** command in user EXEC mode or at the privileged EXEC prompt. The router will place the text displayed on the terminal in the location chosen.

Step 5.   View the output to verify that it was not corrupted.

Step 6.   Choose **Transfer** > **Capture Text**, and then click **Stop Capture**.

Store the text files generated by these tests in a safe location, along with the rest of the network documentation.

Learning About the Nodes on the Network

If an appropriate addressing scheme exists, identifying IPv4 addresses for devices in a network should be simple. Identifying the physical (MAC) addresses, however, can be daunting. You would need access to all the devices and sufficient time to view the information, one host at a time. Because this is not a practical option in many cases, there is an alternate means of MAC address identification using the **arp** command.

The **arp** command provides the mapping of physical addresses to known IPv4 addresses. A common method for executing the **arp** command is to execute it from the command prompt. This method involves sending out an ARP request. The device that needs the information sends out a broadcast ARP request to the network, and only the local device that matches the IP address of the request sends back an ARP reply containing its IP-MAC pair.

To execute an **arp** command at the command prompt of a host, enter the following:

```
C:\> host1>arp -a
```

As shown in Figure 11-15 and Example 11-25, the **arp** command lists all devices currently in the ARP cache, which includes the IPv4 address, physical address, and type of addressing (static/dynamic) for each device.

```
Example 11-25 arp Command Output
C:\> arp -a

Internet Address        Physical Address        Type
10.0.0.2                00-08-a3-b6-ce-04       dynamic
10.0.0.3                00-0d-56-09-fb-d1       dynamic
10.0.0.4                00-12-3f-d4-6d-1b       dynamic
10.0.0.254              00-10-7b-e7-fa-ef       dynamic
```

Figure 11-15 Learning About the Nodes on the Network

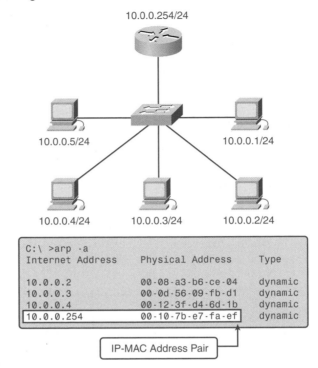

Notice that the IP address 10.0.0.254 is paired with the MAC address 00-10-7b-e7-fa-ef, the MAC address of the router interface in Figure 11-15.

The router cache can be cleared by using the **arp-d** command, in the event the network administrator wants to repopulate the cache with updated information.

Note

The ARP cache is only populated with information from devices that have been recently accessed. To ensure that the ARP cache is populated, ping a device so that it will have an entry in the ARP table.

Ping Sweep

Another method for collecting MAC addresses is to employ a ping sweep across a range of IP addresses. A *ping sweep* is a scanning method that can be executed at the command line or by using network administration tools. These tools provide a way to specify a range of hosts to ping with one command.

Using the ping sweep, network data can be generated in two ways. First, many of the ping sweep tools construct a table of responding hosts. These tables often list the hosts by IP address and MAC address. This provides a map of active hosts at the time of the sweep.

As each ping is attempted, an ARP request is made to get the IP address in the ARP cache. This activates each host with recent access and ensures that the ARP table is current. The **arp** command can return the table of MAC addresses, as discussed previously, but now there is reasonable confidence that the ARP table is up to date.

Switch Connections

One additional tool that can be helpful is a mapping of how hosts are connected to a switch. This mapping can be obtained by issuing the **show mac-address-table** command.

Using a command line from a switch, enter the **show** command with the **mac-address-table** argument:

```
Sw1-2950# show mac-address-table
```

See Example 11-26 for a sample output.

Example 11-26 show mac-address-table Output

```
Sw1-2950# show mac-address-table


Mac Address Table
```

Vlan	Mac Address	Type	Ports
— —	— — — — .	— — — —	— — .
All	0014.a8a8.8780	STATIC	CPU
All	0100.0ccc.cccc	STATIC	CPU
ALL	0010.0ccc.cccd	STATIC	CPU
All	0100.0cdd.dddd	STATIC	CPU
1	0001.e640.3b4b	DYNAMIC	Fa0/23
1	0002.fde1.6acb	DYNAMIC	Fa0/14
1	0006.5b88.dfc4	DYNAMIC	Gi0/2
1	0006.5bdd.6fee	DYNAMIC	Fa0/23
1	0006.5bdd.7035	DYNAMIC	Fa0/23
1	0006.5bdd.72fd	DYNAMIC	Fa0/23
1	0006.5bdd.73b0	DYNAMIC	Fa0/23
1	000e.0cb6.2b51	DYNAMIC	Fa0/2
1	000f.8f28.b7b5	DYNAMIC	Fa0/18
1	0011.1165.8acf	DYNAMIC	Fa0/1
1	0013.720b.40c3	DYNAMIC	Fa0/19

The table in Example 11-26 lists the MAC address of the hosts that are connected to this switch. Like other output in the command window, this information can be copied and pasted into a file. Data can also be pasted into a spreadsheet for easier manipulation later.

An analysis of this table also reveals that the Fa0/23 interface is either a shared segment or is connected to another switch. Several MAC addresses are representing multiple nodes. This is an indication that a port is connected to another intermediary device such as a hub, wireless access point, or another switch.

Summary

This chapter introduced the issues to be considered when connecting and configuring computers, switches, and routers to build an Ethernet-based local-area network. The Cisco IOS Software and the configuration files for routers and switches were presented. This included accessing and using the IOS CLI modes and configuration processes, and understanding the significance of the prompt and help functions.

Managing IOS configuration files and using a methodical structured approach to testing and documenting network connectivity are key network administrator and network technician skills.

The following is a summary of IOS features and commands:

User EXEC mode:

.   **enable:** Enter privileged EXEC mode

Privileged EXEC mode:

copy running-config startup-config: Copy the active configuration to NVRAM

copy startup-config running-config: Copy the configuration in NVRAM to RAM

erase startup-configuration: Erase the configuration located in NVRAM

ping ip_address: Ping to that address

traceroute ip_address: Trace each hop to that address

show interfaces: Display statistics for all interfaces on a device

show clock: Show the time set in the router

show version: Display currently loaded IOS version, hardware, and device information

show arp: Display the ARP table of the device

show startup-config: Display the saved configuration located in NVRAM

show running-config: Display the contents of the currently running configuration file

show ip interface: Display IP statistics for interface(s) on a router

configure terminal: Enter terminal configuration mode

Terminal configuration mode:

hostname *hostname***:** Assign a host name to device

enable password *password***:** Set an unencrypted enable password

enable secret *password***:** Set a strongly encrypted enable password

service password-encryption: Encrypt display of all passwords except secret

banner motd# *message* **#:** Set a message-of-the-day banner

line console 0: Enter console line configuration mode

line vty 0 4: Enter virtual terminal (Telnet) line configuration mode

interface *interface_name***:** Enter interface configuration mode

Line configuration mode:

login: Enable password checking at login

password *password***:** Set line password

Interface configuration mode:

ip address *ip_address netmask***:** Set interface IP address and subnet mask

description *description***:** Set interface description

clock rate *value***:** Set clock rate for DCE device

no shutdown: Set interface to up

shutdown: Administratively set interface to down

Labs

The labs available in the companion *Network Fundamentals, CCNA Exploration Labs and Study Guide* (ISBN 1-58713-203-6) provide hands-on practice with the following topics introduced in this chapter:

Lab 11-1: Network Latency Documentation with Ping (11.4.3.3)

In this lab, you will use the **ping** command to document network latency. You will also compute various statistics on the output of a ping capture and measure delay effects from larger datagrams.

Lab 11-2: Basic Cisco Device Configuration (11.5.1)

In this lab, you will configure common settings on a Cisco router and Cisco switch.

Lab 11-3: Managing Device Configuration (11.5.2)

In this lab, you will configure common settings on a Cisco router, save the configuration to a TFTP server, and restore the configuration from a TFTP server.

Lab 11-4: Configure Host Computers for IP Networking (11.5.3)

In this lab, you will create a small network that requires connecting network devices and configuring host computers for basic network connectivity. The appendix in the lab is a reference for configuring the logical network.

Lab 11-5: Network Testing (11.5.4)

In this lab, you will create a small network that requires connecting network devices and configuring host computers for basic network connectivity. SubnetA and SubnetB are subnets that are currently needed. SubnetC, SubnetD, SubnetE, and SubnetF are anticipated subnets, not yet connected to the network.

Lab 11-6: Network Documentation with Utility Commands (11.5.5)

Network documentation is an important tool for the network administrator. A well-documented network can save network engineers significant amounts of time in troubleshooting and planning future growth.

In this lab, you will create a small network that requires connecting network devices and configuring host computers for basic network connectivity. SubnetA and SubnetB are subnets that are currently needed. SubnetC is an anticipated subnet, not yet connected to the network.

Lab 11-7: Case Study: Datagram Analysis with Wireshark (11.5.6)

Upon completion of this exercise, you will know how a TCP segment is constructed and be able to explain the segment fields. You will also know how an IP packet is constructed and be able to explain the packet fields. You will know how an Ethernet II frame is constructed, be able to explain the frame fields, and know the contents of an ARP Request and an ARP Reply.

Packet Tracer
☐ Companion

Many of the hands-on labs include Packet Tracer companion activities, where you can use Packet Tracer to complete a simulation of the lab. Look for this icon in *Network Fundamentals, CCNA Exploration Labs and Study Guide* (ISBN 1-58713-203-6) for hands-on labs that have Packet Tracer companion activities.

Check Your Understanding

Complete all the review questions listed here to test your understanding of the topics and concepts in this chapter. Appendix A, "Check Your Understanding and Challenge Questions Answer Key," lists the answers.

1. Which command turns on a router interface?

   A. Router(config-if)#**enable**

   B. Router(config-if)#**no down**

   C. Router(config-if)#**s0 active**

   D. Router(config-if)#**interface up**

   E. Router(config-if)#**no shutdown**

2. What is the purpose of the IOS **enable secret** command?

   A. To set password protection on incoming Telnet sessions

   B. To set password protection on the console terminal

   C. To allow a user access to user mode

   D. To allow a user to enter a password that will be encrypted.

3. Which command will display statistics for all interfaces configured on a router?

   A. **list interfaces**

   B. **show interfaces**

   C. **show processes**

   D. **show statistics**

4. What command will display a list of commands available for viewing the status of the router?

   A. Router#**?show**

   B. Router# **sh?**

   C. Router# **show ?**

   D. Router# **help**

   E. Router# **status ?**

5. An administrator configures a new router and names it SanJose. The administrator needs to set a password that will be required to establish a console session with the router. What command should be issued by the administrator to set the console password to CISCO?

   A. SanJose(config)#**enable password CISCO**

   B. SanJose(config)#**line con 0**

      SanJose(config-line)#**login**

      SanJose(config-line)#**enable password CISCO**

   C. SanJose(config)#**enable console password CISCO**

   D. SanJose(config)#**line con 0**

      SanJose(config-line)#**login**

      SanJose(config-line)#**password CISCO**

6. What type of cable is used to initially configure a router?

7. The console port can be used for which of the following? (Choose three.)

   A. Debugging

   B. Password recovery

   C. Routing data between networks

   D. Troubleshooting

   E. Connecting one router to another

8. What do routers use to select best paths for outgoing data packets?

   A. ARP tables

   B. Bridging tables

   C. Routing tables

   D. Switching tables

9. What is setup mode?

Challenge Questions and Activities

These questions require a deeper application of the concepts covered in this chapter.

1. Terminal emulation software, such as HyperTerminal, can be used to configure a router. Which of the following HyperTerminal options, shown in Figure 11-16, are correctly set to allow configuration of a Cisco router. (Choose three.)

Figure 11-16 HyperTerminal

A. Bits per second

B. Data bits

C. Parity

D. Stop bits

E. Flow control

2. A router is composed of many internal components. Where are the main configuration files of the router stored?

3. Select the statement that correctly describes flash memory in a router.

A. Holds the startup configuration by default

B. Stores Cisco IOS Software images

C. Stores routing table information by default

D. Maintains the only copy of an IOS image after the router is booted

To Learn More

The IOS feature set of Cisco routers and switches varies significantly across the model range of these devices. This chapter has introduced some of the basic IOS commands and features that are common across most devices. Although some of the more advanced features are covered in later Cisco courses, often during the regular day-to-day administration of a network, other information might be required more immediately.

The Cisco website, http://www.cisco.com, is the source of the technical documentation used to install, operate, and troubleshoot Cisco networking devices. A free Cisco.com registration provides access to online tools and information. You should register on the website to make use of this resource during your study and to prepare for using it when in the workplace.

An example of the technical documentation available from Cisco.com is the procedure used to recover lost or forgotten passwords on a device. This chapter explained the importance of securing access to the IOS with the use of encrypted passwords. However, for a number of reasons, a password can be lost or forgotten, thereby preventing access to the device.

A search for password recovery documents for the 1841 router and 2960 switch (the current recommended CCNA Exploration lab devices) on Cisco.com returned the following documents that provide the procedures to follow:

- http://www.cisco.com/warp/public/474/pswdrec_1700.pdf
- http://www.cisco.com/warp/public/474/pswdrec_2900xl.pdf

Check Your Understanding and Challenge Questions Answer Key

Chapter 1

Check Your Understanding

1. C. Instant messaging is the only answer that is both text based and real time.

2. B. An extranet provides as-needed access for external vendors and customers to a secure corporate network. An intranet is for internal users.

3. Wikis

4. C. Considering the importance of traffic flow when managing data is a function of a quality of service (QoS) strategy. Network administrators would evaluate the network traffic to determine a QoS strategy.

5. protocols

6. A, B. A quality of service strategy first classifies traffic based on requirements and then assigns priorities to the classifications as needed by the owners of the network. The network administrator can give different priorities to e-mail, web traffic, and movies.

7. media

8. B, D. Two components of a network's architecture are scalability, which is planning for growth, and fault tolerance, which includes redundant links. The other answers describe either users of the network or the product of it (data transfer).

9. icons

10. B, C, and E. Circuit-switched networks did not automatically establish alternative circuits in the event of circuit failure and required that an open circuit between network endpoints be established, even if data was not being actively transferred between locations. Also, the establishment of simultaneous open circuits for fault tolerance is costly.

11. A, B, C. Packet-switched, connectionless data communications technology can rapidly adapt to the loss of data transmission facilities and efficiently utilizes the network infrastructure to transfer data, and data packets can travel multiple paths through the network simultaneously. D and E refer to connections being established, which is not the nature of connectionless data communications.

12. router

13. B. QoS establishes priorities for different communications. It is not required to rate all network communication, just to give priority to what is deemed important.

14. B. Convergence is combining different technologies, such as telephone, video, and text, on one network platform.

15. packets

16. B. Only the cut cable pertains to infrastructure security. The others refer to content security. The unsecured wireless network might be allowed in network plans, but care must be taken to keep sensitive information beyond its reach.

Challenge Questions and Activities

1. B, D. It is possible that music and video downloads could take too much bandwidth and processing, disrupting the conference. Better QoS would give the video session priority over the download and avoid disruption.

2. C. The connection is established and exclusive, so it is privately circuit switched. Circuit-switched connections are connection oriented.

Chapter 2

Check Your Understanding

1. C. IP addressing is a concern of the OSI network layer (Layer 3). Physical addressing happens at OSI Layer 2.

2. channel

3. B, C. A MAC address is the physical address burned on to the OSI Layer 2 network interface card. Logical addressing happens at OSI Layer 3.

4. D. Encapsulating into TCP segments occurs at OSI Layer 4, so the next encapsulation is at OSI Layer 3, which includes adding source and destination IP addresses to the segment headers and converting them into packets. Then the physical addressing is added and the data is converted to bits.

5. B. A protocol describes a specific set of rules for communication, including message formatting and encapsulation.

6. proprietary

7. B. TCP has control features pertaining to OSI Layer 4, FTP is an application (Layer 7), and IP and TFTP are network layer protocols (Layer 3).

8. NIC, or network interface card

9. C. Segmentation, which occurs at OSI Layer 4, is the correct answer.

10. router

11. B. Multiplexing is the correct term.

12. A. IP addressing is an OSI Layer 3 function. All others are OSI Layer 2 functions.

13. B. The correct order is application, presentation, session, transport, network, data link, physical.

14. B. End-to-end message delivery is the concern of OSI Layer 4, the transport layer.

Challenge Questions and Activities

1. B, D, F, G. The OSI presentation and session layers are combined into the application layer of the TCP/IP model. The OSI data link and physical layers are combined into the network access layer of TCP/IP. The transport and network layers have parallel layers in TCP/IP.

2. C, E. LANs are connected by WANs. WANs connect networks through telephone service providers (TSP). Logical addressing is used between networks, and physical addressing, or MAC addresses, are used inside LANs.

Chapter 3

Check Your Understanding

1. D. Layer 7 is the application layer and its components: applications, services, and protocols.

2. B. The functionality of the TCP/IP application layer protocols fits roughly into the framework of the top three layers of the OSI model: application, presentation, and session.

3. C. Hypertext Transfer Protocol (HTTP) is used to transfer files that make up the web pages of the World Wide Web. DNS is used to resolve Internet names to IP addresses, and Telnet is used to provide remote access to servers and networking devices.

4. D. Post Office Protocol (POP) uses UDP port 110.

5. A. GET is a client request for data.

6. D. E-mail, the most popular network service, has revolutionized how people communicate through its simplicity and speed. Choice A. is incorrect, because HTTP is a protocol, not a service.

7. B. To successfully transfer files, FTP requires two connections between the client and the server: one for commands and replies and another for the actual file transfer.

8. C. The Dynamic Host Configuration Protocol (DHCP) enables clients on a network to obtain IP addresses and other information from a DHCP server.

9. A. The Linux and UNIX operating systems provide a method of sharing resources with Microsoft networks using a version of SMB called SAMBA.

10. C. A connection using Telnet is called a VTY session, or connection.

11. eBay is a client/server application. eBay is implemented as a web server that responds to web client (browser) requests using HTTP.

12. client. Even though a device can serve as a client and a server at times, the device requesting a service is defined as the client and the device providing the service is defined as the server.

13. GET, PUT, and POST. GET is a request; PUT and POST provide uploading.

14. Assignment of IP addresses, subnet masks, and default gateway. The protocol automates the assignment of IP addresses, subnet masks, gateway, and other IP networking parameters.

15. FTP stands for File Transfer Protocol. It is used to move files on the network. FTP was developed to allow file transfers between a client and a server. An FTP client is an application that runs on a computer that is used to push and pull files from a server.

Challenge Questions and Activities

1. 1. The user inputs data using a hardware interface.

2. The application layer prepares human communication for transmission over the data network.

3. Software and hardware convert data to a digital format.

4. Application services initiate the data transfer.

5. Each layer plays its role, and the OSI layers encapsulate data down the stack. Encapsulated data travels across the media to the destination. OSI layers at the destination decapsulate the data up the stack.

6. Data is ready to be processed by the end device.

2. Application software has two forms: applications and services:

- Applications are designed to interact with us. Application is software for the user. If the device is a computer, the application is typically initiated by the user. Although there can be many layers of support underneath, application software provides an interface between humans and the hardware. The application will initiate the data transfer process when the user clicks the Send button or performs a similar action.

- Services are background programs that perform a particular function in the data network. Services are invoked by a device connecting to the network or by an application. For example, a network service can provide functions that transmit data or provide conversion of data in a network. In general, services are not directly accessible or seen by the end user. They provide the connection between an application and the network.

3. The source end of data communication is referred to as the *server*, and the receiving end is called the *client*. The client and server processes are application layer services that provide the foundation for data network connectivity.

In some cases, the servers and clients are devices that perform that role specifically and exclusively. For example:

- A central file server can contain an organization's business data files that employees access using their client-only workstation.

- Internet-based examples include web servers and mail servers, where many users access a centrally provided service.

- In other situations, such as file sharing over a home network, individual devices can perform both server and client roles at different times.

   Servers are both a repository and a source of information such as text files, databases, pictures, video, or audio files that have been previously recorded.

   Client processes at the other end of the communication across the data network allow the user to make requests to obtain the data from a server. The client software typically uses a program initiated by a user. The client initiates communication data flow from the server by sending requests for the data to the server. The server responds by starting to send one or more streams of data to the client. In addition to the actual data transfer, this exchange can include user authentication and identification of the data file to be transferred.

Examples of common client/server services include the following:

- DNS (Domain Name Service)

- FTP

- HTTP

- Telnet (Teletype Network Service)

4. Client/server data transfer specifically refers to the centralized source end of data communication as the server and the receiving end as the client.

   With peer-to-peer data transfer, both client and server services are used within the same conversation. Either end of the communication can initiate the exchange, and both devices are considered equal in the communication process. The devices on either end of the communication are called peers.

   In contrast to a client/server model, where a server is typically a centralized repository and responds to requests from many clients, peer-to-peer networking has distributed data. Furthermore, after the communication is established, the peers communicated directly; the data is not processed at the application layer by a third device on the network.

5. Functions specified by application layer protocols include

   - The processes that are to occur at either end of the communication. This includes what has to happen to the data and how the data is to be structured.

   - The types of messages. These can include requests, acknowledgments, data messages, status messages, and error messages.

   - The syntax of the message. This gives the expected order of information (fields) in a message.

   - The meaning of the fields within specific message types. The meaning has to be constant so that the services can correctly act in accordance with the information.

   - The message dialogs. This determines which messages elicit which responses so that the correct services are invoked and the data transfer occurs.

6. DNS, HTTP, SMB, and SMTP/POP use a client/server process.

   - Domain Name System (DNS) provides users with an automated service that matches or resolves resource names and e-mail domains with the required numeric device network addresses. This service is available to any user connected to the Internet and running an application layer application such as a web browser or e-mail client program.

   - HTTP was originally developed to publish and retrieve HTML pages and is now used for distributed, collaborative, hypermedia information systems. HTTP is used by the World Wide Web (WWW) to transfer data from web servers to web clients.

- Server Message Block (SMB) describes the structure of sharing network resources, such as directories, files, printers, and serial ports, between computers.

- Simple Mail Transport Protocol (SMTP) transfers outbound e-mails from the e-mail client to the e-mail server and transports e-mail between e-mail servers and so enables e-mail to be exchanged over the Internet.

- POP, or POP3 (Post Office Protocol version 3), delivers e-mail from the e-mail server to the client.

7. DNS includes standard queries, responses, and data formats. DNS protocol communications are carried in a single format called a message. This message format is used for all types of client queries and server responses, for error messages, and for the transfer of resource record information between servers.

HTTP is a request/response protocol:

- A client application layer application, typically a web browser, sends a request message to the server.

- The server responds with the appropriate message.

HTTP also includes messages to upload data to the server, such as when completing an online form.

SMB messages use a common format to

- Start, authenticate, and terminate sessions

- Control file and printer access

- Allow an application to send or receive messages to or from another device

SMTP specifies commands and replies that relate to session initiation, mail transaction, forwarding mail, verifying mailbox names, expanding mailing lists, and the opening and closing exchanges.

POP is a typical client/server protocol, with the server listening for client connections and the client initiating the connection to the server. The server can then transfer the e-mail.

DNS, HTTP, SMB, and SMTP/POP use client/server, request/response messages. Whereas users see the applications that use HTTP (a web browser), SMB (file manager), and SMTP/POP (e-mail client), a DNS operation underlies these applications and is truly transparent to the user.

Chapter 4

Check Your Understanding

1. B. Port 80 is the standard port number used with HTTP. Port 23 is Telnet, port 20 is FTP, and port 110 is POP3.

2. C. Port number 25 is used for SMTP.

3. A, D. TCP is a reliable, connection-oriented protocol.

4. C. TCP uses flow control to avoid buffer overflows.

5. D. Port numbers 0 to 1023 are the well-known () ports. Port numbers 1024 to 49151 are the registered ports and are used by the host for dynamic port allocation. Port numbers 49152 to 65535 are the private and dynamic ports.

6. D, E. The receiving host has to acknowledge receipt of the packets and then reassemble them in the right order.

7. Answers could vary and could include (a) keeping track of the individual conversations taking place between applications on the source and destination hosts, (b) segmenting data and adding a header to identify and manage each segment, (c) using the header information to reassemble the segments into application data, and (d) passing the assembled data to the correct application.

8. A. Sequence numbers are used in the TCP headers because segments could arrive at their destination in a different order than when they were sent. The numbers allow the receiving host to reassemble them in the proper order.

9. D. In TCP, window size is used to manage flow control.

10. D. Port numbers allow you to track multiple conversations generated by the same host using the same IP address.

11. Segmentation of the data, in accordance with transport layer protocols, provides the means to both send and receive data when running multiple applications concurrently on a computer.

12. Reliability means ensuring that each segment that the source sends arrives at the destination.

13. Web browsing, e-mail, file transfer.

14. DNS, video streaming, Voice over IP (VoIP).

15. The source and destination port number.

16. A sequence number allows the transport layer function on the destination host to reassemble segments in the order in which they were transmitted.

Challenge Questions and Activities

1. 7. The acknowledgment number is always one more than the last segment received.

2. D. A flag is set in the segment header. If this flag actually reads 17, it is identified as a UDP header.

3. B. Port 53 is used for DNS.

4. Netstat lists the protocol in use, the local address and port number, the foreign address and port number, and the state of the connection. Netstat also displays active TCP connections, ports on which the computer is listening, Ethernet statistics, the IP routing table, IPv4 statistics (for IP, ICMP, TCP, and UDP), and IPv6 statistics (for IPv6, ICMPv6, TCP over IPv6, and UDP over IPv6). Used without parameters, the **netstat** command displays active TCP connections.

5. TCP uses the acknowledgment number in segments sent back to the source to indicate the next byte in this session that the receiver expects to receive.

Chapter 5

Check Your Understanding

1. A. IP provides connectionless network layer services. TCP is connection oriented. UDP is connectionless, but it works at the transport layer.

2. **netstat -r** and **route print**.

3. A, C, D. A routing table contains the next-hop, metric, and destination network address. Routers do not need the source address, last hop, or default gateway to find a path to a network.

4. A, B, D. Reduced network bandwidth, increased overhead, and reduced host functions are three potential results of excessive broadcasts. The other answers can be part of a solution to the problem of excessive broadcasts.

5. Purpose, ownership, and geographic location are three key ways to divide a network.

6. C, D. Delivery reliability is a transport layer concern. Application data analysis is a concern of the presentation layer. Routing, addressing packets with an IP address, encapsulation, and decapsulation are functions of the network layer.

7. B, E. IP stands for the Internet Protocol, which operates at OSI Layer 3 (the network layer). IP encapsulates transport layer segments. IP does not look inside the upper-level PDU, so it has no knowledge of the presentation layer data.

8. Decapsulation.

9. C. Routers and hosts use IP. B is incorrect because IP uses addressing information in the header to determine the best path for a packet. D is incorrect because IP is a "best effort" unreliable protocol.

10. A, D. Network layer encapsulation adds a header to a segment and adds both source and destination IP addresses. Network layer encapsulation happens only on the original host; other devices can read the data, but they do not remove or alter it until the destination network is reached. The network layer converts transport layer segments into packets.

11. B, C. TCP is reliable and connection oriented. IP is unreliable and connectionless. IP operates at the network layer.

12. B. IP encapsulates OSI Layer 4 data. IP can carry voice, video, and other types of data, but "media independent" refers to the OSI Layer 1 medium that carries the data across the networks. IP, or any other communication, can occur without a physical (OSI Layer 1) medium.

13. transport

14. 32. There are four octets (8 bits each) in an IPv4 address.

15. C, E. Dynamic routing adds packet-processing overhead, and routers can use static and dynamic routing simultaneously. Static routing does not require a routing protocol. A default route is an example of a static route. Because static routes must be manually configured and updated, they add to administrative overhead.

Challenge Questions and Activities

1. A, C. When the TTL is 1, it has one hop remaining to be either delivered or discarded. IP does not provide return notification of dropped packets. TCP controls at the destination will request a packet retransmission, but the TCP PDU is never accessed en route.

2. D. The destination host will send a request if the packet does not arrive. IP is connectionless, so there is no reliability built into the protocol. Previous packets with TCP information have arrived at the destination host with "expectational" information. Routing protocols, such as RIP, are used by routers to share route information; they are not involved in TCP/IP reliability.

Chapter 6

Check Your Understanding

1. B, D. 192.168.12.64 /26 and 198.18.12.16 /28 are network addresses.

2. B. 172.31.255.128 /27

3. C. 255.255.252.0

4. B. The four networks are .224, .228, .232, and .236.

5. Hosts with the same network portion of their IPv4 address.

6. The three types of IPv4 addresses are

   ■ **Network address:** The address by which you refer to the network

   ■ **Broadcast address:** A special address used to send data to all hosts in the network

   ■ **Host addresses:** The addresses assigned to the end devices in the network

7. C. 255.255.255.224 provides the 16 addresses required. .224 will provide 30. .240 will provide only 14.

8. The three types of IPv4 addresses are

   ■ **Network address:** Lowest address in the network 0 for each host bit in the host portion of the address.

   ■ **Host address:** Host bits are a unique mix of 1s and 0s within a network.

   ■ **Broadcast address:** Uses the highest address in the network range. The host portion is all 1s.

9. Following are the three forms of IPv4 communication:

   ■ **Unicast:** The process of sending a packet from one host to an individual host

   ■ **Broadcast:** The process of sending a packet from one host to all hosts in the network

   ■ **Multicast:** The process of sending a packet from one host to a selected group of hosts

10. Specified private addresses allow network administrators to allocate addresses to those hosts that do not need to access the Internet.

11. A. The host is using a link-local address. Link-local addresses should not be routed.

12. The allocation of addresses inside the networks should be planned and documented for the following purposes:

   ■ Preventing duplication of addresses

   ■ Providing and controlling access

   ■ Monitoring security and performance

13. Administrators should statically assign addresses to servers, printers, LAN gateway addresses on routers, management addresses on network devices such as switches, and wireless access points.

14. Running out of IPv4 addresses is the primary motivation for developing IPv6.

15. Network devices use the subnet mask to determine the network or subnet address of an IP address that the device is processing.

16. Networks are subnetted to overcome issues with location, size, and control. In designing the addressing, consider these factors for grouping the hosts:

    - Grouping based on common geographic location

    - Grouping hosts used for specific purposes

    - Grouping based on ownership

17. Three tests that use the ping utility are

    - Ping 127.0.0.1: Loopback test to test IP operation

    - Ping the host gateway address or another host on the same network: To determine communication over the local network

    - Ping a host on a remote network: Test device default gateway and beyond

Challenge Questions and Activities

1. The reserved and special IPv4 addresses are

    - **Multicast addresses:** Reserved for special purposes is the IPv4 multicast address range 224.0.0.0 to 239.255.255.255.

    - **Private addresses:** The private address blocks are

        - 10.0.0.0 to 10.255.255.255 (10.0.0.0 /8)

        - 172.16.0.0 to 172.31.255.255 (172.16.0.0 /12)

        - 192.168.0.0 to 192.168.255.255 (192.168.0.0 /16)

        Private space address blocks are set aside for use in private networks. Packets using these addresses as the source or destination should not appear on the public Internet. The router or firewall device at the perimeter of these private networks must block or translate these addresses.

    - **Default route:** The IPv4 default route is 0.0.0.0. The use of this address reserves all addresses in the 0.0.0.0 to 0.255.255.255 (0.0.0.0 /8) address block.

- **Loopback:** The IPv4 loopback address 127.0.0.1 is a reserved address. Addresses 127.0.0.0 to 127.255.255.255 are reserved for loopback, where hosts direct traffic to themselves.

- **Link-local addresses:** IPv4 addresses in the address block 169.254.0.0 to 169.254.255.255 (169.254.0.0 /16) are designated as link-local addresses. These addresses can be automatically assigned to the local host by the operating system in environments where no IP configuration is available. These might be used in a small peer-to-peer network or for a host that could not automatically obtain an address from a Dynamic Host Configuration Protocol (DHCP) server.

- **Test-net addresses:** The address block 192.0.2.0 to 192.0.2.255 (192.0.2.0 /24) is set aside for teaching and learning purposes. These addresses can be used in documentation and network examples. Unlike the experimental addresses, network devices will accept these addresses in their configurations.

2. IPv4 is an unreliable best-effort protocol. ICMPv4 provides a means for network problems such as dropped packets or congestion to be reported to the source network or host. Messages include

- Host Conformation

- Unreachable Destination or Service

- Time Exceeded

- Route Redirection

- Source Quench

Chapter 7

Check Your Understanding

1. The data link layer prepares a packet for transport across the local media by encapsulating it with a header and a trailer to create a frame.

2. MAC methods for shared media are as follows:

- **Controlled:** Each node has its own time to use the medium, a ring topology

- **Contention-based:** All nodes compete for the use of the medium, a bus topology

Media access control in point-to-point connections can be one of the following:

- **Half duplex:** A node can only transmit or receive at one time.

- **Full duplex:** A node can both transmit and receive at the same time.

3. In a logical ring topology, each node in turn receives a frame. If the frame is not addressed to a node, the frame is passed to the next node. If there is no data being transmitted, a signal (known as a token) can be placed on the media. A node can place a frame on the media only when it has the token. This is a controlled media access control technique called token passing.

4. Layer 2 protocols include

   - Ethernet

   - PPP

   - High-Level Data Link Control (HDLC)

   - Frame Relay

   - ATM

5. Typical frame header fields include

   - **Start Frame field:** Indicates the beginning of the frame

   - **Source and Destination address fields:** Indicate the source and destination nodes on the media

   - **Priority/Quality of Service field:** Indicates a particular type of communication service for processing

   - **Type field:** Indicates the upper-layer service contained in the frame

   - **Logical connection control field:** Used to establish a logical connection between nodes

   - **Physical link control field:** Used to establish the media link

   - **Flow control field:** Used to start and stop traffic over the media

   - **Congestion control field:** Indicates congestion in the media

6. A. The node drops the frame. The CRC provides error detection, not error correction, so B is incorrect. C is incorrect because the frame is not forwarded. The interface is not disabled, so D is incorrect.

7. C, D. PPP and HDLC are designed as WAN protocols. 802.11 and Ethernet are LAN protocols, so A and B are incorrect.

8. B. The network layer PDU is encapsulated in the frame. The number of bytes in the payload is variable, so A is incorrect. C is incorrect because the Layer 2 source address is in the address field of the frame header. The data from the application undergoes encapsulation before being passed down to the data link layer, so D is incorrect.

9. B. Nodes compete for the media. Option A is incorrect because contention-based is used on shared media. C is incorrect because one of the primary purposes of Layer 2 is MAC. D is incorrect because taking turns is a function of controlled access.

10. B, C. LLC is the upper sublayer, and MAC is the lower sublayer.

11. D. Virtual circuits establish a logical connection between two devices to provide a logical point-to-point topology. Option A is incorrect because CRC is an error-detection technique. Virtual circuits do not provide an encapsulation technique, so B is incorrect. C is incorrect because virtual circuits can be used over multiple types of physical topologies.

12. Header, data, and trailer.

13. C. The data link layer provides the connection between hardware and software. A is incorrect; this is a role of the application layer. B is incorrect; this is a function of the network layer. D is incorrect; this is a function of the transport layer.

14. D. The logical topology influences MAC. The logical topology can be many types of MAC, so A is incorrect. The MAC sublayer provides the physical address, so B is incorrect. The logical and physical topologies are not always the same, so C is incorrect.

Challenge Questions and Activities

1. The media is a potentially unsafe environment for data. The signals on the media could be subject to interference, distortion, or loss that would substantially change the bit values that those signals represent. To ensure that the content of the received frame at the destination matches that of the frame that left the source node, a transmitting node creates a logical summary of the contents of the frame. This is known as the Frame Check Sequence (FCS) and is placed in the trailer to represent the contents of the frame.

   When the frame arrives at the destination node, the receiving node calculates its own logical summary, or FCS, of the frame. The receiving node compares the two FCS values. If the two values are the same, the frame is considered to have arrived as transmitted. If the FCS values differ, the frame is discarded.

   There is always the small possibility that a frame with a good FCS result is actually corrupt. Errors in bits can cancel each other out when the FCS is calculated. Upper-layer protocols would then be required to detect and correct this data loss.

2. Unlike Layer 3 logical addresses that are hierarchical, physical addresses do not indicate on what network the device is located. If the device is moved to another network or subnet, it will still function with the same Layer 2 physical address.

   Because the frame is only used to transport data between nodes across the local media, the data link layer address is only used for local delivery. Addresses at this layer have no meaning beyond the local network. Compare this to Layer 3, where addresses in the packet header are carried from source host to destination host, regardless of the number of network hops along the route.

3. A logical point-to-point topology connects two nodes directly. In data networks with point-to-point topologies, the MAC protocol can be very simple. All frames on the media can only travel to or from the two nodes. The frames are placed on the media by the node at one end and taken off the media by the node at the other end. In point-to-point networks, if data can only flow in one direction at a time, it is operating as a half-duplex link. If data can successfully flow across the link from each node simultaneously, it is a full-duplex service.

A logical multiaccess topology enables a number of nodes to communicate by using the same shared media. Data from only one node can be placed on the medium at any one time. Every node sees all the frames that are on the medium, but only the node to which the frame is addressed processes the contents of the frame. Having many nodes share access to the medium requires a data link MAC method to regulate the transmission of data and thereby reduce collisions between different signals.

4. If a router is interfacing media of different speeds, the router will have to buffer the frames for transmission. If not enough buffers are available, the packets can be lost.

5. The source addresses are used to identify the source node. In most cases, Layer 2 source addresses are not used. The most common use of source addresses is for security or by switches learning where the host exists. The source address is also used in the creation of dynamic maps such as ARP.

   Both ATM and Frame Relay use a single address in the frame header. These technologies use a single number that represents a connection.

6. The full-duplex communication between the two nodes could have twice the throughput of half-duplex and more than twice the throughput of multiaccess. If the underlying physical media can support it, the two nodes might be able to transmit and receive at full media bandwidth at the same time. This would be twice that of half duplex. Because multiaccess has overhead to control media access, the throughput is less than the bandwidth and, in many cases, much less. This would allow full duplex to have more than twice the throughput of multiaccess.

7. As the router receives a frame on one interface, it decapsulates the frame down to a packet. It then refers to the routing table to determine out which interface the packet should be forwarded. The router then will encapsulate the packet into a frame of the appropriate size for the segment connected to the outbound interface.

Chapter 8

Check Your Understanding

1. physical media

2. D. Encoding represents the data bits by using different voltages, light patterns, or electromagnetic waves as they are placed onto the physical media.

3. NRZ (nonreturn to zero) and Manchester

4. D. The chief purpose of the physical layer is to define the functional specifications for links between end systems and the electrical, optical, and radio signals that carry data. Reliability, path selection, and media access are the tasks of other layers.

5. RJ-45

6. B. Crosstalk is reduced by the twisting of cables in the UTP (unshielded twisted-pair) cable. UTP has no cladding, shielding, or grounding points.

7. pinout

8. B, D, F. The advantages of using fiber-optic cabling include immunity to electromagnetic interference, longer maximum cable length, greater bandwidth reception and decoding requirements, and antenna design.

9. wireless. Because wireless is open to anyone with a wireless receiver, it is more susceptible to security breaches than copper or fiber-optic media.

10. C. Cladding helps prevent light loss. No other listed functions pertain to fiber-optic cable.

11. B, C. Rollovers work in Cisco console ports, and crossovers would connect two switches.

12. rollover cable

13. C. Throughput measures actual data rates. Bandwidth is the line capacity, and goodput measures only the rate of usable application layer data bits that arrive.

14. C. 1 Mbps = 1,000,000 (10^6) bps

15. B. Synchronization between devices allows them to know when frames begin and end.

16. B. Bit time changes depending on the speed of the NIC. The time it takes a bit to traverse the network is slot time (which counts bits, not bytes).

Challenge Questions and Activities

1. B. The two hosts with straight-through cables will link to the hub. The third host is using the original cable, which is a crossover cable appropriate for peer-to-peer connections, but will not link to a hub from a host.

2. A, C, E. A: The A wing, having the most connected workers, can have too much traffic on the cable and packets can be getting dropped. C: Refrigerator compressors and microwave ovens can cause interference on a network. E: Because orders are up, the wing's proximity to the manufacturing shed could be because of electromagnetic interference from the machines on the production line.

   Incorrect answers: B: The janitor's actions are intermittent, and the network problems are consistent. D and F: These differences should provide more reliability, not less.

Chapter 9

Check Your Understanding

1. The two data link sublayers are as follows:

   - **Logical Link Control (LLC):** Handles the communication between the upper layers and the lower layers, typically hardware.

   - **MAC:** The Ethernet MAC sublayer has the following responsibilities:

     - Data encapsulation

     - Media access control

     - Addressing

2. A. Poor scalability

3. C. Frame Check Sequence. The FCS (4 bytes in length) field is used to detect errors in a frame.

4. C. An Ethernet MAC address is a 48-bit binary value expressed as 12 hexadecimal digits.

5. An Ethernet MAC address is used to transport the frame across the local media.

6. C. The Ethernet broadcast MAC address is FF-FF-FF-FF-FF-FF. Frames with this destination address are delivered to and processed by all the devices on that LAN segment.

7. B. The jam signal in CSMA/CD makes sure that all sending nodes see the collision.

8. The group of connected devices that can cause collisions to occur with each other is known as a collision domain. Collision domains occur at Layer 1 of the networking reference model.

9. C. Historic Ethernet and legacy Ethernet both use logical bus topology.

10. B. Is a separate collision domain

11. D. Learning. When a frame of data is received from a node, the switch reads the source MAC address and saves the address to the lookup table against the incoming interface. The switch now knows out which interface to forward frames with this address.

12. D. Learning. When a frame of data is received from a node, the switch reads the source MAC address and saves the address to the lookup table against the incoming interface. The switch now knows out which interface to forward frames with this address.

13. When a host has a packet to send to an IP address that does not have a map in the ARP cache.

14. C. Flooding. When the switch does not have a destination MAC address in its lookup table, it sends (floods) the frame out all interfaces except the one on which the frame arrived.

15. B. Timing can be more easily distorted with the shorter bit times.

Challenge Questions and Activities

1. (Can vary.) With the same frame format, different implementations of Ethernet (PHY) maintain compatibility. Changing the frame format would have resulted in different "Ethernets" that were not compatible.

2. (Can vary.) The primary reason is that the frames are not sent to every device. If a device receives a frame, it can be examined to obtain the sensitive information.

Chapter 10

Check Your Understanding

1. C. One of the primary responsibilities of a DCE device is to provide clocking to the routers for synchronization.

2. A. To have at least 100 hosts, your networks must go up by 128. So, you would have to subnet 178.5.0.0/16 to 178.5.0.0/25. This would make your first network 178.5.0.0, your second network 178.5.0.128, your third network 178.5.1.0, your fourth network 178.5.1.128, your fifth network 178.5.2.0, and so on.

3. D. If you increment your network by 32, you lose two (the network and broadcast address), so you must jump up to 64, which equals 128 + 64 = 192.

4. B. A 248 means that you are incrementing your network in steps of 8 (128 + 64 = 192 + 32 = 224 + 16 = 240 + 8 = 248). If you increment in steps of 8, your networks would be 154.65.128.0 to 154.65.136.0, the next network. That would mean 154.65.128.0 would be the network address, 154.65.128.1 to 154.65.128.254 would be the hosts, and 154.65.128.255 would be the broadcast address.

5. D. 100BASE-FX uses fiber cabling and supports full duplex up to a distance of 2000 meters.

6. True.

7. A straight-through UTP cable would be used to connect these devices:

   ■ Switch to router

   ■ PC to switch

   ■ PC to hub (if used)

8. A crossover UTP cable would be used to connect these devices:

   ■ Switch to switch

   ■ Switch to hub (if used)

   ■ Hub to hub (if used)

   ■ PC to PC

   ■ PC to router

9. The terms DCE and DTE are described as follows:

   ■ **Data communication equipment (DCE):** A device that supplies the clocking to another device. It is typically a device at the WAN access provider end of the link.

   ■ **Data terminal equipment (DTE):** A device that receives clocking from another device and adjusts accordingly. Typically this device is at the WAN customer or user end of the link.

   In a lab environment, generally connect two routers with a serial cable, providing a point-to-point WAN link. In this case, decide which router is going to be the one in control of the clocking. Cisco routers are DTE devices by default but can be configured to act as DCE devices.

10. The following criteria should be considered:

- Cost

- Cable/wireless

- Speed

- Ports

- Expandability

- Manageability

- Features

11. End devices requiring IP addresses include

- User computers

- Servers

- Other end devices such as printers, IP phones, and IP cameras

Network devices requiring IP addresses include

- Router LAN gateway interfaces

- Router WAN (serial) interfaces

12. Reasons for subnetting a network include

- Manage broadcast traffic

- Similar network requirements

- Security

13. The five factors to consider are as follows:

- Cable length

- Cost

- Bandwidth

- Ease of installation

- Susceptibility to EMI/RFI

Challenge Questions and Activities

1. C, D, F. A 255.255.255.248 mask would mean that the networks would increment in steps of 8. In other words, the network addresses would be 0, 8, 16, 24, 32, 40, 48, 56, 64, 72, 80, 88, 96, 104, 112, 120, 128, 136, 144, 152, 160, 168, 176, 184, 192 , 200, 208, 216, 224, 232, 240, and 248. Hence:

   A. would not be correct. 192.168.200.87 would be the broadcast address for the network 192.168.200.80.

   B. would not be correct. 194.10.10.104 would be a network address.

   C. 223.168.210.100 is correct, a host on the 223.168.210.96 network.

   D. 220.100.100.154 is correct, a host on the 220.100.100.152 network.

   E. 200.152.2.160 is not correct. It is a network address.

   F. 196.123.142.190 is correct, a host on the 196.123.142.184 network.

2. E. A /20 would yield 4096 possible IP addresses, minus 1 for the network address, minus 1 for the broadcast address, and minus 1 for the host address already used. That would provide you with 4093 IP addresses left for network devices.

3. A. Using the fact that a /27 would increment the networks by 32, you have the following networks, per Figure 10-27: 192.168.102.0, 192.168.102.32, 192.168.102.64, 192.168.102.96, 192.168.102.128, 192.168.102.160, 192.168.102.192, and 192.168.102.224. Option A is correct because the server address of 192.168.102.147 falls out of the 192.168.102.96 network.

4. E. The only option is to use fiber-optic cable. Thinnet and Thicknet would provide EMI protection but could not provide the bandwidth.

5. B, D. Initial configuration of a Cisco router must be accomplished through the console port, and that requires a rollover cable and terminal emulation software.

6. The four types of interfaces are as follows:

   - **Ethernet:** This interface is used for connection of the LAN device, which includes computers and switches. This interface can also be used to connect routers.

   - **Serial:** This interface is used for connection of the WAN devices to the CSU/DSU. Clock rate and addressing are assigned to these interfaces.

   - **Console:** This is the primary interface for gaining initial access to and configuration of a Cisco router or switch and is the primary means of troubleshooting. It is important to note that through physical access to the console interface router, an unauthorized person can interrupt or compromise network traffic. Physical security is extremely important.

   - **Auxiliary (AUX):** This interface is used for remote, out-of-band management of the router. Typically a modem is connected to the AUX interface for dialup access. From a security standpoint, having the ability to remotely dial in to a network device also requires vigilant management.

Chapter 11

Check Your Understanding

1. E. The **no shutdown** command, given at the interface prompt, will bring the interface up. The **enable** command moves you from operating at the user mode to the privileged mode. **S0 active** and **interface up** are not legal IOS commands.

2. D. The **enable secret** command allows you to input a password that will be used to get you from the user to the privilege mode. This password will be encrypted.

3. B. The **show interfaces** command will display statistics for all interfaces configured on a router. It is the only legal command listed.

4. C. The **show** command will provide you with numerous commands that can be used for viewing router status. The **?** will list those commands.

5. D. The administrator should issue the following commands, which are presented in the correct sequence, and the proper format:

   SanJose(config)#**line con 0**

   SanJose(config-line)#**login**

   SanJose(config-line)#**password CISCO**

6. A rollover cable connected to the serial port of a computer is used.

7. A, B, D. The console port is used strictly to access the configuration of the router; it cannot be used for data routing or for connecting one router to another.

8. C. Routers store routing tables that basically match network addresses to the best exit interface.

9. Setup mode allows you to configure a router by answering a series of questions posed to you.

Challenge Questions and Activities

1. B, C, D. Bits per second would have to be set to 9600 to be correct, and Flow control would have to be set to None to be correct.

2. The router stores the running-configuration file in RAM. The router stores the start-up configuration file, the file created when you save the running-configuration file, in NVRAM.

3. B. The IOS is stored in flash and then run and/or uncompressed in RAM. All other choices are stored either in RAM or NVRAM.

4B/5B   An encoding scheme (called 4B/5B coding). 4B/5B uses 5-bit symbols or codes to represent 4 bits of data. 4B/5B is used in 100BASE-TX Ethernet.

ACK   A 1-bit flag in the TCP header that indicates the acknowledgment field is valid.

acknowledgment   A notification sent from one network device to another to confirm that some event (for example, receipt of a message) has occurred.

acknowledgment number   A 32-bit field in the TCP segment header that specifies the sequence number of the next byte this host expects to receive as a part of the TCP session. It is used to recognize lost packets and flow control.

address pool   The range of IP addresses that can be assigned by the DHCP server.

Address Resolution Protocol (ARP)   The method for finding a host's hardware address from its IPv4 network layer address.

administratively scoped address   An IPv4 multicast address that is restricted to a local group or organization. *See also* limited-scope address.

AND   One of three basic binary logic operations. ANDing yields the following results: 1 AND 1 = 1, 1 AND 0 = 0, 0 AND 1 = 0, 1 AND 0 = 0.

argument   Additional data that is provided with a command to provide information used by the execution of the command. IOS command arguments are entered at the CLI after the command.

ARP cache   A logical storage in a host's RAM to store ARP entries. *See also* ARP table.

ARP poisoning   A technique used to attack an Ethernet network by sending fake ARP messages to an Ethernet LAN. These frames contain false MAC addresses that "confuse" network devices, such as switches. As a result, frames intended for one node can be mistakenly sent to another node. *See also* ARP spoofing.

ARP spoofing   A technique used to attack an Ethernet network by sending fake ARP messages to an Ethernet LAN. These frames contain false MAC addresses that "confuse" network devices, such as switches. As a result, frames intended for one node can be mistakenly sent to another node. *See also* ARP poisoning.

ARP table   A logical storage in a host's RAM to store ARP entries. *See also* ARP cache.

association identity (AID)   A number used in the 802.11 header to specify the session between a wireless client and the access point.

asynchronous   Communication that does not use a common clock between the sender and receiver. To maintain timing, additional information is sent to synchronize the receive circuit to the incoming data. For Ethernet at 10 Mbps, the Ethernet devices do not send electrical signals for synchronization.

attenuation   The loss of communication signal on the media. This loss is due to degradation of the energy wave over time.

authentication   A process used to verify the identity of a person or process.

authoritative   A source of information that is highly reliable and known for its accuracy.

backoff algorithm   The retransmission delay used with CSMA/CD when a collision occurs. The algorithm forces each sender that detected the collisions to delay a random amount of time before attempting to retransmit.

bandwidth   In networking, a measurement of the speed of bits that can be transmitted over a particular link. It is the amount of data that can be transmitted in a certain amount of time. For digital bandwidth, it is usually expressed in bits per second (bps).

best-effort   Network protocols or technologies that do not use the acknowledgment system to guarantee reliable delivery of information.

binary   A numbering system characterized by 1s and 0s.

bit   Binary digit used in the binary numbering system. Binary digits are units of information storage and communication in computing. Each bit can be either a 0 or a 1.

bit time   The time required to send a single bit over some transmission medium. The time can be calculated as 1/speed, where speed is the number of bits per second sent over the medium.

blog   A website where entries are made in journal style. A blog is created by the user, who can make changes to the blog through templates or by altering the HTML code of the blog itself. Visitors can leave posts to the blog. Blog is short for weblog.

bridge   A device that connects multiple network segments at the data link layer of the OSI model. Bridges were the predecessor to LAN switches.

bridge table   The table used by a switch or bridge that associates MAC addresses with the outgoing port. The switch or bridge uses this table for its forwarding/filtering decisions. *See also* switch table.

bridging   The process of forwarding frames in a switch or a bridge from one port to another port or from segment to segment.

broadcast   A form of transmission where one device transmits to all devices within the network or on another network.

broadcast address   An address used to represent a transmission from one device to all devices. In Ethernet, the special Ethernet address FFFF.FFFF.FFFF is used as a destination MAC address to cause a frame to be sent to all devices on an Ethernet LAN. In IPv4, each subnet has a single broadcast address, which is more commonly called the subnet or directed broadcast address.

broadcast domain   A logical network composed of all the computers and networking devices that can be reached by sending a frame to the data link layer broadcast address.

burned-in address (BIA)   The MAC address that is permanently assigned to a LAN interface or NIC. It is called burned-in because the address is burned into a chip on the card, and the address cannot be changed. Also called universally administered address (UAA).

cache   A temporary storage where data that has been retrieved or calculated and is accessed frequently can be stored. After the data is stored in the cache, the processes can access the cached copy instead of accessing the original data. A cache reduces the average access time and reduces the overhead of recalculating the data.

carrier   A signal on a medium used to support the transmission of data. Data is "carried" over the medium by modulation (combining the data signal with the carrier signal).

carrier sense multiple access (CSMA)   Media access methodology in which a node wishing to transmit listens for a carrier wave before trying to send. If a carrier is sensed, the node waits for the transmission in progress to finish before initiating its own transmission.

carrier sense multiple access collision avoid (CSMA/CA)   A mechanism used to regulate the transmission of data onto a network medium. CSMA/CA is similar to CSMA/CD except the devices first request the right to send, which hopefully avoids collisions. CSMA/CA is used in 802.11 WLANs.

carrier sense multiple access collision detect (CSMA/CD)   The MAC algorithm used by Ethernet devices in a shared media. The protocol requires a node wishing to transmit to listen for a carrier signal before trying to send. If a carrier is sensed, the node waits for the transmission in progress to finish before initiating its own transmission. If a collision occurs and is detected, the sending node uses the backoff algorithm before retransmitting.

channel   A communication path over a medium used to transport information from a sender to a receiver. Multiple channels can be multiplexed over a single cable.

channel service unit/data service unit (CSU/DSU)   A device that connects a local digital telephone loop for a WAN circuit to a serial interface on a network device, typically connecting to a router. The CSU/DSU performs physical (Layer 1) signaling on WAN circuits.

classful addressing   A unicast IP address that is considered to have three parts: a network part, a subnet part, and a host part. The term *classful* refers to the fact that the classful network rules are first applied to the address, and then the rest of the address can be separated into a subnet and host part to perform subnetting. In the early days of IPv4, IP addresses were divided into five classes, namely, Class A, Class B, Class C, Class D, and Class E. Classful addressing is not generally practiced in current network implementations.

classless addressing   An IPv4 addressing scheme that uses a subnet mask that does not follow classful addressing limitations. It provides increased flexibility when dividing ranges of IP addresses into separate networks. Classless addressing is considered the best in current network implementations.

client   A network device that accesses a service on another computer remotely by accessing the network.

cloud   In networking, a symbol used when drawing network diagrams that represent a part of the network whose details can be ignored for the purposes of the diagram.

coaxial cable/coax   Cable consisting of a hollow outer cylindrical conductor that surrounds a single inner wire conductor. The cable has three different layers of material surrounding the inner conducting material: the outer conductor, the insulator, and the protective outer jacket.

code group   A grouping of code that meets a certain, already specified, condition for entering in that certain group.

collaboration tool   Something that helps people collaborate. Many people use the term *collaboration tool* in a software context, for example, collaboration software such as Google Docs and Microsoft Sharepoint Server. Going back in time, a collaboration tool was a piece of paper that many used and edited.

collaborative   Information systems that allow the creation of a document or documents that can be edited by more than one person in real time.

collision   In Ethernet, the results of two nodes transmitting simultaneously. The signals from each device are damaged when they combine on the media.

collision domain   A physical or logical area in a LAN where the signals sent by the interfaces (including NICs and network device interfaces) may be subject to being combined (a collision). Within a collision domain, if a device sends a frame on a network segment, every other device on that same segment will receive that frame. In an Ethernet network, repeaters and hubs increase the size of collision domains by propagating the signals. LAN switches and bridges separate collision domains.

connection-oriented   Communication where the sender and receiver must prearrange for communications to occur; otherwise, the communication fails.

connectionless   Any communication in which the sender and receiver do not prearrange for communications to occur.

console port   A port on Cisco devices to which a terminal or computer with a terminal emulator is connected to the network device in order to communicate and configure the network device.

control data   Data that directs a process. A flag in a data-link frame is an example of control data.

convergence   Another form of the root word *converge* in the phrase "converged network." This kind of network aggregates various forms of traffic such as voice, video, and data on the same network infrastructure. A more common usage represents the process by which routers recognize that something has occurred that changes some routers' routes, reacts to the event, and finds the now-currently best routes.

crossover cable   A UTP cable used in Ethernet in which some pairs of twisted-pair wires are crossed when comparing the RJ-45 connectors on either end of the cable. 10BASE-T and 100BASE-T crossover cables connect the pair at pins 1 and 2 on each end to pins 3 and 6 on the other end. 1000BASE-T crossover cables also cross the pairs at pins 4 and 5 and pins 7 and 8.

cyclic redundancy check (CRC)   A type of hash function (one-way encryption) that is used to produce a small, fixed-size checksum of a block of data, such as a packet or a computer file. A CRC is computed and appended before transmission or storage, and verified afterward by the recipient to confirm that no changes have happened in transit.

daemon   A computer program that runs in the background and is usually initiated as a process. Daemons often support server processes.

data   Application layer protocol data unit.

data communications equipment (DCE)   The devices and connections of a communications network that comprise the network end of the user-to-network interface. The DCE provides a physical connection to the network, forwards traffic, and provides a clocking signal used to synchronize data transmission between DCE and DTE devices. Modems and interface cards are examples of DCE. Compare to DTE.

data network   A digital network used to send data between computers.

data terminal equipment (DTE)   Device at the user end of a user-network interface that serves as a data source, destination, or both. DTE connects to a data network through a DCE device (for example, a modem) and typically uses clocking signals generated by the DCE. DTE includes such devices as computers, protocol translators, and multiplexers. Compare to DCE.

decapsulation   A process by which an end device, after it receives data over some transmission medium, examines the headers and trailers at each successive higher layer, eventually handing the data to the correct application. Sometimes called de-encapsulation.

default gateway   A device on a network that serves as an access point to other networks. A default gateway is used by a host to forward IP packets that have destination addresses outside the local subnet. A router interface typically is used as the default gateway. When the computer needs to send a packet to another subnet, it sends the packet to its default gateway. Also known as default router.

default route   Routing table entry that is used to direct frames for which a next hop is not explicitly listed in the routing table. This route is used to forward a packet when no other known route exists for a given packet's destination address.

delimiter   This field of a frame signals the beginning or end of a frame.

destination IP address   The Layer 3 address to which the data is going.

deterministic   Refers to whether the performance of a device, attached to a particular type of LAN, can be accurately predicted (determined). Token Ring LANs are deterministic, but Ethernet LANs are nondeterministic.

digital logic   Also known as Boolean algebra. These consist of the AND, OR, and IF operations.

directed broadcast   A term that describes IPv4 packets sent to all hosts in a particular network. In a directed broadcast, a single copy of the packet is routed to the specified network, where it is broadcast to all hosts on that network.

directly connected network   A network that is connected to a device's interface. For example, networks that interface with the router are known to be directly connected. Devices learn their initial IP routes based on being connected to these subnets.

dispersion   The spreading of a light signal caused by light signals traveling at different speeds through a fiber.

distributed   A method of computer processing in which different parts of a program run simultaneously on two or more computers that are communicating with each other over a network.

DNS resolver   The client part of the DNS client-server mechanism. A DNS resolver creates queries sent across a network to a name server, interprets responses, and returns information to the requesting programs.

domain name   A name, as defined by DNS, that uniquely identifies a computer in the Internet. DNS servers can then respond to DNS requests by supplying the IP address that is used by the computer that has a particular domain name. This term also refers to the part of a URL that identifies a single company or organization, such as ciscopress.com.

Domain Name System (DNS)   An Internet-wide system by which a hierarchical set of DNS servers collectively hold all the name-IP address mappings, with DNS servers referring users to the correct DNS server to successfully resolve a DNS name.

dotted decimal   A convention for writing IP addresses with four decimal numbers, ranging from 0 to 255 (inclusive), with each octet (each decimal number) representing 8 bits of the 32-bit IP address. The term originates from the fact that each of the four decimal numbers is separated by a period (or dot).

download   To transfer data from the computer functioning as a server to the client computer you are using.

Dynamic Host Configuration Protocol (DHCP) A protocol used to dynamically assign IP configurations to hosts. The services defined by the protocol are used to request and assign an IP address, default gateway, and DNS server address to a network host.

dynamic or private ports   TCP and UDP ports that range from 49152 to 65535 and are not used by any defined server applications.

dynamic routing   Routing that adjusts automatically to network topology or traffic changes.

electromagnetic interference (EMI)   Interference by magnetic signals caused by the flow of electricity. EMI can cause reduced data integrity and increased error rates on transmission channels. The physics of this process are that electrical current creates magnetic fields, which in turn cause other electrical currents in nearby wires. The induced electrical currents can interfere with proper operation of the other wire.

enable password   Unencrypted password used to allow access to privileged EXEC mode from IOS user EXEC mode.

encapsulation   The process by which a device adds networking headers and trailers to data from an application for the eventual transmission of the data onto a transmission medium.

encode   To change the energy levels transmitted over some networking medium to transmit bits over that medium.

encryption   The process of obscuring information to make it unreadable without special knowledge, sometimes referred to as scrambling. The process takes the data to be encrypted and applies a mathematical formula to it along with a secret number (called an encryption key). The resulting value, which is called an encrypted packet, is sent through a network.

end device   A device such as a desktop or mobile device that is used by an end user.

Ethernet PHY   The physical interface transceivers. It deals with Layer 1 (the physical layer, hence the PHY) of Ethernet.

extended star   A network topology characterized by a central location connected to multiple hubs. In an extended star, these interconnected hubs may be connected to more hubs. It is essentially a hierarchical topology but typically is drawn with the central site in the center, with the rest of the topology radiating outward in all directions. This is sometimes called a *hierarchical star*.

extranet   Part of a company's intranet that is extended to users outside the company (that is, normally over the Internet).

Fast Ethernet   A common name for Ethernet technology that operates at 100 Mbps.

fault tolerance   The design on networks that can continue to operate without interruption in the case of hardware, software, or communications failures.

fiber-optic cable   Physical medium that uses glass or plastic threads to transmit data. A fiber-optic cable consists of a bundle of these threads, each of which is capable of transmitting data into light waves.

fiber-optics   The glass fibers inside certain cables over which light is transmitted to encode 0s and 1s.

filtering   In Ethernet, the process performed by a bridge or switch when it decides that it should not forward a frame out another port.

FIN   A 1-bit field in the TCP header that is used by a device that wants to terminate its session with the other device. This is done by inserting the FIN flag in the flag field found in the TCP segment.

firewall   Any combination of hardware device and/or software application designed to protect network devices from outside network users and/or malicious applications and files.

flash   A removable component that has memory space for storage. Used on the router or switch for storing the compressed operating system image.

flooding   A process used by a switch or bridge to forward broadcasts and unknown destination unicasts. The bridge/switch forwards these frames out all ports except the port on which the frame was received.

flow control   The management of data flow between devices in a network. It is used to avoid too much data arriving before a device can handle it, causing data overflow.

forwarding   In Ethernet, the process performed by a bridge or switch when it decides that it should send a frame out another port.

fragmentation   The dividing of IP datagrams to meet the MTU requirements of a Layer 2 protocol.

frame   The Layer 2 PDU that has been encoded by a data link layer protocol for digital transmission. Some different kinds of frames are Ethernet frames and PPP frames.

full duplex   Communication that allows receipt and transmission simultaneously. A station can transmit and receive at the same time. There are no collisions with full-duplex Ethernet transmission.

gateway   Normally, a relatively general term that refers to different kinds of networking devices. Historically, when routers were created, they were called gateways.

Gigabit Ethernet   Ethernet that transmits data at 1,000,000,000 (one billion) bits per second.

global configuration mode   From the privileged mode, you can enter the device's global configuration mode. From global configuration mode, you can configure global parameters or enter other configuration submodes such as interface, router, and line configuration submodes.

globally scoped addresses   Unique addresses that are public domain addresses.

goodput   Application-level throughput. It is the number of useful bits per unit of time from a certain source address to a certain destination, excluding protocol overhead and excluding retransmitted data packets.

half duplex   Communication that only allows one station to receive while the other station is transmitting.

hierarchical addressing   An addressing scheme in which a network is partitioned into sections, with the section identifier forming one part of each destination's address and the destination identifier forming another.

high-order bit   The portion of a binary number that carries the most weight, the one written farthest to the left. High-order bits are the 1s in the network mask.

hop   The passage of a data packet between two network nodes (for example, between two routers).

host   A network device that has an IPv4 address assigned to it to communicate over a network.

host address   IPv4 address of a network host. When talking about host addresses, they are the network layer addresses.

host group   A group defined by a class D address (multicast, ranging from 224.0.0.0 to 239.255.255.255), whereupon hosts can pertain to multicast groups. Hosts that have the same multicast address are part of the same host group.

hub   In Ethernet, a device that receives an electrical signal in one port, interprets the bits, and regenerates a clean signal that it sends out all other ports of the hub. Typically, it also supplies several ports, which are oftentimes RJ-45 jacks.

hybrid fiber-coax (HFC)   A network that incorporates both optical fiber along with coaxial cable to create a broadband network. Commonly used by cable TV companies.

Hypertext Transfer Protocol (HTTP)   Defines the commands, headers, and processes by which web servers and web browsers transfer files.

instant messaging (IM)   Real-time communication between two or more people through text. The text is conveyed through computers connected over a network such as the Internet. Files can also be transferred through the IM program to share files. A good example of an IM program is Microsoft Messenger.

Institute of Electrical and Electronics Engineers (IEEE)   An international, nonprofit organization for the advancement of technology related to electricity. IEEE maintains the standards defining many LAN protocols.

interframe spacing   A time period between Ethernet frames that allows fairness with the CSMA/CD algorithm. Without a space between frames—in other words, without some time with no frames being sent—a NIC might always listen for silence, never hear silence, and therefore never get a chance to send a frame.

intermediary device   A device that connects end devices to the network or interconnects different networks. A router is an example of an intermediary device.

International Organization for Standardization (ISO)   An international standards body that defines many networking standards. Also, the standards body that created the OSI model.

Internet   The network that combines enterprise networks, individual users, and ISPs into a single global IP network.

Internet Assigned Numbers Authority (IANA)   An organization that assigns the numbers important to the proper operation of the TCP/IP protocol and the Internet, including assigning globally unique IP addresses.

Internet backbone   A high-speed line or series of connections that forms a major pathway within a network. The term is often used to describe the main network connections comprising the Internet.

Internet Control Message Protocol (ICMP)   As part of the TCP/IP Internet layer, ICMP defines protocol messages used to inform network engineers of how well an internetwork is working. For example, the **ping** command sends ICMP messages to determine whether a host can send packets to another host.

Internet Engineering Task Force (IETF)   The standards body responsible for the development and approval of TCP/IP standards.

Internet service provider (ISP)   A company that helps create the Internet by providing connectivity to enterprises and individuals, as well as interconnecting to other ISPs to create connectivity to all other ISPs.

internetwork   A combination of many IP subnets and networks, as created by building a network using routers. The term *internetwork* is used to avoid confusion with the term *network*, because an internetwork can include several IP networks.

Interpret as Command (IAC)   In the Telnet application, commands are always introduced by a character with the decimal code 255, known as an Interpret as Command (IAC) character.

intranet   A corporate system such as a website that is explicitly used by internal employees. Can be accessed internally or remotely.

IP (Internet Protocol)   Network layer protocol in the TCP/IP stack offering a connectionless internetwork service. IP provides features for addressing, type-of-service specification, fragmentation and reassembly, and security. Documented in RFC 791.

IP address   A 32-bit number, written in dotted decimal notation, used by the IP to uniquely identify an interface connected to an IP network. It is also used as a destination address in an IP header to allow routing, and as a source address to allow a computer to receive a packet and to know which IP address to send a response to.

IP header   The header defined by the IP. Used to create IP packets by encapsulating data supplied by a higher-layer protocol (such as TCP) behind an IP header.

jam signal   In a shared media Ethernet network, a signal generated by the transmitting devices that detects the collision. The jam signal will continue to transmit for a specific period to ensure that all devices on the network detect the collision. The jam signal is a part of CSMA/CD.

keyword   Used in the CLI following the command. Keywords are parameters that are used with the command from a set of predefined values.

kilobits per second (kbps)   A unit of measurement of the number of times 1000 bits can be transmitted in 1 second. 1 kbps = 1000 bps.

latency   The time that passes while some event occurs. In networking, latency typically refers to the time that occurs between when something is sent in a network until it is received by another device.

layered model   A model that consists of various layers that enable the development and explanation of technology to be done on a modular basis. This allows interoperability among different technologies among the different layers.

limited broadcast   A broadcast that is sent to a specific network or series of networks.

limited-scope address   An IPv4 multicast address that is restricted to a local group or organization. *See also* administratively scoped address.

link-local address   An IPv4 address in the range of 169.254.1.0 to 169.254.254.255. Communication using these addresses is used with a TTL of 1 and limited to the local network.

local-area network (LAN)   A network created for devices located in a limited geographic area, through which the company owning the LAN has the right to run cables.

locally administered address (LAA)   A MAC address that can be configured on a device. The LAA can be used in place of the BIA. This means that you can replace a NIC or use a substitute device without changing the address used by the network to access the station.

Logical Link Control (LLC)   The IEEE 802.2 standard that defines the upper sublayer of the Ethernet Layer 2 specifications (and other LAN standards).

logical network   A group of devices associated by the arrangement of a hierarchical addressing scheme. Devices in the same logical network that share a common network portion of their Layer 3 addresses.

logical topology   A map of the devices on a network representing how the devices communicate with each other.

loopback   A special reserved IPv4 address, 127.0.0.1, that can be used to test TCP/IP applications. Packets sent to 127.0.0.1 by a computer never leave the computer or even require a working NIC. Instead, the packet is processed by IP at the lowest layer and is then sent back up the TCP/IP stack to another application on that same computer.

low-order bit   Represents the 0 in the binary number. In an IP subnet mask, the low-order bits represent the host portion. Sometimes called the host portion of bits.

MAC table   On a switch, a table that lists all known MAC addresses, and the bridge/switch port out which the bridge/switch should forward frames sent to each MAC address.

Mail User Agent (MUA)   Program used to download and send e-mail. E-mail clients use POP3 to receive e-mails and use SMTP to send e-mails. Also called an e-mail client.

Manchester encoding   Line code in which each bit of data is signified by at least one voltage level transition.

maximum transmission unit (MTU)   The largest IP packet size allowed to be sent out a particular interface. Ethernet interfaces default to an MTU of 1500 because the data field of an Ethernet frame should be limited to 1500 bytes, and the IP packet sits inside the Ethernet frame's data field.

Media Access Control (MAC)   The lower of the two sublayers of the IEEE standard for Ethernet. It is also the name of that sublayer (as defined by the IEEE 802.3 subcommittee).

media independent   The networking layers whose processes are not affected by the media being used. In Ethernet, these are all the layers from the LLC sublayer of data link upward.

media-dependent interface (MDI)   The normal operation of Ethernet ports on a hub. In this mode, the mapping of the wire pairs used in the hub port is in a normal configuration. Some hubs provide a media-dependent interface/media-dependent interface, crossover (MDI/MDIX) switch. This switch is usually associated with a particular port. With this switch set correctly, you can connect a network device to the associated port using a straight-through Ethernet cable rather than a crossover Ethernet cable.

media-dependent interface, crossover (MDIX)
MDIX is an alternative operation of Ethernet ports on a hub. In this mode, the mapping of the wire pairs used in the hub port is in a crossover configuration. This allows you to use a straight-through cable to interconnect the hub to another hub.

megabits per second (Mbps) A unit of measurement of the number of times 1,000,000 bits can be transmitted in 1 second. 1 Mbps = 1,000,000 bps.

metropolitan-area network (MAN) A network with a geographic size between a LAN and a WAN. Typically used by service providers to create a high-speed network in a major metropolitan area where many customers might want high-speed services between large sites around a city.

most significant bit The bit position in a binary number having the greatest value. The most significant bit is sometimes referred to as the leftmost bit.

multicast client A member of a multicast group. Every multicast client in each group has the same IP address. Multicast addresses begin with 224.*.*.* and end with 239.*.*.*.

multicast group A group that receives a multicast transmission. The members of a multicast group have the same multicast IP addressing to receive the same transmission (a one-to-many transmission).

multiplexing A process where multiple digital data streams are combined into one signal.

network 1. Collection of computers, printers, routers, switches, and other devices that can communicate with each other over some transmission medium. 2. Command that assigns a NIC-based address to which the router is directly connected.

network address A dotted decimal number defined by the IPv4 protocol to represent a network or subnet. It represents the network that hosts reside in. Also called a network number or network ID.

Network Address Translation (NAT) Translation of RFC 1918 addresses to public domain addresses. Because RFC 1918 addresses are not routed on the Internet, hosts accessing the Internet must use public domain addresses.

network baseline A collection of data that establishes a reference for network performance and behavior over a period of time. This reference data is used in the future to assess the health and relative growth of network utilization.

network interface card (NIC) Computer hardware, typically used for LANs, that allows the computer to connect to some networking cable. The NIC can then send and receive data over the cable at the direction of the computer.

network segment A part of a computer network that every device communicates with using the same physical medium. Network segments are extended by hubs or repeaters.

Network Time Protocol (NTP) A protocol for synchronizing the clocks of computer systems over packet-switched data networks. NTP uses UDP port 123 as its transport layer.

node A data link layer term describing a device connected to a network.

noise In networking, a general term referring to any energy signal on a transmission medium that is not part of the signal used to transmit data over that medium.

nonreturn to zero (NRZ) Line code in which 1s are represented by one significant condition and 0s are represented by another.

nonvolatile RAM (NVRAM) Random-access memory that does not lose its contents when the computer is shut down.

nslookup A service or a program to look up information in the DNS (Domain Name System).

octet A group of 8 binary bits. It is similar to, but not the same as, a byte. One application in computer networking is to use octets to divide IPv4 addresses into four components.

Open Systems Interconnection (OSI)
International standardization program created by ISO and ITU-T to develop standards for data networking that facilitate multivendor equipment interoperability.

Optical Time Domain Reflectometer (OTDR) A popular certification method for fiber systems. The OTDR injects light into the fiber and then graphically displays the results of the detected reflected light. The OTDR measures the elapsed transit time of reflected light to calculate the distance to different events. The visual display allows determination of loss per unit length, evaluation of splices and connectors, and fault location. OTDR zooms in to certain locations for a close-up picture of portions of the link.

Organizational Unique Identifier (OUI) The first half of a MAC address. Manufacturers must ensure that the value of the OUI has been registered with the IEEE. This value identifies the manufacturer of any Ethernet NIC or interface.

overhead Resources used to manage or operate the network. Overhead consumes bandwidth and reduces the amount of application data that can be transported across the network.

packet When used generically, this term refers to end-user data along with networking headers and trailers that are transmitted through a network. When used specifically, it is end-user data, along with the network or Internet layer headers and any higher-layer headers, but no lower-layer headers or trailers.

Packet Tracer A drag-and-drop network simulator developed by Cisco to design, configure, and troubleshoot network equipment within a controlled, simulated program environment.

Pad A part of the Ethernet frame that fills in the data field to ensure that the data field meets the minimum size requirement of 46 bytes.

peer A host or node that participates in some form of a group. For example, peer-to-peer technology defines a group of peers that participate jointly in the same activity, each one having a server and client component.

physical address A data link layer address, for example, a MAC address.

physical media The cabling and connectors used to interconnect the network devices.

physical network The connection of devices on a common media. Sometimes a physical network is also referred to as a network segment.

physical topology The arrangement of the nodes in a network and the physical connections between them. This is the representation of how the media is used to connect the devices.

ping sweep A network scanning technique used to identify which host IP addresses are operational.

pinout   Defines which wires in a cable should connect to each pin on the connectors on both ends of a cable. For example, a UTP cable used for Ethernet, using a straight-through cable pinout, connects the wire at pin 1 on one end with pin 1 on the other end, the wire at pin 2 on one end with pin 2 on the other, and so on.

plug-in   In a web browser, an application the browser uses, inside the browser window, to display some types of content. For example, a browser typically uses a plug-in to display video.

podcast   A digital media file or files that are distributed over the Internet using syndication feeds, for playback on portable media players and personal computers.

port   In networking, this term is used in several ways. With Ethernet hub and switch hardware, port is simply another name for interface, which is a physical connector in the switch into which a cable can be connected. With TCP and UDP, a port is a software function that uniquely identifies a software process on a computer that uses TCP or UDP. With PCs, a port can be a physical connector on the PC, like a parallel or USB port.

positional notation   Sometimes called place-value notation, this is a numeral system in which each position is related to the next by a constant multiplier, a common ratio, called the base or radix of that numeral system.

Post Office Protocol (POP)   A protocol that allows a computer to retrieve e-mail from a server.

prefix length   In IP subnetting, this refers to the portion of a set of IP addresses whose value must be identical for the addresses to be in the same subnet.

priority queuing   A routing feature in which frames in an interface output queue are prioritized based on various characteristics such as packet size and interface type.

private address   Defined in RFC 1918, an IP address that does not have to be globally unique because the address exists inside packets only when the packets are inside a single private IP internetwork. Private IP addresses are popularly used in most companies today, with NAT translating the private IP addresses into globally unique IP addresses.

protocol   A written specification that defines what tasks a service or device should perform. Each protocol defines messages, often in the form of headers, plus the rules and processes by which these messages are used to achieve some stated purpose.

protocol data unit (PDU)   A generic term from OSI that refers to the data, headers, and trailers about which a particular networking layer is concerned.

protocol suite   A delineation of networking protocols and standards into different categories, called layers, along with definitions of which sets of standards and protocols need to be implemented to create products that can be used to create a working network.

proxy ARP   A process that uses the same ARP messages as normal ARP, but by which a router replies instead of the host listed in the ARP request. When a router sees an ARP request that cannot reach the intended host, but for which the router knows a route to reach the host, the router acts on behalf of the host and responds to the ARP request with the router's MAC address listed in the ARP reply.

PSH   A 1-bit flag in the TCP header that is used to request to the higher layers for immediate delivery of the packet.

public address   An IP address that has been registered with IANA or one of its member agencies, which guarantees that the address is globally unique. Globally unique public IP addresses can be used for packets sent through the Internet.

pulse amplitude modulation (PAM)   A form of signal modulation where the message information is encoded in the amplitude of a series of signal pulses. It transmits data by varying the amplitudes (voltage or power levels) of the individual pulses. This is now obsolete and has been replaced by pulse code modulation.

quality of service (QoS)   A control mechanism that can provide different priorities to different users or data flows, or guarantee a certain level of performance to a data flow in accordance with requests from the application program.

query   A request for information. Queries are answered with replies.

radio frequency interference (RFI)   Radio frequencies that create noise that interferes with information being transmitted across unshielded copper cabling.

radix   The number of various unique digits, including 0, that a positional numeral system uses to represent numbers. For example, in the binary system (base 2), the radix is 2. In the decimal system (base 10), the radix is 10.

random-access memory (RAM)   Also known as read-write memory, RAM can have new data written to it and can have stored data read from it. RAM is the main working area, or temporary storage, used by the CPU for most processing and operations. A drawback of RAM is that it requires electrical power to maintain data storage. If the computer is turned off or loses power, all data stored in RAM is lost unless the data was previously saved to disk. Memory boards with RAM chips plug into the motherboard.

read-only memory (ROM)   A type of computer memory in which data has been prerecorded. After data has been written to a ROM chip, it cannot be removed and can only be read. A version of ROM known as EEPROM (electronically erasable programmable read-only memory) can be written to. The basic input/output system (BIOS) in most PCs is stored in EEPROM.

real-time   Events or signals that show output as fast as possible, or as they happen.

redundancy   A network architecture designed to eliminate network downtime caused by a single point of failure.

Regional Internet Registries (RIR)   Organizations that are responsible for the allocation and registration of Internet number resources within a particular region of the world. These registries include the American Registry for Internet Numbers (ARIN) for North America; RIPE Network Coordination Centre (RIPE NCC) for Europe, the Middle East, and Central Asia; Asia-Pacific Network Information Centre (APNIC) for Asia and the Pacific region; Latin American and Caribbean Internet Address Registry (LACNIC) for Latin America and the Caribbean region; and African Network Information Centre (AfriNIC) for Africa.

registered ports   Using values between 1024 and 49,151, these numbers are equivalent to well-known ports in concept, but they are specifically used for nonprivileged application processes.

Requests for Comments (RFC)   A series of documents and memoranda encompassing new research, innovations, and methodologies applicable to Internet technologies. RFCs are a reference for how technologies should work.

reserved link-local addresses   The IPv4 multicast addresses 224.0.0.0 to 224.0.0.255. These addresses are to be used for multicast groups on a local network. Packets to these destinations are always transmitted with a Time to Live (TTL) value of 1.

resource records   DNS data records. Their precise format is defined in RFC 1035. The most important fields in a resource record are Name, Class, Type, and Data.

RJ-45   A rectangular cabling connector with eight pins, often used with Ethernet cables.

rollover cable   A UTP cable pinout that specifies that the wire at pin 1 of an RJ-45 connector on one end of the cable connects to pin 8 on the other end; the wire at pin 2 connects to pin 7 on the other end; pin 3 to pin 6; and pin 4 to pin 5. This cable is used for Cisco console cables for routers and switches.

round-trip time (RTT)   The time required for some networking PDUs to be sent and received, and a response PDU to be sent and received. In other words, the time between when a device sends data and when the same device receives a response.

route   Path through an internetwork through which packets are forwarded.

router   A network device, typically connected to a range of LAN and WAN interfaces, that forwards packets based on their destination IP addresses.

routing   The process by which a router receives an incoming frame, discards the data-link header and trailer, makes a forwarding decision based on the destination IP address, adds a new data-link header and trailer based on the outgoing interface, and forwards the new frame out the outgoing interface.

routing protocol   A protocol used between routers so that they can learn routes to add to their routing tables.

routing table   A list that a router holds in memory for the purpose of deciding how to forward packets.

RST   A 1-bit flag in the TCP header that is used to request that a connection be re-established.

runt frame   An Ethernet frame that is less than 64 bytes in size (which is the minimum frame size in an Ethernet network). Runts are caused by collisions and are also known as collision fragments.

scalability   The ability of a protocol, system, or component to be modified to fit a new need.

scheme   A plan, design, or program of action to be followed. Sometimes an addressing plan is called an addressing SCHEME.

scope   The extent of a certain item. For example, an address scope is also known as a range of addresses from the beginning of the range to the end.

Secure Shell (SSH)   (Secure Shell Protocol) A protocol that provides a secure remote connection to a host through a TCP application.

segment   1. A collision domain that is a section of a LAN that is bound by bridges, routers, or switches. 2. In a LAN using a bus topology, a segment is a continuous electrical circuit that is often connected to other such segments with repeaters. 3. When used with TCP, the term *segment* (verb) refers to the work TCP does to accept a large piece of data from an application and break it into smaller pieces. Again with TCP, used as a noun, segment refers to one of those smaller pieces of data.

segmentation   In TCP, the process of taking a large chunk of data and breaking it into small-enough pieces to fit within a TCP segment without breaking any rules about the maximum amount of data allowed in a segment.

selective forwarding   The forwarding of packets where the forwarding decision is taken dynamically, hop by hop, based on the conditions of downstream forwarding nodes.

server   Can refer to computer hardware that is to be used by multiple concurrent users. Alternatively, this term can refer to computer software that provides services to many users. For example, a web server consists of web server software running on some computer.

Server Message Block (SMB)   An application-level network protocol mainly applied to shared access to files, printers, serial ports, and miscellaneous communications between nodes on a network.

session   A related set of communications transactions between two or more network devices.

shielded twisted-pair (STP) cable   A type of network cabling that includes twisted-pair wires, with shielding around each pair of wires, as well as another shield around all wires in the cable.

signal   The optical or electrical impulse on a physical medium for purposes of communication.

Simple Mail Transfer Protocol (SMTP)   An application protocol typically not used by end users. Instead, it is used by the network management software and networking devices to allow a network engineer to monitor and troubleshoot network problems.

single point of failure   A system or network design characterized by one or more major components that are required to maintain operation.

slash format   A method of expressing a network prefix. It uses a forward slash (/) followed by the network prefix, for example, 192.168.254.0 /24. This /24 represent the 24-bit network prefix in slash format.

slot time   The minimum time a NIC or interface can take to send an entire frame. Slot time, then, implies a minimum frame size.

source   The origin of the PDU. This can be a process, a host, or a node, depending on the layer to which you are referring.

source device   The device that is originating the PDU.

source IP address   The IP address of the originating host that is placed into the IP packet header.

spam   Unsolicited commercial e-mail.

standards   An internationally recognized definition of technical specifications that ensure worldwide consistency.

static route   An entry in an IP routing table that was created because a network engineer entered the routing information into the router's configuration.

store and forward   A method of internal processing by LAN switches. The switch must receive the entire frame before it sends the first bit of the frame. Store-and-forward switching is the method used by Cisco switches.

straight-through cable   A UTP cable pinout that specifies that the wire at pin 1 of an RJ-45 connector on one end of the cable connects to pin 1 on the other end, the wire at pin 2 connects to pin 2 on the other end, pin 3 to pin 3, and so on. Ethernet LANs use straight-through cable pinouts for cables connecting PCs to hubs or switches.

strong password   A password that is complex and has a minimum of eight characters. A strong password uses both alphabetic and numeric characters.

subnet   A group of IP addresses that have the same value in the first part of the IP addresses, for the purpose of allowing routing to identify the group by that initial part of the addresses. IP addresses in the same subnet typically sit on the same network medium and are not separated from each other by any routers. IP addresses on different subnets are typically separated from one another by at least one router. Subnet is short for subnetwork.

subnet mask   A dotted decimal number that helps identify the structure of IP addresses. The mask represents the network and subnet parts of related IP addresses with binary 1s and the host part of related IP addresses with binary 0s.

subnetwork   *See* subnet.

switch   In Ethernet, a Layer 2 device that receives an electrical signal in one port, interprets the bits, and makes a filtering or forwarding decision about the frame. If it forwards, it sends a regenerated signal. Switches typically have many physical ports, oftentimes RJ-45 jacks, whereas bridges traditionally have two ports.

switch table   The table used by a switch that associates MAC addresses with the outgoing port. A general term for the table that a LAN bridge uses for its forwarding/filtering decisions. The table holds a list of MAC addresses and the port out which the bridge should forward frames for those frames to reach the correct destination. Also called a CAM table when referring to the switch table on Cisco LAN switches. *See also* bridge table.

symmetric switching   In LAN switches, a reference to cases in which a frame is forwarded, or switched, when the incoming and outgoing interfaces use the same speed. It is the opposite of asymmetric switching.

SYN   A 1-bit flag in the TCP header used to indicate the initial value of the sequence number. The SYN flag is only set in the first two segments of the three-way TCP connection establishment sequence.

synchronous   Communication that uses a common clocking signal. In most synchronous communication, one of the communicating devices generates a clock signal into the circuit. Additional timing information is not required in the header.

syntax   The structure and order of words in a computer language.

TCP (Transmission Control Protocol)   A Layer 4 protocol of the TCP/IP model, TCP lets applications guarantee delivery of data across a network.

TCP/IP (Transmission Control Protocol/Internet Protocol)   A network model defined by the IETF that has been implemented on most computers and network devices in the world.

terminal emulator   Network application in which a computer runs software that makes it appear to a remote host as a directly attached terminal.

test-net addresses   The IPv4 address block 192.0.2.0 to 192.0.2.255 (192.0.2.0 /24) that is set aside for teaching and learning purposes. These addresses can be used in documentation and network examples.

Thicknet   A common term for 10BASE5 Ethernet, referring to the fact that 10BASE5 cabling is thicker than the coaxial cabling used for 10BASE2 (Thinnet).

Thinnet   A common term for 10BASE2 Ethernet, referring to the fact that 10BASE2 cabling is thinner than the coaxial cabling used for 10BASE5 (Thicknet).

throughput   The actual data transfer rate between two computers at some point in time. Throughput is impacted by the slowest-speed link used to send data between the two computers, as well as myriad variables that might change during the course of a day.

Time to Live (TTL)   A field in the IP header that prevents a packet from indefinitely looping around an IP internetwork. Routers decrement the TTL field each time they forward a packet, and if they decrement the TTL to 0, the router discards the packet, which prevents it from looping forever.

token passing   An access method used with some LAN technologies by which devices access the media in a controlled manner. This access to the LAN is managed using a small frame called a token. A device can send only when it has claimed the use of the token.

tracert (traceroute)   A command on many computer operating systems that discovers the IP addresses, and possibly host names, of the routers used by the network when sending a packet from one computer to another.

transparent bridging   The learning of source addresses on incoming frames and adding them to the bridging table. After the table has been completed and when a frame is received on one of the bridge's interfaces, the bridge looks up the frame's destination address in its bridging table, and the frame is forwarded out the indicated port.

universally administered address (UAA)   *See* burned-in address (BIA).

UNIX   A multiuser, multitasking operating system originally developed in the 1960s and 1970s by a group of AT&T employees at Bell Labs, including Ken Thompson, Dennis Ritchie, and Douglas McIlroy. Today UNIX systems are split into various branches, developed over time by AT&T, as well as various commercial vendors and nonprofit organizations.

unshielded twisted-pair (UTP) cable   A general type of cable, with the cable holding twisted pairs of copper wires and the cable itself having little shielding.

URG   A 1-bit flag in the TCP header used to indicate that the receiving host should notify the destination process to do urgent processing.

user executive (EXEC) mode   The limited CLI mode where the commands available to the user are a subset of those available at the privileged level. In general, use the user EXEC commands to temporarily change terminal settings, perform basic tests, and list system information.

virtual circuit   A logical connection between devices in which the frames are passed between the devices. Virtual circuits are independent of the physical structure and may be established through multiple physical devices.

virtual local-area network (VLAN)   A network of computers that behave as if they are connected to the same network segment, even though they might be physically located on different segments of a LAN. VLANs are configured through software on the switch and router (IOS on Cisco routers and switches).

virtual terminal line (vty)   The reference to text-based logical interfaces on an IOS device. These are accesses using Telnet or SSH to perform administrative tasks. VTY lines are also called virtual type terminal.

Voice over IP (VoIP)   Voice data encapsulated in an IP packet that allows it to traverse already implemented IP networks without needing its own network infrastructure.

well-known ports   Used by TCP and UDP, with values between 0 and 1023, these ports are allocated by high-privilege processes. They are used so that all clients know the correct port number to connect to.

wiki   A website that lets visitors add, edit, and delete content, typically without the need for registration. A good example of this is the site Wikipedia.com, where visitors can access the website and add their commentaries to already written articles or create a new article.

Winchester connector   A 34-pin female v.35 serial cable connector.

window size   As filed in the TCP header that is set in a sent segment, signifies the maximum amount of unacknowledged data the host is willing to receive before the other sending host must wait for an acknowledgment. Used for flow control.

wireless   *See* wireless technology.

wireless technology   Technology that allows communication without needing physical connectivity. Examples of wireless technology include cellular telephones, personal digital assistants (PDA), wireless access points, and wireless NICs.

Numerics

1-Gbps Ethernet, 323-324

10-Mbps Ethernet, 344

10GbE, 346-347

100-Mbps Ethernet, 344-345

1000-Mbps Ethernet, 345-346

100BASE-FX standard, 345

100BASE-TX standard, 344

802.11 standard, 302

    frame format, 265-266

802.15 standard, 302

802.16 standard, 302

1000BASE-SX Ethernet, 346

1000BASE-T Ethernet, 345

A

abbreviating commands, 425

accessing CLI, 411

    via AUX port, 413

    via console, 411-412

    via SSH, 412

    via Telnet, 412

acknowledgments, selective, 122

address assignments, calculating, 209-211

address management, 150-152

address pools, 201

addressing, 55, 137, 260

    IP addressing, 56-57

        hosts per subnet, calculating, 388-389

        subnet masks, 390

        subnets per network, calculating, 389

        subnetting, 391-394, 397-398

        VLSM, 394-396

    physical addresses, 55

aging process of LAN switches, 354

Alohanet, 320

amplitude, 285

ANDing, 207-209

application layer (OSI model), 65-67

    encapsulation, 66

    protocols, 71-74

        DHCP, 87-89

        DNS, 77-81

        examples of, 76-77

        Gnutella, 90

        HTTP, 81-83

        POP, 83

        SMB, 89

        SMTP, 83

        Telnet, 91-92

    services, 70, 73-74

        file-sharing, 89

        P2P, 90

        Telnet, 91-92

    software, 69

application layer protocols (TCP/IP model), 68

applications, P2P, 75-76

architecture. *See* **network architecture**

arguments, 418

ARP (Address Resolution Protocol), 356

    address mappings, removing from table, 360

    IPv4 addresses, resolving to MAC addresses, 355-356

    MAC address resolution, 357-359

    security issues, 361

    table entries, adding, 356

arp command, 461-462

ARP spoofing, 361

assigning

    names to devices, 429-431

    IP addresses, 198-200

        dynamic assignment, 201

        static assignment, 200

asynchronous communication, 339

attenuation, 294, 377

authentication, 24

authoritative DNS servers, 81

AUX interfaces, 400

    CLI, accessing, 413

availability, 25

B

backbone cabling, 375
backing up configuration files, 437-439
backoff procedures, 265
backoff timing, 340-342
bandwidth, 21, 378
    units of measurement, 290
banners, configuring, 434-435
baselines, establishing, 458-459
best-effort protocols, 141
BIA (burned-in address), 327
binary-to-decimal conversion, 175-177
    positional notation, 174
bit time, 285-286, 339-340
bits, 12
blogs, 4
Bluetooth, 302
broadcast addresses, 184-185, 189
broadcast domains, 149
broadcast MAC addressing, 332
bytes, 329

C

cabling
    attenuation, 377
    backbone cabling, 375
    bandwidth, 378
    copper, 293
        coax, 297
        HFC, 298
        safety, 299
        STP, 299
        UTP, 294-296
    cost of, 377
    crossover cables, 382
    ease of installation, 379
    fiber, 299, 302
    horizontal cabling, 375
    interference, 380
    length of, 377
    raceway, 379
    straight-through cables, 381
    telecommunications room, 375
    UTP interfaces, 381

    WANs, V.35-compliant, 387
    work areas, 374
calculating
    address assignments, 209-211
    hosts per subnet, 389
    subnets per network, 389
capturing baseline information, 458-459
career opportunities in networking, 27
categories of UTP cable, 295
circuit-switched networks, 19
Cisco IOS Software, 410, 414
    command prompts, 416
    commands
        CLI help system, 420-422
        conventions, 418-420
        editing shortcuts, 423-426
    hierachical model structure, 415, 418
        EXEC modes, switching between, 417
        global configuration mode, 428-429
        privileged EXEC mode, 417
        user EXEC mode, 416
classful addressing, 196-197
    limitations of, 198
classifying traffic, 22
classless addressing, 198
CLI (command-line interface), accessing, 411
    via AUX port, 413
    via console, 411-412
    via SSH, 412
    via Telnet, 412
client/server model, 72
clients, 37
    UDP processes, 126-127
coax cabling, 297
code groups, 288
collaboration tools, 5
collision detection, CSMA/CD, 335
collision domains, 337
collisions, 253
commands
    abbreviating, 425
    arguments, 418
    arp, 461-462
    CLI help system, 420
        command syntax check, 421-422
        context-sensitive help, 420
        editing shortcuts, 423-426

conventions, 418-420
copy running-config tftp, 437
copy startup-config tftp, 437
editing shortcuts, 423-426
enable secret, 433-434
erase startup-config, 438
hierachical model structure, 415, 418
ipconfig, 156, 330-331
keywords, 418
netstat, 112
nslookup, 78
prompts, 416
reload, 436
service password-encryption, 434
show commands, 426-427
show interfaces command, 427
show ip route, 157
show mac-address-table, 463
show version command, 427-428
syntax check, 421-422
tracert, 453-458
    output, interpreting, 459-461
communication
channels, 35
elements of, 35
external factors, 9
internal factors, 10
Internet as change agent, 3
messages
    multiplexing, 36
    segmentation, 35-36
networks, 10
    convergence, 15-18
    devices, 14
    elements of, 10-11
    layered models, 47-48
    media, 12, 39-40
    messages, 11-12
    rules, 14-15
popular tools
    blogs, 4
    IM, 4
    podcasting, 5
    wikis, 5
protocol suites, 46
protocols, 8-9, 44-47
confidentiality, 24
configuration files, 413
backing up, 437-439
managing, 436

restoring, 440
running-config, 414
startup-config, 414
configuring
banners, 434-435
    MOTD, 435
interfaces, 441
passwords, 431-432
    enable secret, 433-434
    on console port, 433
    on VTY lines, 434
router interfaces
    Ethernet, 441
    serial, 441-442
switch interfaces, 443-444
congestion control, TCP, 123-124
connection establishment/termination (TCP), 118-120
three-way handshakes, 116-118
connection-oriented networks, 19, 114
connectionless networks, 19-20, 140
connectivity
loopback testing, 445-446
of gateway, testing, 451-453
of local network, testing, 449-450
of routers, testing, 447
of switches, testing, 447-449
ping/trace results, interpreting, 444-445, 453-458
router remote connectivity, testing, 453
connectors, 304-306
for WANs, 384-386
console interfaces, 399
CLI, accessing, 411-412
passwords, configuring, 433
contention-based access for shared media, 253
context-sensitive help, 420
control data, 106
controlled access, 253
convergence, 15-18
future trends, 25
    devices, 26
    increased service availability, 26-27
    mobile users, 26
QoS, 21-23
conversations, 104
converting between decimal and hexidecimal, 329-330

copper media, 293

    coax, 297

    HFC, 298

    safety, 299

    STP, 299

    UTP, 294-296

copy running-config tftp command, 437

copy startup-config tftp command, 437

CRC (cyclical redundancy check) value, 261

crossover cables, 297, 382

crosstalk, 295

CSMA/CD (carrier sense multiple access with collision detection), 253-254, 334

    collision detection, 335

    hubs, 337

    jam signals, 336

Ctrl-C command, 425

Ctrl-R command, 424

Ctrl-Shift-6 x command, 425

D

data encapsulation, Layer 2, 318

data integrity, 24

data link layer, 244

    addressing, 260, 331

    data encapsulation, 318

    frames, 248, 258-259

        802.11, 265-266

        Ethernet, 263-264

        fields, 248-249

        PPP, 265

        sample frames, 262

        trailers, 260-261

    LLC sublayer, 250, 317

    MAC sublayer, 317-319

    media access control, 247-248, 252

        contention-based, 253

        controlled access, 253

        for nonshared media, 255

        for shared media, 252

    network topologies, 255

        logical, 256-258

    NICs, 250

    services performed by, 245-246

    standards, 251

data networks, 3, 42

data-carrying capacity of physical layer media, 290-292

datagrams, 107

    reassembly, 125

DCE/DTE (data communication equipment/data termination equipment), 386

decapsulation, 51, 139, 269-273

decimal-to-binary conversion, 1780-183

default gateway, 153-156

default routes, 161, 194

describing interfaces, 442-443

destination IP addresses, 137

Destination Unreachable messages (ICMP), 233

devices, 14

    addresses, selecting

        firewalls, 203-204

        intermediary devices, 38, 202

        routers, 203-204

        servers, 202

    banners, configuring, 434-435

    end devices, 37

    future trends, 26

    naming, 429-431

    network device symbols, 12

    passwords

        configuring, 431-434

        enable secret, 433-434

    terminal emulation, 401

DHCP (Dynamic Host Configuration Protocol), 87-89

directed broadcasts, 185

directly connected networks, 138

DNS (domain name service), 77-78

    caching, 79

    name resolution, 79

    structure, 79-81

DNS resolver, 78

domain names, 77

dotted decimal format, 173

downloads, 72

DTE (data termination equipment), 386

dynamic address assignment, 201

dynamic routing, 164

E

editing shortcuts, 423-424, 426

e-mail, MDA/MTA processes, 84-86

EMI (electromagnetic interference), 380

enable secret passwords, configuring, 433-434

encapsulation, 51, 66, 137, 142

    Layer 2, 318

    source host encapsulation, 268-273

encoding

    messages, 39

    physical layer, 284, 287-290

end devices, 37

erase startup-config command, 438

erasing configuration files, 438

error correction, 261

error detection, 261

error recovery, 104

establishing network baselines, 458-459

Ethernet

    10GbE, 346-347

    addressing, 331

    asynchronous communication, 339

    backoff timing, 342

    bit times, 339-340

    framing, 263-264, 324-325

    hexidecimal addressing, 328-330

        MAC address, viewing, 330-331

    history of, 320-321

        Fast Ethernet, 322-323

        Gigabit Ethernet, 323-324

        legacy Ethernet, 321-322

    interfaces, 399

        configuring, 441

    interframe spacing, 341

    jam signal length, 341

    latency, 338

    Layer 2

        LLC sublayer, 317

        MAC sublayer, 317-319

    Legacy Ethernet, hubs, 347, 349

    MAC addressing, 326-327

        broadcast, 332

        multicast, 333-334

        unicast, 332

    media, 292

    media access control, 334

        CSMA/CD, 334-337

    physical implementations, 319-320

    physical layer, 342-343

        10 mbps, 344

        100 mbps, 344-345

        1000 mbps, 345-346

    slot time, 340-341

    switching, 349-351

        aging process, 354

        directly connected nodes, 349-351

        filtering, 354

        flooding, 354

        learning process, 353

        MAC tables, 352-353

        selective forwarding, 351-354

    synchronous communication, 339

examples

    of application layer services and protocols, 76-77

        DHCP, 87-89

        DNS, 77, 79, 81

        Gnutella, 90

        HTTP, 81-83

        POP, 83

        SMB, 89

        SMTP, 83

        Telnet, 91-92

    of network layer protocol, 140

EXEC modes, switching between, 417

expectational acknowledgment, 120

experimental IPv4 addresses, 192

extended star topology, 337

external communication factors, 9

extranets, 7

F

Fast Ethernet, 322-323, 344

fault tolerance, 17

FCS (Frame Check Sequence) field, 261

fiber media, 299, 302

fields

    of data link layer frames, 248-249

    of Ethernet frames, 325

    of frame trailers, 260-261

    of IPv4 header, 143-144

file-sharing services, 89

filtering, 354

firewalls, 25

    addresses, selecting, 203-204

flash memory, 410

flooding, 354

flow control, 104, 122-123

fragmentation, 142

frames, 55, 248

    802.11, 265-266

    encapsulation, 269-273

    Ethernet, 263-264, 324-325

    fields, 248-249

    media access control, 252

        contention-based, 253

        controlled access, 253

        for nonshared media, 255

        for shared media, 252

    PPP, 265

framing, 258-259, 318

    sample frames, 262

    trailers, 260-261

full-duplex communication, 255

G

gateway connectivity, testing, 451-453

GET requests, 82

Gigabit Ethernet, 323-324

global configuration mode, 428-429

Gnutella, 90

goodput, 291

graphic image formats, 68

grouping network hosts, 145-147

    reasons for, 148-152

GSM (Global System for Mobile Communication), 302

H

half-duplex communication, 255

    slot time, 340-341

headers, 248, 259

    IPv4, 143-144

hexidecimal addressing, 328-330

    MAC addresses, viewing, 330-331

HFC (hybrid fiber coax) cabling, 298

hierarchical addressing, 150-152

hierarchical modal structure of Cisco IOS Software, 415

    privileged EXEC mode, 417

    EXEC modes, switching between, 417

    global configuration mode, 428-429

    user EXEC mode, 416

high-order bits, 174

history of Ethernet, 320-321

    Fast Ethernet, 322-323

    Gigabit Ethernet, 323-324

    legacy Ethernet, 321-322

hops, 138

horizontal cabling, 375

host addresses, 174, 189

    address range, calculating, 211

    hosts per subnet, calculating, 389

host names, assigning, 429-431

host routing table, 158-159

host-to-switch mappings, discovering, 463

hosts, 37

hot keys, 423-426

HTTP (HyperText Transfer Protocol), 46, 81-83

    GET requests, 82

HTTPS (HyperText Transfer Protocol-Secure), 82

hubs, 337

    in Legacy Ethernet, 347, 349

HyperTerminal, restoring/backing up configuration files, 438-440

I

IAC (Interpret as Command) character, 91

IANA (Internet Assigned Numbers Authority), 110, 204

ICMP (Internet Control Message Protocol), 232-234

IDLE symbols, 346

IEEE (Institute of Electrical and Electronic Engineers), 46

IETF (Internet Engineering Task Force), 46

IM (instant messaging), 4

interfaces, 43

    AUX, 400

    configuring, 441

    console, 399

    describing, 442-443

    Ethernet, 399

        configuring, 441

    serial, 399

        configuring, 441-442

    switch interfaces, configuring, 443-444

interference, 380

interframe spacing, 341

intermediary devices, 38

    addresses, selecting, 202

internal communication factors, 10

Internet, 3, 42

architecture, 17-18
network security, 23-25
QoS, 21-23
scalability, 20-21
as change agent for communication, 3
benefits to businesses, 6-7
collaboration tools, 5
online learning, 5-6

internetworks, 17
devices, 368

interpreting
ping/trace results, 453-458
tracert output, 459-461

intranets, 7, 42

intranetwork devices, 369

IP (Internet Protocol), 47

IP addressing. *See* **IPv4 addressing**

ipconfig command, 156, 330-331

iPods, podcasting, 5

IPv4 addressing, 56-57, 173

decimal-to-binary conversion, 178-183
address assignments, 198-200
calculating, 209-211
dynamic assignment, 201
static assignment, 200
ANDing, 207-209
binary-to-decimal conversion, 175-177
positional notation, 174
broadcast addresses, 189
broadcast communication, 184-185
characteristics, 140-142
classful addressing, limitations of, 198
default routes, 194
directed broadcast communication, 185
dotted decimal format, 173
encapsulation, 142
experimental addresses, 192
host addresses, 189
host portion, 174
ICMP, 232-234
ISPs, 205-206
legacy addressing, 196
classless addressing, 198
network classes, 196-197
limited broadcast communication, 185-186
link-local addresses, 194-195
loopback addresses, 194
multicast communication, 186, 188

network addresses, 189
network prefixes, 190
subnet masks, 190-192
network layer, testing, 228-232
network portion, 174
packet header, 143-144
private addresses, 192-193
public addresses, 192-193
resolving IP addresses to MAC addresses, 355-356
selecting addresses for devices, 202-204
subnetting, 211-220
VLSM, 220-227
test-net addresses, 195-196
unicast communication, 183

IPv6, 235-236

IRC (Internet Relay Chat), 4

ISPs (Internet service providers), 42

services, 205
tier 1, 206
tier 2, 206
tier 3, 206

IT (information technology) career opportunities, 27

J-K-L

jam signals, 336, 341

keywords, 418

LAA (locally administered address), 327

LAN switching. *See also* **LANs**

aging process, 354
filtering, 354
flooding, 354
learning process, 353
selective forwarding, 354

LANs, 41

backbone cabling, 375
cabling
bandwidth, 378
cost of, 377
ease of installation, 379
horizontal, 375
interference, 380
length of, 377
devices
internetwork devices, 368
intranetwork devices, 369

routers, selecting, 373
switches, selecting, 370-372
telecommuniations room, 375
work areas, 374

latency, 338

Layer 1. *See* **physical layer**

Layer 2. *See* **data link layer**

Layer 3. *See* **network layer**

Layer 4. *See* **transport layer protocols**

Layer 7. *See* **application layer**

layered network communication models, 47-48

OSI model, 53-54
PDUs, 51
TCP/IP model, 48-52

learning process of LAN switches, 353

leased lines, 41

least significant bits, 211

legacy Ethernet, 321-322

hubs, 347, 349

legacy IPv4 addressing

classless addressing, 198
network classes, 196-197

limited broadcasts, 185-186

link-local addresses, 194-195

LLC sublayer, 317

local network connectivity, testing, 449-450

logical networks, 245

logical topologies, 255

multiaccess, 257
point-to-point, 256
ring, 258

loopback addresses, 194

testing with ping, 445-446

low-order bits, 176

M

MAC addressing, 263, 326-327

address, viewing, 330-331
broadcast, 332
multicast, 333-334
unicast, 332

MAC sublayer, 250, 317-319

MAC tables, 352-353

managing configuration files, 436

Manchester encoding, 286

MANs (metropolitan area networks), 319

MDA process, 84, 86

MDI (media-dependent interface), 381

MDIX (media-dependent interface, crossover), 381

media, 39-40

media access control, 247-248, 252, 334

addressing, 260
contention-based, 253
controlled access, 253
CSMA/CD, 334
collision detection, 335
hubs, 337
jam signals, 336
for nonshared media, 255
for shared media, 252
framing, 258-259
802.11, 265-266
Ethernet, 263-264
PPP, 265
sample frames, 262
trailers, 260-261

media connectors, 304, 306

media-independent protocols, 141

memory, NVRAM, 414

messages, 11-12

encoding, 39
ICMP, 232-234
multiplexing, 36
segmentation, 35-36

mobile users, 26

most significant bits, 178

MOTD banners, configuring, 435

MTA (mail transfer agent) process, 84-86

MTU (maximum transmission unit), 141

MUA (mail user agent), 83

multiaccess topologies, 257

multicast MAC addressing, 333-334

multicasts, 186-188

multimode fiber-optic cable, 302

multiplexing, 36

N

name resolution, 79

naming devices, 429-431

NAT (Network Address Translation), 193

netstat command, 112

network access layer (TCP/IP model), 251

network access protocols, 47

network addressing, 55, 189

addresses, calculating, 209
IP addressing, 56-57
physical address, 55
prefix, 190
subnet masks, 190-192

network architecture, 17-18

circuit-switched, connection-oriented, 19
packet-switched, connectionless, 19-20
QoS, 21-23
scalability, 20-21

network device symbols, 12

network layer, 136, 144, 331

addressing, 137, 331
connectivity, testing, 228-232
decapsulation, 139
default gateway, 155-156
encapsulation, 137
example protocol, 140
IPv4
characteristics of, 140, 142
encapsulation, 142
packet header, 143-144
network hosts, grouping, 145-147
reasons for, 148-152
packet forwarding, 162-163
packets, 154-155
routing, 138, 159
dynamic routing, 164
static routing, 163
routing protocols, 164-165
routing table, 156-159
default route, 161
entries, 160
next hop, 161
subnets, 145

network portion of IPv4 addresses, 174

networks, 3

benefits to businesses, 7-8
career opportunities, 27
communication, 10
components of, 37
convergence, future trends, 25-27
elements of, 10-11
devices, 14
medium, 12

messages, 11-12
rules, 14-15
entertainment uses of, 8
extranets, 7
intranets, 7
logical topologies
multiaccess, 257
point-to-point, 256
ring, 258
media, 40
P2P, 74-75
applications, 75-76
security, 18, 23-24
availability, 25
confidentiality, 24
data integrity, 24
segments, 245
subnetting, 152
topologies, 255

next hop, 161

testing, 452

NICs (network interface cards) , 43, 250

nodes, 245

noise, 294

nonshared media, media access control, 255

NRZ (nonreturn to zero), 286

nslookup command, 78

NVRAM (nonvolatile RAM), 414

O

online learning, 5-6

benefits to businesses, 6-7

OSI model, 49, 53

application layer, 65-67
protocol functions, 71
services, 70
software, 69
comparing with TCP/IP model, 54
data link layer
802.11, 265-266
addressing, 260
Ethernet, 263-264
framing, 248-249, 258-261
media access control, 252-255
media access control method, 247-248
network topologies, 255-258
NICs, 250

PPP, 265
sample frames, 262
services performed by, 245-246
standards, 251
sublayers, 250
encapsulation process, 66, 268-273
network layer, 136, 144
   addressing, 137
   decapsulation, 139
   default gateway, 155-156
   dynamic routing, 164
   encapsulation, 137
   IPv4, 140-144
   network hosts, grouping, 145-152
   next hop, 161
   packet forwarding, 162-163
   packets, 154-155
   protocol example, 140
   routing, 138, 159
   routing protocols, 164-165
   routing table, 156-161
   static routing, 163
   subnets, 145, 152
physical layer
   data carrying capacity of media, 290-292
   encoding, 284, 287-290
   media connectors, 304-306
   physical media, 283, 292-299, 302
   purpose of, 280-281
   signaling, 281, 284-286
   standards, 282-283
   wireless media, 302-304
presentation layer, 67
session layer, 68
transport layer
   purpose of, 101-105
   SAR, 112-114
   TCP, 107, 114-124
   UDP, 107, 124-127
OTDR (Optical Time Domain Reflectometer), 306
OUI (Organizational Unique Identifier), 326

P

P2P networks, 74-75
   applications, 75-76
   services, 90
packet-switched networks, 19-20
packet forwarding, 162-163

Packet Tracer, 6
packets, 19, 154-155
PAM5, 345
passwords
   configuring, 431-432
      on console port, 433
      on VTY lines, 434
   enable secret, configuring, 433-434
PDUs, 51
   frames, 55
   segmentation and reassembly, 112, 114
performance, establishing network baselines, 458-459
photodiodes, 300
physical addresses, 55
physical Ethernet implementations, 319-320
physical layer, 280
   data-carrying capacity of media, 290-292
   encoding, 284, 287-290
   Ethernet, 342-343
      10 Mbps, 344
      100 Mbps, 344-345
      1000 Mbps, 345-346
   physical components, 283
   physical media, 292
      copper, 293-299
      fiber-optic, 299, 302
      media connectors, 304, 306
      safety, 299
      wireless, 302-304
   purpose of, 280-281
   signaling 281, 284-286
      Manchester encoding, 286
      NRZ, 286
   standards, 282-283
physical networks, 245
physical ports, 43
physical topologies, 255
ping
   connectivity, testing, 444-445
   loopback, testing, 445-446
   network layer, testing, 228-230
   results, interpreting, 453-458
ping sweeps, performing, 462
pinout, 296
podcasting, 5
point-to-point topologies, 256
POP (Post Office Protocol), 83

port addressing, 108-109

port numbers, 76, 104

PPP (Point-to-Point Protocol) frame format, 265

Preamble, 339

presentation layer, 67

priority queuing, 22-23

private addresses, 192-193

privileged EXEC mode, 417

processes, 69

   TCP, 115

prompts, 416

protocol suites, 45-46

protocols, 8-9, 14-15, 44-46

   application layer. *See* application layer
   technology-independent, 47
   transport layer. *See* transport layer

proxy ARP, 358

public addresses, 192-193

Q-R

QoS (quality of service), 21-23

queuing, priority queuing, 22-23

raceway, 379

Redirect messages (ICMP), 234

redundancy, 17

reference models, 48

registered ports, 111

reliability, 114-115, 261

reload command, 436

remote connectivity, testing, 453

removing address mappings from ARP table, 360

resolving MAC addresses, ARP, 357-359

resource records, 78

restoring configuration files, 440

RFCs (Requests For Comments), 49, 68, 81

RFI (radio frequency interference), 380

ring topologies, 258

RIRs (Regional Internet Registries), 204

RJ-45 connectors, 304, 380

rollover cables, 297, 401

routers

   addresses, selecting, 203-204
   connectivity, testing, 447, 453
   interfaces
      describing, 442-443
      Ethernet, configuring, 441
      serial, configuring, 441-442
      verifying, 446-447
   selecting, 373

routing, 136-138, 159

   dynamic routing, 164
   hops, 138
   static routing, 163

routing protocols, 164-165

routing table, 156-159

   default route, 161
   entries, 160
   next hop, 161

RTT (round-trip time), 231

rules, 14-15

running-config, 414

   backing up, 437-439
   erasing, 438
   managing, 436
   restoring, 440

runt frames, 342

S

SAMBA, 89

SAR (segmentation and reassembly), 112-114

SC (Subscriber Connector) connectors, 306

scalability, 17, 20-21

security, 18, 23-24

   availability, 25
   confidentiality, 24
   data integrity, 24

segmentation, 35-36

selecting

   routers, 373
   switches, 370-372

selective acknowledgments, 122

selective forwarding, 351-354

serial interfaces, 399

   configuring, 441-442

server daemon, 73

servers, 72

  addresses, selecting, 202
  authoritative, 81
  UDP processes, 126

service password-encryption command, 434

services, application layer, 69-70, 73-74

  DHCP, 87-89
  DNS, 77-81
  examples of, 76-77
  file-sharing, 89
  HTTP, 81-83
  P2P, 90
  POP, 83
  SMB, 89
  SMTP, 83
  Telnet, 91-92

services performed by data link layer, 245-246

session layer, 68

session termination, TCP, 118-120

sessions, 264

shared media

  contention-based access, 253
  media access control, 252

shortcuts for command editing, 423-426

show commands, 426-427

show interfaces command, 427

show ip route command, 157

show mac-address-table command, 463

show version command, 427-428

signaling, 284. *See also* **encoding**

  physical layer, 285
    Manchester encoding, 286
    NRZ, 286

single points of failure, 25

single-mode fiber-optic cable, 302

slot time, 340-341

SMB (Server Message Block), 89

SMTP (Simple Mail Transfer Protocol), 83

sockets, 109

source host encapsulation, 268-273

source IP address, 137

Source Quench messages (ICMP), 234

SSH (Secure Shell), 92

  CLI, accessing, 412

ST (Straight Tip) connectors, 306

standards, 11

  for wireless communication, 302
  for WLANs, 304
  physical layer, 282-283

startup-config, 414

  backing up, 437-439
  erasing, 438
  managing, 436
  restoring, 440

static address assignment, 200

static routing, 163

store-and-forward switching, 352

STP (shielded twisted-pair) cabling, 299

straight-through cables, 297, 375, 381

sublayers of data link control layer, 250

subnet masks, 190-192, 390

subnetting, 145, 152, 211-220, 391-398

  subnets per network, calculating, 389
  VLSM, 220-227, 394-396

switched Ethernet, 349, 351

  aging process, 354
  directly connected nodes, 349-351
  filtering, 354
  flooding, 354
  learning process, 353
  MAC tables, 352-353
  selective forwarding, 351-354

switches

  connectivity, testing, 447-449
  host-to-switch mappings, discovering, 463
  interfaces, configuring, 443-444
  selecting, 370-372

switching between EXEC modes, 417

symbols for network devices, 12

synchronous communication, 339

syntax check help, 421-422

T

tabs, 424

TCP (Transmission Control Protocol), 107, 114

  expectational acknowledgment, 120-121
  congestion control, 123-124
  expectational acknowledgment, 120
  flow control, 122-123
  port addressing, 108-109
  registered ports, 111

reliability, 114-115
retransmission, 121-122
server processes, 115
session termination, 118-120
three-way handshakes, 116-118
well-known ports, 110

TCP/IP model, 48-49

application layer, 67-71
communication process, 50-52
comparing with OSI model, 54
network access layer, 251

technology-independent protocols, 47

telecommunications room, 375

Telnet, 91-92

CLI, accessing, 412

TeraTerm, backing up configuration files, 438-439

terminal emulation, 401

terminal emulator, 400

test-net addresses, 195-196

testing

gateway connectivity, 451-453
local network connectivity, 449-450
    ping, 444-445
loopback with ping, 445-446
network layer, 228-232
next hop, 452
router connectivity, 447
switch connectivity, 447-449

Thicknet, 320

Thinnet, 320

three-way handshakes, 116-118

throughput, 291

tier 1 ISPs, 206

tier 2 ISPs, 206

tier 3 ISPs, 206

Time Exceeded messages (ICMP), 234

token passing, 258

topologies, 255

logical
    multiaccess, 257
    point-to-point, 256
    ring, 258

tracert command, 453-458

output, interpreting, 459-461
network layer, testing, 231-232
results, interpreting, 453-458

traffic classification, 22

trailers, 248

fields, 260-261

transparent bridging, 352

transport layer protocols, 101-107

port addressing, 108-109
registered ports, 111
SAR, 112-114
TCP, 107, 114
    expectational acknowledgment, 120-121
    retransmission, 121-122
    congestion control, 123-124
    flow control, 122-123
    reliability, 114-115
    server processes, 115
    session termination, 118-120
    three-way handshakes, 116-118
UDP, 107, 124
    client processes, 126-127
    datagram reassembly, 125
    server processes, 126
well-known ports, 110

transport protocols, 46

TSP (telecommunications service provider), 41

TTL (Time To Live), 231

U-V

UAAs (universally administered addresses), 327

UDP (User Datagram Protocol), 107, 124

client processes, 126-127
datagram reassembly, 125
port addressing, 108-109
registered ports, 111
server processes, 126
well-known ports, 110

unicast addresses, 183

unicast MAC addressing, 332

UNIX OS, 89

up- and down-arrow keys, 425

uploads, 72

URLs, 81

user EXEC mode, 416

UTP (unshielded twisted-pair) cabling, 294-296

crossover cables, 382
straight-through cables, 381

V.35-compliant cables, 387

verifying router interfaces, 446-447

viewing MAC address with ipconfig command, 330-331

virtual circuits, 257

VLSM (Variable-Length Subnet Masking), 220-224, 226-227, 394, 396

VoIP (Voice over IP)

   QoS, 22

vty (virtual teletype) sessions, 91, 412

   passwords, configuring, 434

W-X-Y-Z

WANs, 41

   cabling, V-35 compliant, 387

   connectors, 384-386

   DCE/DTE, 386

well-known ports, 110

Wi-Fi, 302

wikis, 5

WiMAX (Worldwide Interoperability for Microwave Access), 302

Winchester connector, 385

window size, 121

wireless media, 302

WLANs (Wireless LANs), 303-304

work areas, 374

WPAN (Wireless Personal Area Network), 302